S0-BZZ-261

THE ANGLICAN CHURCH IN NINETEENTH CENTURY BRITAIN

Hymns Ancient and Modern (1860-1875)

THE ANGLICAN CHURCH IN NINETEENTH CENTURY BRITAIN

Hymns Ancient and Modern (1860-1875)

by

Susan Drain

Texts and Studies in Religion

Vol. 40

The Edwin Mellen Press
Lewiston/Lampeter/Queenston

Library of Congress Cataloging-in-Publication Data

Drain, Susan.
The Anglican Church in the 19th century Britain : hymns ancient and modern, 1860-1875 / by Susan Drain.
p. cm. -- (Texts and studies in religion ; vol. 40)
Bibliography: p.
ISBN 0-88946-829-X
1. Hymns ancient and modern. 2. Hymns, English--History and criticism. 3. Church of England--Hymns--History and criticism. 4. Anglican Communion--Hymns--History and criticism. 5. Church of England--History--19th century. 6. Anglican Communion--England--History--19th century. 7. England--Church history--19th century.
I. Title II. Series : Texts and studies in Religion ; 40.
BV370.A1D73 1989
264'.03082--dc20
89-34070
CIP

This is volume 40 in the continuing series
Texts and studies in Religion
Volume 40 ISBN 0-88946-829-X
TRS Series ISBN 0-88946-976-8

A CIP catalog record for this book
is available from the British Library.

The Edwin Mellen Press
Box 450
Lewiston, NY
USA 14092

The Edwin Mellen Press
Box 67
Queenston, Ontario
CANADA L0S 1L0

The Edwin Mellen Press, Ltd.
Lampeter, Dyfed, Wales,
UNITED KINGDOM SA48 7DY

Printed in the United States of America

TABLE OF CONTENTS

Chapter Three
The Publication of *Hymns Ancient and Modern*

Chapter Four
Editorial Policy and Practice

Chapter Five
The Inculcation and Reflection of Anglican Attitudes

Chapter Six

THE ANGLICAN CHURCH IN NINETEENTH CENTURY BRITAIN

Hymns Ancient and Modern (1860-1875)

Acknowledgements

Without the generous permission of the Proprietors of Hymns Ancient and Modern to use the archive, this study would not have been possible, and I am therefore entirely in their debt. I am particularly grateful for the kind enthusiasm with which Canon Cyril Taylor greeted my work. I should add, however, that the views and opinions expressed in this book are my own, and not those of the Proprietors. In addition, I wish to thank the following people for their help and encouragement at various stages of the study, both as thesis and as book: my supervisors, Professor Roger Sharrock, the Reverend Canon Geoffrey Cuming, and Mr. Patrick Yarker of King's College, University of London; Dr. Robindra Biswas of the University of Leicester, who pushed me to begin this study when the idea first occurred to me; the Reverend Dr. Samuel Fogal of Hartford, Connecticut, whose sympathetic support during the writing of much of it was invaluable.

Many friends and colleagues have contributed to this work in diverse ways, as have the staffs of several libraries, and I am grateful to them all. In particular, the Director and staff of the Royal School of Church Music made me welcome and comfortable at Addington Palace for many winter weeks.

Grateful thanks are also due to the British Council and the Association of Commonwealth Universities for the Commonwealth Scholarship which I held when I began the work, and to the Social Sciences and Humanities Research Council of Canada for the Doctoral Fellowship which enabled me to complete it. In addition, I am grateful for the support of the Research and Publications Committee of Mount Saint Vincent University for a grant toward the manuscript preparation. It should here be noted that a portion of Chapter Three was previously published as "An 'Incomprehensible Innovation': the Application of Copyright Law to Hymn-Publishing in the Church of England" in Publishing History XV (1984), 65-90.

My parents and my husband have never faltered in their belief that the work was worthwhile; this book is only a poor return for that steadfastness.

Preface

An idle curiosity and a modern hymnbook initiated this study, though the interest soon became a serious one, and the Victorian original of the hymnbook became its subject. The development of that interest and the pursuit of that study revealed a rich field for exploration, but the present work has been shaped largely by the existence of the archive belonging to the Proprietors of *Hymns Ancient and Modern*, and containing documents relating to the early and continued publication of the book. I am, therefore, deeply indebted to the Proprietors for their kind permission to use those papers freely in my study, and I am most grateful to them for their generosity.

I have drawn heavily upon the documents in that archive for evidence and for illustration. A great deal of the manuscript material has never been published and, particularly in the case of the actual editorial work, I have thought it worthwhile to quote at length and sometimes in entirety various drafts, revisions, and criticisms, preferring the risk of repetition and the charge of dullness to the danger of misrepresenting the editors, whose understanding of the importance of their own work, all-pervading sense of responsibility, and thoroughness in performing the task they had set themselves, are at once the most significant and the most attractive characteristics of the whole endeavour.

More than any other period, the nineteenth century offers the opportunity to make the acquaintance, sometimes the intimate acquaintance, of people of little or no importance to formal history. It is even possible to trace individual lives within the generally faceless ranks of the working classes, and by diligent pursuit of these individual traces, modern historians have been able to correct many misapprehensions, or to redeem whole areas of knowledge from ignorance or condescending generalization. It is among the middle classes, however, that acquaintance can most easily be made, for it is their letters, diaries, and account books which have survived in large numbers to give us first-hand records of their lives.

Even the business papers, such as those in the _Hymns Ancient and Modern_ archive, are surprisingly personal and individual. They are, of course, handwritten, and the pains and pleasures of deciphering, and eventually of recognizing, each writer's hand form a large part of the researcher's satisfaction. As befits an enterprise of amateurs and acquaintances, the early letters are sometimes surprisingly unselfconscious, and leave their hymnological subjects to purvey clerical gossip, or voice gentle complaints, or indulge in reminiscence. The tone begins to change when the greater responsibilities of the project become apparent, and large numbers of strangers, most humble but some eminent, are associated with it.

Like so many Victorians, they built, not better than they knew, for they were shrewd enough, but as well as they knew. More than a century later their book is at once a thriving concern, and a monument to a particular era and a particular group of men. The composition and construction of that monument is detailed in the chapters which follow, but it is the memory of the men that I wish to evoke here. They were quite extraordinarily ordinary men, idealistic, irascible, confident of their vision, and conscious of their limitations, unrelentingly clerical and gentlemanly and Victorian, but undeniably human. Let this preface end, not with the monument, but with a glimpse of two clerical friends met to discuss their project in a Kentish rectory on a summer's day, a scene called up in the post-script of a letter:

> If ever you can come to me from London again do, and I will promise not to drench you with cider or ginger beer as I did last time.[1]

[1] A.P., Letter, July 23 [1858], Francis Murray to HWB.

Note on the Archive Material

The archive relating to the publication of *Hymns Ancient and Modern* is the property of the Proprietors, and is housed at the Royal School of Church Music, Addington Palace, Croydon. The parts of the archive relevant to this study are three. First, there are letters written by and to the Compilers, divided into groups by subject or by correspondent. Second, there are the Minute Books, which record the business of the general meetings of the Proprietors from 1863. The information contained in these books is very uneven: at times they note only motions passed and sums spent, but sometimes they contain a summary of the various view-points presented in general discussion. Conclusions drawn from information in the Minute Books must frequently be modified from information in the letters, especially as the Chairman assumed a greater role and more independence of action. Many business facts, especially with regard to grants of books, are to be found in the Minute Books. Third, there is a collection of notes and documents relating to the publication of the book, including, for example, an annotated specimen volume, some proofs with and without emendations, circulation statistics, legal documents, and a number of press cuttings, the source or date of many of which is unidentified. The archive is thus by no means a complete record, though the later years are more fully documented in, for example, comprehensive scrap-books of press cuttings for the New edition of 1904. The relative scarcity and haphazard assortment of materials for the early years of Hymns Ancient and Modern are evidence for the unpretentious beginnings of the book.

References to unpublished material will be inden-tified by the location of the archive, the section of the archive (letter, minute book, document), by date, and in the case of a letter, by the names of the writer and the recipient. For example:

[1] A.P., Letter, July 23, [1858], Francis Murray to H.W.B.

[2] A.P., M.B., April 12, 1877.

[3] A.P., Specimen Book, preface dated May 20, 1859.

A note on the use of abbreviations follows.

All quotations from manuscript are rendered exactly as found in the original papers. Errors in spelling, peculiarities of punctuation, omissions of words, and individual marks of expression are unal-tered, except that double-underlining is indicated by the combination of single-underlining and bold print.

Standard Terms and Abbreviations

Wherever possible I have tried to standardize many of the terms used in this study. For example, a hymnbook is consistently a printed collection of hymns for any purpose, scholarly or practical. A hymnal is a hymnbook intended for use in congregational worship, and thus, it was the ideal of the Compilers of Hymns Ancient and Modern that the Church of England have an authorized hymnal. When quoting letters or the titles of books, I have let others' usages stand.

The three terms, editor, compiler, and proprietor, must each be distinguished. In general, the term editor is used when editorial functions, especially in textual alterations, are of chief concern. The term compiler is intended to be relatively neutral, identifying one who publishes a collection of hymns most of which were written by other people. The same word with an upper-case initial refers to those who made a significant contribution to the first edition of Hymns Ancient and Modern. The editorial control of the book was in the hands of a Committee of Compilers, most of the members of which invested in the publication of the book and thus became its Proprietors. These distinctions are of importance chiefly in Chapter Three, on the publishing history of the book, and are summarized again there. Elsewhere the words Compilers and Proprietors refer to the same group of men in their different functions. The use of the term Compilers is thus intended to emphasise the editorial and publishing concerns; the term Proprietors stresses instead their legal and financial concerns, as in the exercise of copyright law. In most cases, the usage is clear from the context.

Apart from those in common use, only one abbreviation is found in the text of this study. Henceforward, Hymns Ancient and Modern is referred to as A&M. (In quotations from letters, the title also appears as H.A.M. or another variant, which is easily recognizable.) The Reverend Sir Henry Williams Baker, Bart. is referred to in the text as Sir Henry, and in the notes only as H.W.B. Other abbreviations in the notes are:

A.P. A&M archive at Addington Palace
M.B. Minute Book

In all other cases, short forms of reference are used in preference to abbreviations.

When a hymn which is printed in A&M is referred to in the course of discussion, its first line is used as the title, and is followed by two numbers in parentheses. The first number refers to the 1860 edition (1-273) or the Appendix (274-386); the second number refers to the 1875 edition. If a hymn is omitted from either edition, the relevant space is left blank, thus (--/160) or (160/--).

Chapter One
General and Historical Introduction

1. General Introduction

A list of names, the Index of Authors and Translators in the most recent revision of A&M, provoked the interest which led to this study. Among the names in that index were those of Addison, Blake, Carlyle, Cowper, Herbert, Keble, Kingsley, Milton, Newman, Christina Rossetti, Scott, and Vaughan: over a dozen names with a fame which owed nothing to their hymns, and would not be found together in any other context. Included quite naturally among those names were those of saints -- Ambrose, Patrick, Thomas Aquinas and Thomas A Kempis, and others more obscure, such as Joseph the Hymnographer. A third prominent element in the list was the high Victorian: names, sometimes with a clerical title, whose dates of birth and death fell within the last three-quarters of the nineteenth century. The principles of compilation which could bring together in one book the works of three such different groups of people must be a remarkable one. From that interest in the principle of compilation grew this study of the publishing of A&M, its purpose, its achievement, and its evolution.

Most anthologies of verse exhibit a perceptible unity, based on historical period, language, literary form, theme, or purpose. The limitations of hymn compilations are relatively few: the historical period is the Christian epoch; the language is any of the ancient or modern tongues of Christendom; the literary form is determined only by the demands of singing and ready comprehension -- not too long, not too irregular, not too complex, not too obscure. The thematic unity is large indeed, being the praise of God, but the individual themes of the hymns may be very different one from another, including the full range of human religious needs and responses, and the aspects and attributes of God. The purpose of a hymn book, to enhance and extend the worship and praise of God, is as general as its theme, but it may have a more particular purpose, whether historical, liturgical, or even literary: to revive neglected uses, to promote private or supply public devotions, to propagate better translations or introduce new hymns. Each hymn within a collection has its own purpose and its intended use, whether to teach, to proclaim, or to give communal expression to the aspirations and emotions of the Christian life.

A hymnal is thus an unusual anthology in the relative freedom with which its principles of unity and compilation may be understood or applied, and in the eclecticism of its contents. A hymnal has two further unusual characteristics.

First, a hymnal is primarily a practical book. If it is relegated to the library shelves or left to moulder in the vestry, it is a failure. Some hymn collections, it is true, are compiled for scholarly reasons, and for the use of other hymnologists and compilers. It is not with this kind of book that this study is concerned, though some of these books are worthy of, and indeed, must be given, attention. The practicality of a hymnal means that it is subject to unusual pressures. Some of the pressures are musical: the most effective hymnals are those the editors of which have borne in mind the important relationship between words and melody, the need for a responsible choice of appropriate music, and the congregation's ability and enthusiasm for singing. The nature of congregational music itself poses special problems and requires a nice balance between intensity and sincerity of feeling, as well as propriety of expression.

A hymnal must also appeal across cultural barriers, to evoke a popular response without offending the more fastidious, to speak to the educated without bewildering the simple, and to encourage the unity of Christ's people within a society manifestly divided, both ignorant of, and sadly, hostile to, one another.

The second unusual characteristic of a hymnal is the degree of editorial interference perceptible therein, which can be very great indeed. In general, the editors of more modern hymnals have been more scrupulous and more careful in wielding their powers of abridgement and alteration than were earlier editors. These were no less responsible than their successors, but they counted their responsibility to liturgical, theological and hymnological standards more important than merely literary responsibility to an author.

The early editions of A&M offer rich material for

the study of all these aspects of hymn collections. As the prominence of Victorian names among the authors indicates, A&M was originally a Victorian conception and publication. It is the product of the confluence of a number of forces, historical, theological, ecclesiastical, social and literary. Historically it marks the coming of age of Anglican hymnody, in that until its publication, hymn-singing (and hymn-publishing) was largely a local, haphazard, amateur, and above all, recent phenomenon. The success of A&M proved that hymns had a place in the worship of the whole Church of England, and that in their dual nature of ancient tradition revived and popular demand supplied, they were a unifying means within a church extremely conscious of its parties and internal divisions.

Despite the best efforts of its Compilers, however, and a partial success,[1] A&M could not succeed in standardizing Anglican hymnody: the ancient tradition was too rich, the modern interest too enthusiastic, the range of taste (both aesthetic and theological) too broad. There were and still are too many serious competitors for any of them to be accepted officially as a book of common praise.

Why study A&M? First, it was an astonishing success: how the Compilers achieved, promoted, protected, and exploited that success is in itself an unusual publishing story. Second, it marks a moment in the history of the Victorian church, in the relationships between clergy and congregation, between parish priest and hierarchy, between the church and the people of the nation as a whole. To use a fanciful metaphor, the hymnal is a node in the system of nerves which binds together church and people: here cross many of the threads of sensitivity which extend throughout both groups -- spiritual vision, spiritual need, social conscience both individual and collective, ecclesiastical politics, theological controversies, the exigencies of scholarship, and the aesthetics of popularity. Third, it is a remarkable literary project. At first the Compilers exercised little more than the undergraduate skills of their classical education and their own enormous confidence, but they quickly perceived, and began to meet, the increasing need for meticulous linguistic, historical, and theological scholarship, for greater editorial responsibility and modesty. Fourth, A&M is worth looking at for its adaptations of the particular forms and limitations of hymn-writing and hymn-editing. Fifth, A&M is remarkable for something which is hard to analyze or even to isolate, but which may be called its imaginative effect, that is, its undeniable but strictly unaccountable hold over priest and people alike. Their belief in its effectiveness and its importance in the worship of God by a Victorian congregation is far stronger than could be justified by any reference to statistics on church attendance, conversion, or recidivism. A&M's general effect is in fact an extension of the seriousness with which the project was taken by its own Compilers, who never forgot that they were about their Lord's business, and who began each Committee meeting with an appeal to the Holy Ghost. The feeling of the Compilers for their book is what speaks most strongly from their records, a feeling compounded of earnestness, anxious attention to correctness of detail, eagerness (sometimes seen as arrogant) to promote their views, sensitivity to criticism and defensiveness under attack, an old-fashioned faith in tradition and a bold sense of innovation, dedication to the service of God, and a highly acute commercial sense. Such a blend of contraries and complementaries can be seen in all the actions and decisions of the Compilers, so that the study of A&M is also the study of an extraordinary working relationship among men of different tastes, talents, and temperaments. It is the study of a book in the process of becoming, and of changing, subject to and reflecting many different demands and influences. In the course of that study the book itself, something often taken for granted or examined only in idle curiosity, appears to be, as it rightfully is, an extraordinary accomplishment in its own right.

In choosing the aspects of A&M for particular study, the guidelines for selection have been, first, the intrinsic interest of the hymns themselves and of the special concerns of the hymn editors, and second, the wider interest of the relation of the hymnbook to its age. In all aspects it has not necessarily been more important to establish facts and measure effects than to consider intentions and to appreciate motives. This is primarily a literary study: the words and thoughts of the people involved are its materials, and such materials are notoriously difficult to evaluate objectively. There is a heavy emphasis throughout on attitude and expectation, for the fact that a clergyman may have been mistaken, when he claimed that hymn-singing in the parish church had reduced the incidence of crime in the parish alleyways, is of less concern than that the clergyman honestly believed that to have been the case.[2]

The study is organized in the following way. The present introductory chapter concludes with a sketch of some of the important concerns in Anglican church history immediately prior to and at the time of the publication of A&M. Chapter Two deals with hymnody and hymnology as a literary study, especially with the distinctions between hymns and other religious verse, and with the purposes for which hymns have been and may be intended. In addition, the English, and specifically, the Anglican, tradition of hymnody is traced to its culmination in A&M, the first of a new kind of hymnal. Chapter Three examines in detail the publishing history of A&M until 1875, and many of the practical aspects of nineteenth-century publishing, editions, revisions, the variety of available formats, pricing, advertising, sales, and the laws of copyright, which A&M exploited with a new determination and thoroughness. In Chapter Four are discussed editorial problems of sources, translations, alterations, and improvements, theological difficulties and the problem of avoiding offense to anti-Papist sensibilities, and the development of a sense of editorial and scholarly responsibility which begins to balance the sense of clerical duty with which the project had been undertaken. Chapter Five is a study of the attitudes which informed the book, partly deliberately and partly unconsciously. Only a few of the many possible areas are explored, and those through thematic groups of hymns. The sixth and final chapter deals with the expectations aroused by A&M, and with its general effect and appeal, by which is meant not so much the measurable success of the book as the faith its Compilers and its users had in it and in its value to the Church of England.

The study covers the first three volumes of A&M, that is, the Original edition of 1860/1861, the Appendix of 1868, and the Revised edition of 1875. Reference is made occasionally to the Supplement of 1889, but the inclusion of that volume in this study would have swollen it beyond reasonable or manageable proportions. Moreover, one of the chief concerns of the following chapters is to trace the changes from one volume to the next. With the publication of the Revised edition, the direction of A&M is confirmed, and the Supplement is only an extension, not a modification, of it. The next major change is with the publication of the New edition in 1904, and though some of its characteristics are foreshadowed in 1875, it clearly falls outside the limits of Victorian hymnody. It is insofar as it represents that area, that A&M has its chief interest here.

2. Historical Introduction

To try to understand what A&M was, or what it did, would be futile without some appreciation of the state of the Church of England in the nineteenth century or at least a catalogue of those characteristics and preoccupations of the Victorian church which relate to the practice of hymn-singing. The actual place, legal, traditional, and popular, of hymn-singing in Anglican worship is discussed separately in Chapter Two. What is of concern here are those issues which influenced or provided a background to the assumptions and decisions of the Compilers of A&M.

Which aspects of Victorian church history are relevant to A&M? There are four general areas: the Oxford Movement, Ritualism and Ceremony, relations with the Roman Catholic Church, and social responsibility. In many ways these areas overlap. One cannot, for instance, discuss either the Oxford Movement or Ritualism without some reference to the Roman Catholic Church, for not only were English churchmen influenced by Roman Catholics, but the evidence of that influence also provoked considerable anxiety in the hearts of their more Protestant compatriots.

The Oxford Movement was, of course, a major influence on the Compilers of A&M. Their understanding of the nature of the Church of England itself was shaped by the writers of the Tracts for the Times, with their emphasis upon the Catholic and Apostolic nature of the English church. Both geographical and historical limits were pushed back: the Church was encouraged not to repudiate, but instead to claim proudly its history and heritage of the pre-Reformation centuries. The rediscovery of the Church's mediaeval tradition is obviously reflected in the work of the hymnologists. The very title of Hymns Ancient and Modern proclaims their repossession of mediaeval hymnody. The enthusiasm for old service-books, for variations in local uses, and for accurate and poetic translations, was so great as almost to overwhelm their own judgement; any verses in Latin, even those of dubious antiquity, attracted eager translators and publishers.

The Tractarians' concept of the priesthood also affected the Compilers. Their own sense of priestly identity and of the sacred responsibility of their priestly function informed all their activities with a high seriousness at once self-conscious and selfless. Their hymnological project was not the casual indulgence of an idle antiquarian interest, but a part of their vocation to save souls and glorify God.

Their theology, too, was strongly influenced by the Tractarians, in its emphasis upon the sacraments and on the Church of Christ rather than on personal conversion and election. The Compilers were themselves High Churchmen, moderate Anglo-Catholics, who had no difficulty in accepting expressions which others found suggestive of Popery. They were accustomed to careful interpretation and the weighing of implication, so that Protestant conscience and Catholic truth might maintain a peaceful and vital co-existence.

Throughout this study there is evidence of the Compilers' debt to the Tractarians in both immediately identifiable matters, such as their espousal of the principle of Reserve, and also in less demonstrable ways. Their chief debt, however, is to the Tractarians as forerunners in controversy: the storm of public debate broke over the heads of an earlier generation. Their spiritual heirs found it easier to follow and consolidate where they had gone before. Practices that had provoked acrimony and even violence in the 1830s and 1840s passed without remark, or were admitted to be matters of aesthetics and taste rather than orthodoxy, in the 1860s and 1870s. That is not to say that there were not bitter arguments and debates between the Compilers and other churchmen. The difference is that the Compilers knew they had real support for their point of view and for their practices, and were not subject to the same pressures as the innovators.

Some of the most violent controversies in religious matters had been over aspects of what has been called ritualism, but ought more accurately to be called ceremonialism. It was not so much the ritual, that is, the form of worship of the Church of England, that was questioned,[3] as the ceremony that attended it. Differences of opinion about the propriety and even the legality of various practices sometimes escalated into actual violence, as at Exeter in 1845-1848, and in London, at St. Barnabas, Pimlico, in 1850 and at St.

George's-in-the-East in 1859. The reasoning behind ceremonial innovations was both theoretical and pragmatic. In theory, the emphasis on ceremony, involving such practices as the use of candles, lighted or unlighted, flowers, surplices for preachers and for choristers, incense, and the eastward position at the altar, could be seen as part of the antiquarianism associated with the Oxford Movement. The interpretation of the Ornaments Rubric in the Prayer Book depended upon a knowledge of historical practice,[4] the details of which were not common knowledge. In keeping also with the strong sacramentalism of Tractarian theology, the use of ceremony to indicate reverence could be interpreted as being only right and proper in celebrating such mysteries. Pragmatically, there was a strong belief among Anglo-Catholics that the colour and light and music of an elaborate ceremony were very attractive to the working classes, and would draw to worship those who would be indifferent to plainer services. Whether this belief was true is open to question. It is likely[5] that working people were not so much attracted by the trappings of the services as by the character of the clergyman, many Anglo-Catholic priests being extremely hard-working and devoted to the parishioners and their causes.[6]

To the beauty of Anglican ceremony and ritual the use of hymns added a further element, the heart-stirring strength of many voices raised in song. Congregational hymnody was part of a conscious attempt to appeal to the working classes, in whom loyalty might be inculcated through a sense of active participation and their own role in the service. The hymns were intended not only to attract urban heathen, but also to recall the errant.

The use of congregational hymns is only part of the great interest in the place of music in Anglican worship. The phenomenon is admirably documented in Bernarr Rainbow's _The Choral Revival in the Anglican Church 1839-1872_ (1970), in which he traces the two streams of musical interest which contributed to the revival. One of these was the antiquarian and scholarly interest in early music, an interest which was part of the enthusiasm for ecclesiology and all matters related to the decorous conduct of worship which was associated with Cambridge, and found formal expression in the Cambridge Camden Society and later, the Ecclesiological Society. An unfriendly observer drew an analogy between the Oxford Movement and the ecclesiological enthusiasm which holds, though their purposes may have been misinterpreted, that Romanism was taught "_Analytically_ at Oxford . . . _Artistically_ at Cambridge."[7]

The Ecclesiologists' musical concerns were chiefly in the hands of John Mason Neale and Thomas Helmore, who prepared for the society the _Hymnal Noted_ (1851 and 1854), a two-part collection of ancient hymns set to their original music, transcribed with some inaccuracy from old manuscripts into modern notation. Neale and Helmore were committed to the use of the proper tunes, Gregorian chants for the most part, for the ancient hymns. Their influence was immense and can easily be seen even in A&M, the Compilers of which were not so thoroughly averse to the notion of modern tunes for old hymns.

Thomas Helmore's name is associated not only with scholarship through his pioneering work on Gregorian chant, but also with popular musical education.[8] Teaching singing had come to be considered important during the 1830s, either as a means of improving the morals of schoolchildren and others (William Hickson's lecture on the "Use of Singing as Part of the Moral Discipline of Schools," 1838), or as a way of improving the singing of psalms in church (Sara Glover's Scheme to Render Psalmody Congregational, 1835). In the 1840s John Hullah's mass singing classes at Exeter Hall trained hundreds of schoolteachers to sing, and to teach singing by the same method (Hullah's) by which they had learned. By the end of 1841, Hullah estimated that fifty thousand London children would be learning to sing from his teachers.[9] Various methods of teaching and different kinds of musical notation were invented, and singing classes were held all over England. The Tonic Sol-fa system of notation, a synthesis of various methods of notation, was perfected by John Curwen, and became the most widely used form of non-traditional notation. School songbooks and church service-books were issued in the new notation; devotees of the system begged permission to "translate" popular music into Tonic Sol-fa. An edition of A&M in Tonic Sol-fa appeared in 1869.[10]

The Church of England took advantage of the enthusiasm for singing: John Hullah was hired to instruct student teachers at the National Society's training school of St. Mark's, Chelsea. The teachers were subsequently expected to train their pupils and the choir members in the parishes where they worked, thus improving at once the congregational and the choral music of their parish churches. Other singing-masters toured the country, sometimes staying long enough to establish a local church choir, sometimes only stopping to coach and encourage an already existing one. In this work, Thomas Helmore's brother Frederick was deeply involved.

If one group laboured to improve congregational music and to increase its importance in Anglican worship, another group was concerned to limit the participation of the congregation, and to improve the music of the church choir. These church musicians, chief among them Samuel Sebastian Wesley, wanted to establish a cathedral-type service in every parish large enough to provide a choir, so that music, even the chanting of psalms, was performed for the congregation and not by them. Curiously, Neale and Helmore's revival of the Gregorian tones was not intended as one might think for these choral services: Gregorian tones, they contended, were easier for congregations to sing, and would return to the people the music that was rightfully theirs. Though they were to some extent successful in promoting the use of Gregorian tones, especially after Helmore's Manual of Plainsong was published in 1849, there was not the general adoption that Neale and Helmore had hoped. Styles of music diverged: the "Anglican chants" favoured by the cathedral-service men became the norm for psalms, and modern tunes, related to popular and sometimes sentimental part-songs, were the generally accepted fare for hymns, with a few notable exceptions where an ancient hymn, together with its proper plainsong, had caught on.

That there was reason to be concerned for the improvement of church music is not open to doubt. The disparities of musical standards in the church before the choral revival explain the fervour with which musicians and ecclesiologists sought to improve them. The cathedrals had individual histories, but with their choirs and choir schools they could maintain an acceptable standard in their services. Parish churches, especially rural churches, were in very much worse straits: they relied for music upon a band of local instrument-players, and a choir whose sense of self-importance was rarely equalled by the quality of their singing. Largely illiterate congregations had either to listen to the choir's performance of the metrical psalms, or submit to the clerk's "lining-out" the psalm, a process which destroyed both rhythm and sense, though it did allow a kind of participation. In parishes where there were no local instrumentalists, or where the incumbent wished to suppress their individuality, a barrel organ might be introduced, providing consistency, at least, in accompaniment. The choice of tunes available, of course, was limited to the number of barrels the parish could afford to buy.[11]

The organ gradually became commonplace in parish churches through the middle of the nineteenth century, ending the era of the band and the choir, and enabling the ecclesiologists to call for the removal of the west-end galleries which had been built to contain them. Writers such as George Eliot and especially Thomas Hardy have given sympathetic portraits of parish clerks and musicians to set against the often extreme caricatures drawn by the ecclesiologists and those clergy whose sense of refinement had been offended by their robustness.

Given this situation, it is hardly surprising

that two schools of thought should arise concerning the best way to improve parochial worship. The cathedral-service standard certainly had its own advantages, as professionalism always has, but it also denied the essentially congregational nature of parish services, and reduced worshippers to spectators. Those who responded to the challenge to incorporate parishioners fully into the services -- by training sober surpliced choirs to lead them, by providing hymn-books with music, by training them and their children to sing, and by offering them frequent chances both within and beyond the formal services of the church to practise and enjoy their singing -- took the harder, and perhaps the better way. The Compilers of A&M were among them.

The relations between the Church of England and the Roman Catholic Church were extremely complex in the nineteenth century, mostly because it was not only the clergy and hierarchies who were drawn in, but ordinary church members also. The most interesting aspects of this matter are, first, the intellectuals' attraction and sometimes conversion to Roman Catholicism, and second, the popular suspicion of Roman subversion or aggression. It is enough just to recall the shock and the resulting uncertainty which Newman's conversion had occasioned. When a man of his stature repudiates what he has long been concerned to protect and improve, the consequences are not confined to his own life. Other conversions followed Newman's, until it seemed as if the _Tracts for the Times_ had been written to benefit Rome, and not to stir up Anglicanism. The theological and historical enthusiasms of Tract readers led them to a better knowledge of the similarities between the two communions, and to load all the responsibility for the differences upon far fewer points than had been assumed. It needed a rigorous, as well as an acute, mind to say "thus far do I carry my understanding of a doctrine, and no farther." The seeming rapprochement of Roman and Anglo-Catholics caused a real weakening in the Church of England by threatening the flexibility of its traditional via media and insisting upon stricter definitions and interpretations of doctrine. The Church of England's special status as a national church requires a certain flexibility in order to preserve its genuinely national character: too much definition inevitably restricts its appeal. Again and again in the correspondence relating to A&M is heard the plea not to define what has traditionally been left undefined, not to specify what has been general, not to offend or anger unnecessarily.

Offense might easily be taken. Anti-Popery sentiments were often directed not against Papists themselves but against Anglo-Catholics whose ceremonialism was misinterpreted. With the exception of the nervousness occasioned by the institution of a British hierarchy in 1850, a move immediately dubbed Papal Aggression, the English were more ready to imagine schemes and plots than to detect outright missionizing if and when it occurred. If Francis Close detected Popery in the restoration of churches, there were others who saw it in the publication of A&M. The accusations of one of these critics are discussed in detail in Chapter Four.

The church's sense of social responsibility became more acute as the century progressed. The concern found expression in many ways, from the

Ecclesiastical Commission's encouragement of new church building in the 1830s, to the appointment of suffragan bishops to look after missions on a diocesan level. Clergy came to rely on the help of district visitors, missioners, and lay readers to identify their parishioners' needs and respond effectively and immediately to them. University settlements were founded in slum areas to supply a constant source of practical help and godly influence. The range of projects initiated by individuals and committees was immense. Not all met with the same success; in fact, regarded practically, most of the ambitious and idealistic schemes were failures, though no clergyman would count them so as long as he felt he was doing his duty and preparing the salvation of even one soul. Some of the most admirable work was done by individuals who sought to work within the limits of the parochial system, idealistically believing that its centuries-old structure could accommodate the needs of nineteenth-century urban and industrial society. The cynical dismiss many of their attempts as mere gestures, futile or, worse, deceptive, but that judgement is unduly harsh. The more convenient time-tabling of weekday services so that devout working people could attend had a demonstrably good effect on church attendance. Whether or not parochial missions had any long-term effect is, on the other hand, more doubtful. The adoption of services such as the one for harvest and of such activities as choral festivals, may not have attracted many newcomers to church but did reflect a new awareness of popular tastes and interests. Hymn-singing was also one of the ways in which the clergy attempted to adapt traditional forms of service to new tastes: it is undeniably a gesture, but a grand one, intended to advertise the presence and the vitality of the church, and to draw both the waverers and the faithful together in the communion of song. Behind all the scholarly and hymnological enthusiasm of the Compilers of A&M can be detected that serious social purpose -- to do whatever was possible to ensure that "kings of the earth and all people; princes and all judges of the world; young men and maidens, old men and children, praise the Name of the Lord."[12]

Not all the issues touched on in the preceding pages are directly or immediately relevant to the publication or importance of A&M, and even those that are (Popery and social responsibility, for instance) are much larger subjects than can be discussed here. Social responsibility, for instance, is less a practical aspect of the hymn-book than an attitude to be detected in the editorial decisions of its Compilers, and, as will be seen, by no means a consistent attitude. Nevertheless, even to mention some of the issues of nineteenth-century ecclesiasical history serves to remind the reader that A&M was published in a complex and exciting period. It is sometimes easy to be deceived into thinking of the preparation and publication of such a book as a peaceful pursuit remote from the controversies with which the century was rife. That misconception will not survive long. The hymnbook was the occasion of much debate, some of it acrimonious, for it was a real product of its age, and through a study of its pages it is possible to see that age, and the churchgoers who peopled it, from a new perspective, and at the same time, soundly in context.

NOTES

[1] As a result of conscientious effort and the exercise of copyright law, the A&M Compilers did succeed in establishing their versions or translations of a number of hymns.

[2] See Chapter Six.

[3] There was, in fact, real pressure for the revision of the Book of Common Prayer from both within and without the Church, culminating in the Royal Commission on Ritual of 1867. The issues of revision were more complex, and less easily polarized in popular opinion, than those of ceremony.

[4] "Provided always, and be it Enacted, That such Ornaments of the Church and of the Ministers thereof, shall be retained, and be in use, as was in this Church of England, by Authority of Parliament, in the second year of the Reign of King Edward the Sixth, until other Order shall be therein taken by the Authority of the Queen's Majesty," etc. An Act for the Unity of Common Prayer, etc., Book of Common Prayer.

[5] For details, see Owen Chadwick, The Victorian Church II, 2nd edition (1972), 311-313, and K.S. Inglis, Churches and the Working Classes in Victorian England (1963), 46.

[6] Beresford-Hope argued that it was not, in fact, the working classes to which ceremony appealed, but that class "which, without sharing in the easy circumstances of the so-called upper and upper middle classes, has the disadvantage of being, by the stern laws of conventionality, compelled to burden itself with the characteristic dress of those classes - clerks, dressmakers, the young men and women employed in the wholesale establishments and so on." In the course of their business they come into contact with people and objects which give them "glimpses of beauty and ideas of refinement, which they cannot follow out or gratify with their own resources." The church allows them to bask in, and feel at home with, sensual magnificence. A.J.B. Beresford-Hope, Worship in the Church of England (1874), 248-249.

[7] Rev. Francis Close, "The Restoration of Churches is the Restoration of Popery: Proved and Illustrated from the Authenticated Publications of the 'Cambridge

Camden Society.' A Sermon Preached in the Parish Church, Cheltenham, On Thursday, November 5th, 1844," quoted in James White, The Cambridge Movement (1962), 142.

[8] See Bernarr Rainbow, The Land Without Music (1967).

[9] Rainbow, The Land Without Music, 125.

[10] See Chapter Three, 2, ii.

[11] In 1862, when the Rev. E.D. Burrows came to his parish church at Wareham in Dorset, the musical resources of the congregation were limited to one barrel, offering three tunes and two chants. (A.P., Letter, May 8, 1876, E.D. Burrows to H.W.B.)

[12] Psalm 148: 11-12, Book of Common Prayer.

Chapter Two
Hymnody and Hymnology

1. The Theory and Function of Hymnody

i. Preamble

To this point the word hymn has been used, as it is commonly understood, to mean a piece of regular versification sung, stanza by stanza to a recurring tune, by the people in the course of a service of worship. Such a circumstantial description in no way defines what a hymn is, and it is the purpose of this chapter to examine the nature of a hymn, its characteristics of excellence, and the uses to which it may be put. This examination will be conducted under three main heads: first, the general meaning of the term, and some of the simpler formal distinctions; second, the important and vexed problems of the relationship of hymnody to religious poetry; and third, some Victorian descriptions in which suitability and practicality of use are as important as any more theoretical formulations. Part One of this chapter concludes with a discussion of the role of emotion in hymn-singing, and of the didactic and propagandistic function of hymns.

ii. The Definition of a Hymn

Over the essential definition of a hymn there is no disagreement: the Oxford English Dictionary calls it a "song of praise to God," and Saint Augustine, "the praise of God in song."[1] The singing or composition of such songs of praise is hymnody, and by extension, the body of such songs composed or sung is also hymnody.

St. Augustine's definition is generic. Hymns can be further distinguished according to a number of criteria, such as the source of the words, the language used, the music, the singers, or the occasion of singing. Some of these distinctions overlap.

The source of the words distinguishes scriptural from non-scriptural texts, or paraphrases from original hymns. Psalmody comprises both the chanting of the psalms and the singing of metrical versions of them. The importance of psalmody is that of tradition at its most significant: the psalms were part of the celebration of principal Jewish festivals, and in continuing their use, the church emphasizes its derivation from a Judaic tradition, and continues a Christian one.[2] Indeed, the prejudice against importing non-scriptural words into the liturgy of the church made psalmody dominant for centuries, at first in the Roman church,[3] and, after the Reformation, among those Protestants who were influenced by Calvinism.

Psalmody is not the only scriptural hymnody. Many passages of the Bible have been paraphrased for singing. It is not always easy to determine when a paraphrase becomes a commentary, and ought properly to be considered original. The hymns of Isaac Watts often pose this problem.[4]

Language is also a criterion of distinction: hymns may be written in a liturgical language such as Latin, or in the vernacular. An important characteristic of carols, for instance, though not a necessary one, is that they are written in the vernacular, suitable to a popular rather than a liturgical use. For in carols, mediaeval hymnody found its popular form, with a greater emphasis on gospel, or even apocryphal, narrative or human glimpses than on theological niceties. They were written in a dance rhythm and often had a refrain which could easily be joined. Not all carols are folk-song: many were deliberately written to supplement the more staid services of which the people were spectators only. Nor were all such art-carols written in the vernacular: some were all in Latin, and some were macaronic, with lines in both Latin and the vernacular.

In the Church of England, the Reformers' insistence upon the use of English in worship meant that Latin hymns were excluded from public use along with Latin prayers, and that, with the exception of some choral pieces in the cathedrals, Anglican hymnody has been exclusively English.

Some kinds of hymnody are characterized by the music to which they are sung. Again, carols furnish an example, for they were originally written to dance tunes, and, indeed, the word can mean a round dance with singing. Another example is the German chorale, a hymn set to an often traditional melody harmonized in four or more parts. Bach wrote many chorales: they have a deliberate grace, given authority by the certainty of the harmony, and lightness by the movement of the inner voices. Even when the hymn is sung in unison, it is immediately recognizable in its resonance.

The fourth criterion mentioned is the singers. Songs of praise may be sung by anyone or any number, but some formal distinctions can be made. Usually, for instance, hymns and anthems are differentiated: primarily, the people in the nave sing hymns, while those in the choir or chancel sing anthems. Anthems are, after all, only the more complex songs of praise, requiring rather better-trained singers.[5]

The occasion of a hymn's use is closely related to its function and purpose within the service of worship. Broadly speaking, however, one may distinguish between hymns used liturgically, that is, with direct reference to the office or service of worship, and those used *ad libitum*, according to the worshippers' needs or wishes, or the clergy's intention. Thus, a service may include an office hymn, appropriate to the day or hour, and a "general" hymn, the theme of which may reflect or illustrate some local circumstance or a particular sermon.

The distinctions outlined above are largely formal rather than essential. It is akin to a discussion of poetry which carefully presents the differences between epic and lyric, sonnet and *vers libre*, without touching upon the difference between poetry and mere versification. The essence of hymnody is almost as difficult to define as the essence of poetry, although descriptions abound, and there exist a number of undisputed touchstones, in the Arnoldian sense, to serve as reminders, examples, and counter-examples.

A final comment upon the definition of a hymn must here be made. St. Augustine's definition is both general and impossibly narrow, depending as it does upon the meaning of the word praise. A literal interpretation will limit a song of praise to the _Sanctus_, for it is impossible for finite beings adequately to "commend the merits," as the O.E.D. puts it, of an infinite and ineffable being, and they can only echo the song of the heavenly host. It is difficult for human beings to conceive of God's majesty, save in comparison with their own littleness, or of divine mercy, except by contrast with their own unworthiness. Human beings cannot even apprehend God save as the Creator is manifest in the creation, or in Providence, demonstrably operating in the history of the chosen people, or most wonderfully in the Incarnation. In short, the praise of God cannot be disinterested, and its human terms of reference, and limitations, must be accepted. What St. Augustine's definition excludes is undue emphasis upon the human rather than the divine element of worship, upon the worshippers rather than the Deity. It is a point made again and again by writers upon the subject.

iii. Hymnody and Religious Poetry

A hymn must be considered a form of religious poetry, which has itself long been a special case in criticism. The first question which arises in discussing religious poetry is, ought religious poetry to be properly considered under the head of religion, or of poetry? Is the religious poet one who infuses all subjects with a religious spirit, or one who writes about the topics of religion? Religion and poetry are very close in their essential function, defined by Helen Gardner as "ordering and interpreting . . . experience and rendering it in moving and expressive symbols."[6] If poetry is also special insight, what distinguishes it from revelation or prophecy? It is the quality of the insight, and the resultant ordering and interpretation of experience, which is important, not the name by which the source of insight is called.

One consequence of this line of argument is that religion and poetry may be seen to be interchangeable -- or rather, that if the forms that religious insight takes are no longer acceptable or comprehensible (perhaps because its symbols are no longer "moving and expressive," or are drawn from a cultural background outgrown), forms of poetic insight may take over. This takeover is what Matthew Arnold predicted in his essay "The Study of Poetry," when he wrote that poetry would inherit the mantle of religion:

> More and more mankind will discover that we have to turn to poetry to interpret life for us, to console

> us, to sustain us. Without poetry, our science will appear incomplete; and most of what now passes with us for religion and philosophy will be replaced by poetry.[7]

Arnold does not mean that priests would be ordained on the strength of their versification, or that a rhyming dictionary would replace the Thirty-nine Articles, but that poetic insight would afford a new order and interpretation of human experience, in newly moving and expressive symbols.

John Keble, unlike Arnold, did not consider that the symbols of his religion were in any way losing significance, for he believed them to express ultimate insight -- Truth. The insights of poetry are a forerunner of the revelation of religion, writes Keble, citing Virgil in the fortieth of his Lectures on Poetry, and, in discussing Lucretius, he associates Nature with poetry, and declares:

> ...the Great and Good God ordained him to be a shining witness, in what high and special reverence we should hold both all the form and feature of the world around us, and that region of Poetry, in particular, which is most deeply concerned with them. In truth, I firmly believe that all these things were granted as a solace of sorrowing mortals till such time as true Religion should be revealed, and that minds

> which have been imbued with divine truth should look on them as a valuable means, for they are fraught with the sense of piety.[8]

For Keble, the insights of the pagan poets are like the theories of primitive people who, out of the alternations of darkness and light, declared that the sun circled the earth in a predictable course. Divine revelation is like the scientific discovery that the earth revolves around the sun; it is a deeper truth, the appreciation of which does not alter day and night, but only the context in which people perceive them. Both theories make sense of the observable phenomena, and the discrediting of the first can only come through information, such as the mathematics of the orbits of the planets, which the non-mathematician and the non-astronomer must accept as a kind of authoritative revelation.

This argument has emphasized the similarities between poetry and religion in order to underline the difficulties which arise when one wishes to write specifically religious poetry, that is, to apply poetic insight to that part of human experience which deals with the numinous. The intellectual problems of the task are enormous; as an example, consider what it is to write a poem about the Eucharist. To write such a poem is to construct a system of verbal symbols for an act, which is in fact the re-enactment, using symbols of bread and wine for the body and blood of Christ, of an event, the sacrifice of the Son of God, which is itself a metaphor for the triumph of good over evil, of mercy over justice, of life over death. To consider all the levels of symbolism and metaphor in religious poetry would bewilder all but the most clear-headed and theologically-minded critic. The reader of the poem must accept the theological metaphors as the foundation upon which the poet has built, and consider only the soundness of the construction. As Helen Gardner puts it, the religious poet asks the reader to accept "truths which are not presented as personal discoveries, values that are not his individual values, and to measure the experiences treated against standards that the poem itself does not create but whose existence it takes for granted."[9] Religious poets make this demand even when they choose a subject not specifically religious, for the poem is nonetheless informed by the attitudes they bring to the task.

The need has already been expressed to distinguish between what may be called religious poetry and the poetry of religion. The first is written out of a religious commitment, but does not necessarily deal with any overtly religious subject, though it is informed by a religious as well as a poetic insight. The poetry of religion, on the other hand, is specifically about religion in its theological essence or in human experience. Samuel Johnson distinguishes three kinds of poetry of religion, didactic verse, praise, and devotional verse.

Didactic verse is straightforward: as Johnson observed, "the doctrines of religion may indeed be defended in a didactick poem; and he who has the happy power of arguing in verse, will not lose it because his subject is sacred."[10] There is a strong didactic element in hymnody, though it is rarely found there unmixed. The didacticism of hymnody is discussed more fully below in section four of this chapter.

In addition to didactic verse, Johnson admits that verse that praises the "Maker for His works" may also be successful. This element is undeniably the principal one in hymnody, according to the essential definition discussed above. As Johnson says, "the subject of the disputation is not piety, but the motives to piety; that of the description is not God, but the works of God."[11] Two works of God are principally remembered in hymns, the creation and redemption of mankind, both of which are, in Johnson's phrase, excellent "motives to piety."

What Johnson cannot accept is "poetical devotion," that is to say, "contemplative piety, or the intercourse between God and the human soul" in poetical form. "Man admitted to implore the mercy of his Creator, and plead the merits of his Redeemer, is already in a higher state than poetry can confer."[12] His argument is couched in the terms of eighteenth-century criticism, as when he declares that the "essence of poetry is invention," and that the "topicks of devotion [being] few, and . . . universally known . . . can be made no more; they can receive no grace from novelty of sentiment, and very little from novelty of expression."[13] In this, however, he has the support of the Victorian Palgrave, who remarked in his _Treasury of Sacred Song_ that sacred verse had a very limited sphere, at least, in comparison with the "many provinces" of secular verse.[14]

The forms of intercourse between God and the

human soul are fourfold, according to Johnson, and he dismisses them all as subjects for poetry.

> The employments of pious meditation are Faith, Thanksgiving, Repentance, and Supplication. Faith, invariably uniform, cannot be invested by fancy with decorations. Thanksgiving, the most joyful of all holy effusions, yet addressed to a Being without passions, is confined to a few modes, and is to be felt rather than expressed. Repentance trembling in the presence of the judge, is not at leisure for cadences and epithets. Supplication of man to man may diffuse itself through many topicks of persuasion; but supplication to God can only cry for mercy.[15]

Johnson is saying that poetry cannot be expected to substitute for prayer, which is the proper name for pious meditation. Furthermore, "of sentiments purely religious, it will be found that the most simple expression is the most sublime."[16] Or, as Helen Gardner says, prayer at its most intense passes beyond words into silence, and that is why there is a conflict between poetry and prayer, for poetry aims at the highest possible articulateness.[17] The conflict, however, is needless, and has arisen out of the confusion of the functions of poetry and prayer. Johnson has glanced at the important distinction, but failed to make of it what it deserves. "All that pious verse can do," he says, "is to help the memory, and delight the ear, and for these purposes it may be very useful; but it supplies nothing to the mind. The ideas of Christian Theology are too simple for eloquence, too sacred for fiction, and too majestick for ornament."[18]

Pious verse or devotional poetry, however, does more than help the memory and delight the ear: by these means it prepares believers to worship. Its articulation of the needs and weaknesses of the human soul is not intended for the ears of God; its enumeration of the works of Creation cannot please God;[19] its formulation of the ideas of Christian theology is hopelessly inadequate to the expression of the Divine Mind -- but the intended effect of all these is upon the worshippers themselves. Their insight into the inadequacy of heart and of mind prepares them and moves them to address their souls to God, and when the soul speaks, it speaks in prayer. Johnson wrote that pious poetry cannot "animate devotion"; if he meant that poetry was not the essence, soul, or *anima* of devotion, then he was right, but even in his own dictionary he does not define "animate" thus. He does, however, define it as "to encourage, to incite," and that is precisely the function that devotional poetry does perform.

Thus we may speak of devotional poetry not as a mode of worship, but as an aid to devotion or a means to worship. Keble confirms this conclusion, saying (of all poetry, but the specific application is justifiable) that the "very practice and cultivation of Poetry will be found to possess . . . the power of guiding and composing the mind to worship and prayer."[20]

What relation, however, does hymnody bear to devotional poetry? Clearly, the same relation as the prayers of the Book of Common Prayer bear to the individual's devotions. That is to say, hymns are a public form of devotional poetry, as common prayer is a public form of devotion.

Common or congregational forms of expression are subject to specific limitations. Public worship is quite distinct from individual devotion (the intercourse between God and the human soul) though it may provide the framework for such an experience. Public or congregational worship means rather the "reverent homage or service" rendered to God, and is an affirmation of the church of Christ on earth and of the communion of saints. Questions are immediately raised about the insincerity of public worship and public prayers. The formal prayers of public worship concentrate on the shared elements of Christian faith in general confession and common supplication. Both prayers and hymns ought to function in public worship precisely as does the Apostles' Creed, which is a statement of the *sine qua non* of Christian belief. It is by no means an exhaustive statement: the Nicene Creed is a much more full version. The Apostles' Creed holds its central place in morning and evening prayer because it is the minimum statement: the congregation may and must profess it in all sincerity, though their individual creeds might contain many more clauses, not all of them equally acceptable to all individuals.

Since it is shared, common prayer assumes some of the characteristics of poetry rather than prayer. Its highest value is articulateness, and not necessarily the simplest articulation, though it may appear simple. Those who wrought the prayers for the Anglican services laboured over them as long and as intelligently as any poet over fanciful decorations and leisured epithets. The measure of their poetic craft is the authority of their phrases, smoothed with use to the simple perfection of familiarity so that the congregation is neither distracted by novelty or ingenuity, nor lulled out of meaning by a facile formula long committed to memory and lost to understanding.

It is not possible for hymns to attain quite the same excellence of formal expression, because that excellence depends to such an extent upon familiarity as well as upon the careful choice of word and phrase. Only in the case of those songs of praise which are an integral part of morning and evening prayer, the *Te Deum* or the *Jubilate*, the *Magnificat* or the *Nunc dimittis*, is that public sense of immutable rightness achieved. Even the most frequently sung of metrical hymns, because they are a variable part of public worship,[21] are inevitably touched with particular associations from the circumstances of their singing, and thus lose the universality of the formal prayers. Their particularity may in fact be an important strength, but an emotional and individual one, rather than an objective and general one.

Nevertheless, the function of hymns in public worship is an important, varied, and occasionally subtle one. Like devotional poetry, hymns are rather preparatory to worship than an effusion of worship itself. It has already been noted that hymns can play an undoubted didactic role; in this they are like the sermon. They are also a chief expression of common praise: the people are brought to think of the glory of God, to magnify God to the limits (aforementioned) of their beings.

It has been argued above that devotional poetry does not express faith, thanksgiving, repentance, or supplication as much as it animates these forms of devotion. Hymns perform the same function in public worship, always subject to the same constraints as public prayers. The faith, thanksgiving, repentance and supplication which are reinforced by hymns must be common rather than individual, expressed in terms that are not incongruous in the context of congregational worship. The hymn-writer writes out of individual devotion, but writes for common worship.

The relation of hymnody to religious poetry is not a simple subject to discuss, for it inevitably leads to an examination of the meaning of such key words as worship and devotion, and the important differences between public and private forms of both prayer and praise. Once the terms are distinguished, however, and the relations sketched out, they may be compared and contrasted with what Victorian writers said on the same subject, with their own meanings and uses in mind. Some Victorian descriptions of hymnody, in theory and practice, are discussed in the section which immediately follows.

A final note must be made about the adoption, or adaptation, of poems for use as hymns. Obviously not every hymn in A&M was originally intended for public worship; many, like Keble's "New every morning" (2/4) were published in collections for private use. As long as they comply with the standards of general suitability outlined above, it is a simple matter to include them in a hymnal. Often they need only abridgement, or a change of pronoun, though sometimes more extensive alterations may be carried out.[22] Such adapted hymns present no real problems. Increasingly, however, nineteenth-century hymn editors included in their pages poems which were the private thoughts of their authors, beginning with Newman's "Lead, kindly Light" (342/266) and eventually including poems by George Herbert and even Tennyson. Nor were these poems much altered to make them conform to the standards of public use, partly because of the increasing editorial respect for an author's text, and partly because the verses were so thoroughly un-hymn-like that they resisted, and made to look foolish, any attempts to "hymnodize" them. Fortunately such poem-hymns are not a great feature of the editions of A&M under consideration here, and it is not necessary to seek editorial justification for their use. Even "Lead, kindly Light" may be acceptable; its more personal details are recognizable if not common, and more than compensated by the emotional and spiritual truth it presents. Editors may of course find excellent hymns outside the ancient hymnals or the contemporary books of private devotional verse which are the usual sources. Newman's second hymn in A&M is "Praise to the Holiest in the height" (305/172), which the editors took from "The Dream of Gerontius," for which it was written as a genuine song of praise, the triumphant conclusion of the poem.

iv. Some Victorian Descriptions

The hymn-writers whose opinions are discussed below often seem to have a very utilitarian approach to their subject. They are not as much interested in what a hymn is, as in what it does, and in how well it achieves its purpose. Thus the descriptions are largely concerned with how suitable a hymn is for its use in congregational worship, and a hymn's excellence is judged in proportion to that suitability.

The Rev. L.C. Biggs, whose annotated edition of A&M was published in 1867, discussed in his preface to that book[23] the chief characteristics of good hymns, and concluded that, though a strict canon was impossible to draw, they must be devotional, intelligible, and earnest. By devotional he meant that hymns should bring the "soul of the singer into communion with God,"[24] that is, to perform the preparatory, animating function analyzed above. Intelligibility is essential to this end, for "an involved construction, a foreign phraseology, an allusion unexplained or misunderstood, will at once paralyse the devotional power of a hymn."[25] Earnestness he equates with sincerity, for he attributes a lack of earnestness to a writer's trying to describe "what he has only imagined, not felt, in the way of spiritual experience," and likens it to "affectation," or "visible artifice."[26]

Biggs's straightforward assessment of a good hymn is echoed by other Victorian writers. Dr. Boyd Carpenter, writing about the hymns of W.W. How, called "devotional feeling" and "good sense" the chief requisites of good hymns. Brilliancy or eccentricity, he declared, was the ruin of a hymn.[27] Anything unusual which provokes questions or criticism among those who read or sing a hymn will necessarily distract from the primary purpose of bringing the soul into communion with God. It is for this reason that Tennyson is reputed to have lamented that "a good hymn is the most difficult thing in the world to write. In a good hymn you have to be commonplace and poetical. The moment you cease to be commonplace and put in any expression at all out of the ordinary, it ceases to be a hymn."[28] One could reasonably object that Tennyson's statement is exaggerated, and that the common stock of language and thought upon which a hymn may draw is anything but commonplace, including as it does the richness of Biblical diction and imagery, and the ideas of Christian theology both simple and majestic. It is entirely appropriate to draw upon these sources, for they are the possessions of the congregation even when other education has been denied them.

Furthermore, the form of a hymn must be simple enough to allow its material to be immediately comprehensible, for a hymn is a song, and music waits for no one to fathom complicated sentence structure. It is not necessary to agree with Auden entirely in his observations on lyric and song,[29] but it is true that the immediacy of the music does compel the words.[30]

When Biggs writes about earnestness or sincerity, he is making a point of great importance about hymns in public worship. Just as the prayers in the church service voice common concerns, so hymns derive their force from common experience. Reference has already been made to creation and salvation as two motives to piety, shared by all Christians, which find expression in hymns of thanksgiving. Similarly, as sin is also a common human experience, penitential hymns may be written, preparing Christians for the confession of their sins. A penitential hymn ought, however, to be no more specific than the general confession of the prayer book, ("We acknowledge and bewail our manifold sins and wickedness, Which we, from time to time, most grievously have committed, By thought, word, and deed, Against thy Divine Majesty") as in the following stanza of a Lenten hymn:

> With self-accusing voice within,
> Our conscience tells of many a sin
> In thought and word and deed:
> O cleanse that conscience from all stain,
> The penitent restore again,
> From every burthen freed.[31]

It would be an obvious affectation in all but a very few individual cases to sing of idiosyncratic depths of sinfulness, and mere sensationalism to dwell upon any depravity which ordinary Christians ought to have repudiated, if they ever knew it.

On the other hand, it may be permissible to sing of heights of aspiration, beyond the experience and perhaps beyond the reach of the congregation, as the affirmation of an ideal which Christians by definition and by profession acknowledge, and attempt, however imperfectly, to achieve. The singing of such a hymn unites the individual members of the church, inspiriting and encouraging them, until what may have begun as a gesture ends in conviction. Further discussion of sincerity in hymnody follows in section v of this chapter.

Other hymn-writers were even more strict than Biggs in outlining what does and what does not constitute a good hymn. Canon John Ellerton, one of the co-editors of the S.P.C.K.'s Church Hymns,[32] was himself a most conscientious hymn-writer. The following statement sets forth his views.

> Hymns may express adoration, thanksgiving, commemoration of God's mercies; they may be prayers, penitential, supplicatory, intercessory; they may be devout aspirations after God; but in any case they must be forms of worship. It is not enough that they suggest devotion, they must be capable of expressing it. The observance of this rule would clear the ground at once of much irrelevant matter with which the hymn books of every Church and sect are at present encumbered. The whole multitude of didactic and hortatory verses, the addresses to sinners and saints, the paraphrases of Scripture prophecies, promises and warnings, the descriptions of heaven and hell, the elaborate elucidations of the anatomy and pathology of the soul; all these ... ought utterly and for ever to be banished from the choir.[33]

On first reading it appears that Ellerton's views contradict the understanding reached in the discussions above, where it was argued that hymns, as a kind of devotional poetry, are not a form or mode of worship, but a means to worship, and a preparation for it. Yet Ellerton specifically says that hymns must be forms of worship, and must express, not merely suggest, devotion. Furthermore, he identifies hymns with prayers, whereas it was argued above that there is an essential conflict between poetry and prayer. He has, however, exaggerated his point in order to emphasize his chief plea, that hymns be always directed to their proper end, the praise of God. Therefore he rejects material which he considers irrelevant, though not everyone would agree with his judgment. Certainly his scorn of the "elaborate elucidations of the anatomy and pathology of the soul" is justified; such material, being far too individual, is already condemned by the standard of congregational suitability. The other things he condemns are not so much irrelevant as peripheral, or better, subordinate to the chief end. Didactic and hortatory verses have exactly the same right to a place in a service of worship as has the sermon: that is to say, the sermon cannot be said to be an act of devotion in the same way as can the prayers, but it is an opening of the minds of the people to receive instruction and to offer their finite understanding, that they may worship with the mind as well as with the heart and soul and voice. Ellerton is unnecessarily strict in excluding the didactic and hortatory elements of hymnody: he would, if he could, confine all hymns to a simple shout of praise, but how limiting that would be. One of his own translations in A&M 1868 is of "Alleluia piis edite laudibus" (336/296):

Sing Alleluia forth in duteous praise,
Ye citizens of Heav'n; O sweetly raise
An endless Alleluia.

While Thee, by Whom were all things made,
we praise
For ever, and tell out in sweetest lays
An endless Alleluia. (stanzas 1,8)

The endless alleluia is Ellerton's ideal of praise; ironically, however, he must incorporate it in a metrical hymn. Moreover, the first seven of the hymn's nine stanzas are addressed to the citizens of heaven, in direct contradiction of Ellerton's proscription of addresses to sinners and saints. Perhaps, after all, he will allow that such addresses are not irrelevant.

The "paraphrases of Scripture prophecies, promises and warnings, the descriptions of heaven and hell" are also familiar in hymnody. Why did Ellerton object to this large if vague group of hymns? In Chapter Five there is a discussion of the hymns of paradise, which contains some of the background for Ellerton's objection. To revel in the imagined details of a local paradise is to escape the pressing realities of an actual existence. To think about the world to come, whether in prophecy or promise or warning, is to be distracted from the Christian's immediate responsibility, which is, to live well in this world. Despite Ellerton, and despite those hymn-writers who deliberately used escapism and distraction, hymns which concern themselves with the world to come can also be concerned with what Ellerton described as "devout aspirations after God," or the soul's longing for closer communion with God. Nowhere can hymns more effectively perform their preparatory function as means to worship than in such a context. Doubt legitimately arises when it seems that it is the primary aim of a hymn to provoke the emotional thrill of yearning, and in doing so, slight the all-important end which is the praise of God.

The descriptions of Ellerton and Biggs are closer than is immediately apparent. Both make the spirit of devotion the primary characteristic of a good hymn. Ellerton stresses the variety of forms that spirit may take (adoration, thanksgiving, penitence, supplication, aspiration), and warns of the extreme forms which may supplant devotion. Biggs sets up standards of intelligibility and sincerity to measure all hymns, and by those standards excludes much of what Ellerton criticizes. Thus, though a good hymn may be penitential, it cannot be abysmally so, for then it would be an exploration of the pathology of the soul, in Ellerton's phrase, or an affectation, in Biggs' terms.

Having looked at the categories and standards delineated by Ellerton and Biggs, the would-be hymnologist is advised to consider J.M. Neale's condemnation of excessive codification, epitomized by the rules of hymnody devised by Faustinus Arevalus, regularizer of the ancient hymns in the Spanish Breviary. Neale's comment is indignant:

> First of all, think what a hymn is: the dearer, the warmer, the more unfettered elevation of the soul to that Human Soul which wrought out

> our redemption, even than prayer can be, -- and will you rather ridicule or be disgusted with the laws of this critic?[34]

Arevalus' rules are directions for the manufacture (Neale's word) of acceptable hymns, by the correct use of rhyme, metre, music, style, and standard structure. It is in reaction to such a formal and rigid code that Neale puts his emphasis upon the spiritual and emotional essence of a hymn. He echoes the conviction of George Herbert, whose poem "A True Hymn" dismisses the Arevalian hymn:

> He who craves all the minde,
> And all the soul, and strength, and time,
> If the words onely ryme,
> Justly complains, that somewhat is behinde
> To make his verse, or write a hymne in kinde.
>
> Whereas if th' heart be moved,
> Although the verse be somewhat scant,
> God doth supplie the want.
> As when th' heart sayes (sighing to be approved)
> O, *could I love*! and stops: God writeth, *Loved*.[35]

The conclusion is clear: despite the best efforts at definition and description, hymnody remains a special critical case. The tools of literary criticism serve an important purpose in analyzing and in producing the precise effect wanted in worship, but there is a limit to their usefulness, for there is a point where the soul's expression is unfettered, the heart is moved, and the communion of the human soul with God takes place. Toward this moment, the hymn in its literary form can only point.

v. Emotion and Emotionalism

At several points in the discussion above, the question of sincerity or emotion has arisen, and an attempt must now be made to clarify what is one of the more controversial aspects of hymnody. The terms with which this section will concern itself are emotion, emotionalism, and reserve; subjectivity and objectivity; sentimentalism and sincerity.

Since the eighteenth century there have been those who distrusted enthusiasm, finding it unbecoming at best. The distrust attached itself to whatever was conducive to enthusiasm, as the following entry in an early nineteenth-century journal reveals:

> At times during the service, had a joyful sense of the divine presence, but as it was chiefly during the hymns, I think these affections suspicious.[36]

Emotion cannot be removed from hymnody: praise is a joyous activity. The contemplation of the infinite mystery of God cannot but evoke strong feelings of wonder and gratitude, awe and humility. The problem is not so much emotion as emotionalism, that is, emotion for its own sake: not the genuine overflow of powerful feeling, but the titillation of the sensibilities. Many catchphrases in the criticism of hymnody have their origin in the need to distinguish emotion from emotionalism.

During the preparation of A&M, and especially during its revision, several correspondents wrote to the Compilers urging objectivity in hymns as what the Catholic party wanted. There were also requests for more subjective hymns.[37] It would be very difficult to classify any hymn as objective or subjective with any degree of accuracy, for there are hardly any hymns which are wholly objective. One might identify songs of praise such as Heber's Trinity hymn, or some of the psalm paraphrases, or narrative hymns, or predominantly doctrinal hymns. Almost always, however, an element of human experience intrudes. Bishop Mackarness of Oxford, writing to the Compilers, distinguished glibly enough between hymns "suitable for worship, dwelling on the majesty and mercy of God," and those which expressed the "experiences and feelings of men."[38] It is to some extent a false distinction, for, as noted above in the second section of this chapter, a hymn cannot objectively dwell on the infinite qualities of God which finite humans cannot know save through their own necessarily subjective experience of them. The two are inevitably and inextricably bound up.

Take for an example a hymn by H.F. Lyte, "Praise, my soul, the King of heaven" (198/298). The fact that this hymn is a paraphrase of Psalm 103 is irrelevant to the present discussion. What is important is that Lyte cannot separate his praise of God from his experience of Him:

> Praise, my soul, the King of heaven,
> To His feet thy tribute bring;
> Ransomed, healed, restored, forgiven,
> Who like me His praise should sing?

That fourth line can be read as a sharing of the knowledge of God's mercy: the writer looks beyond the limits of his own experience both upward toward God and outward to his fellow human beings. Unfortunately, the Compilers did not understand it so, but objected to the obtrusion of personality. The lines in the A&M version read:

> Ransomed, healed, restored, forgiven,
> Evermore His praises sing,

which is flat and uninspired after the fervour of the original. Even with that alteration, the Compilers have not succeeded in making the hymn objective: the link between the ransom and the praise is both emotional and necessary, and gives the experience of worship its impulse and its validity.

A hymn can be relatively (if it cannot be absolutely) objective by the subordination of the personal and emotional elements, as Lyte put praise first and his feelings second in his hymn. In the preface to his _Lyra Catholica_ (1849), Edward Caswall praised the objectivity he found in the ancient Latin hymns, an objectivity which he discerned in their "exceedingly plain and practical character" and their "perpetual reference to action."

> Their tendency is, to take the individual out of himself; to set before him, in turn, all the varied and sublime Objects of Faith; and to blend him with the universal family of the Faithful. In this respect they utterly differ from the hymn-books of modern heretical bodies, which, dwelling as they do, almost entirely on the state and emotions of the individual, tend to inculcate the worst of all egotisms.[39]

Caswall's judgments are somewhat extreme: the reference to action in ancient hymns is hardly "perpetual," nor is all Protestant hymnody as damnable as he declares. Nevertheless, his understanding of what is objective is valid, and is a useful standard, in that he never repudiates the human element: his objectivity is simply a larger concern, the common interest of the universal family of the faithful, as opposed to the individual and egotistic. Others were not so willing to recognize ancient virtues in modern times. The arch-ecclesiologist Benjamin Webb feared that the age of hymns had passed, for even Neale, he claimed, could only imitate and approximate the ancient hymns.

> I don't believe that we subjective men <u>can</u> write hymns, which should be altogether objective. . . . The

> ancient hymns are bald, meagre, rude, etc., but with all this there is in them a simplicity, a vigour, a heart, that one loves them.[40]

Webb dismissed Neale's interest in hymnody as merely a stubborn remnant of his Evangelical background. Webb even rejected translations of the ancient hymns, complaining that "translation into English reduced everything to common sense."[41] He had, in fact, an imperfectly reasoned, though nonetheless fervent, dislike of all hymns, and it is this dislike which provoked his comments to Neale. Caswall, on the other hand, would presumably approve of common sense in the modern language of hymns, as akin to the plainness and practicality he admired in the ancient.

The Tractarian principle which underlies the distaste for emotion and the call for objectivity in hymns is that of reserve. It was the subject of the eightieth and the eighty-seventh of the <u>Tracts for the Times</u>, "On Reserve in Communicating Religious Knowledge," by Isaac Williams, published in 1838 and 1840. Williams' thesis is that "there is . . . in God's dealings with mankind, a very remarkable holding back of sacred and important truths, as if the knowledge of them were injurious to persons unworthy of them."[42] Williams uses this thesis to inculcate a proper humility before the problems of theology, suggesting that if one does not understand some point, it is a reflection of one's own unworthiness, rather than of some intellectual weakness in the theological argument. "God punishes with blindness those who approach sacred truths with a speculative mind."[43] It is an ingenious defence of the mystique of the theologian and the authority of the priest, but what is of immediate interest is the kind of humility Williams advocates, and its reference to hymn-writing and hymn-singing. He detects a reserve or "retiring delicacy" which "always accompanies all strong and deep feeling" and serves to " protect . . . all sacred and virtuous principle."[44] He criticizes the lack of awe and the excessive familiarity with which his contemporaries use Scripture and publish abroad the mysteries of faith under the sceptical and irreverent gaze of the ungodly.[45] Extending this principle, he questions attempts to lure the heathen into church by means of showy preaching, splendid ceremony, and music of all kinds, including popular hymnody. To do so is to degrade the sacred to the level of popular taste, and defile its "chaste reserve".[46] Williams could not countermand Christ's own commission to take the gospel to all nations, but his doubts probably restrained some of the more extreme methods of evangelizing and helped maintain the dignity which befitted the established church. Thus, when home missions had their vogue,[47] they were comparatively modest affairs. Certainly even the Anglican missions included an element of showmanship -- some strong preaching and emotional hymns -- but were free of the hoopla which surrounded some of the revivals and meetings.

In the expression of religious feeling, Williams calls for restraint and delicacy, that expression neither outstrip feeling nor cheapen it. He defines enthusiasm as "a state of mind when the feelings are strongly moved by religion, but the heart is not adequately purified nor humbled."[48] What is dangerous about this kind of emotional imbalance is that it threatens to exalt the one who feels, rather than the inspiration of the feelings. In short, such enthusiasm in a hymn distracts from the object of that hymn, which is the praise of God.

The term reserve occurs frequently in hymn criticism, where, however, it tends to suggest a lack of exuberance rather than a proper humility before sacred subjects. W. Priest, whose long commentary on the second specimen of the Original edition is discussed in Chapter 3, voiced some general misgivings, one of which was "the effect, for congregational use, of passages such as the following . . . 'There Jesus shall embrace us/ There Jesus be embraced'":[49]

> Such passages are of frequent occurrence, and, in the earlier days of the Church movement, would, I think, have been looked upon with uneasiness, from their want of 'reserve'. Public service need not be cold and heartless; but surely even the most perfunctory service is better than the obtrusion of <u>personal</u> feeling, either by the congregation or clergy.[50]

Priest has not chosen a very good example: the lines do not really express a personal feeling, meaning the particular, or perhaps idiosyncratic sentiments of an individual, but an unusually direct physical notion which he finds distasteful. In this case, the reserve Priest is advocating really the shyness of one who fears to be presumptuous, and is sure that a heavenly hug is an unpardonable liberty.

The principles of objectivity and reserve are intended to limit the extent to which the human elements of personality and emotion infuse divine worship. Hymn critics are concerned not only to limit these elements, but also to ensure that worship is appropriate and decorous. The key word is sincerity.

Biggs wrote of the need for sincerity, or earnestness, on the part of hymn-writers, so that they not write about what they only imagined, but about what they had experienced. This stricture is not as severe as it appears, and does not prohibit the play of poetic imagination in the areas of metaphor, imagery and other matters of language. What it does expressly condemn is the assumption of attitudes and feelings which are not a writer's own, but which the writer either wants or feels obliged to express. It is a kind of hypocrisy and can be detected in a certain unease of expression or a lack of serenity in the conviction. Those who espouse the principle of reserve, however, warn not to confuse a reservation of feeling, which is part of proper humility, with the uncertainty of insincerity. Illustrations of sincere, insincere, or reserved expressions in hymns are difficult to choose: it is a subtle matter, requiring on the part of the critic long and sympathetic acquaintance with the language of devotion. Even then, a charge of insincerity may be unanswerably challenged by the query, whether one can be sure that the writer has not felt what the words express. It may, after all, be a case of blindness divinely inflicted upon a too speculative critic.

Insincerity may also afflict the hymn-singer. Any public form of words carries a real danger of insincerity or sheer inappropriateness. The choice of a hymn must take into account all the circumstances of its use: the identity and experience of the singers and the occasion of the service. On the whole, common sense adequately determines the choice. It is not necessary, however, to be strictly literal in choosing what is suitable. The hymn need not always reflect what its singers are; it may reflect what they aspire to be, and thus be an affirmation both of individual and of common purpose, and a statement of faith in what is greater than themselves.

In fact, it may be wrong to insist that a hymn express only that to which most individuals can assent, or which they can make their own. Helen Gardner asserts that a hymn is not intended to express "the personal situation or personal warmth of feeling of an individual singer, but a common ideal of Christian feeling and sentiment which the congregation acknowledges as ideal."[51] Sincerity is measured by how wholeheartedly the singer accepts the ideal. For this reason the expression of the ideal ought not to be too idiosyncratic, too much the product of an individual mind. An unusual image or an exaggerated phrase will cause unease among the singers, distracting them from worship or undermining that "sense of belonging to a continuing fellowship"[52] which it is the purpose, according to Helen Gardner, of a hymn to create.

In this, there is more than an echo of Caswall's emphasis upon the universal family of the faithful. Here is the chief function that the expression of emotion in hymns serves: the shared feeling strengthens the sense of community. The stirring up of feelings opens the way to conviction and resolution, or even, in the case of hymns in mission services, to conversion. An emotional understanding may be more powerful than an intellectual one, and more immediate. Never, however, does the emotion substitute for the understanding or the conviction.

A hymn which deliberately arouses emotion but keeps it in check is Milman's "Ride on! ride on in majesty" (87/99) for Palm Sunday. It echoes, even imitates, the shouts of triumph at Christ's entry into Jerusalem, making a sharp contrast with the Lenten hymns which precede it and the Passion hymns which follow. The emotion of the acclamation is controlled by the irony of the words themselves, which point the irony of the situation:

> Ride on! ride on in majesty!
> In lowly pomp, ride on to die;
> Bow Thy meek Head to mortal pain,
> Then take, O God, Thy Power, and reign.
> (stanza 5)

The emotion must always be consonant with the situation which produces it, and no greater than is warranted. As an emotion can be said to have its objective correlative through which it finds expression, an object or a situation might be said to have its subjective correlative -- the emotional response which is sufficient, appropriate and necessary to it. An excessive, or inappropriate, or unnecessary emotion destroys the correlation and upsets the balance which is sincerity. That excessive emotion is what is meant by emotionalism. The theme of and ideas in a hymn seem incapable of supporting the weight of feeling with which the writer has invested it. The hymn seems to have been written for the sake of the emotion itself. The best example in A&M of such indulgence is Faber's hymn on the Passion (100/114). Its first line betrays it: "O come and mourn with me awhile." The hymn is discussed at length in Section 6 of Chapter Four.

Sentimentalism is a form of emotionalism which is extremely hard to judge objectively. What may be perfectly acceptable in one age may be scorned in another, and one must be wary of grounding one's judgment solely on literary fashion. The same impulse which criticizes the death of Little Nell may be behind the criticism of Faber's hymn. Both were obviously widely acceptable in their time. What ultimately condemns Faber's hymn, however, is the self-consciousness of the emotion. The mourner is so much in the foreground that he loses his sense of proportion, so that he seems to pity Christ. And to pity God is, as Erik Routley says, the one entirely inappropriate human response.

Sentimentalism may also be detected in the use of cliché, for the unimaginative use of language often reveals insensitivity, in this case to emotional balance. The use of cliché in hymnody, however, is not very revealing, for it is a characteristic of hymns that they deal in stock symbols, standard phrases and formula epithets. These are frequently but not always Scriptural: they may have the resonance of epic device, or they may be merely feeble and flat. They often form part of a stock rhyme, as, for example, the phrase "meek and mild"[53] is commonly used to describe the boy Jesus, because "mild" rhymes with "child." In one hymn the phrase is used to describe Eli, the priest whom Samuel served, again for the sake of the rhyme, as the awkwardness of the syntax reveals:

> The old man, meek and mild,
> The priest of Israel, slept;
> His watch the Temple child,
> The little Levite, kept.[54]

The rhyme association of "meek and mild" with child is an unfortunate one, for it reinforces a potentially sentimental picture of a namby-pamby Messiah, especially in children's hymns, which often focus on the childhood of Jesus. The translation of de Santeuil's "Divine crescebas puer" in the first specimen of A&M reads:

> In stature grows the heavenly Child,
> With death before His eyes;
> A Lamb unblemished, meek, and mild,
> Prepared for sacrifice.[55]

In 1860 the Compilers' alteration both brought the translation closer to the Latin and presented a much more vigorous image than that of the sacrificial lamb. They did not, however, manage to improve the rhyme in the second and fourth lines:

> The heavenly Child in stature grows,
> And growing learns to die;
> And still His early training shows
> His coming agony.[56]

lines as "Meek and lowly may I be;/ Thou art all humility" (stanza 3).

The whole subject of the place of emotion in worship and particularly in hymnody is a complicated one. Many catchphrases have attached themselves to the relevant criticism: several have been discussed above. It has finally to be admitted that any judgment must itself be subjective, depending upon prevalent standards and individual taste. A hymn will almost certainly vary in effect from one occasion to another. What is certain is that there is no such thing as a perfectly objective or dispassionate hymn, and that a hymn's excellence depends equally upon the quality of its writing, the appropriateness of its occasion, and the response it evokes in its singers. George Herbert summarized that final requirement in his poem "A True Hymn":

> The finenesse which a hymne or psalme affords
> Is, when the soul unto the lines accords.[59]

vi. Propaganda and Didacticism

> Hearken unto a Verser, who may chance
> Ryme thee to good, and make a bait of pleasure.
> A verse may finde him, who a sermon flies,
> And turn delight into a sacrifice.[60]

A second hymn in the First specimen contains the same convenient rhyme, in the last stanza of "See, amid the winter's snow":

> Teach, O teach us, Holy Child,
> By Thy Face, so meek and mild,
> Teach us to resemble Thee
> In Thy sweet humility![57]

The unusual expression "to teach by one's face" must be part of the reason for the omission of the hymn from A&M 1860, and indeed, from the later volumes.

In the matter of stock epithets, however, it is necessary to examine each hymn individually, for some writers manage not to be compelled by their clichés, but to keep the full meaning of the words. Charles Wesley's hymn "Lamb of God, I look to Thee" can be strongly criticized for its perpetuation of the stereotype of bland perfection in the boy Jesus, but it is clear that Wesley's portrait is deliberate, however unattractive:

> Lamb of God, I look to Thee,
> Thou shalt my example be:
> Thou art gentle, meek and mild,
> Thou wast once a little child.[58]

The ensuing stanzas elaborate each of the attributes, so that one knows that this is no stock phrase, but one the meaning of which Wesley wishes to emphasize. At least the imagery is not sentimental: whatever tender emotion adheres to the phrase in the first stanza quickly dissipates in the bleak perfection of such

Herbert was not of course the first to seize the instructional opportunity which verse presents. In classical criticism it has long been stated that poetry has a two-fold purpose, to delight and to instruct. Add to the delights of verse those of music, and it is easy to see why hymn-singing has from the earliest years of the Christian church been used to reaffirm conviction and conquer disbelief. "The folksong of the church militant"[61] is what Erik Routley has called hymns, and as such they are a tool and a device hard to overlook but easy to underestimate.

Within the church, hymns were used in the great doctrinal controversies of the early Church: both heretics and the orthodox took advantage of the literally propagandistic qualities of song. Songs are more widely repeated than sermons, and more memorable than any tract. Arius made sure that his anti-Trinitarian <u>thalia</u> would be remembered, by setting them to secular melodies, which may or may not have had licentious associations as the Trinitarians claimed. The Arian heresy provoked considerable hymn-writing: St. Gregory of Nazianzus and St. Hilary of Poitiers, at distant ends of Christendom, wrote hymns to combat the Arian heresy. In Constantinople a musical battle was waged in the streets. St. Chrysostom, tired of competing with the Arian hymns sung outside the churches, sent the faithful marching through the city, with full pomp of torches and crosses, and in full orthodox voice, until the procession disintegrated in clamour and confusion. St. Ambrose, the father of Church song, first wrote hymns under the stimulus of the controversy, when driven with his followers into the safety of the cathedral at Milan by the supporters of the empress Justina.

Hymns have rarely been quite such explicit propaganda since those early years, though they have certainly had their place whenever a group of Christians banded together with a common purpose. Hymns have especially been associated with reforming movements: Italian *laudi spirtuali* accompanied the growth of the Franciscan order in the thirteenth century; in the fifteenth century hymnody flourished in Bohemia among the Hussites. With such precedents it is hardly surprising that Luther made use of as powerful a supplement to debate as hymn-singing with the bold reinforcement of secular melody.

In the nineteenth century, Neale published a collection of verses which he did not call hymns, but which clearly derive from the disputatious tradition of hymnody. The book, *Songs and Ballads of the People* (1843), reflects Neale's ecclesiological and Tractarian convictions, with its verses on "The Teetotallers," "The Church Rate," "Why are you a Dissenter," and that special ecclesiological bogey, "Pews." One of the poems is called "The Church of England," and its lesson is clear, though Neale's use of the first person pronoun is not entirely convincing:

> The good old Church of England!
> With her priests through all the land,
> And her twenty thousand churches,
> How nobly does she stand!
> Dissenters are like mushrooms,
> That flourish but a day;
> Twelve hundred years, through smiles and tears,
> She hath lasted on alway!

God bless the Church of England!
The poor man's Church is She;
We were nourish'd at Her bosom,
We were fondled at Her knee,
God bless the Church of England!
The good, the true, the brave!
She baptis'd us in our cradle;
She shall bear us to our grave.[62]

Such outright propaganda had little place in the mainstream of English hymnody; nevertheless, didacticism is a very strong element. On the whole it may be said that the Dissenters valued hymns more highly than did the established church, and attached greater importance to their use. It has been said by Bernard Manning that hymnody supplies for Dissenters the place that the liturgy of the Prayer Book holds for the Anglican: it is a framework for the service of worship, and is itself charged with meaning.[63] John Wesley spoke of his 1780 _Collection of Hymns for the Use of the People called Methodists_ as a "body of experimental and practical divinity":

> In what other publication have you so distinct and full an account of the heights and depths of religion, speculative and practical; so strong cautions against the most plausible errors . . . ; and so clear directions for making your calling and election sure, for perfecting holiness in the fear of God?[64]

For Wesley, his hymnbook contained "all the important truths of our most divine religion."[65]

Hymnal editors have been greatly concerned over the lesser truths of religion also, quick to excise alien sectarian allusions and to "correct" statements of dogma. The exercise of these editorial powers in A&M is examined in Chapter Four. Other hymns are specifically and intentionally didactic, as in C.F. Alexander's collection of Hymns for Little Children (1848) containing verses on the phrases of the Creed, the Lord's Prayer, and the Ten Commandments. These hymns teach not only the elements of religion, but also good manners and the behaviour appropriate to Anglican ceremonial. Her hymn on "The Holy Catholic Church" contains the following instructions:

> Little children must be quiet,
> When to holy Church they go,
> They must sit with serious faces,
> Must not play or whisper low.
>
> They must walk in reverent order,
> Stand for praise, and kneel for prayer,
> For the Church is God's Own Temple,
> And His Presence dwelleth there.[66]

Such hymns had no place in congregational worship, but were used in Sunday schools or catechism classes. There was no relenting of the firmly prescriptive tone "must . . . must not."

Geoffrey Faber has criticized the Tractarian poetry of Keble and Newman for being merely assertive, a matter of obvious ideas in metrical shape,[67] and Tractarian hymns share that characteristic. Their apologists would claim that there is no place in worship for anything which would suggest uncertainty or the possibility of dispute. As a result there may be a certain blandness of tone in the Anglican collections influenced by Tractarianism, when idiosyncrasy gives way to authority.

Examples of didacticism in A&M hymns are easy to find, especially in hymns written on ticklish theological topics. The hymns for Holy Communion, for example, are most carefully worded. Among the five hymns in A&M 1860 were two by Thomas Aquinas, one of which, his "Pange lingua" ("Now my tongue the mystery telling" 203/309) caused considerable debate among the Compilers of the book, and its doctrinal implications are discussed at some length in Chapter Four. Nor were Aquinas' hymns the only controversial ones containing expressions which were open to misinterpretation. To balance any questionable material, the Compilers printed in the Appendix hymns which are plainly assertive of Anglican doctrine. William Bright's hymn "Once, only once, and once for all" (347/315) expounds the doctrinal point of the Thirty-first article:

> The Offering of Christ once made is that perfect redemption, propitiation, and satisfaction, for all sins of the whole world, both original and actual; and there is none other satisfaction for sin, but that alone. Wherefore the sacrifices of Masses, in the which it was commonly said, that the Priest did offer Christ for the quick and the dead,

> to have remission of pain or guilt, were blasphemous fables, and dangerous deceits.

Bright's hymn phrases it as follows:

> Once, only once, and once for all,
> His precious life He gave;
> Before the Cross our spirits fall,
> And own it strong to save.
>
> 'One offering, single and complete'[68]
> With lips and heart we say;
> But what he never can repeat
> He shows forth day by day.
> (stanzas 1,2; emphasis added)

Bright's insistence underlines the Protestant concept of the Eucharist as a commemoration rather than a re-enactment of the sacrifice of Christ's death. The Compilers, anxious that there should be no doubt about the matter, altered Bright's fourth stanza, avoiding the phrase "Priest and Victim" and the slightly awkward construction of the first and second lines:

> Our Priest and Victim, adding nought
> To His atonement's power,
> Presents Himself for those He bought
> In that dark noon-tide hour.

The first two lines of the stanza in the A&M version read: "So He, Who once atonement wrought,/ Our Priest of endless power." The theme is a favourite one with Bright, and it informs another of his Eucharistic hymns, printed in the Revised edition (--/322):

> And now, O Father, mindful of the love
> That bought us, once for all, on
> Calvary's Tree,
> And having with us Him that pleads above,
> We here present, we here spread forth
> to Thee
> That only Offering perfect in Thine eyes,
> The one true, pure, immortal
> Sacrifice. (stanza 1)

These hymns are certainly assertive, but their assertiveness is still subordinate to the thanksgiving and the supplication which are the primary purpose of the hymns. A hymn which is unrelievedly didactic has nothing to recommend it, and the Compilers recognized that when they omitted from all subsequent editions of their book a hymn for Trinity which had appeared in the Original edition, "Blest Trinity from mortal sight" (133/--). As a late Latin hymn by C. de Santeuil, it had not even the authority of antiquity to recommend it. The first stanza is a profession of faith in the doctrine of the Trinity, the second a series of exclamatory apostrophes to the various Persons of the Trinity, and the third and fourth stanzas contain a summary utterly without imaginative force of what is one of the Church's most difficult concepts. A written-to-order doxology snugly concludes an entirely unexceptionable and uninspired hymn.

> Blest Trinity, from mortal sight
> Veiled in Thine own eternal Light,
> We Thee confess, in Thee believe,
> To Thee with loving hearts we cleave.

O Father, Thou most Holy One!
O God of God, Eternal Son!
O Holy Ghost, Thou Love divine!
To join them Both is ever Thine.

The Father is in God the Son,
And with the Father He is One:
In both the Spirit doth abide,
And with them both is glorified.

Such as the Father, such the Son,
And such the Spirit, Three in One:
The Three one perfect Verity,
The Three one perfect Charity.

Eternal Father, Thee we praise;
To Thee, O Son, our hymns we raise;
O Holy Ghost, we Thee adore;
One mighty God for evermore.

A hymn may not only teach doctrine, but in narration recall the stories of Scripture and the lessons they embody. Narrative form is often used in A&M for occasions less well-known than the chief festivals. The hymns for the Apostles are particularly good examples. Mrs. Alexander's "The Shepherd now was smitten" (--/405) tells the story of the conversion of Saint Paul, and Henry Alford's "Brightly did the light Divine" (--/412), for Saint Barnabas, is a reminder of just who that Apostle was, and what he did. A more difficult challenge is presented by Saint Bartholomew, about whom there are no stories. John Ellerton solves the problem by making Bartholomew the type of all forgotten saints whose reward is none the less for being unknown on earth. The hymn, "King of Saints, to Whom the number" (--/419), is a little masterpiece. Consider the second stanza, Ellerton's eight-line paraphrase of the simple fact that "we know nothing of him."

> In the roll of Thine Apostles
> One there stands, Bartholomew,
> He for whom today we offer,
> Year by year our praises due;
> How he toiled for Thee and suffered
> None on earth can now record;
> All his saintly life is hidden
> In the knowledge of his Lord.

The need for something more particular is still felt, and without making any identifications, Ellerton suggests some gospel incidents with which Bartholomew might be associated:

> Was it he, beneath the fig-tree
> Seen of Thee, and guileless found;
> He who saw the good he longed for
> Rise from Nazareth's barren ground;
> He who met his risen Master
> On the shore of Galilee;
> He to whom the word was spoken,
> 'Greater things thou yet shalt see?'
> (stanza 3. Punctuation as in A&M)

There is a testimonial to the didactic value of narrative which deserves full quotation. It comes from the Reverend Sabine Baring Gould, himself a hymn-writer, and is a plea for the continued use of the full hymn "O sons and daughters, let us sing" (108/130):

> The original form contains the whole story of the Resurrection, & is very popular with children & with villagers. I have found it very useful for conveying the whole story to the memory of ploughboys & the like. I think country people & the poor generally like a good long narrative hymn. With the poor A&M is hardly popular, much being beyond them, but 'O filii et filiae' I find they always delight in . . . . They soon learn it by heart, & I hear it sung about the fields.[69]

It has been said above that hymns are commonly used to unite and encourage the members of the church on earth. There is an increasing element in A&M, and in Victorian hymnody generally, of militancy. The metaphors of warfare have been part of the language of Christianity since the letter to the Ephesians,[70] but were never so strongly taken up as in the latter part of the nineteenth century. The Church of England turned from its internal reforms to the task of re-establishing its place as the national church. Other groups, determined to take the gospel to the cities, felt the need of solidarity and strength in invading what must have truly seemed "the darkness of this world." In hymn-writing there was also a reaction against the tenderness bordering on sentimentality of writers such as Faber, and the new spirit of resolution and determination had much in common with muscular Christianity.

Many of the most famous militaristic hymns were written or published within a few years of one another: "Stand up, stand up for Jesus" in 1858, "Fight the good fight" in 1863, "Onward Christian soldiers" and "For all the saints who from their labours rest" in 1864. Christian militarism was thoroughly established with the increasing regimentation of William Booth's evangelist movement, declared the "Salvation Army" in 1878. The popularity of the Army led to its imitation by groups within the Church of England, and these groups came after 1882 to be called, unimaginatively, the Church Army. The A&M Supplement of 1889 reflected this new spirit with a whole subsection of militaristic general hymns (numbers 540 to 543) and others for missions,[71] only one of which was written before 1858. The militaristic hymns had been increasingly a feature of A&M from its first edition. That had contained Charles Wesley's hymn "Soldiers of Christ, arise" (181/270), a paraphrase of the passage from Ephesians, and printed under the motto "Put on the whole armour of God." The Appendix showed the first sign of contemporary militarism with Baring Gould's "Onward Christian soldiers" (385/391), but there was also J.H. Clark's translation "Soldiers who are Christ's below" (316/447) from a Latin hymn of 1734. It is in 1875 that there is a real increase of modern militarism, with hymns such as "Through the night of doubt and sorrow" (--/274), a translation by Baring Gould from the Danish of B.S. Ingemann, "For all the saints" (--/437) by W.W. How, "Forward! be our watchword" (--/392) by Henry Alford, and W.D. Maclagan's "The Saints of God! their conflict past" (--/428). Not all these hymns employ the metaphor consistently; indeed, in the Latin one, it is only a prelude to the description of the "pledged reward" that awaits the victors. In other hymns the metaphors of soldiering are mingled with those of pilgrimage, and the army of God seems rather to be engaged in constant marches and manoeuvres than in any pitched battles. Maclagan's hymn has a different metaphor in each of its four (excluding the doxology) stanzas: of battle, of pilgrimage, of sea-voyage, and of vigil. What all these hymns share is the tone of outgoing determination and resolution, and an invincible sense of shared conviction.

One area where the Church's didacticism is apparent, though less militantly so, is in its hymns for children.[72] The instruction of children in their faith is an important responsibility, so important that at their baptism they are given godparents to ensure their Christian upbringing. The Book of Common Prayer provides in the Catechism a form for their religious instruction. Furthermore, the church had long been a major force in national education through its voluntary day schools, and in the nineteenth century through the Sunday schools. Teaching was thus an important and familiar function of the church.

Hymn-singing quickly found its way into public schools early in the nineteenth century, and schools such as Rugby had their own hymn collections.[73] A&M included three hymns for school festivals in its first edition, but they are more suitable for the use of school visitors than for pupils. The later editions replaced the school festivals section with one of "hymns for the young," but the air of benign and condescending authority in the first hymns persisted, although they were increasingly ousted by hymns written for children themselves to sing.

It is these hymns which present a special challenge, a challenge to which hymn-writers responded in different ways. Several collections of verses and hymns for children had already been published; notable among them were such books as J.M.Neale's *Hymns for Children* (1842), C.F. Alexander's *Hymns for Little Children* (1848), Keble's *Lyra Innocentium* (1846), and Mrs. Yonge's *The Child's Christian Year* (1841). These books were intended for private rather than public use, and more for instruction than for devotion. They strongly influenced the A&M hymns, some of which were drawn from their pages.

Instructiveness in the A&M children's hymns varies from prescription without much enthusiasm to a shared expression of faith. Keble had set a high standard for children's hymns when he wrote the preface for his friend Mrs. Yonge's *The Child's Christian Year*:

> The first impression on looking over this little book, will probably be that the hymns are too difficult. . . . It should be . . . considered that such subjects cannot be lowered to the level of childish minds without more or less of irreverence; and if we observe the Church's method of teaching, we shall find that she places in the memories of her young members a form of sound words, the full understanding of which neither they nor their teachers can arrive at.[74]

Keble saw hymns as a teaching device, to be used in connection with the services of the day, and to lead to questions and explanations. The A&M hymns are not suitable for such a catechistic purpose, but they are intended to reinforce, sometimes explicitly, sometimes more subtly, the lessons children were to learn. They were also intended to be remembered outside the class and the church, to be the "sound words" stored in the memory to be pondered and appreciated. In this, hymns perform the primary propaganda function discussed at the beginning of this section: reaching and remaining with young minds more effectively than other forms of teaching.

The writing of children's hymns is thus a special responsibility: their effect must be both immediate and resonant. They must be comprehensible without being overly simplified, their language attractive but not pretty or puerile. A variety of devices can be employed to attract and keep the child's attention: picturesque imagery, frequent use of the first person pronoun, pleasant rhymes, and refrains. The hymns which are most successful, however, are those which are not obviously for children only; their language is as simple and strong as the best English style, and they are informed with a deep respect for the child's intelligence. Such hymns are often found among the adult hymns of other collections, for they are classics. Hymns which illustrate all the above characteristics are discussed in Chapter Five.

Although the Proprietors of A&M recognized that the standard hymn collection did not supply the needs of children, and gradually increased their provision for their needs, they kept children's hymns within the framework of their book. They discussed the possibility of publishing a separate children's book,[75] but decided against it, partly because at the time of the discussion they were rather timidly recovering from the death of their bolder chairman, but also partly because it was not their intention to provide books for special groups and purposes. Their plan was to provide a single book for general congregational use, and although they acknowledged that the Church's activities and responsibilities extended beyond the sanctuary itself (and in some cases the Proprietors provided for them), in general the limit they set on A&M was that of congregational worship. The congregation, and its worship, was to be a higher priority than the instruction of children.[76]

In addition to the explicit didacticism and the propaganda function discussed in this section, there is a whole range of implicit didacticism in all hymns. Implicit in every hymn, of course, is the Christian faith which informs it, and the drama of sin and redemption which is the larger context for every hymn. Furthermore there are matters of attitude which have perhaps less to do with the lessons being taught than with the schools in which the teachers learned. It is in the assumptions and prejudices of the writers of the hymns that most is revealed about the Church's role in its Victorian society, at least from the viewpoint of the clergy. Sensitivity and insensitivity, authority and irresponsibility are all to be found in the hymns of the Church of England, and not the less in A&M. Some of these matters of attitude and implicit didacticism are examined in Chapter Five.

2. Anglican Hymnody

i. The English and Anglican Tradition

The adoption of hymns by the Church of England was a late development in the history of English hymnody. To place the achievement of A&M in its rightful context requires a brief history of the English hymn.

Before the Reformation, hymns had their place in the Latin liturgy of the English church, but, with the sole exception of the "Veni Creator" in the Ordinal, hymns were omitted from the translations of the liturgy which became the Book of Common Prayer. Translations of the Latin hymns were found in the various Primers (devotional books for lay use), both authorized[77] and unauthorized.

The omission of hymns from common worship, and their relegation, at best, to manuals of private devotion, is the result of the influence of Calvin upon the English Reformation. That influence was reinforced when the reformers took refuge at Geneva during the Marian persecutions. Calvin's proscription of anything but the divinely inspired word of God in the liturgy gave rise to many paraphrases, chiefly of the psalms, wherever his influence reached. Thomas Sternhold's nineteen psalm paraphrases were published in 1549; after the Marian exile, encouraged by the example of the Geneva Psalter of Clément Marot and Théodore de Bèze, other writers continued the task of an English paraphrase. After Elizabeth's succession, the growing collection of paraphrases was authorized for use in services, and by 1562 the book was complete: _The Whole Booke of Psalmes, collected into Englysh metre by T. Starnhold, I. Hopkins, and Others_. This book is the standard edition of what came to be known as "Sternhold and Hopkins," or "Day's Psalter," after the publisher of an edition with music, and later, as the "Old Version" of the psalms. The collection supplied the musical needs of English congregations for generations, until the "New Version" of the Poet Laureate Nahum Tate and Dr. Nicholas Brady was allowed by William III in 1696 as an alternative. Great discussion of the relative merits of the two versions ensued. Some were rightly pleased to be rid of the worst awkwardnesses of the Old Version, but some, such as the squire in Hannah More's "Florio,"

> fear'd 'twould show a falling State,
> If Sternhold should give way to Tate:
> The Church's downfall he predicted,
> Were modern tunes not interdicted.[78]

Although Calvin's influence was strong in England, that of Luther was not entirely unknown. Unlike Calvin, Luther embraced hymn-singing with enthusiasm, took hymns from many sources, including his own pen, and borrowed tunes from the devil and the dance alike. Following his example, German hymnody has a rich tradition, though only a little found its way to England, and that little chiefly the music rather than the words. Miles Coverdale's Goostly Psalmes and Spirituall Songes (not before 1543) was an attempt to introduce Lutheran hymnody, though its pieces were not intended for liturgical use, but to oust "balettes of fylthynes" and be godly pastime for youth.[79] After Coverdale, it was not until John Wesley became fascinated with Moravian hymns and the Pietists that German influence was again strongly felt.

For a century and a half English hymnody was dominated by the Bible, though the versifiers could not always do justice to the wealth of language and imagery found therein. Towards the end of the nineteenth century hymn-writers began to free themselves from the scriptural strictures, and their hymns were used in Nonconformist churces. Benjamin Keach championed the use of hymns in Baptist worship, and effectively split the Baptists into two factions, the singing and the non-singing, despite a rebuke from their General Assembly in 1692. At the same time Independent congregations adopted hymn-singing, and Isaac Watts is traditionally supposed to have begun his hymn-writing career when challenged by his father to provide better verses than his Southampton congregation already had.

Watts's first book of hymns (though not his first volume of verse) was Hymns and Spiritual Songs (1707) in three parts. The first part contained hymns "Collected from the Scriptures," that is, paraphrases; the second and third parts were original hymns on "Divine Subjects" and "For the Lord's Supper." Two points are here of interest. First, Watts's hymns were clearly intended for congregational and liturgical use. Second, his hymns mark a half-way point between paraphrase and original hymnody. Not only do his books contain both, but his paraphrases are increasingly original. The title of another hymn collection makes the nature of this originality clear: The Psalms of David Imitated in the Language of the New Testament, And Apply'd to the Christian State and Worship (1719).[80]

It was in the eighteenth century that the distinctive character of English hymnody was formed. Even before his conversion, John Wesley felt a need for hymn-singing: his first Collection of Psalms and Hymns was published in 1736-1737 when he was in Georgia. After their conversion in 1738, John and Charles worked hard to supply hymns for the use of their Methodist followers, and succeeded so thoroughly that Methodist hymnody may almost be said to be theirs alone. They not only wrote, but also collected, hymns and in 1780 John Wesley compiled a huge collection (525 hymns) for general use in all his societies. This book may be called the standard collection, though it was by no means a static one. Wesley himself revised it, and various Methodist groups compiled their own supplements. A hundred years later it still formed the core of the Wesleyan Conference's Methodist Hymn Book.[81]

The Church of England had not the same enthusiasm for hymn-singing as had the Wesleyans, but interest grew in the course of the eighteenth century, and several important collections were published: Martin Madan's in 1760, Augustus Toplady's in 1776, and John Newton's and William Cowper's in 1779. Until this period, original Anglican hymns were intended solely for private devotional use, as Thomas Ken's morning and evening hymns were recommended for daily private recitation by the scholars of Winchester, in whose *Manual of Prayers* they were printed. The eighteenth-century collections were partly intended for public use: Toplady entitled his book *Psalms for Public and Private Worship*. Newton intended his *Olney Hymns* for use in his weekday study class, not in his Sunday services, though many of them were perhaps more suitable for private use. The Foundling Hospital in London published the *Psalms, Hymns and Anthems* sung in its chapel, but services there were not typical, but more like performances and charity concerts by which visitors might be persuaded to more generous support of the institution.

The hymn had no official status in congregational worship, however, except insofar as Queen Elizabeth's Injunction to the Clergy of 1559 allowed "an hymn or such-like song" to be sung "for the comforting of such as delight in music . . . in the beginning or end of Common Prayer either at Morning or Evening," the music being the "best that may be conveniently devised," and the sense of the words clearly "understood and perceived."[82] This lack of prescription allowed considerable variation in the nature and use of the hymns which were chosen. The two main impulses for the adoption of hymn-singing were quite distinct. Probably the earlier was a popular demand influenced by the practice of the Dissenters, and accepted by Evangelical clergy, and the later impulse was a Catholic and clerical one. In either case, hymn-singing was initially and primarily a local phenomenon, determined by the talents and prejudices of both clergyman and congregation.

period, original Anglican hymns were intended solely for private devotional use, as Thomas Ken's morning and evening hymns were recommended for daily private recitation by the scholars of Winchester, in whose _Manual of Prayers_ they were printed. The eighteenth-century collections were partly intended for public use: Toplady entitled his book _Psalms for Public and Private Worship_. Newton intended his _Olney Hymns_ for use in his weekday study class, not in his Sunday services, though many of them were perhaps more suitable for private use. The Foundling Hospital in London published the _Psalms, Hymns and Anthems_ sung in its chapel, but services there were not typical, but more like performances and charity concerts by which visitors might be persuaded to more generous support of the institution.

The hymn had no official status in congregational worship, however, except insofar as Queen Elizabeth's Injunction to the Clergy of 1559 allowed "an hymn or such-like song" to be sung "for the comforting of such as delight in music . . . in the beginning or end of Common Prayer either at Morning or Evening", the music being the "best that may be conveniently devised", and the sense of the words clearly "understood and perceived".[82] This lack of prescription allowed considerable variation in the nature and use of the hymns which were chosen. The two main impulses for the adoption of hymn-singing were quite distinct. Probably the earlier was a popular demand influenced by the practice of the Dissenters, and accepted by Evangelical clergy, and the later impulse was a Catholic and clerical one. In either case, hymn-singing was initially and primarily a local phenomenon, determined by the talents and prejudices of both clergyman and congregation.

Julian's incomplete list of books published between 1820 and 1860 numbers one hundred and twenty-one, an average of three collections a year. Some of these were collections already in local use; others were compiled according to some principle of the editor's own, and offered as an improvement upon existing collections. Later books were the product of the new scholarly interest fired by the Tractarians, and were not always for practical use, but for the elevation of hymnological standards and the improvement of popular taste.

With so many books available, it must have been bewildering to the cleric, who, having made the decision to forsake Tate and Brady or Sternhold and Hopkins,[85] was faced with the task of choosing a hymnbook. The organist or choirmaster had also the task of selecting one or more tune books for the new hymns from among the dozens available. It is in this context that the decision of a handful of hymnal editors to sacrifice their own books in order to collaborate on a single improved volume, which might attain a wider circulation than any of the suppressed books, must be seen. The history of the compilation and publication of that book is detailed in the chapter which follows, together with an account of its compilers' increasing ambition for it.

The publication of A&M in 1860-1861 marks the beginning of a period of consolidation in hymn-publishing. The hundreds of collections began to give way to half a dozen books, and increasing efforts were made to improve those few books with supplements and revision. Eventually, by the end of the century, most churches in England used one of those few collections,[86] of which A&M was the predominant. Anglican hymnology was still characterized by a spirit of enterprise and competition, though less frequently an individual effort, and often a competition regulated by party preferences. The ideal of an authorized hymnal characterized by unexceptionable doctrine and impeccable taste seemed not unattainable. Some discussion about adopting A&M as the basis of a hymnal compiled by and for Convocation took place, but the proposal fell through. In the following decade, the first of the twentieth century, A&M's predominance was undermined, first by the unpopularity of its own New edition, and second, by the publication of the English Hymnal. Outside England, the Anglican communion has several books of local authority, but at home, the Church of England retains a freedom of choice, though among fewer possibilities than previously.

ii. Some Predecessors, Sources, and Models of Hymns Ancient and Modern

In the preceding section mention was made of some of the early Anglican hymnbooks, and of the hundreds of collections published in the nineteenth century. The purpose of this section is to show some of the characteristics of the Anglican tradition out of which A&M grew and from which it diverged.

The local nature of early Anglican hymnody has already been noted, and is exemplified in the Olney Hymns of 1779. These hymns were specifically written for use at weekday meetings in the Buckinghamshire parish of Olney, whose clergyman was the redoubtable John Newton. His taste for hymn-singing can be traced to two influences of his boyhood and manhood -- a pious Dissenting mother, and the experience of conversion, which left him a fervent Evangelical. Having decided that his parishioners were to sing hymns, Newton set about providing them with their own collection, and enlisted the aid of his neighbour, the poet William Cowper. The published book contained 348 hymns in three parts: the first contains hymns based on passages of Scripture; the second contains occasional hymns roughly following the Church year; the third contains hymns "on the progress and changes of the spiritual life" under various headings. Most of Cowper's hymns are found in the first and third parts, and it is the hymns of the third section which reflect most clearly Cowper's distressful personal faith. His "God of my life, to Thee I call," for instance, is printed under the heading "Looking upwards in a storm." This section has a closer affinity with private devotional verse than with public song, and thus reinforces the subjective strain of Anglican hymnody.[87]

Newton's hymns in the collection exemplify another side of Evangelicalism, its enthusiasm and its conviction. Newton's hymns are somewhat rough and ready,[88] but sometimes achieve a virtue in their simplicity or borrow the grandeur of the psalmist's language.

The important characteristics of the _Olney Hymns_ are thus, an Evangelical impulse, a three-part arrangement, and an intended use outside the Sunday services. The important collections published in the first half of the nineteenth century differ on most of these points: a Tractarian influence is discernible, the most usual arrangement is seasonal, and the books are meant for and used within the Prayer Book services.

Heber's _Hymns Written and Adapted to the Weekly Church Service of the Year_ was published in 1827, after the bishop's death. The book had, however, been compiled earlier, but left unpublished when his attempt to have it authorized by the Archbishop of Canterbury in 1820 failed. The book is noteworthy, not only in that it follows the Church calendar, but also in that its hymns were written or chosen by Heber to illustrate the epistles and gospels of the liturgy. It was Heber's practice to preach upon a subject suggested by the readings, and his hymnbook is thus part of his plan to unify thematically three parts of Anglican worship, the liturgy of the Prayer Book, the sermon of the preacher, and the singing of the people.

In the same year as Heber's _Hymns_, there appeared a collection of "thoughts in verse," John Keble's _The Christian Year_, which proved immensely popular. Entirely of his own composition, the book was intended for private meditation and devotion, but its verses were soon ransacked for stanzas which might be sung. Its influence was immense, chiefly in its focus upon the Anglican calendar as an organizing principle of the Church's worship and of hymnbooks that might assist that worship. Keble's book and the Tractarian antiquarian enthusiasm awakened a strong interest in fasts and festivals, and in translations of breviary hymns that might fitly mark them.

Thirty-five years later, a book on similar lines to those of the Christian Year was published, Christopher Wordsworth's The Holy Year (1862). It was definitely hymnodic in intent and content, though far too large and expensive for most to purchase, and thus it served as a source-book for other compilers, rather than as a practical hymnal. The hymns in The Holy Year, more than half of them by Wordsworth himself, do not belong to the subjective branch of hymnody; they are rather doctrinaire in content, and (to judge from some of the first lines) a little imperative in tone: "Hark the sound of holy voices," "Heavenly Father, send Thy blessing," "See the Conqueror mounts in triumph."

The many hymn collections published up to 1860 may be divided into three groups: the practical hymn-book for use in worship, the source-books of original verse, paraphrase, or translation, and the books which resulted from increasingly scholarly research in hymnology.

Noteworthy among the practical books were Edward Bickersteth's Christian Psalmody (1833), W.J. Hall's Psalms and Hymns Adapted to the Services of the Church of England (1836), known as the "Mitre" from the symbol on its cover, and William Mercer's Church Psalter and Hymn Book (1854).

Bickersteth's book was Evangelical in inspiration, modelled after Cotterill's suppressed book, and borrowed largely from the Wesleyan collection. It was dedicated to the Bishop of London, and achieved notable success, especially after its enlargement in 1841. Revised by his son, it was published as _Psalms and Hymns based on the Christian Psalmody_ in 1858, and eventually superseded by the same son's _Hymnal Companion to the Book of Common Prayer_ (1870 and 1876).

The "Mitre" hymn-book was known as a high-church collection, though it contained no hymns for saints' days. Its editor had been editor of the _Christian Remembrancer_, in the columns of which many of its hymns had appeared and many letters about hymnody published. Its psalm paraphrases were grouped together, and its hymns, a high proportion of them modern and original, were arranged in Prayer Book order. Most of its contents were abridged and altered, but it sold approximately four million copies, partly because of the published approval of Bishop Blomfield.

Mercer's hymnal was large: it contained the entire psalter, and the canticles pointed for chanting, and 400 hymns, including Wesleyan hymns and translations from German and Latin. It was further enlarged in 1856, and given an appendix in 1872, but did not increase the popularity it initially had. It was among the first books to publish music and words together.

Among the source-books may be noted Henry Lyte's _Spirit of the Psalms_ (1834 and 1836), a collection of relatively free paraphrases for use in his own Devon Church. Volumes of verse by C.F. Alexander, Henry Alford, and others provided many hymns for editors. Frances Cox published her translations of German hymns,

Sacred Hymns from the German, 1841 and 1864; Catherine Winkworth's Lyra Germanica (two series, 1855 and 1858) and her Chorale Book for England (1863) also provided German translations. The increasing interest in the ancient church, and in the breviaries and liturgical books of Roman Catholicism, led to the publication of many translations from Latin, by Isaac Williams (Hymns Translated from the Parisian Breviary, 1839), John Chandler (Hymns of the Primitive Church, 1837), William Copeland (Hymns for the Week, and Hymns for the Seasons, 1848), Edward Caswall (Lyra Catholica, 1849) and John Mason Neale (Mediaeval Hymns and Sequences, 1851).

The source-books of translations are all the result of hymnological research, but the real examples of this newly serious study were the works of Neale. He published volumes not only of original verse,[89] but also of translations from Latin and, more unusually, from Greek, with commentaries (Hymns of the Eastern Church, 1862). His most important hymnological work was probably the Hymnal Noted (1851 and 1854), the model collection of ancient hymns and music mentioned in the discussion of the choral revival in Chapter One. It provided careful and accurate translations which editors delighted to use, though they did not always respect them.[90]

The Compilers of A&M benefited from many of the books mentioned above: on many points, such as the order of the contents, or the publication of both music and words, they found precedents to follow. They were able to borrow excellent material from many sources, and they enlisted the aid of editors, writers, and translators themselves. Then they published a book which met a need hitherto only inadequately met: a book for non-Evangelicals who were yet unwilling to go to the extreme of the Hymnal Noted. Julian characterized the original A&M as "moderate, definite, and popular" -- moderate in avoiding both the Bickersteth and the Neale extremes, definite in its standards of doctrine and congregational suitability, and popular beyond any popular success yet achieved. The following chapters analyze more accurately the elements of the character of A&M, and of its appeal and effect.

NOTES

[1] In his commentary on Psalm 148:14. Quoted in Bernarr Rainbow, "Hymns," A Dictionary of Liturgy and Worship, edited by J.G. Davies (1972), 194.

[2] Still one of the best books on the place of the psalms in Christian tradition is R.E. Prothero, The Psalms in Human Life, first published in 1903.

[3] Benedict (c.480-c.550) made provision for the use of non-scriptural hymns in all the hours of the divine office, but they were not admitted into the secular office until the twelfth century.

[4] See also Chapter Four, 7.

[5] In this passage, the common distinction is being made in using the word anthem to mean the special musical offering of a choir, rather than its musicologically correct definition, the responsive or antiphonal performance of a piece of music. Even in the latter case, however, one may infer that the singers have to be rehearsed.

[6] Helen Gardner, Religion and Literature (1971), 122.

[7] Matthew Arnold, "The Study of Poetry," Prose and Poetry, ed. A.L. Bouton (New York, 1927), 76-77.

[8] E.K. Francis, tr. Keble's Lectures on Poetry 1832-1841 (1912), II, 368.

[9] Gardner, Religion and Literature, 135.

[10] Samuel Johnson, "Life of Waller," Works (1787), II, 266-267.

[11] Johnson, Works, II, 267.

[12] Johnson, Works, II, 267.

[13] Johnson, Works, II, 267.

[14] Quoted in F.J. Gillman, The Evolution of the English Hymn (1927), 26.

[15] Johnson, Works, II, 268.

[16] Johnson, Works, II, 268.

[17] Gardner, Religion and Literature, 189.

[18] Johnson, Works, II, 268.

[19] In the matter of pleasing, compare C.S. Lewis in English Church Music (April 1949): "We must beware of the idea that our music can 'please' God as it would please a cultivated human hearer. That is like thinking, under the old Law, that he really needed the blood of bulls and goats. . . . All our offerings, whether of music or martyrdom, are like the intrinsically worthless present of a child, which a father values indeed, but values only for the intention." Quoted in Erik Routley, Hymns and Human Life, second edition, (1959), 307.

[20] Keble's Lectures on Poetry, II, 482-483.

[21] Office hymns, of course, were intended to be familiar through regular use in close association with the liturgy. See also Chapter Four, 1, on Victorian attempts to make hymns as familiar as the collects.

[22] See Chapter Four, 6.

[23] L.C. Biggs, ed., Hymns Ancient and Modern for Use in the Services of the Church, with Annotations,

Originals, References, Authors' and Translators' Names and with some Metrical Translations of the Hymns in Latin and Greek (London, 1867).

[24] Biggs, A&M Annotated, vi-vii.

[25] Biggs, A&M Annotated, vi-vii.

[26] Biggs, A&M Annotated, vi-vii.

[27] F.D. How, Bishop Walsham How: A Memoir (1899), 412.

[28] Tennyson in conversation with Dr. Warren, quoted in H.A.L. Jefferson, Hymns in Christian Worship (1950), 221.

[29] "Poetry is in its essence an act of reflection, of refusing to be content with the interjections of immediate emotion in order to understand the nature of what is felt. Since music is in essence immediate, it follows that the words of a song cannot be poetry. Here one should draw a distinction between lyric and song proper. A lyric is a poem intended to be chanted. In a chant the music is subordinate to the words which limit the range and tempo of the notes. In song, the notes must be free to be whatever they choose and the words must be able to do as they are told." W.H. Auden, "Notes on Music and Opera," The Dyer's Hand (1962), 472.

[30] Not, however, at the expense of sense, the importance of which is paramount in hymnody. One of the strong points of Anglican hymn tunes was the avoidance of the upper and lower voices and fugue-entries of popular Methodist tunes, which often produced verbal nonsense, as in "Bring down Sal-- Bring down Salvation from on high." See A. Hutchings, Church Music in the Nineteenth Century (1967), 135.

[31] "O Thou Who dost to man accord" (77/86), a translation by J.W. Hewett of "Summi largitor praemii," an ancient hymn in English use from the eleventh century.

[32] He had two hymns in the A&M Appendix, and eight new ones in the Revised edition.

[33] Quoted in H.A.L. Jefferson, Hymns in Christian Worship (1950), 177.

[34] J.M. Neale, Christian Remembrancer, vol. xlvi, no. cxxi (July 1863), 125-126.

[35] F.E. Hutchinson, ed., The Works of George Herbert (Oxford, 1941), 168.

[36] Journal of Henry Martyn, June 24, 1804. Quoted in L.E. Elliott-Binns, The Early Evangelicals (1953), 438.

[37] See Chapter Three, 1, iii.

[38] A.P., Letter, January 29, 1872, the Bishop of Oxford [J.F. Mackarness] to W. Pulling.

[39] E. Caswall, Lyra Catholica (1849), viii-ix.

[40] Quoted in E.A. Towle, J.M. Neale, D.D.: A Memoir (1907), 208. Webb's emphasis.

[41] Towle, Neale, 208.

[42] Isaac Williams, "Tract 80: On Reserve," Tracts for the Times, vol. 4 (1838), 3.

[43] Williams, "Tract 80", 45.

[44] Williams, "Tract 80", 53.

[45] Williams, "Tract 80", 62, 70.

[46] Williams, "Tract 80", 69.

[47] See Chapter Five, 5.

[48] Williams, "Tract 80", 55.

[49] The lines are the first of the eighth stanza of "Brief Life is here our portion" (142i/225) as given in the specimen books. The stanza is omitted from A&M 1860.

[50] A.P., Letter, March 27, 1860, W. Priest to H.W.B.

[51] Gardner, Religion and Literature, 156.

[52] Gardner, Religion and Literature, 156.

[53] Variations of this formula are "meek and lowly" and "meek and gentle," as "Jesu, meek and lowly" (152/88) and "Jesu, meek and gentle" (189/194). In the second of these hymns the usage is particularly inept, as the rest of the hymn celebrates the power of Christ -- "Pardon our offences,/ Loose our captive chains,/ Break down every idol/ Which our soul detains" (stanza

2) -- but the writer, G.R. Prynne, does not bring out as he might have done the implicit paradox of the gentle conqueror.

[54] Stanza 2, ll. 1-4 of "Hushed was the evening hymn" by J.D. Burns, no. 574 in the 1889 Supplement. As the use of cliché and set epithet is a general issue in hymn criticism, the choice of apt illustrations has not been restricted to the first three editions of A&M.

[55] First Specimen (1859), no. 23. Translation based on John Chandler's.

[56] "The heavenly Child in stature grows" (62/78), stanza 1.

[57] First specimen (1859), no. 18, stanza 6. The hymn is given for "Christmas, For Children." White's copy bears the marginal note "general if at all."

[58] Stanza 1, no. 568 in the 1889 Supplement.

[59] F.E. Hutchinson, ed., _The Works of George Herbert_ (1941), 168.

[60] "The Church-porch," _The Temple_, in Hutchinson, ed., _The Works of George Herbert_ (1941), 6.

[61] Erik Routley, _Hymns and Human Life_, second edition (1959), 3.

[62] First and last stanzas, quoted in A.G. Lough, _The Influence of J.M. Neale_ (1962), 100-101.

[63] Quoted in W.K.L.Clarke, _One Hundred Years of Hymns Ancient and Modern_ (1960), 2. See Bernard Manning, _The Hymns of Wesley and Watts_ (1942).

[64] Preface, dated October 20, 1779. Quoted in John Julian, ed., _A Dictionary of Hymnology_, second edition (1907), 1257.

[65] Quoted in F.J.Gillman, _The Evolution of the English Hymn_ (1927), 28.

[66] C[ecil] F[rances] H[umphreys] [C.F. Alexander], _Hymns for Little Children_ (1848), no. 16 (stanzas 1,4), 37.

[67] Geoffrey Faber, _Oxford Apostles_, second edition (1936), 92-93.

[68] A reference to the Prayer of Consecration in the Book of Common Prayer: "who made there (by his one oblation of himself once offered) a full, perfect, and sufficient sacrifice, oblation, and satisfaction."

[69] A.P., Letter, March 11, 1873, Sabine Baring Gould to [H.W.B.]. Comments on proof-sheets of the Revised edition.

[70] Ephesians 6:11-17, beginning "Put on the whole armour of God."

[71]
540 "Fight the good fight," J.S.B. Monsell
541 "We are soldiers of Christ," T.B. Pollock
542 "Stand up! stand up for Jesus!," G. Duffield
543 "There's peace and rest in Paradise," J.R. Vernon
586 "Lift up your head, ye gates of brass," J. Montgomery
588 "Soldiers of Christ, arise!" W.W. How

[72] For further discussion of children's hymns, see Chapter Five, 4.

[73] *Rugby School Hymn Book* (1824, revised 1843).

[74] Mrs. Yonge, *The Child's Christian Year: Hymns for Every Sunday and Holy-day, Compiled for the Use of Parochial Schools* (1841), v.

[75] See Chapter Three, 2, ii.

[76] For further discussion of the Proprietors' policies in compiling, publishing, and revising A&M, see Chapter Three *passim*.

[77] One primer, however, that published in 1553 at the time of the death of Edward VI, contained no translated hymns, marking a high point of Calvinist influence.

[78] Quoted in L.E. Elliott-Binns, *The Early Evangelicals* (1953), 374.

[79] Title page address. For further details, see Chapter Four, 2.

[80] For further discussion of originality in paraphrase, see Chapter Four, 7.

[81] See G.J. Stevenson, ed., *The Methodist Hymn Book, Illustrated with Biography, History, Incident, and Anecdote* (1883).

[82] Quoted in K.H. MacDermott, The Old Church Gallery Minstrels (1948), 48.

[83] John Julian, editor of A Dictionary of Hymnology (1892 and 1907), which is still the hymnologist's essential reference work.

[84] For example, J. Bickersteth's Psalms and Hymns Selected and Revised for Public, Social, Family or Secret Devotion (1819).

[85] The decision was not an easy one. Harcourt's authorization of one book did not make hymn-singing immediately or widely acceptable. Debate continued in the columns of the press, the British Critic, for instance, stating its objection in 1840 to the "passionate fervour and self-confidence" of hymns, which it found at odds with the tone of the Prayer Book. Two years later the same paper declared that "there cannot be a more miserable bondage than to be compelled to join in the so-called hymns that now infest our church." This indeed is what the Ecclesiastic of 1850 called "a stiff and sullen Anglicanism [which] proscribed all metrical hymns as savouring of the conventicle." On the other hand, there were those who called for the rejection of metrical psalmody (as perverse and wretched), and the reinstatement of mediaeval hymns (Christian Remembrancer, 1849). See W.K.L. Clarke, One Hundred Years (1960), 18-19.

[86] The best of which are A&M; The Hymnary, 1872 (Cooke and Webb); Church Hymns, 1871 (S.P.C.K.); Hymnal Companion, 1870, 1876 (Bickersteth); The Church of England Hymn-Book, 1882 (Thring).

[87] Indeed, when the Compilers printed that hymn in A&M, they thought it necessary to replace the first person singular with the plural, and to conclude three Cowper stanzas with a more confident fourth from another source.

[88] "Though I would not offend readers of taste by a wilful coarseness and negligence, I do not write professedly for them. I have simply declared my own views and feelings, as I might have done if I had composed hymns in some of the newly-discovered islands in the South Sea, where no person had any knowledge of the name of Jesus but myself." Preface to Olney Hymns, quoted in The Life of John Newton (1855), 242.

[89] Volumes which show a wide field of interest,

though none of them was intended for use in regular church worship: Hymns for Children, Intended chiefly for Village Schools (1842); Hymns for the Young (two series, 1844 and 1846); Hymns for the Sick (1843 and 1849), in which he took special pains to avoid regular rhythms which would jog mercilessly through the head of a fevered patient; and Songs and Ballads for Manufacturers (1844).

[90] See Chapter Four, 4.

Chapter Three
The Publication of *Hymns Ancient and Modern*

1. Compilation

i. Original Edition, 1860-1861

In August 1862 the *English Churchman* published a letter signed "An Englishman," which referred sarcastically to "this hymn-book-making age" in which:

> Every Clergyman now-a-days seems to pride himself on having '*his own*' selection of hymns, compiled probably by his wife and eldest daughter, and the music for it selected perhaps by some young 'Tommie' [simpleton] who has just learned to play a double-chant, and sing boy-alto in his schoolchoir. No doubt it is well to let gentlemen have a vent for their genius, and perhaps a hymnbook is after all more harmless (?) [sic] than a volume of bad sermons printed 'at the request' of personal admirers![1]

The writer went on to say:

> I very well know how difficult a thing it is to bring out a good [hymnbook]. As for a hymnal to suit all tastes, or to be universal, let no one dream of producing such a work; still less let any imagine that 'Hymns A & M' will ever become _generally_ liked.[2]

What success A&M had achieved by this time was ascribed to its "myriad contributors," with the implication that the contributors had exploited their local influence to push the book beyond the circulation it would have achieved on its own.

The fact is that A&M did differ from other hymnbooks precisely in the way "An Englishman" described. It was not the work of an amateur enthusiasm nor the expression of an individual vanity. It was the work of a committee and, as such, prone to the faults to which the works of committees are liable. At the same time, it owed its virtues to the consultations which the committee made possible, and to that extent, its success was indeed due to the number of its contributors.

A&M differed from other Anglican collections because its aim was higher. As it has been seen, most hymnbooks were either collections of favourites, or works of scholarship intended to introduce or revive the hymnody of other languages and times. A&M was intended to combine both functions, for the benefit both of congregation and of choirmaster, thus overriding the differences which the Choral Revival had rather too strongly emphasized. To be an improvement upon the collections which every Vicar and his daughter were printing required greater resources than those upon which every Vicar and his daughter could call. An individual of great learning and considerable leisure might be able to complete the task: no doubt J.M. Neale's Hymnal Noted, which reintroduced ancient hymns and Gregorian tones to mid-Victorian churchgoers, owed as much to Neale's near-sinecure as Warden of Sackville College, (which gave him a living), and to Bishop Gilbert of Chichester's inhibition of his clerical functions in that diocese between 1847 and 1861 (which forced him into other activities than preaching and celebrating), as to his great scholarship. The clergy who conceived A&M, however, were none of them as remarkable characters as Neale. They were all clergy in parishes which presented practical problems as well as spiritual needs. Pragmatism tempered their scholarship; they were less concerned with authoritative versions of ancient hymns than with the need for singable translations which would reveal the treasures of mediaeval hymnody to nineteenth-century congregations. The effects of this concern are examined in the next chapter. They were busy men, and they turned naturally to committee work and consultation to achieve their goal. They did not hesitate to request the help of scholars and experts when they felt that help to be necessary, but the final criterion in any judgment was neither poetic nor scholarly, but one of clerical common sense and parochial experience. Initially, and perhaps finally as well, the committee succeeded because its members had made real commitments: they were preparing to sacrifice their own interests in favour of a larger venture.

A&M was not the first hymnbook to be compiled by a committee, but it was the first collection entirely the work of a committee. The S.P.C.K.'s collection was Psalms and Hymns, the 1859 edition of which was in preparation when A&M was conceived. The editors of the S.P.C.K. collection were required to submit their work to the stringent criticisms of the Society's episcopal referees, whose views were not always those of the lower clergy and laity who were the editors. The A&M committee, on the other hand, was its own first and last judge.

Nor was A&M the first hymnbook for which wider co-operation was sought beyond the editors' own circle of acquaintance. The Advertisement to Cooke and Denton's Church Hymnal sounds much like the preliminary appeals which Sir Henry wrote on behalf of the A&M Committee. It is not surprising, for Denton was present when A&M was conceived.

> Feeling the want of a good HYMNAL in their own Churches, some Clergymen have united for the purpose of compiling one which shall be suited to general use, either in town or country parishes. They feel that such a Work will be equally interesting to hundreds of their brother Clergymen, and cordially invite co-operation and assistance.
>
> They are not desirous of merely adding ANOTHER to the many Hymn-Books already in use; but believe that if they can obtain the

> co-operation of a large number of Clergymen, this will supersede many of those already published, and will be found so suited to the use of the Church at large, that it will be adopted by many Clergymen who have not yet introduced Metrical Hymns into their services and having the sanction of a large number of Clergymen, the Work will have an authority, the best that, under present circumstances, can be given to any such collection.[3]

The editors offered to send proof-sheets to any clergyman who would read and correct them, and announced their intention of printing a first part of their book for trial use before continuing the publication.[4] Their plan seems to have been just as well thought-out as A&M's: in this as in a number of ways it is clear that A&M was not an innovation, but a combination and consolidation of innovative features, and that its consequent success has nearly obliterated all trace of its more tentative predecessors.

The idea of A&M was first mooted in the early summer of 1858, as the Rev. Francis Murray recalled in a letter to the Rev. W. Denton in 1862:

> You will remember our conversation in the train on the Great Western, the proposal (made by which of us I do not recollect) that present Editors should unite in abandoning, as

> far as they could, interest in their books, and unite in an endeavour to promote one good one. We parted with an assent to this idea. Sir H. Baker had for some time pressed on me the thorough revisal of my own book, but I had shrunk from the labour. When an opening was made for joint labour and the co-operation of many skilled hands, I gladly took up the project and wrote to Sir H.B.[5]

Murray was the Rector of Chislehurst, and the editor, together with the Rev. Christopher Harrison (who had been his curate) of a *Hymnal for Use in the English Church*, which he had published in 1852, and which had achieved some small success. Denton was Vicar of St. Bartholomew's, Cripplegate, and one of the editors of the widely used *Church Hymnal*, published in full in 1853. The Rev. Sir Henry Baker was Vicar of Monkland, a rural Herefordshire parish, where he was both squire and parson. He had been a contributor to Murray's book. At this time he was planning a hymnbook of his own, the chief known characteristic of which was to have been its price of sixpence.[6]

Murray wasted no time in writing to Sir Henry:

> It was seriously proposed to me the other day by Denton that he White and we should endeavour still to amalgamate in a new edition: and for our part [Murray and Harrison] we should be glad to do so: I do

> not know if White wd. There are serious difficulties in the way of such doings in respect of a Hymnal, which I need not say is unlike many other books, that alterations subject former possessors and congregations to such great inconvenience, and if the plan of Denton's or the one to which you before urged me [the revision of the Hymnal for Use in the English Church], was carried out, Denton White and we must still at the same time each keep on a continued edition of each book for the sake of those who now use it. This is a serious matter, but one of course which can be done. . . . When White returns from his holiday I mean to try him upon the subject. Our 3 books are in so many respects so similar that they ought not to go on along 3 paralell [sic] roads.[7]

The White to whom Murray refers was the Rev. George Cosby White, editor of Hymns and Introits (1852). Almost a contemporary of Sir Henry at Cambridge, he had been curate at Chislehurst, and in 1858 he was Curate-in-charge of the formerly controversial parish of St. Barnabas, Pimlico. It was White who convened the first meeting to discuss the proposal, a meeting which was attended by Sir Henry, Harrison, Murray, and the Rev. William Pulling, Sir Henry's friend and neighbour. Surprisingly, Denton did not attend, and it is now very difficult to discover the true reason for his absence, for the conflicting accounts are further confused by a welter of misunderstanding and injured feelings. Denton claimed that he had not been invited, because no one but Murray really wished to include him in the project.[8] Murray claimed that when Denton did not appear at the meeting as he had been expected to do, he rushed to the City to request his attendance, and that Denton refused to come.[9] The letters prove that more than three years later, the misunderstanding was unresolved. What is certain is that Murray reported that Denton had refused because he would not agree to an entirely new collection, but wished to work from an already existing book, and that preferably his own. Denton expressed this view in a letter to the Rev. W. Upton Richards, Vicar of All Saints, Margaret Street, where White's Hymns and Introits was in use. Richards had been invited to join the committee, and Denton wrote to urge his view, unsuccessfully, upon him:

> It is a pity & I think a great waste of strength & injurious to us all to multiply books. . . . Can anything be done to make 'The Church Hymnal' usable for a larger number. Its claims are to a larger sale than all other Church hymnal [sic], put together although it has been a shorter time in the field. We have sold 32,000 copies, our sale has every year increased, it is now about 6000 yearly, & rising. It is taken in every diocese of England -- to my knowledge -- except Carlisle of which I am not sure. . . . It is

> official to one Colonial diocese. . . . Now under these circumstances would it not be better to make as far as we can this one perfect by an appendix rather than start a new one.[10]

Thirty-two thousand was indeed a respectable sale for a hymnbook: Murray's book, by comparison, had sold twenty thousand in three editions. A&M's success, however, was unprecedented, with a sale of 100,000 in its first year.[11]

Although Denton remained intractable and never joined the committee, the Compilers found no lack of other help from other hymnbook editors, and among their own friends. For the sake of clarity, a distinction is henceforward made between the Compilers and the Committee: the former comprises all who helped in the compilation of A&M; the latter, those Compilers who formed the editorial nucleus of the enterprise. The Compilers were no formal body: they never met altogether, though the Committee met frequently. The Compilers made their suggestions, submitted their own hymns, and commented upon the sheets sent to them; the Committee made the final choices and decisions. They were the most committed to the book: eleven of them invested in it not only their time but also their money, and became by Trust Deed the Proprietors of A&M. There were nearly three times as many Compilers who advised regularly, though some of them withdrew after disagreements over editorial policy or party alignment. The critics of A&M wrote of them as the Forty Thieves, with slightly more accurate reference to their number than to their methods.

The Committee included White, Murray, Harrison, Pulling, Richards, and Baker, the last of whom became by common consent the Secretary. His was the only name made public: it appeared in the advertisements, and all enquiries were to be directed to him.

Sir Henry was a keen lover of hymns, a writer of verse, and an amateur musician; his enthusiasm led him to urge a bolder project than others of his talents would have dared; his zeal and his occasional high-handedness carried A&M through many of its early difficulties. His colleagues were too honest not to record in the obituary note in their Minute Book that there had been differences of opinion, but they gave him full credit for "inward cordiality" and "unflagging zeal."[12] The Committee was justified in appointing him Secretary and later Chairman of the Proprietors: the work of co-ordinating the labours of approximately forty Compilers was enormous, but so was his energy. To read the pencilled drafts of his many letters is to see his mind at work: he often wrote without pausing to deliberate, especially when his temper was roused. Phrase upon phrase is scrawled in haste; much is cut out but very little altered. He makes frequent reference to the conduct befitting gentlemen and clergy when he is angry, and not a few of the quarrels between the Proprietors and other editors were exacerbated by Sir Henry's style. Nevertheless, his labours were greatly appreciated by his colleagues, who eventually left most of the correspondence and administration to him. After publication the Proprietors met once a quarter to ratify what Sir Henry had done in the interim. He did regularly consult one or two of the Proprietors before making far-reaching decisions, but it was not until

1870 that a formal Standing Committee of the Chairman and two annually elected members was established to transact jointly all business between general meetings.

The other Proprietors were also all clergymen. George William Huntingford spent twenty-one years at Littlemore, near Oxford, where J.H. Newman had built the church and established his community, and whence he had been received into the Roman Catholic Church. Huntingford's ministry there must have been a period of peace after the bewilderment and excitement his congregation had undergone.

William Hearle Lyall was also an Oxford man, and became Rector of St. Dionis-Backchurch in the City of London in 1853, where he served for twenty-four years. Subsequently he caused considerable anxiety to A&M by going over to Rome in 1879 and refusing to give up his Proprietorship. He never again attended the general meetings, but continued to take his share of the profits. The other Proprietors were anxious lest the public should discover that a Papist had an interest in their hymnbook, and denounce them. Antipapist feeling, though never again as high as in the fifties, was not to be disregarded.

Thomas Ashley Maberley was ten years older than most of the Committee. His thirty-six year ministry at Cuckfield in Sussex confirmed him in his retiring ways: his role was less to initiate than to encourage. After his death, his colleagues wrote that

> ... mainly from his humble estimate
> of his own capabilities, he did not

> take a prominent part in the work committed to us, but his genial kindness to each and all of us and hearty support of every measure which he thought would conduce to the great end wh we have in view can never be forgotten.[13]

William Henry Perceval Ward, Rector of Compton-Valence, Dorchester, for over thirty years, resigned his Proprietorship in 1863 when a revision of the Salisbury Hymnal was proposed, for he felt that he could not refuse the assistance requested of him.[14]

John Murray Wilkins was approximately the same age as Maberley; as the Rector of Southwell he had become involved with A&M when he wrote to enquire about the proposed hymnbook. His own church had no hymnal, for none suited his musical judgment.[15] His chief concern was the Music edition of 1861, which was financed separately from the Words edition, and the Proprietorship of both was amalgamated only in 1863.[16] Poor Wilkins was declared insane in 1877.

One of the Committee who did not become a Proprietor but who devoted much labour to A&M was the Rev. James Russell Woodford of Kempsford in Gloucestershire, later Bishop of Ely. He had edited a hymnbook entitled _Hymns arranged for the Sundays and Holy Days of the Church of England_, two editions of which were published, in 1852 and 1855. In 1858 he wrote that he was considering a new edition:

> ... only 250 copies remain, and we

> are in doubt what preparation to make in order to be ready for the time when that shall have been used up. The experience of the three years has I think left us satisfied with the book as far as it goes, but proven also the need of more hymns. When you have looked it over I should be very glad to hear whether you think it ought to be taken as the basis of a larger book in which case I should be very happy to co-operate with you in getting out such a book. I had thought of at once beginning to prepare another and much enlarged edition, but [would] much prefer to join with another like your self in so doing.[17]

The characteristic features of his hymnal, according to Woodford, were first, the exclusion of "every technical or scholastic word" and "any verse in which the allusions seemed too remote for popular appreciation," and, second, the admission of "no second rate hymn," though this last, he confessed, had not been entirely achieved.

Many of the Compilers answered the advertisement which the Committee placed in the Guardian on October 20th and 27th 1858. It was worded as openly as possible to encourage a wide range of responses.

> To the CLERGY and OTHERS interested in Hymnology. -- The Editors of

> several existing HYMNALS being engaged, with others, in the compilation of a Book which they hope may secure a more general acceptance from Churchmen, would be very thankful for any suggestions from persons interested in the matter.[18]

The Committee had already some definite principles concerning a hymnbook to secure general acceptance, but they were not deaf to other views. It was the similarities between their own collections which had drawn them together, though White was originally an exception in being "rather dogged against modern hymns."[19]

The response to the Guardian advertisement was extremely gratifying: more than two hundred clergymen wrote to Sir Henry with general or specific suggestions and offers of help. Many of the issues raised in correspondence are discussed in Chapter Four.

The recruitment of Compilers is clearly illustrated in the case of the Rev. William Wigan who wrote to Sir Henry with some suggestions. Sir Henry replied, thanking Mr. Wigan and requesting his continued help, but Mr. Wigan was too modest to involve himself further:

> Many thanks for your offer of sending Hymns for Criticism. I am not competent to give an opinion; so pray do not put yourself to that trouble and expense.[20]

Encouragement came from clergymen who wrote in support of the Committee's basic principles. The aim of reducing the number of hymnals in current use was already being achieved when individuals gave up their own works in deference to the larger project. The unselfishness manifested in such a letter as this one from the Rev. J. Hamilton, another country rector, not only reveals the readiness of the parishes to accept a general book, but also pays silent tribute to the tact with which Sir Henry could dissuade potential rivals.

> The motives wh have led you to undertake the publication of a new Selection are so completely my own, & the principles you have laid down for your guidance, are so much in accordance with those I have endeavoured to act upon, in forming the collection, I have now on hand, that I am quite disposed to postpone its publication, until I have seen that which you are preparing & should be most happy to co-operate with those, who are working on the new Book, if you would let me know, how I could most effectually assist them.[21]

Others regretted that it was now too late to halt the publication of their own books, but were eager to share their experience.

One example of the co-operation which was secured through the Guardian advertisement is well documented. The Vicar of the North Yorkshire parish of Easingwold wrote immediately to Sir Henry:

> I have just seen your Advertisment in the Guardian about a new Hymnal -- and having been for more than a year occupied, with several other Clergymen, in the compilation of a Hymnal I send you the following particulars. Out of a body of twelve Clergymen, all sound Churchmen, And forming a Clerical Society in the neighbourhood of York, four persons were deputed to consider and select suitable Hymns. These selected Hymns were then submitted from time to time to the whole body, discussed and approved or rejected. Very great pains have been taken and much anxious labour bestowed upon the work. We have selected and approved about 140 Hymns chiefly from the various published Hymnals, of which a very great variety have been examined. We propose to add a certain number of Psalms -- from the Old & New Versions, the Oxford and Cleveland Psalters chiefly. . . . Some of the selected Hymns may yet be rejected on revision -- and a few others added. I am writing this without the opportunity of consulting any of my brethren -- but in the hope of giving and receiving assistance.[22]

Sir Henry asked Mr. Braithwaite to send him a list of their selected hymns, and on that evidence of their similarity of purpose, proposed that the two committees combine their efforts. Braithwaite reported that co-operation might be possible.

> I read your letter to my brethren at our last meeting, and I am requested to communicate to you our unanimous wish to make an attempt at co-operation . . . . We think that when we have seen something of each other's work we should be able to judge what are our chances of ultimate agreement. If this should seem probable -- some one or other of our members would probably be able to meet you in London after Xmas. . . . The last two years have added very greatly to the number of Church Hymnals -- and altho' most contain some bad Hymns -- most contain some, & many a large collection of good ones. The work certainly progresses -- and the time seems not unfavourable to some such effort as you are making. There should be no unnecessary delay in the matter, as many persons are introducing Hymnals, which cannot be readily displaced -- and others will hardly be prevailed upon to wait long.[23]

The points upon which the Yorkshire clergymen and the A&M Committee disagreed were two important ones: the inclusion of metrical psalms, and the relative proportion of ancient and modern hymns for the seasons. These issues are discussed in section 3 of Chapter Four. Eventually, despite the recurrent doubts mentioned in Braithwaite's letters, the Yorkshire clergymen decided to give up their book, and were enrolled as Compilers of A&M, through a committee of six who were invited to attend meetings of the Committee.[24] The Proprietors formally recognized Braithwaite's "services rendered in Compilation" with a grant of ten pounds for his parish,[25] which Sir Henry rightly considered ungenerous, and contrived to increase to a grant of one hundred pounds to the Yorkshire Committee as a whole.[26]

A note may here be fitly made on the subject of payment. The publication of A&M was a co-operative venture, impossible without the goodwill of the Compilers and the financial gamble of the Proprietors. When the gamble was proved successful, the Proprietors began to realize profits which they quite naturally felt to be the reward for their foresight, labour, and investment. They had not paid very much for copyrights, or for permission to print, and had greatly benefited from the generosity of their living authors, and from the silence of the dead. As they paid themselves increasing dividends, they began also to recognize their debts to their contributors and fellow compilers. Sometimes, as in Braithwaite's case, a gift was given for parish rather than personal use; at other times the gift was outright. In 1864, J.M. Neale was "requested to accept the sum of £100 as a slight token of the deep sense which the Committee [Proprietors] entertain of the value of his labours in the field of Hymnology of which they have by his own kind permission so largely availed themselves in the Compilation of their Book."[27] Similarly a £50 token of "the deep sense [of the] value of his labour in the Cause of Church Music" was given to Neale's colleague in the Hymnal Noted, Thomas Helmore.[28] A slight problem arose in the case of Caswall, who wrote to the Proprietors requesting a grant "in aid of the erection of a Calvary on his property in consideration of the Hymns wh he had allowed the Compilers to take."[29] The Proprietors seemed a little embarrassed, both by the request and by its object. They gave Caswall fifty pounds, with the note that

> ... as a Committee they feel they cannot enter into any question as to how you may wish to dispose of any money but they have much pleasure in making a similar acknowledgement of an obligation to your works, as we [sic] have done to Mr. Helmore, Dr. Neale, and others.[30]

Sir Henry's original ideas on the content and ordering of the book were strongly influenced by the suggestions he received, though usually only in details. It was his practice to digest the many opinions he heard, and present revised proposals to the Committee. An example of his method is this letter to Richards.

> The result of correspondence & thought hitherto has led me to 2 or 3 conclusions which I think it would be well if you & the rest of the committee would think over before

> our next meeting --
> 1st I propose that all hymns wh we take from the **Sarum** Breviary (and perhaps Roman also) be translated in the metres of the original: & if they are given in the Hymnal Noted that they be made to suit the tunes there but that with regard to hymns from other ancient sources the Paris e.g. we [?] liberty to do as we like -- This is a modification of my original idea which was to adhere invariably to the old metres -- and I make it because practically it wd not do to have scarcely anything except long measures in hymns for the Seasons, for those who do not use the old tunes -- It is a sort of compromise -- but I think a good one --.[31]

The issue of the metres of translation is considered in Chapter Four: at this point it is sufficient only to recognize how the compromise is reached in order to please as many as possible, and to note how Sir Henry's energy breaks through in this informal letter in dashes, underlining, sprawling sentences, and indecipherable words. The very page is a reminder of the excitement the project could arouse and the pleasure its projector found in working out the problems involved and seeing through to their solutions.

Sir Henry's dealings with the Committee and the Compilers are also revealed in the same letter.

> 2nd. that it would be well in the course of 3 or 4 months -- say about Easter -- to print some proofs (roughly) of hymns that we have agreed to -- those proofs being of different parts of the book as e.g. hymns for days -- Advent Christmas & Easter -- Sundays after Trinity & modern hymns -- Special occasions like Harvest etc -- so as to give some idea of what it will be -- and send to all who have answered the advertisement or whom we know of as wanting a Hymnal -- partly in order to get their criticisms and partly to keep up their expectations & interests -- I have ventured almost to promise this in some instances. For this reason I have sent a few hymns now for Trinity etc instead of going straight on only -- [32]

The third suggestion in Sir Henry's letter betrays the real practicality which coexisted with the antiquarian and hymnological passion he felt.

> 3rd. to <u>profess</u> to give, amongst the general or Trinitylike hymns, some that would be suitable for singing in mission rooms, at lectures in cottages, [houses -- deleted] or meetings of brotherhoods etc rather than in church -- We want such -- and this would give us <u>good grounds</u>

> on which to admit some as to which we should otherwise feel bound to be more strict -- It wd be a popular characteristic of the book too --[33]

Here is early evidence of concern that the proposed book should do more than embody true doctrine and conform to exact standards in ritual: it should be a part of the mission to the working classes. The language suggests the rural rather than the urban godless masses: "mission rooms" and "cottages" have little in common with the great Exeter Hall missions and the slums and rookeries of London. It is not surprising that Sir Henry, a country parson himself, should think in such terms, but it is also symptomatic of the slowness with which the Church of England as a whole came to appreciate the scale and complexity of the problem.[34]

Sir Henry's choice of the verb "to profess" sheds an interesting light on his suggestion to Richards. At first sight there is an implication of insincerity in the intention but it is clearly not so, for the suggestion was indeed enacted. Thus it can only be that Sir Henry wishes to use it in its emphatic, quasi-religious sense -- to declare or affirm openly. It is then a much more positive statement, with even a note of defiance in its tone which suggests that Sir Henry is anticipating objections from the stricter antiquarians and ritualists.

The sample of proofs which Sir Henry ventured almost to promise was duly printed and sent out for criticism. It contained the texts of thirty-four hymns and the first lines of another sixteen, most of them for seasons, and the rest General Hymns. All the hymns selected for Advent were printed in this Specimen, together with a sample for Christmas, Circumcision, Epiphany, Septuagesima, and Lent.

The preface to the Specimen called for criticism of the hymns, though with less urgency than the _Guardian_ advertisement.

> Some of the translations given in this specimen are, it is confidently hoped, superior to any now existing; but any criticisms on them, especially after careful comparison with the originals, would be acceptable; as well as general suggestions.[35]

The extent to which the Specimen was altered bears witness to the enthusiasm of the Committee even after seven months of labour. White's copy of the Specimen in the Addington archive contains a number of pencilled emendations and comments. Four hymns were altered, some drastically, and seven of the suggested hymns were finally omitted.

The preface to the Specimen book, in addition to calling for criticism, was also a prospectus:

> The following hymns are printed as a specimen of the New Hymn Book now in preparation by a committee of about twenty Clergymen, including the Editors of several existing Hymn Books.

> The best edition will correspond in type with this edition. The cost of the cheap edition wll be 6d. A text will be printed at the head of each hymn, as of the first hymn given here: marginal references added occasionally: copious indices, etc. Ample provision will be made not only for seasons of the Church's year, weeks after Trinity, Saints' Days, etc; but also for Morning, Evening, etc, Baptisms, Confirmations, Holy Communion, Harvest-thanksgivings, School-feasts, Funerals, Fast and Thanksgiving Days, Missionary Sermons, Meetings, etc. . . . An accompanying Book of Tunes is also in preparation, under the superintendence of an eminent and well-known Church Musician. Any persons likely to use the Book (which will be ready, it is hoped, by Advent) would confer a favour on the Editors by sending their names, and the number of copies (either of words or music) they will probably require, to the Secretary of the Committee, the Rev. H.W. Baker.[36]

Of course, the hymnbook was not ready as soon as the Committee hoped: the revisions they undertook prevented its early appearance. Nor was there a book of tunes, as such, but instead a full Music edition, which was undertaken as a separate venture by Sir

Henry, and W.H. Monk, Organist and Director of the Choir at King's College, London, with the help of the Rev. Sir Frederick A. Gore Ouseley, and financed separately by Sir Henry and Wilkins.

A second specimen book was considered necessary six months after the first, when it became clear that yet another delay was inevitable. Sir Henry was fully aware that possible buyers might grow impatient before the book was ready. There were many who felt as did this clergyman:

> I quite hope to be able to postpone the adoption of any hymns until I have seen yours -- but it does seem rather a long time to go on with 'Tate & Brady' when once my mind has been made up to dispense with those functionaries.[37]

The temptation to Sir Henry to complete the book without waiting for full agreement from his colleagues must have been great, but his first concern was for a book to win general acceptance, and a book over which its own Compilers were not in accord could hardly recommend itself to the Church at large. The second specimen was again intended to keep up expectations and interest. It was much larger, containing 138 hymns, and set in print by Novello.

> These hymns are printed for temporary use, and as a specimen, still open to revision, of the Hymn Book now in course of preparation by a

> Committee of Clergymen, the publication of which has been postponed to Advent, 1860.[38]

The Compilers emphasized again the variety of occasions for which hymns were provided, realizing that one of the great attractions of hymn-singing for congregations which had not adopted the practice was that hymns could provide colour and a chance to participate not only in the Prayer Book services, but also on other occasions where no service was appointed. They also wished to emphasize that their book would be comprehensive, and therefore suitable to supersede other volumes which might already be in use.

The Second Specimen in its turn evoked considerable criticism: it must have been disheartening even for Sir Henry to receive the packet of closely written comments which one W. Priest sent him. Priest's main objection was that too little of the collection could be called "_finished English poetry_, or at least, _versification_":

> It is an invidious task to criticise, but I do not really see how any person of cultivated tastes can approve of the majority of the pieces, or even read some of them with patience.[39]

Nevertheless, he undertakes the invidious task with a will. One of the defects he notices, for example, is "the tendency to what, for want of a better name, has been tolerably defined as the 'Brady & Tate' school," which he illustrates with no fewer than thirteen quotations from the Second Specimen. Hardly a hymn escaped Priest's displeasure: it would have been impossible to revise sufficiently thoroughly to please him, especially as Priest himself felt that editors should not tamper with an author's own words. If Priest had suggested how improvements might have been effected, the Committee might have been more open to his criticisms. As it was, the Committee disregarded his recommendation that the book be "submitted to some more competent judge, (say, for instance, Mr. M. Arnold) and the whole carefully recast in accordance with his criticisms."[40] The Committee had too practical a sense of what hymns might be, and what purposes they might serve, to delude themselves into thinking that they might also be, in anything more than rare cases, outstanding poetry.

As late as October 1860, the contents of the book were still not final. On October 22, 1860, Catherine Winkworth wrote granting permission to include six hymns from her Lyra Germanica, Second Series, with due acknowledgment. (Only five actually found a place in the 1860 edition; the sixth, after considerable revision, was included in the 1868 Appendix. It may be surmised that a lack of time to seek her approval of the alterations prevented its inclusion with the others.) By the end of the month, however, Sir Henry was able to declare the book complete, and to announce its publication with subdued triumph in a circular sent to the many people who had shown interest in the work:

> The Hymn Book that we have been so long in preparing is now in the press, and will be ready by Advent

> Sunday. . . . We shd be much obliged if you cd let me know soon how many, if any, copies you wd require. An edition is also in the press with an accompanying tune to each hymn.
>
> Believe me, dear Sir,
>
> Faithfully yours.[41]

The words-only edition duly appeared in December 1860, and the complete Music edition followed in March 1861.

The full title of the book is _Hymns, Ancient and Modern, for Use in the Services of the Church_. W.H. Monk is generally credited with the suggestion of the title, but it is by no means original. William Sandys, a lawyer and antiquarian, had published a collection of folksong carols, which he considered sorely neglected, as _Carols Ancient and Modern_, in 1833. E.H. Bickersteth pointed out another similarity in the title of Dr. Callcott's tune book prepared in 1840 for Bickersteth's father's hymn book. That title was _Ancient and Modern Psalm and Hymn Tunes for the Christian Psalmody_.[42]

In the preface to his _Hymns of the Primitive Church_ (1837) John Chandler wrote of the Church's need for the standardization of its hymnody, and offered his book as a first step:

> Thus are set forth in one view the _Hymns, Ancient and Modern_, which are the peculiar property of the Church of Christ -- those which she had before the Papal Apostasy, and those

> which have been added to her collection since. Here is a nucleus which, in proper hands, may be added to, and amended in such a way from more modern sources, as to form a Hymn-Book in every respect worthy of our Church.[43]

That was the challenge to which the compilers of A&M responded.

ii. Appendix, 1868

The Compilation of the Appendix was undertaken to supply the deficiencies of the Original edition which had become apparent after publication. The progress of the Appendix is recorded in the Minute Book, and in the correspondence between the contributors and the Proprietors.

The first steps were taken at a meeting of the Proprietors (Richards and Maberley were not present) on April 12, 1864 at which it was decided to send letters to "certain persons interested in hymnology," to ascertain the desirability of publishing an Appendix while keeping the Original edition available unaltered, and to ask for suggestions for new material. The list of interested people to be consulted included Richard Trench, newly consecrated Archbishop of Dublin; J.S.B. Monsell, whose most recent collection of hymns and religious verse (Hymns of Love and Praise for the Church's Year) had been published in 1863; Richard Littledale, whose translations (Offices of the Holy Eastern Church, 1863) had been praised by Neale; Benjamin Webb, one of the founders of the Cambridge Camden, later Ecclesiological, Society, and one of the editorial committee for Hymnal Noted; William John Copeland, whose translations of Latin hymns were published even before Caswall's and were very influential; John Keble, Christopher Wordsworth, and John Mason Neale. Their replies to the Proprietors' letters were filed and discussed at a later meeting.[44]

The Appendix was delayed for some months while a proposal to amalgamate the Salisbury Hymnal and A&M was discussed.[45] When the project was abandoned, the Proprietors returned to work in earnest on the Appendix.

A sub-committee of three (Sir Henry, Harrison, and White) was appointed.[46] They met for several days at a time, and printed for circulation the hymns they proposed for inclusion in the Appendix. At the general meetings, the Proprietors discussed and considerably altered the sub-committee's proposals, omitting several suggested hymns and adding others. As late as July 8, 1868, for example, they approved four additions, one of them Sir Henry's own version of the twenty-third Psalm, "The King of love my Shepherd is" (330/197).

They also made many alterations to the texts of their proposed hymns, and because many of these were modern, the alterations, and at a later stage proofs, were submitted for approval to the authors of the originals.[47] Not all authors were as obliging as Matthew Bridges, three of whose hymns were included in the Appendix:

> By all means do whatever you wish with my poor little pieces: for in your hands I doubt not one is quite safe from unfair alterations or modifications. I am only too happy when pious individuals inside or outside my own communion [Bridges joined the Roman Catholic Church in 1848] can condescend to find or feel edification in any thing I have written.[48]

Indeed, it seems to be a curious fact that the Roman Catholic contributors were extremely generous and co-operative in sharing hymns, while the most warmly expressed disagreements and difficult obstacles were those between fellow Anglicans.

The chief aim of the Proprietors in compiling the Appendix was simply to broaden the scope of the collection. In doing so, they could silence several of the complaints which had been heard of the Original edition. For instance, to include Greek hymns would satisfy Neale, who claimed that the treasures of Eastern Orthodox hymnody were unfairly neglected. To increase the element of modern hymns in the collection would prevent the frequently-heard charge that the book's sympathies were too High church. How the

Proprietors achieved their aim is discussed in the comparative study of the contents of the books in Chapter Four, 3.

Although the Music edition was no longer a separate venture, the Proprietors did not interfere too much with it, leaving it to Sir Henry's amateur enthusiasm and Monk's professional experience. They did, however, insist that Monk not dominate the project entirely, by passing the following resolution:

> ... with a view to greater variety and as complete perfection as possible to the Music of the Appendix it is desirable that one or two competent assessors be associated with Mr. Monk in editing the Appendix tunes.[49]

A measure of Monk's importance, however, is the sum of £350 he received for his work and his copyrights. Dr. Dykes received £100.[50] Most composers received two or three guineas for their contributions, although Samuel Sebastian Wesley asked for and got 25 guineas for two tunes, one of which was the very popular "Aurelia." A proposal to offer prizes for "any competitive original Tunes for any Hymn for which we cannot otherwise procure perfectly satisfactory accompaniments" was rejected.[51] Half the hymns in the Appendix had new tunes, so that the purchase of copyrights was a large item in the accounts for the Appendix. The sums spent to secure copyrights of words are fewer,[52] mostly because many authors were beneficed clergymen who did not depend on their income from writing, or who felt strongly that the buying and selling of copyrights was incompatible with the worship of God.[53]

iii. Revised and Enlarged Edition, 1875

Almost immediately after the publication of the Appendix in Advent 1868, the Proprietors began to think of amalgamating and revising their two volumes. In February 1869 they ordered interleaved copies for themselves. They were at this time much distracted by the transfer of their printing from Novello to Clowes, but a year later they appointed a subcommittee, consisting of Sir Henry, Pulling, Harrison, Murray, and White, to "commence the work of revising the present book, and to report to the next general meeting."[54] In May 1871 the subcommittee reported that it had met five times and had drafted a volume of suggested emendations and omissions. At the same time John Stainer was asked to join the Music Committee for the Revised edition.

The revision was carried out in the same way as the Appendix was compiled: the subcommittee circulated its proposals,[55] which were discussed at the general meetings.[56] By August 1874, the Revised book was considered settled to the end of the section for the Burial of the Dead,[57] and by October the revision was declared complete. The printer, however, announced that it could not be published for Advent of that year, but that the principal formats would be ready by February 1, 1875.

As before, the Compilers received both solicited and unsolicited suggestions. Not everyone was as convinced as they were of the need for revision. R.W. Hutton wrote to his friend Godfrey Thring about the project, and his letter is worth quoting at length as an illustration of the widespread interest the book could arouse, and of the ambivalent attitude toward its Compilers of many who both approved the task and envied the achievement.

> Your news about the H.A.M. Committee interests me much. I presume they are stirred up by the activity of Novello, & the S.P.C.K. [Novello had recently published The Hymnary in competition with A&M which they no longer printed; the S.P.C.K.'s greatly revised Church Hymns was published in 1871] -- 'and not before time'. But judging from their performances in their Supplement [i.e. Appendix] I have no hope of their doing anything really good. If they are going to issue a new book altogether, they may, by leaving out about 3/4 of the old one, do real good service. But surely they don't mean to do this? They would raise such an outcry among the congregations as well as the parsons as

> they can have but little idea of, if they are proposing such a measure. I have held this morning . . . a caucus meeting of several divines using H.A.M. & they instruct me to impress strongly upon you to use your very best endeavours to obtain the publication of an Appendix to H.A.M. <u>not a new book</u>. And they further tell me to state that a much greater number of Evening Hymns is wanted. So much for them -- now for me by myself. I don't say anything about omissions, for three reasons -- 1st, you would get tired of reading, & I of writing my list, -- 2nd, I can't think they mean a new book; 3rd, I have too strong an idea of their belief in their own infallibility (at any rate the old lot of them) to imagine they would omit anything on the advice of an outsider. I confine my valuable services, therefore, to suggestions of additions. [He recommends some thirty hymns for inclusion.] . . . In the highly improbable event of their adopting any of the hymns I have mentioned, I could be of use about the tunes; but don't mention my name, and don't shew my book.[58]

Most of the advice received was equally conflicting, though not so negative in tone. The letters of advice from High churchmen had a common theme: "Do not by any means consent to water down the Book."[59] The Rev. E. Hoskins, associated with All Saints, Margaret Street, put the Anglo-Catholic views on A&M in some detail. He recommended:

> That the Book should be, wherever possible, of a more Catholic character by the introduction in preference to others of Hymns which are translations of Catholic Hymns, or framed on Catholic models.[60]

In Hoskins' use, "Catholic" is quite clearly a party term, indicating the body of men grown up under the protection of the Tractarians, who came to their Catholic and Apostolic position without the bitter struggles which had attended the Oxford Movement well over a generation earlier. Their partisan sense was very strong: Hoskins warned Sir Henry that "the book will not be accepted by a large portion of the Catholic party of my age and certainly not by the younger Clergy unless the wants I have stated in this letter are met," and goes on to say that:

> ... if such Clergy as these are not satisfied with the Book and they are an increasing number, I think only few will, for Bickersteth Book [sic] seems to be meeting the wants of the Low Church, & the S.P.C.K. of the moderate people; no doubt those who use your old Book with or without the Appendix would take the new Book

> but you have a book already for them in that one, & why have a second.[61]

One of Hoskins' general recommendations on behalf of the Catholic party was "that the tendency should be to make the book more objective."[62] In this opinion he was joined by the Bishop of Oxford, John Fielder Mackarness, who was known as a liberal High Churchman.

> In general, I should have been disposed to question the fitness of introducing a class of _sentimental_ hymns, such as 'Hark, hark my soul'. I should have preferred that the book should consist _mainly_ of hymns suitable for worship, dwelling on the majesty and mercy of God, rather than on experiences and feelings of men. Bp Heber's Trinity Sunday Hymn ['Holy, Holy, Holy! Lord God Almighty'] is just what I mean.[63]

The subjective and the sentimental, however, also had their advocates, among them Edward Husband, compiler of the _Mission Hymnal_, published in 1874.

> I am only one of a large and increasing body of men in the Church of England, who . . . like a hearty, fervid hymn, in addition to those you so strongly approve of, in which, 'we can breathe forth the deep-felt needs of our souls'. I don't want a Hymnal entirely

> composed of subjective hymns, but I do want a book in which subjective hymns are fairly represented.[64]

It is tempting but inaccurate to identify the call for objectivity with the Catholic party, and subjectivity with Low church or Dissent. Probably the most sentimental writer in A&M is F.W. Faber, who is represented in the 1860/1868 collection by seven hymns, and in 1875 by eight, and who admits that his models were the Olney Hymns and those of the Wesleys.[65] The problems of the *via media* are nowhere more clearly exemplified than in the extreme delicacy with which the Anglo-Catholics held themselves aloof from the emotional excesses of both Protestant and Papist.

The extent to which hymn-writing as well as the practice of hymn-singing could be partisan is illustrated by a letter from Frances Havergal, who was first represented in A&M in the 1875 edition. It was always to the Compilers' great credit that they looked beyond party divisions to bring together writers of faith and talent. The policy of anonymity within the volume, of course, made it easier to assemble a mixed company. Havergal wrote to Sir Henry to express her pleasure that her hymns should find a wider circulation through A&M. She continues:

> For the last two or three years I have been I may almost say 'petted & spoiled' by the Evangelicals; everything I have brought out, whether verse or prose has been reviewed & praised & furthered by pretty well

> all their papers or periodicals. . . they circulate my leaflets by hundreds of thousands, and recommend my books right & left. But so far as I know, not one High Church paper, (such as the Guardian, etc) has ever taken the least notice of anything, nor have I ever had such a cordial & sympathetic greeting as you gave me from any one else on your side. What wonder then that I supposed high churchmen as a rule had not the warm sympathies with topics dearer than life to me, which you expressed so gladdeningly! Especially as I have never written anything the least controversial or antagonistic wh could account for the one party taking me up with almost overwhelming kindness, & the other entirely ignoring me. So you have, unwittingly, taught me a lesson of charity![66]

When the book was published, the Proprietors felt the need to preface it with the following explanation:

> The Compilers of Hymns Ancient and Modern are well aware that it is no light matter to put forth a revised and enlarged Edition of their Book. It is too widely used, and (perhaps they may add) too much loved, to allow of any change being made without

good cause. But the very fact of its larger circulation is their best apology for revision. It is a simple debt which they owe to the Church. The thirteen years which have passed since their first copy was published have seen a great change in opinion on many points. For example, it is not necessary now, as it was thought to be then, to print an altered or shortened form of a good Hymn simply because it happened to be so used by certain congregations. No one wishes now to reprint tunes with unsatisfactory harmonies because we have been accustomed to them.

The general desire is rather to have a Hymn as its author wrote it; and Compilers are not expected to make changes in it without strong reason. The best Musicians of the day are writing new Tunes and re-harmonising old Melodies. New Hymns have been written to meet [,to some extent,] admitted needs. It would surely then have been [something like ingratitude to God, and] almost a dereliction of their duty to the Church, if the Compilers of _Hymns Ancient and Modern_ had not taken advantage of those altered circumstances.[67]

The examination of editorial policy and practice in Chapter Four will show most clearly how the Compilers responded to the altered circumstances which they perceived. Suffice it to say here that the 1875 edition was not only a revised, but also an enlarged edition. Ninety-three new hymns and a section of eleven litanies, ten of which were appearing in A&M for the first time, were added to the collection, and eighteen hymns were omitted, bringing the total number of hymns in the book to 473.[68]

The Revised edition is a consolidation rather than an innovation or extension. Although the tendency toward modern and English hymns was pursued, and the choice of ancient Latin hymns was more discriminating, the balance between sources of different ages and denominations was largely unaltered. The basic principle had been established, and the Compilers modified matters of detail. As hymnology became an increasingly serious study, the Compilers began to take their editorial responsibilities even more seriously, and to attempt a satisfactory adjustment between the practical demands of hymn-singing and conscientious scholarship. Hence their cautious recognition in their Preface that textual alterations were not as frequently necessary as their previous practice had suggested.

The Music edition was prepared by a Tunes Committee, which included for the first time Stainer, who was to epitomize Victorian church music for later generations. Sir Henry continued to exercise his tireless enthusiasm and interest, and in addition, the committee was required to submit its work "from time to time to a suff[t] number of professional musicians."[69] Apart from improving technically the previously published tunes, the committee's work was to find new tunes for old and new hymns. The book bears most strongly Monk's stamp, and for his labours and his copyrights the Proprietors paid him one thousand pounds. No wonder Thomas Hardy was later to refer ironically to the period of "the great choral reformation and the rule of Monk."[70]

The musical character of the Revised edition was acutely summarized by an anonymous clergyman who sent his comments to the Proprietors after publication.

> The nervous vigour of the Gregorian Tunes, the old "Psalter" Tunes, & the German Chorales, seems sadly lacking, and the tendency is toward the modern Part-song, & even the sentimental ballad.[71]

He observed sharply that although there was much choice, there was little variety. It is a fair criticism, but on the whole the volume appealed to the musical tastes of that Mendelssohn-steeped generation, and was received with enthusiasm.

The Revised edition was the first printed by William Clowes and Sons, and the accounts reveal not only how expensive, but also how profitable, the venture was. Monk's fee was enormous: in contrast, the Proprietors paid the members of their own revision subcommittee one hundred pounds each, in addition to their dividends.[72] Those dividends from the Original edition and the Appendix decreased as the expenses of revision mounted: when the extra payment was made, the dividend for the previous half year (to December 31st 1873) had been two hundred. They paid themselves £100 each for the next half year; the half-year ending December 31, 1874 paid nothing; at the end of June 1875 there was a balance against the Proprietors after Clowes presented their account, but six months later the Proprietors could afford to pay themselves a dividend of £330 each.[73] Their decision to undertake a revision, and to change printers, was most satisfactorily proven sound.

iv. A Note on the Music Edition and the Character of Sir Henry Baker

The Minute Book words the transfer of the Music edition from Sir Henry and Wilkins to the Proprietors in the following way:

> Sir H.W. Baker and Mr. Wilkins most kindly expressed their wish that the Proprietorship of the Words and of the Tunes should be amalgamated from this date. The Committee accepted this offer with thanks.[74]

No mention is made of their receiving any reimbursement for giving up their venture. Monk asked for and received £250 for his "share of the property in the Tune Book."[75] It seems, however, that both Sir Henry and Wilkins received five hundred, and thereafter were to be treated exactly as every other Proprietor. In 1869, however, in the middle of the confusion over the proposed transfer of the printing from Novello to Clowes (a subject upon which Sir Henry found himself at odds with his fellows), he wrote to Wilkins proposing a new arrangement. He asked Wilkins to second the following motion at the next meeting of the Proprietors:

> ... that Sir Henry Baker and Mr. Murray Wilkins were at first the sole Proprietors of the Tune edition of HAM -- That they merged their separate rights in those of the general body of the Proprietors on the understanding, which then existed that (with the exception of a small dividend once a year and travelling expenses) the Profits of the Book should not be distributed to or by each Proprietor separately. That lately this understanding has not been acted on -- and that therefore now and for the future it is only just that one of the following propositions be accepted 1st that Sir H. Baker & Mr. Wilkins become again sole Proprietors of the Tune Editions of HA&M <u>Or</u> 2nd that in the distribution of dividends a double (or I think <u>treble</u>) share be allotted to each of them.[76]

Wilkins was puzzled. "I don't see your object. -- Surely it is not that you desire to have sole disposal of the proceeds of H.A.& M.? If not this, what is it?" but with a mixture of good humour and plain speaking he dissuaded Sir Henry.

> I don't think it would do for us to act like the little boy who gave away his Cake & then asked for it back again. . . . I may be sorry for not having made a better bargain -- but I consider it now a 'fait accompli', and therefore not to be recalled. (at least not by us, I should be quite willing if the other 8 pressed on us double shares!!) I know nothing of any understanding about only a small dividend & travelling expenses. I know that I was glad of my £500, and there was nothing said about 'no profits' then.
>
> Excuse my frankness -- but I think you are taking rather a wrong line, & it is very unpleasant year after year to have differences on money matters wh we need not have if you would have any faith in other men's consciences. . .
>
> You had much better accept the situation -- give the 10 shares to the 10 shareholders & they will doubtlessly spend them as

> conscientiously as our own honoured Chairman himself.[77]

Sir Henry's motives are no clearer now than they were when he wrote to Wilkins, but it is one of those "at times passing differences of opinion" which he and his colleagues experienced.[78] Sir Henry's objection seems to have been that all the A&M profits were divided equally among the Proprietors, and that the body exercised no control over how each Proprietor spent his dividend, instead of sharing out only a small portion of the profits, and then spending the rest in charitable and hymnological objects in the name of the Proprietors as a whole. He was incensed by the talk of Novello's excessive profits which exercised the Proprietors for most of 1868. He seems to have felt that his colleagues were unbecomingly concerned with profits, and that if they insisted on altering the existing arrangements, they should not greatly benefit themselves. That is the kindest interpretation, but feelings were running high among the Proprietors at this time: Sir Henry did not chair the meeting of February 4, 1869 at which the decision, which he deplored, to remove the printing of A&M from Novello was taken. Harrison referred to his "desertion of [his] post as Chairman," and ventured to reprimand him:

> If a minority and most of all a minority of <u>one</u> is not bound by the decision of a majority, what must become of all transactions whether in business or in honour?[79]

This rift was eventually mended, but the

Proprietors were never on quite the same business terms again. The Finance subcommittee which had overseen the transfer was replaced by the Standing Committee consisting of the Chairman and two annually elected members, to transact jointly all business between general meetings. The opportunity for another major difference of opinion was to be avoided, for not always could Sir Henry be as well handled as by Wilkins in the matter of the Music edition.

2. Printing History

i. Formats

A detailed printing history of A&M is of little interest. A few points, however, about the physical format of the book are worth noting.

A&M was originally printed for the Proprietors by Novello, Ewer and Co. It seemed natural to them to issue the book in a number of formats, of different qualities and at different prices, so that, while the book was available to the many, it could also appeal to the discriminating few. In this respect, hymnals are like the Prayer Book and the Bible itself: a variety of bindings disguises a single purpose.

Hymnbooks were intended both for private and for congregational purchase. Indeed, the idea of a book for every churchgoer was a novel one. Although one could expect one's poorer parishioners to be familiar with the services of the prayer book through long acquaintance, or even with the words of many of the metrical psalms, one could not expect them to sing hymns without prompting, and the principle of congregational hymn-singing was threatened if a large portion of one's congregation kept silence. It was therefore necessary to provide editions either cheap enough for the poor to buy,[80] or sturdy enough to survive general public use. The Proprietors did both.

When the book was first issued, it was offered for sale in sheets at 4 1/2d. and 5 1/2d., depending upon the quality of the paper, or in cloth covers on thin paper at 6d., or in limp roan on better paper for a shilling.[81] The cheap fourpenny edition was printed over a year later, and although fourpence was no negligible sum, it was certainly a most reasonable price for a book. The first Music edition was expensive at 4s 6d, but cheaper editions of separate voice parts were later issued.

By 1870, the Proprietors offered A&M and its Appendix, separately or bound together, in twenty-two different formats, of different sizes, types, and qualities of binding and paper.[82] The cheap words-only edition was small, printed in double columns on medium 32mo paper, and stitched. The usual edition bought for congregational use was also words-only, printed in long primer on "second paper," demy 18mo, with cloth covers of an undistinguished brown. All Music editions were larger and more substantial than the words-only ones, bound in brown cloth boards for choirs, or in best morocco with gilt edges for private musicians.

In 1868, before the publication of the Appendix, the Proprietors began to question the profit Novello was making from A&M, and after much debate and some disagreement, the printing was transferred to William Clowes and Son on March 25, 1869, with the final agreement on costs and charges being signed on May 19, 1870. The printing of A&M has been entrusted to this firm ever since.

ii. Other Publications

In addition to the words-only formats and the Music edition, the Proprietors concerned themselves with a number of other projects related to A&M.

An early project was the publication of a volume of _Introits for Use throughout the Year_, which was issued concurrently with the hymnbook itself until after 1875. Its plainsong tones were adapted and accompanied by Monk. It was not as great a success as had been hoped, and from 1869 "any person so desiring could have Introits included in any copies of words without additional charge."[83] With the addition of a set of anthems, the book was issued in conjunction with the Revised edition, but was eventually allowed to go out of print.

In 1864 the Proprietors ordered the printing of their hymns on separate sheets for special occasions, such as Confirmation, Harvest festivals, and Mission meetings.[84] This innovation may be seen as a response to the frequent requests from clergymen for permission to print a few A&M hymns for local use: where the Proprietors were unable to sell the whole book they could henceforth sell selections of their hymns. The success of this scheme was such that the Proprietors later published orders of service for Confirmation, Baptism, and Burial, with appropriate hymns.[85]

A similar project was the publication of Hymns for Mission Services in 1877, a collection primarily for use at special missions, but which the Proprietors hoped would have a more general use as well.[86] This collection had no pleasant beginning: in correspondence with William Walsham How, Sir Henry learned that How was preparing an enlarged edition of the S.P.C.K.'s Hymns for Parochial Missions. At this time, that is, during the winter of 1875-1876, the Proprietors were feeling hardpressed by the S.P.C.K., whose new collection, Church Hymns, was proving a rival to A&M. Sir Henry wrote in his least patient tone of voice to How, refusing A&M copyright hymns to any S.P.C.K. project.[87] In addition, he claimed that the Proprietors were contemplating their own mission collection; this news came as a surprise to How,[88] and may well have been Sir Henry's invention. The first mention of such a mission book in the Minute Book is not until May 1876, when it is recorded that a mission book was "under consideration after correspondence with How," and Sir Henry was authorized to "proceed as necessary."[89] Sir Henry had already offered to publish How's collection after learning that the S.P.C.K. had decided against it.[90] Thus A&M took over How's work; the Proprietors sent out a letter asking for assistance,[91] and when the book appeared, How's help was acknowledged with thanks in the preface. Nearly 34,000 copies, words only, were sold in the first six months at 2d a copy.[92]

Hymns for Mission Services is a good example of Sir Henry's opportunism and initiative: at one stroke A&M was able to fulfil a particular need, and to eliminate a competitor. It was not his most gentlemanly act, but it was certainly in character, and one of the last projects he saw completed before he died on February 11, 1877.

After Sir Henry's death, and Harrison's in September of the same year, the Proprietors lacked the same enthusiasm for new ventures. The Minutes record a request from Mrs. Carey Brock for permission to insert "certain Children's hymns in a Hymnal for Children," but the ensuing debate concerning the possibility of a Children's A&M ended with the following decision:

> ... on the ground that she had already secured the co-operation of the greater number of persons to whom they would have looked for help, it was thought better to abandon the idea, and to concede to Mrs. Brock the use of the hymns for which she asked.[93]

Sir Henry, one feels sure, would at least have tried to persuade Mrs. Brock to turn over her selection and her contributors' good will to the Proprietors.

The teaching of music to large groups of uneducated people had been a particular nineteenth-century concern from the time John Hullah conducted his singing classes in Exeter Hall in the 1840s.[94] Of all the schemes to supplant classical musical notation, and there were many, Tonic Sol-fa method was one of the most popular. Sir Henry recognized the potential of a Tonic Sol-fa edition, and in 1869 he published a Music edition, "translated" into Tonic Sol-fa notation by Mr. Kitchin of Sydenham. The publication was a separate venture, and it was not until 1877, after Sir Henry's death, that the Proprietors took it over at the request of Sir Henry's sister.[95] The edition was not cheap: the full four-part score cost half a crown. A "translation" of the Revised edition, improved according to the latest refinements of the method, was equally expensive, but when the Proprietors took over the project, they authorized the publication of a book with alto and treble parts only, which would be sold in paper covers for sixpence, or in better bindings up to 1/3.[96] In this case the Proprietors were responding at last to an increasingly vocal demand, exemplified by the letter from Mr. Holloway, Curate of St. Saviour's, Hoxton:

> The Sol-fa copies of the old edition were more than double the price they need have been -- poor working girls, mill-hands & the like cannot afford to pay 3/6 [sic] for a hymn book, and it is just these classes who sing from Tonic Sol fa. The first tune book published in that notation was 'The People's Service of Song' 212 tunes Treble & Alto for <u>6d</u> -- <u>25 years ago</u>. If Hymns A & M could be brought out as cheap relatively, what a boon it would be to poor people & children! There is

nothing that would help the cause of 'people's music' like a very cheap Hymns A & M in Sol fa. It may be objected that the old notation editions are cheap enough. That is very true but the poorer classes of people do not sing from the old notation whereas they do use Sol fa very extensively. The London School Board teach it very carefully in all their schools. I teach it in our own parish schools & I have a large class on Wednesday evenings of the young men & women of our congregation. If I could put a cheap copy of the tunes into their hands I should have hundreds of pupils in a very short time, & our services in Church would assume a very different aspect.[97]

3. Sales and Circulation

i. Sales, Grants, and Circulation

Sales figures for the early years of A&M are hard to find. That the book had an immense success is clear: it was reckoned to have sold 100,000 copies in its first year[98] before the cheapest format was published, and nearly to have doubled that figure in a further six months.[99] By 1868 it had sold four and a half million copies.[100] After the publication of the Appendix, which was sold separately to purchasers of the Original edition, sales of the combined volumes remained more or less constant (average annual sales of 1,200,000) until 1874, just before the publication of the Revised edition, when approximately 800,000 copies were sold. The Revised edition itself sold over 800,000 copies in its first year, and the Original edition a further 500,000. Over the next ten years the combined sales of both editions never fell below one million per year, nor did they again achieve the 1875 figure. The Original edition's share of sales fell steadily until in 1885 it sold only 20,197 of the year's total of 1,218,205.

The success of A&M was largely due to the extent

to which it met the new demands for hymn-singing in the Church of England, but the suitability of the moment would not have been enough without some astute marketing. The Proprietors had not the established organization of the S.P.C.K. to help them, but they took advantage of the press, the resources of a well-known printer, and the law, as well as their own book. The role of the law, that is, the law of copyright, in the publication of A&M is examined at length in the section immediately following.

The account of the compilation of the Original edition reveals the preliminary steps the Proprietors took to ensure the financial as well as the critical success of the book: the advertisements in the press and the distribution of circulars to build interest and expectation, while discouraging would-be-rivals, and Sir Henry's assiduous cultivation of any individual who showed interest in the project, and who might be flattered into pushing the book.

Sir Henry was especially anxious to secure episcopal recommendation, as even an unofficial imprimatur would have a good effect upon sales, at least according to the bishop of Sir Henry's own diocese:

> I remember when I was in the Diocese of Oxford, we had a Collection of Hymns made by two Clergymen of Oxford [Edward Denison and Walter Kerr Hamilton] . . . which, I think had much circulation, and that had simply the recommendation of a dedication to the Bishop of Oxford, or

> rather an Inscription rather than a <u>dedication</u>. Something like that, I shd think, would be quite sufficient for your purpose: merely saying that to the Bp of the Diocese this Collection, (or whatever term you prefer), is 'intended' (or 'dedicated') by the Editors.[101]

Sir Henry's attempts to obtain official episcopal sanction were not very successful. The Bishop of Llandaff, Alfred Ollivant, was pleased to report that the Chapter had approved A&M for use in public worship in the cathedral, but he declined any "further expressions of my feeling and opinion respecting the book."[102] The Bishop of Fredericton, New Brunswick, British North America, regretted that his diocese had already its approved book, though he had ordered A&M for his cathedral choir.[103] The highest episcopal approbation A&M received was equally informal: the Archbishop of York, Charles T. Longley, pencilled a note to a clergyman uneasy about references to the Virgin Mary in A&M, that he did not find the references objectionable, and concluded "You need never fear censure from me in the use of that Hymn Book."[104]

That these expressions of approval[105] were unofficial and informal did not prevent Sir Henry from letting them be known, unofficially and informally. The tactics are revealed in a letter from Warwick R. Wroth, who had spoken against a proposed new S.P.C.K. hymnbook, one of his arguments being that A&M was already so firmly established that S.P.C.K. could not hope to displace it.

> I mentioned . . . that if [A&M] had received the imprimatur (Lyall kindly shewed me y letter) of Archbp of York, Bps of Llandaff & Hereford, & that it was not likely that these Bps & all these clergy wd now give up this book for the sake of one emanating from S.P.C.K.[106]

A deliberate effort to extend the book's popularity was made in 1864, when the Proprietors sent a copy of the Music edition to each of the Colonial Bishops.[107]

Sir Henry's willingness to make use of every possible method to push the book is vividly illustrated in a letter written twenty-five years after his death. It is a begging-letter from one J. Charlesworth to White, appealing for aid in buying a pony and conveyance so he will no longer have to walk seven miles on Sundays. He had been organizing choir-master to the Herefordshire choral union from 1861, and had lived at Monkland until Sir Henry's death.

> During the first two years of my work as organizing choir master, I carried about in my bag -- at Sir Henry Baker's request -- specimen copies of the hymn book, and it was greatly owing to my exertions in making known the book, that it had such a speedy introduction into the Hereford Diocese.[108]

This unabashed use of local influence was characteristic of Sir Henry, and it may be predicted that similar local influence was exerted by each of the Proprietors, and by many of the Compilers.

Success breeds success, as a Norfolk clergyman made clear:

> I have ordered 100 copies of the two cheapest editions, and hope to introduce them on Sunday week.
>
> I have lately obtained, through a letter published in the Norfolk Chronicle, some returns as to the relative circulation of Hymns A & M and Hymns S.P.C.K. in the Diocese. The former are to the latter as 6 to 1, and this fact has had much weight in my decision.[109]

Although there certainly were cases where A&M's success was its warmest recommendation, the Proprietors had nevertheless to be careful of arousing the resentment of those who felt that the book was being forced upon the Church. This resentment will be further discussed in the following section.

Most sales were either to individuals or to congregations of the Church of England, but A&M quite rapidly obtained a place in the middle-class musical life outside that communion. By 1876, it could be said, without deliberate insincerity, by "a Wesleyan minister of some experience" that:

> ... in no circles has your Collection commanded a truer appreciation than in our Connexion. In our public services we are restricted to the uniform use of our own Hymn Book. But there are few Wesleyan <u>homes</u> in this country, with any pretension to the love of sacred song, where there is not at least one copy of 'Hymns Ancient and Modern' . . . which in social and domestic life they have learned to love.[110]

Young was referring to the music of the book, which was a strong attraction. The Proprietors consistently refused to publish a volume of tunes only, so that, even if the book were bought for its music alone, closer acquaintance and ease of reference might make the words accepted where they would otherwise not have penetrated.

By twentieth-century standards, the Proprietors did not take the advertisement of their book very seriously. In fact, the amount spent on advertising was less than 1% of the cost of the Revised edition -- £169.7.6 of £18,130.11.11, although a similar amount (£170.3.2.) was spent on presentation copies which, by securing the goodwill of the volume's compilers and contributors, were no doubt just as important in extending the circulation of the book.[111] The single measure, however, which most aided the circulation of the book was the system of grants which the Proprietors operated through the printer.

When A&M was first discussed, W.W. How wrote expressing his interest in the project, and describing how the "very large sale" of his hymn book was in part achieved.

> I send you the cheapest form of the Hymnbook, as being the last, & stereotyped, edition. It is priced 4d. The proprietor of the Book, Mr. John Morgan, is a very liberal man, & makes a present to any Church adopting the book of as many copies as are ordered in the 1st instance for gratuitous distribution to the poor, & the Schools, or, if preferred, charges the first number ordered at half price.[112]

The grant system was not immediately adopted, though Novello gave clerical discounts. The standard A edition was sold at sixpence each to clergy, with an extra copy for every two dozen ordered, and no charge for postage and packing. An even better offer was advertised to encourage the adoption of the Music edition.

> Clergymen wishing to introduce the book into their churches may also be supplied at the same rate [3/6 a copy instead of 4/6], or may obtain 30 copies for £5 (package included), on application to Rev. Sir Henry Baker, Bart.[113]

Grants of books were first made upon the personal recommendation of a Proprietor, and were awarded to the parishes of compilers and contributors. Grants were at first small and miscellaneous; at one meeting the following grants were approved: one of 200 copies of the standard A format to a Wolverhampton church, and another of 50 copies of the same to a church at Lerwick; 70 A's, 20 cheaper cloth bound words-only formats (AA), and 10 books with a treble voice part to a church in Glasgow, and 10 copies each of 2 Music editions, to the cathedral at Gilbraltar, no doubt for the use of the cathedral choir, with the Proprietors' hopes for a subsequent general adoption.[114] Credit at Novello's was also granted, usually five pounds at a time. The support of Edward Twells, who had assisted the compilation while Perpetual Curate of St. John's, Hammersmith, was wooed as soon as he became Bishop of the Orange River State in 1863: he was immediately granted the sum of fifty pounds for his diocese, and "as many copies of H.A.&M. as he requires for the use of his diocese,"[115] and the following year a further twenty pounds' worth of books.[116]

By 1870 the grant system had been revised. Only one hundred pounds' worth of books had been granted in 1869, and Sir Henry was given permission to make grants at his own discretion. The discovery that the S.P.C.K. gave grants on the same terms as the proprietor of W.W. How's book twelve years earlier (that is, they matched the original order, or sold at half price, "regardless of the relative wealth of the parish"[117]), stimulated the Proprietors to issue a circular to the "Clergy of England, Ireland, and Scotland," announcing the availability of grants, and as a result they received "a very large application."[118] In 1871 Sir Henry made grants to the value of £768.6.11.

The Proprietors did not change the discretionary nature of their grants, though Sir Henry remained indignant over the S.P.C.K. system, which he considered "grossly unfair to our Book, & to all other Hymnals":

> It never crossed our minds that, supported as the Society is partly by our own contributions and those of the compilers of other Hymnbooks, it should push its Hymnbook in every possible way to our disadvantage -- week after week it advertizes in the most prominent way that it will let the Clergy have the Book at half-price if they will but use it -- Why at half price? Why not at the same discount as other books which the Society publishes?[119]

In 1875 the Proprietors themselves advertised their Revised edition in the newspapers, setting out the terms upon which they offered grants:

> Liberal grants of the Revised Book, without any restriction as to choice of Editions [i.e. expense] are made to FACILITATE ITS FIRST INTRODUCTION; and also in other cases where the assistance of a Grant is specially required. Also 20% discount to clergy for cash.

Application Form for Grant:
Parish or District of ----
1. Population.
2. Chief Occupation and Trades.
3. Average Congregation.
4. How far Poor.
5. Any other particulars strengthening claim for grant.
6. What Hymn Book is now in use in your Church?
7. What is the total expenditure intended on first introducing this Hymn Book?*

*This question _must_ be clearly answered, as Grants are made in proportion to the expenditure and to the circumstances of a Parish.[120]

The value of grants awarded rose steadily over the next five years: in 1875 grants of the Revised edition totalled £618.12.3; two years later, this amount had increased by approximately two-thirds to £1094.8.4. The average grant was worth £2.3.9 1/2. The Minute Book begins to record with subdued statistical triumph how A&M was establishing itself: in 1879, most of the 550 grants had been to replace the Original edition with the Revised edition, but in 96 churches, other collections had been ousted. That same year _Mackeson's Guide to the Churches of London_ recorded A&M in use in 421 out of 872 (48.3%) London congregations. In 1880, other hymnbooks were ousted from another 119 churches; Mackeson found A&M in 450 out of 887 (50.7%) London churches. In 1881, 105 new churches received grants, and 475 out of 916 (51.8%) London churches used A&M.[121] The progress was slow but steady, and by 1889 57% of the London churches listed in the Guide (580 out of 1016) were using A&M. It was a satisfactory achievement, and largely due to the Proprietors' practice of encouraging applications for grants "as much as possible, as every Grant extends the net-work of the use of H.A.&M. which now spreads over the whole United Kingdom and the Colonies; and so carries out the purpose for which H.A.&M. were [sic] originally designed in promoting a more uniform Hymnological use in all English-speaking Churches."[122] The two remaining sections of this chapter pursue the question of "uniform Hymnological use" as conceived by the Proprietors.

ii. Copyright

One of the more curious aspects of the publication of A&M is the legal and moral question of copyright. In the nineteenth century, international copyright hardly obtained, and British authors, most notably Dickens perhaps, were plagued by foreign publishers' pirated editions. Within Britain, however, British authors were protected by British law. The Copyright Act of 1842 stated that an original work belonged to its author, or, after death, to the author's representatives, for forty-two years or for the remainder of the author's life plus seven years, whichever was the longer period.

The chief problems A&M faced arose from the fact that many people felt that hymns should be exempt from the law of copyright. So general was this feeling that the laws were largely ignored. Hymnbooks were understood to be compiled by gentlemen whose sole purpose in writing, printing and publishing was to glorify God, and whose only interest, after recovering their costs, was to see their work as widespread as possible. Such gentlemen were sufficiently humble to acknowledge that their verses were inadequate to the task of praising God, and were therefore willing for others to attempt improvements upon them. Francis Pott was not expressing a new idea when he wrote to Sir Henry:

> It is and always has been my theory and feeling that hymns and other devotional writings are -- or ought to be -- an exception to the laws of copyright and property. They are I think written 'pro bono Ecclesiae' and ought to be considered as public Church property.[123]

Pott was writing his resignation from the Committee of Compilers, but he wished it to be understood that the Compilers were welcome to any of his translations, and reciprocally, that he might make use of the Compilers' work in any future hymnbook he might edit, for he should "greatly regret perpetuating inferior translations (when better ones exist) even in one or two congregations."[124]

There are of course two sides to copyright, as Pott's letter shows. For the compilers of a hymnbook, which is to a very large extent the work of other people, copyright limits the material from which they may freely choose, and may even prohibit the use of a piece they particularly wish to include. Once their book is compiled and published, it is itself protected by copyright as far as the original work goes. Strictly, the law protects as original alterations made to another's work by the compilers, and the form in which the material is ordered and presented, if it can be shown to be an innovation. In brief, copyright affects first, the sources of the book, and second, the book itself, and these two areas will be considered in turn.

The problems which copyright could present to the Proprietors were recognized very early. In 1858, Sir Henry wrote to Wilkins setting before him the tentative plans for a comprehensive book. Wilkins replied:

> Your plans appear to me very sound & promising, but there are many difficulties in the way, wh no doubt you are well aware of -- I shd think one of y greatest will be the law of copyrights & the 'vested interests' of publishers -- How shall you get over this? One reason for my delay in writing to you was my wish to read the letter on Hymnals by Mr. Blew whom you mention. . . . In the 1st part of his letter he advocates very properly selecting the hymns

> from the best sources, & at the end he inveighs against piracy of other men's labours -- How he wd do the former without the latter I know not.[125]

A&M was undertaken with the aim of including the best hymns of the Church in all ages. The more recent modern hymns were still copyright: Keble, for example, was still alive, and his Christian Year consequently protected. Even Heber's Hymns, published posthumously in 1827, were still within the forty-two year period protected by the Copyright Act. The mediaeval hymns were no less of a legal problem: though the Latin texts were common property, good translations of them were recent work, being the product of the great revival of interest in ancient hymnody concurrent with the Oxford Movement.

Determining authorship was a problem in itself. Sometimes a hymn was drawn from the published collection of a writer's own verse, and in such cases there was no doubt as to authorship. More frequently, the Compilers searched through other hymnbooks, which might be largely original, or entirely borrowed. More than half of Heber's Hymns were written by Heber himself, and in this collection at least there was little difficulty about attribution, for the initials of the author were given. In most of the hymn collections the Compilers examined, the authors were not acknowledged. Perhaps it was not considered consistent with the purpose of congregational worship to point out that in the act of common praise the Church was indebted to any individual. For whatever reasons, anonymity was the general rule in publishing hymnbooks: A&M itself did not publish authors' names, except for some specific acknowledgements in the Preface, until the Revised edition of 1875, and then only in the index. There was in general no immediate way of discovering whether any hymn in a collection was the original work of the editor, or whether it had simply been borrowed from another anonymous hymnbook. Another favourite form of publication was in periodicals and papers, and in these cases not even the editor always knew the contributor. Occasionally an author would claim verses which had been admired, but all too often there was no way to discover who was responsible for any hymns thus published.

In all cases the Proprietors wished to obtain permission from the authors to print their hymns or their translations. As this policy was consistent, illustrations will be drawn from the editions of 1860 and 1875, and the 1868 Appendix.

In many cases permission to print was implied. When the announcement was made in the Guardian that a new hymnbook was being considered and suggestions were called for, more than one editor of a hymnbook sent the book to Sir Henry. For example, W.W. How wrote:

> I have heard that you are preparing a Hymnal for your Church. I am taking a great liberty in writing to you, but having for years taken a deep interest in the subject, I trust you will forgive me for sending you one I was mainly

> instrumental in bringing out, & which is now having a large sale. I send it simply thinking you wd like to have all the material you can get before you, & may possibly find in it some hymns you may like to have.[126]

When the Proprietors wished to include a hymn published elsewhere, they asked only permission to print it. They did not attempt to claim copyright except over any alterations that they made in the original version. The question of alterations is an interesting and controversial one, discussed at length in Chapter Four. In the context of copyright, it is first to be noticed that in requesting permission to print others' hymns, the Proprietors often neglected specifically to ask permission to make alterations in the received text.

In 1868, Godfrey Thring replied as follows to a request from the Proprietors for the Appendix:

> I have no objection to your taking any of my hymns for H.A.&M. -- on the one condition that the text is not altered -- as I am of opinion that this shd never be done without the authors [sic] express permission -- and the sooner that all copyright of hymns used expressly for public Worship is given up the better.[127]

Thring's position is odd but not uncommon: he is ready

to waive any legal copyright, while clinging to the moral right of an author to preserve the integrity of the text. It could be argued that he cannot really be thinking of the good of the Church as a whole, as long as he is unwilling to sink his own work in the greater endeavours of the Church as a whole in the field of hymnody. Be that as it may, Thring so impressed upon the Proprietors his reluctance to alter his text that they were careful to submit to him any changes they proposed. Letters passed between Thring and Sir Henry to within a few weeks of publication: single words were changed, and whole stanzas redrafted, but reluctantly: "I dislike very much altering anything once in print . . . but I suppose I must give in."[128] The Proprietors claimed copyright over the altered versions. The thoroughness with which the Compilers approached their task of improving the hymns they wished to print is discussed at length in the section on editing.

Not everyone was as jealous as Thring of his compositions. Neale renounced his rights in his translations in order to further the cause of Anglican hymnody:

> I have been asked more than once whether I had any objection to my own hymns being altered, as might suit the Committee's taste. And I have always answered 'Not the least'. I do not imagine, indeed, I hardly wish, that we should see an authorised Hymnal in our own day; and therefore the more people try

> their hand at improving, the more those who are concerned in its final compilation will have to choose from.[129]

He did not, however, renounce his right to criticize alterations to his hymns, and the comments of one so influential in the revival of ancient hymnody and the choral service were not easy to disregard, however mildly expressed:

> I will freely & thankfully allow that, in some of your translations I think you have improved on our versions. . . . But, as is only natural, I think that sometimes you have sadly spoilt what you have taken in hand. . . . Many of these things must be matters of taste: but there are some which are not so; & which show that those who made the alterations had not studied Hymnology.[130]

Neale's modest comments are a pleasant contrast indeed to the self-importance of other hymn-writers. He subscribed to the principle that hymns should be exempt from copyright, though he must have been tempted to invoke legal protection for some of the fruits of his painstaking work, when he saw its logical beauties destroyed by more ignorant editors.

> A man cannot without previous study sit down & translate, or correct the translation of one of these hymns.

> In several instances *you* have given as a correction a reading *we* [the editors of the *Hymnal Noted*] had deliberately & unanimously rejected on grounds which could be very easily explained.[131]

The contrast between Neale's attitude and that of Christopher Wordsworth, soon to be examined, may be symbolic of the contrasts inherent in a collection which embraced old and new. Neale was a classical scholar; his work and his chief joy lay in obscure and often anonymous hymns which were written to glorify God and to strengthen the Church on earth. Neale seems to have taken on the self-effacing qualities of the ancient authors, but then he was a very lowly clergyman, who languished under episcopal disfavour. Christopher Wordsworth, on the other hand, subscribed cheerfully to his post-Romantic concept of the poet. In addition to his bardic authority, he came to assume that of a bishop: there is little which is self-effacing about Wordsworth.

The disagreement between Wordsworth and the Proprietors over the alterations to Wordsworth's hymns in the Appendix was entirely unworthy of any of the participants. The correspondence dealing with the inclusion of the hymns is unfortunately incomplete, but it is clear that the association was never a happy one. In 1862 Sir Henry wrote to Wordsworth to complain that several copyright hymns from A&M had been printed in the recently published Supplement to Wordsworth's *Holy Year*. Wordsworth explained that a friend had collected many hymns from which Wordsworth had made his selection for the Supplement, and, as borrowing was the general practice for compilers, he had not thought to query the sources of the hymns he chose. Copyright hymns belonging to A&M would not be reprinted in any further edition.[132] Sir Henry replied that Wordsworth could keep the hymns with a proper acknowledgement, as long as he did not alter them: "What we might refuse to other books very similar to our own & by younger men we may well grant to a Book so original as yours & to yourself."[133] Wordsworth eventually accepted Sir Henry's terms.[134]

Six years later, the Proprietors requested Wordsworth's permission to include eight of his hymns in their forthcoming Appendix, and encountered considerable reluctance. His objections were twofold: doctrinal, and practical. He wondered with what other hymns his own would be printed, for he was afraid of being associated with some "erroneous & dangerous doctrine, introduced into the service of the Church, by means of Hymnology."[135] His other concern was the extent to which the Appendix would encroach upon the sales of his own book: at 2/6 for the cheapest edition, the _Holy Year_ was a much more expensive book than A&M, and Wordsworth feared that if the best and most popular of his hymns were readily available in a cheaper collection, sales of the _Holy Year_ would decline.[136] In compensation for his loss, he told Sir Henry, he would be willing to accept a share in the profits of the Appendix.[137]

Sir Henry found it hard to credit Wordsworth's objection: he reminded him of the approval A&M had won from bishops and archdeacons, and even from the government,[138] and of its acceptance "more widely than any other by moderate men of all schools in the Church -- And you suspect us of heresy!"[139] He went on to say that the Holy Year could never have been intended but as a source book for original English hymns, and that to consider A&M a competitor was seriously to misrepresent the aims and achievements of each book. Sir Henry offered not a share in the profits, but a sum in recognition of their debt to him, and reminded him that he had given his hymns to "the only Hymn book that is a rival to Hymns Ancient & Modern, from bearing a considerable resemblance to it, I mean the Salisbury Hymnal -- and yet you demur to giving the same leave to us -- to us only, who treated you generously."[140] This obvious reference to the 1862 situation in which the relative positions were reversed seems to have had some effect upon Wordsworth: after examining rough proofs of other hymns in the Appendix, he announced that he would not withhold consent.[141] Sir Henry replied: "It pains me to accept the permission you now give us . . . but I was cheered by the strong conviction that it is right."[142]

Thereafter Wordsworth was sufficiently reconciled to the inclusion of his hymns to be concerned to improve them, particularly his hymn "Heavenly Father, send Thy blessing" (364/338). He suggested several amendments to the original, but very few of them appear in the published version. There are no further letters in this series save Wordsworth's polite acknowledgement of a copy of the Appendix sent him, but the story is not yet concluded.

The Proprietors' attitude to Wordsworth is not

much different from their attitude to any of the other contributors, but it is more marked because of the unexpected opposition they encountered. When the project was undertaken, those involved were much more cautious or even more tactful than they came to be later. The project had been originally conceived as an amalgamation of several books, the editors of which were to sink their own interests in the joint venture. On the whole, conflicting interests were diplomatically settled. The response to their advertisement, announcing their larger intentions and soliciting help, was extremely gratifying. As the undertaking grew in scope and their own plans grew clearer, and as they received generous support in the venture, their confidence increased. After the success of the first edition, and the popular demand for an Appendix, the Proprietors began almost to take for granted that, within their own party of the Church at least, they would encounter nothing but encouragement in their plans.

It came as rather a shock to them, therefore, to discover that Wordsworth looked upon his book as anything other than the source book which the Proprietors considered it. Sir Henry's tone is at first incredulous: "You don't really mean to refuse the permission I asked: do you?"[143] and then righteous on behalf of sound theology and the wide acceptance which A&M had met.

In pursuing their aim of establishing A&M as the most widely used Anglican hymnbook and the precursor of an official hymnal, the Proprietors had adopted a policy which contradicted the views of many of their contributors, that is, the policy of maintaining strict legal copyright. They supported themselves in the face of criticism on the claim that they had always acted by the law: never knowingly printing anything without permission, and never allowing anything of theirs to be printed without their permission. The consistency upon which they prided themselves was an attempt to be business-like, to bring some order into the publishing chaos which was nineteenth-century hymnology. Even concessions and exceptions were part of the policy: note Sir Henry's appeal to Wordsworth to remember the Proprietors' generosity. Indeed, their confidence justified itself, as the success of their hymnbook proved.

It did, however, overreach itself occasionally, and such was the case in the final stage of the Wordsworth affair. It has already been said that the Proprietors were not always careful enough in the matter of alterations, not specific enough in their requests for permission to print.

The disagreement is in many ways inexplicable. Nearly three years after the publication of the Appendix, Wordsworth, now Bishop of Lincoln, wrote to Sir Henry to complain of the omission of two stanzas from his hymn "O Lord of heaven and earth and sea" (370/365), explaining that he was writing privately before taking "public steps to have the injury redressed."[144] The Proprietors were "surprised & pained . . . by the tone of your Lordship's letter," because he had made no complaint after seeing the proofs of the Appendix.[145] Wordsworth claimed that the proofs sent to him had not included his own hymns.[146] In October, the Bishop

Church Congress, and a report of his speech was published in the Guardian, October 18, 1871. J.B. Dykes, who was sitting on the platform during the speech, described in a letter to Sir Henry the embarrassing situation in which he had been placed. Dykes had spoken on Church Music, and then the Bishop delivered the closing address:

> The Bp referred to Hymns & Tunes and Editors: and then spoke about Editors taking liberties with the Hymns they introduced into their books -- he spoke of needless alterations & wanton curtailments. . . . He could not let the opportunity pass without publicly arraigning the compilers [of A&M] for the treatment his own Hymn had received at their hands: he specially alluded (he said) to their heartless & fatal mutilation of his almsgiving Hymn. . . . He then turned round & apostrophised myself -- and asked me if, as a Churchman, I could fail to feel for, & sympathise with him at having to find himself the virtual teacher of heresy -- . . . He did not suppose there was any wish that the Hymn shd teach heresy: but the Compilers found it just a little too long for their page so they took a pair of scissors, & cut it shorter -- never even heeding that they were sacrificing the very kernel & heart of the whole Hymn.[147]

Dykes advised that, since the speech had been made before two thousand people, the Bishop had better be "quietly & respectfully answered." The Proprietors' answer was to request permission to publish the letters they had exchanged in July together with a "statement of facts" from the Compilers.[148] In his reply, the Bishop referred again to the proofs he had been sent, in which, he declared, no attention had been drawn to the omissions, "but I may have been too careless in the matter, and if so, I beg pardon for my negligence." He raised an important question:

> Even on the supposition that I gave an express consent (which I doubt) to mutilation of my Hymns in 'Hymns Ancient and Modern,' is not an Author to be allowed to have any opportunity of reconsidering such a consent; and is he to lose for ever all control over his own Hymns, as far as that work is concerned?[149]

The answer to this twofold question reveals some of the difficulties in the exercise of copyright. To the first query the Proprietors answered, no: they had acted upon express permission and produced a version which was now their own. The author might regret having consented, but nevertheless lost control of the new version. The answer to the second query is, yes: permission to print, once given, is irrevocable. It might be possible for authors to persuade those to whom they have already given a hymn that a later version is preferable, but they have no right to adopt the A&M version as their own, as William Whiting discovered.

He had found the Compilers' alterations to his hymn "Eternal Father, strong to save" (222/370) preferable to his original, and so, when asked by other editors for his hymn, he gave them the A&M version. He too referred to the common idea of copyright exemption for hymns in excusing himself:

> Hymns which are used in Collections seem to be quite regarded as common property, and editors neither think of the rights of Authors nor of those of other Editors: they are like tunes which every one thinks himself at liberty to use as he pleases.

He had only hoped to circulate the hymn in

> ... its best shape. But if this vexes you, and is not thought quite fair, I am willing to be more careful for the future.[150]

This particular case was amicably settled, when Whiting expressed his willingness to sell the copyright of his hymn in its A&M form to the Compilers for "a couple of guineas."[151]

Sir Henry's actual reply to Wordsworth's query ("Is [the Author] to lose for ever all control over his own Hymns, as far as that work [A&M] is concerned?") was straightforward: "Yes; so far as that work is concerned."[152] Sir Henry also sought to justify the alterations on several grounds: first, as regards the legal right, he observes that Wordsworth had not seemed careless or negligent of his hymns in 1868, rather the contrary, and so he had seemed to permit the version to which he subsequently objected so strongly. On doctrinal grounds, Sir Henry claimed that there was sufficient reference to grace and redemption in the shortened version to prevent the charge of heresy; on musical grounds, he defended the minor alterations as easier to sing than the original, and finally, he denied that the size of the page had led to the omissions, as longer hymns than Wordsworth's had been set in type on one page. Sir Henry is clearly trying to be as sweetly reasonable as possible, as no doubt befits a rural clergyman when contradicting a bishop, but the matter came to an impasse: the correspondence of July to October 1871 was printed in the Guardian, but neither side changed its views.

In 1874, Wordsworth wrote again to Sir Henry to ask for the restoration of his hymns to their "authentic form" in the Revised edition.[153] Sir Henry replied that it was too late to add to or alter the hymns, but that (no doubt in deference to Wordsworth's persistence) the omitted stanzas had been restored, although the alterations to the refrain had been retained.

Considerable detail has been given to this case of Wordsworth's hymns because it is indicative not only of how strongly the Proprietors defended the legality of their actions, but also of how slow, or how careless, they could be in establishing their rights.

Gradually they became more business-like and thorough, and more and more often they sought to secure their rights by obtaining outright the copyright of hymns they published. It was easier to do this for hymns published for the first time in A&M than in any other case, and as the proportion of modern hymns in the collection increased (see Chapter Four, 3), so did the number of hymns belonging exclusively to A&M.

They clarified the legal position with regard to some of their hymns. For instance, W. Chatterton Dix's hymn "As with gladness" (64/79) had won great popularity, and began to appear in other collections. Dix hastened to assure Sir Henry:

> I shall, if asked, for the hymn refer to you for your permission -- thereby vesting the copyright with the committee -- in the [word illegible] way wh you suggest. I have always understood that I gave you the hymn & that it is your property (if such it can be called). . . . I think that I have made clear that I wish you to be the owners of the hymn.[154]

C.F. Alexander was another the copyright of whose hymns the Proprietors were anxious to obtain. She wrote several new hymns for the Revised edition, and the Proprietors paid her for her trouble; in a postscript Sir Henry added:

> I am not quite sure whether you consider the copyright of the Hymns written <u>expressly</u> <u>for</u> <u>us</u> is ours or

> not -- We are always glad if it can be so: as to Words or Tunes. As a mere matter of business will you kindly say so in your letter if you did mean to give it us.[155]

She replied that she had no objection.[156]

The principles which guided the Proprietors in their exercise of copyright were consistent, but their practice was not so straightforward. Their purpose was always to improve Anglican hymnody, and the reduction of the number of available hymnals was a first step in such an improvement, for it would facilitate the wide acceptance of a body of hymns written on correct Anglican principles. From its very inception, A&M was intended to be not just another hymnbook, but an improvement upon and single successor to existing books. This policy (the deliberate discouragement and displacement of possible competitors) the Proprietors shared with one of their chief competitors, the S.P.C.K.'s Church Hymns. W.W. How, who was one of the editorial committee for the new edition of Church Hymns, harped on this string when he asked one of A&M's contributors for permission to print a hymn:

> Our hope is that, if we are successful, Hymns A&M & the S.P.C.K. book may ultimately occupy so large a proportion of the country, as to become practically the two books of the English Church, and then it may not be so vain to talk about an 'Authorized Hymnal', not that I am

> at all sure that such a book will ever be really practicable or desirable.[157]

How is sufficiently cynical to admit that an authorized hymnal is only a business monopoly by another name, and that, though the idea may not be entirely practicable, it justifies the position taken by the S.P.C.K. and by the Proprietors of A&M. The Proprietors set about their purpose in a thoroughly business-like way: first, as detailed above, they produced cheap editions and offered introductory grants to parishes in order to encourage wide circulation and general acceptance, and second, they protected the special qualities of their book from any imitation which might encourage competition. In other words, they decided deliberately to go against common practice in exercising whatever legal rights they possessed, first, in prosecuting infringements of their copyright, and second, in bestowing the favour of permission to print their hymns.

The cases of infringement are many, and some of them thoroughly documented, but only a few can be examined in these pages.

The first case, that of the Rev. Francis Pott, is one of particular bitterness. Pott was a young clergyman with a great interest in translations of Latin hymns, and so had become one of the extended committee of compilers to whom new versions and suggested alterations were sent for comments. His association lasted only a year; by February 1860 he was sufficiently disillusioned on doctrinal grounds, and doubtful of the success of the book, to resign from the committee. He then undertook to complete a hymnbook begun by his friend Mr. Hamilton before his death, "more as a memorial to [him] than as a publication to pay its own way."[158] For this book, he requested permission to print some of the hymns upon which he had worked in committee with the A&M Compilers.

The correspondence was carried on for over a year, during which time A&M was published, and Pott's attitude toward his book began to change: he no longer saw it as an act of piety to the memory of a dead friend, but as a book to supply a need which he considered A&M did not meet.[159]

> Now I have looked at your book I see no reason to regret my [resignation from the compilers]; because although I think it far the best book out, it still violates those principles for which I raised my voice, I had hoped intelligibly. . . . It was only for those who, like me, would be quite prevented on the same principles from accepting your book, otherwise so good, that I proposed to print mine.[160]

He still does not see it as a competitor: "I am therefore sorry that you will look on it as an opposition."[161]

The agreement reached between Pott and Sir Henry was that Pott could have no original hymns written for A&M, but that he might have, upon certain conditions, a number of translations from the 1859 Specimen books which he had helped produce. Those certain conditions were almost certainly the usual ones of an acknowledgement to the Proprietors, and no alterations to be permitted. Pott's side of the correspondence, which is all that survives up to this point, is conducted in a uniformly pleasant way. He is self-deprecating ("I had hoped intelligibly") and politely acquiescent ("I quite appreciate your distinction between the translations and the original hymns, and if it had occurred to me I would not have given you the trouble of declining to give me the latter").[162] There is considerable indication that Sir Henry never relaxed his suspicion of Pott's motives ("I am therefore sorry that you <u>will</u> look on it as an opposition") and that he was by no means eager to grant Pott's requests ("your hint about 'tolerable moderation in my <u>demands</u> (?)'" [sic]).[163] Sir Henry's suspicions seemed confirmed in November 1861 with the publication of <u>Hymns Fitted to the Order of Common Prayer</u>, a copy of which Pott sent him with a final disclaimer of rivalry and congratulations on A&M's success. Sir Henry replied, nearly spitting with rage. The letter is quoted at length because it reveals the jealousy with which Sir Henry defended the A&M copyrights, a jealousy which is not so apparent in other letters where he is in better control of his pen. In this case, however, Sir Henry felt that his committee and his book had been betrayed.

> I had already seen your book. An indignant letter from one of our committee had called my attention to it, & a copy reached me the morning before yours came. I could hardly

> believe my eyes: & now as I look at the 2, side by side, and see type size cover prices exactly alike, I marvel at the possibility of your thinking you have acted fairly by us -- Except that the word 'Hymns' is higher up in your copy than in those I have of our own, I should not know which is yours or ours -- And the contents are worse -- Not satisfied with what we gave you, you have pillaged wholesale -- taken whole verses, texts, arrangements without the least compunction; some verses which are my own & which I never would have allowed you so to use -- . . . in a word if ever any one infringed copyrights unfairly you have done it -- I expect to meet some of the committee at St Barnabas on Thursday, & we shall then talk over what steps to take -- I will only now say that had we had the least idea of what you intended, we shd never have given you a single hymn -- It is not that we are afraid of you as a rival -- a book that was really different to and superior to our own I hope we shd all be glad to see -- but no-one likes to be pirated and spoiled.[164]

And again, witness the depth of Sir Henry's feeling:

> I should be willing to appeal to almost anyone you could name as to whether it is courteous & gentlemanly to work with a committee for a long while, leave them without any tangible reason, (or if you like for a tangible reason,) & then use <u>private information gained as a member of that committee</u> for your own book.[165]

Sir Henry's charges are often matters of detail, and illustrate both the extent to which the Proprietors would press their claims, and also the difficulties inherent in pressing such claims on hymnologists, who were heirs to all ages, and engaged in co-operative labours. Sir Henry's character is revealed in his dealings in these cases: his temper, his insistence upon detail, and his unquestioned standards of behaviour as a clergyman and a gentleman. Those standards made him reluctant to stoop to a court of law when an appeal to a tribunal of peers was possible, though he was ready enough to go to law to remedy what he considered injustice.

Pott's explanations are a catalogue of small misunderstandings, assumptions and oversights: for example, the printer had not consulted him before selecting a type, and Pott had not thought it worthwhile to object. Commented Sir Henry: "A publisher is no judge of what a gentleman should do."[166] In general, Pott pleads that the similarities of the book are due to the common principles and the common work which Pott and the Compilers shared after a year's co-operation. He is willing, however, to make any alteration Sir Henry demands, regardless of expense, but *cui bono*?[167]

By the time the Proprietors eventually met on December 11th, Sir Henry had been considerably mollified, and was ready to discuss practical means to deal with the case. They requested Pott to desist from general circulation of his book, which should henceforth be for his own and his parishioners' use only, and available only privately from Pott himself. Any direct or indirect publicity would cause the Committee to "feel at liberty ...to prevent the sale."[168] The tone of this minute is remarkably mild after Sir Henry's fulminations; it is formal and regretful, and the more offensive and unneccessary jibes have been scored out of the draft. Several months later, Sir Henry and Pott finally agreed to drop the fruitless correspondence about plagiarism, and Pott wrote a formal acceptance of terms to G.C. White:

> I now write to declare finally through you to the Committee that we agree to the proposed understanding, as follows: -- We undertake not to press the sale of our book, not to advertize nor to issue any prospectus, nor to send copies as specimens to any except our own private friends, nor to take any steps to put our book into competition with yours in any parish.[169]

The outcome of this case was, as far as the

Proprietors were concerned, successful. It was one of the earliest cases brought to their attention, and it was sufficiently important to establish a precedent, and at the same time, small enough to remain a relatively private affair, which could be adequately conducted by personal correspondence, and concluded by gentleman's agreement. The Proprietors were unanimous in support of their principle of reducing the number of hymnbooks. Pott's book they considered unnecessary: it was too similar to be either an improvement of old, or a source of new, material. It could only be a matter of private interest, intended to satisfy the doctrinal standards of its editor alone, and as such could only be printed as a private and strictly limited venture.

Other cases involved considerable publicity, and were dealt with differently. The Proprietors and the Rev. R.R. Chope crossed swords more than once: the first occasion was the publication of the second edition (1862) of Chope's Congregational Hymn and Tune Book. In November Wilkins wrote to Sir Henry about the forthcoming book:

> Our illustrious Committee I have heard irreverently spoken of as the '40 Thieves' -- but our petty larcenies are a joke to the garotting principle of Chope (or Choke) & Co. Their avowed principle has been to take 'Hymns A & M' as their groundwork & model & endeavour to improve thereon Hymn by Hymn & Tune by Tune. -- With what success they have

> accomplished this we shall see in a few days, but for one, I am not at all alarmed.[170]

The first objections were raised by Novello and Co., who claimed that Chope had infringed the copyright of the _Hymnal Noted_ which the Ecclesiological Society had assigned to Novello. Chope replied that he had not borrowed from the _Hymnal Noted_ because it was unfit for congregational use, and charged in his turn that A&M, which was printed by Novello for the Proprietors, had infringed the copyright of the first edition of his book. Chope published, without leave, Novello's letter and his reply to it in the _Guardian_. Novello and the Proprietors, outraged by this step, put the case before their solicitors, who said that Chope could not be compelled to withdraw his charge, and recommended a letter to the _Guardian_ as "the best and simplest remedy," and "abstaining from any communication or collision with him, so long as this may be practicable."[171] The case ended in formal letters declining further correspondence.

The Chope case is important because the Proprietors had recourse to legal advice, and it is significant that the case was allowed to drop with only a protest that Chope's charge was unfounded. It was unlike the Proprietors not to pursue the matter of Chope's borrowings, and it is tempting to see the explanation in Wilkins' letter quoted above. For there is no doubt that, despite the care taken by the Proprietors to obtain permission to print hymns in A&M, certain "petty larcenies" did take place, either through ignorance or carelessness, and passed largely unnoticed or at least unprotested, because of the impenetrability of the prevailing anonymity, and of the general feeling that hymns should be exempt from copy-right. Chope, however, was clearly not one to let any borrowing pass unremarked, especially when the bor-rowers complained of being borrowed from. He had indicated clearly enough that he knew the effective channels of publicity, such as published letters in the Guardian, and he was sufficiently established as an editor (his own book had gone into its second edition) to warrant respect. A "forty thieves" scandal could not but injure the circulation and general acceptance of A&M, and with a show of dignity and a gesture of confidence, in consulting the solicitors, the affair was allowed to lapse. It was a case more of expediency than of "those high principles of right and good faith, which as gentlemen and Clergymen . . . they had a right to expect" and which they had claimed in the Pott case.[172]

The Proprietors were always sensitive to publi-city, both favourable and, especially, unfavourable. They were always careful to retain their anonymity, only the Chairman being known publicly, although oc-casionally Pulling or White conducted correspondence for him. When Chope's book appeared, and charges were being made, the Proprietors were already in the middle of an affair of considerable adverse publicity and acrimony.

In August 1862, there had been a number of letters printed in the English Churchman about the impossibility of any hymnbook being acceptable to all tastes. It was alleged by an anonymous "Englishman," and supported by J.B. Trend, that even some of the compilers of A&M would not allow it to be used in their churches.[173] Novello and Co. denied the assertion,[174] but Trend insisted that A&M had "failed to give that general satisfaction, even amongst those who were engaged in its compilation, which was at first expected."[175] The editor of the English Churchman noted that Trend gave no grounds for his assertion, and closed the correspondence.

At first, the Proprietors were content to consider the correspondence "contemptible & below notice," as Edward Twells assured them,[176] and to satisfy themselves with Novello's published denial. Maberley very acutely suggested that Trend's assertion might be a repercussion of the Pott case, but considered that the "least said the better on all such occasions."[177] In October, however, Sir Henry discovered in Trend's new hymn collection several A&M hymns.[178] The correspondence which ensued was particularly bitter: Sir Henry's first letter was extremely strong, and Trend took violent exception to it. Sir Henry demanded that the English Churchman statement be retracted, and that the sale of Trend's book be stopped. Trend upheld the truth of his statement, and denied that he had stolen any hymns from A&M. He was supported in his stand by the Rev. H.B. Walton, Fellow of Merton College and Incumbent of St. Cross, Holywell, Oxford, who assured him that the Proprietors could not claim copyright over verbal alterations, ancient hymns being the "heritage and property of the Church at large," and further, that their legal case was weak: "They have besides, reared an edifice too brittle, (& withal too recent) for them to throw stones!"[179] Trend enclosed this letter when he wrote to Sir Henry on November 1st; with such a warning before them, it is little wonder that only a few weeks later, the Proprietors should have been reluctant to cast stones at Chope.

Trend threatened to publish the correspondence unless Sir Henry apologized for his language. The Rev. Henry Bailey, Warden of St. Augustine's College of which Trend was a Fellow, wrote privately to Pulling in an attempt to settle the dispute:

> I dare say [Trend's letter in the English Churchman] was juvenile and indiscreet. But it was nothing to the offensive terms in wh Sir H.W. Baker opened his fire upon Mr. Trend. terms & language wh I have no hesitation in saying ought not to have been used by any clergyman to any person, still less to a brother clergyman, a stranger, & I may add most keenly felt by the gentle unassuming person to whom they were addressed. . . . I accounted for it myself, by the supposition of the writer's brain being affected in consequence of his sad fall. [Baker had had an accident early in the summer, and was recuperating at Brighton while Pulling dealt with most of his correspondence.] I feel confirmed in that supposition by a letter I had myself from him . . . . containing a threat which I wd not condescend to notice. [This letter has not survived.][180]

The correspondence, having reached an impasse, was put into the hands of the solicitors, who drew a case for Counsel's opinion. It is unfortunate that the Opinion of Mr. Gifford, Q.C., has not survived, but it was strongly in favour of the Proprietors' case. Trend gave up. The printed correspondence had already been withdrawn after a formal apology from the solicitors on Sir Henry's behalf; the sale of Trend's book was stopped. Secure in their rights, the Proprietors could afford to be magnanimous: they gave Trend leave to print three A&M hymns, with proper acknowledgement, in any future edition, and, to save him pecuniary loss, they allowed him to insert a flyleaf acknowledgement in the remaining stocks of his first edition, and to resume its sale.

It has been shown how the Proprietors protected their book against infringements; they also had the task of answering requests for the use of copyright material. It is a measure of their success in the improvement of Anglican hymnody that they should receive so many requests, and it was no doubt an encouragement to them to consider their book the precursor of an authorized hymnal.

The Proprietors' general rule was to refuse permission, and their justification was summarized by Sir Henry in a letter to the Rev. B.F. Carlyle, who had requested six tunes and three hymns for a revised edition of his _Manual of Psalmody_.

> Our Book was compiled with the distinct & avowed object of diminishing the existing diversity of Hymnals --

Two or three compilers of books that had attained a wide circulation, feeling strongly the evils of that existing & increasing diversity, and having also a good hope that united prayer & counsel would produce something better than had been done by separate individual efforts, agreed (as I was not one I may say that it was a considerable sacrifice of personal feeling and interests) to give up the use of their own books & to discourage their further sale, in favour of one new & common Book, in the compilation of which they invited, by further advertisements, other churchmen to join them. The result, I think one may fairly say, shows that we were right. . . . We should surely then be contradicting our own principles & showing want of faith in our purpose, if we were to permit some of our new & best Tunes & Hymns to be added to existing collections intended for general use; although for Choral Festivals, or even for parochial use where special circumstances make it impossible to adopt our Book, we should give & have given that permission; and although if ever Convocation were to take up the matter, we should cheerfully place whatever we have done at its disposal.[181]

Not everyone had the same view of the Proprietors' motives: here is an anonymous clergyman, himself the editor of a little hymnbook, writing to the editor of the Literary Churchman:

> I do not know -- I had rather not know -- who the gentlemen are who have compiled and issued [A&M]. But I confess I cannot understand Clergymen consenting to impose any restrictions -- after once cost is paid, which must have been long ago -- on the freest possible use of hymns written by them for the sole purpose, one must suppose, of glorifying God. One would have thought that they would have desired to see, and be thankful to see, that their labours were bringing forth fruit for His service, as widely and freely as possible, without an intention of making money by their publication. . . . What the compilers say is, in effect, you shall have this whole collection, or none of it. . . . The only hope is, that the compilers of 'Hymns Ancient and Modern', after the enormous sale they have had, may be brought to alter their course; or, that the question of copyright in such a work may be tried.[182]

By the time this criticism appeared in print, the

Proprietors had already had cause to examine their policy. The Rev. H.W. Beadon had written to request the use of several A&M hymns in a revised edition of the Parish Hymn Book, and on being refused, protested vigorously. The Proprietors were being inconsistent in making free use of other sources, including the Parish Hymn Book, and refusing similar help to other editors, he claimed, but his real objections were on general grounds:

> Assuming it to be desirable in the present state of the Church of England to promote uniformity of use in Hymns, we distinctly refuse to recognize the right of any body of Clergymen however numerous and respectable to attempt to impose their hymnal on the acceptance of the Church.[183]

Pulling's reply claimed that:

> ... the usual practice . . . of individual Editors permitting selections from their books is inapplicable to a case where a numerous body of Clergymen made large sacrifices of time & labour, many mutual concessions, surrender of Hymnals already in extensive use, in order to act in union with others, whose co-operation was very earnestly invited.[184]

One of Beadon's colleagues in the revision of the Parish Hymn Book was the Rev. J.R. Woodford, who had been a Compiler, but did not become a Proprietor. If he had not been involved, the Proprietors would probably have done no more than reiterate their dislike of too many hymnbooks, but they took this opportunity to "touch up" (White's words) Woodford for "seceding." They took the criticism seriously enough to discuss the matter at a general meeting, where they decided that the sales of their book proved that uniformity was being achieved, but that, because their purpose was being misunderstood, a change of policy was in order. They announced, therefore, that henceforward

> ... they [would] not adhere to their rule, hitherto observed, of refusing permission in all cases to use their copyright Hymns. But whilst they expect this permission to be asked, . . . they [would] meet such applications in a friendly spirit, whenever they are similarly, & with good reason, made.[185]

The new ruling came too late to benefit the Parish Hymn Book, but that it was put into practice is attested by the numbers of entries in the Minute Book in which applications are granted. For the most part, they allowed the use of their hymns in local or private collections, but not when new books were being planned. They were by no means generous, for they were still primarily concerned with the uniformity of hymnody, but they could afford such gestures of magnanimity as that towards Trend at the conclusion of that unhappy case.

One of their most common stipulations was that copyright words and tunes associated in A&M should not be separated: this proviso did not affect words-only collections, but was the ground for refusals for tune-books. Not all requests for tune-books were refused: in 1876, they allowed a number of tunes to the Wesleyan Conference Tune Book in order not to separate hymns already in the Wesleyan book from what the Proprietors considered their proper tunes. The decision was an easy one: there could be no competition within the Church of England from a publication which was "an official publication of the Wesleyan Conference, for the exclusive use of Wesleyan congregations";[186] and the Proprietors could claim that they were not narrowly sectarian in their aims to improve hymnody.

The absence of any element of competition was still the strongest claim the Proprietors recognized. They had granted permission to the Irish Church Hymnal, but they withdrew it for a later edition on the grounds that, despite an assurance to the contrary, copies of the book had been sold in England, and were thus in competition with A&M.[187]

On occasion they could be stern, as when, for example, Novello and Co. proposed in 1870 to publish a hymnbook and to include copyright hymns from A&M, only two years after the Proprietors had transferred the printing of A&M from Novello to William Clowes Ltd. Sir Henry was not slow to impute mean motives to Novello in publishing The Hymnary:

> [Your book] comes . . . before us as a commercial undertaking and in a

> character quite different from that of other Hymnals assisted by them, so far as they know -- As such they do not feel called upon to assist a book which does not represent any special needs of the Church, and which without any sufficient reason is at variance with the principle [uniformity in Church hymnody] on which they have hitherto endeavoured to act. Nor can they conceal from themselves the apparent fact that your proposed Publication is the result of their having withdrawn their own Book from your Firm, and is designed, so far as it may be able, to diminish the usefulness of H.A.& M.[188]

Sir Henry exemplifies how widely pervasive in his age commercialism could be spread, in that he could in all sincerity criticize The Hymnary for being a commercial venture, while at the same time doing all within his not inconsiderable power to further the commercial success of his own book. He never wavered in his high purpose, but he recognized early that to achieve it, he must enter the worldly field of publishing, there to use worldly methods to further his own ends. It is pragmatic Christianity, or more accurately, pragmatic Churchmanship, and it was no novel experience for a Victorian clergyman of the Established Church.

Occasionally pragmatism prevailed upon the Proprietors to reverse a decision. In 1874 they refused some copyright tunes to a proposed Uppingham School Hymn Book, but changed their minds after a protest from the headmaster of Uppingham, Edward Thring, who claimed that the singular nature of a school congregation made a miscellaneous collection unsuitable for its use. It is a strong argument, especially with regard to tunes for the use mainly of trebles. Thring considered the Proprietors' policy unfair, and reminded Sir Henry of the "hundreds that go out from our schools" who would "carry this idea with them all over the world."[189] Thring denied that he had intended a threat, but it is a striking instance of the power, even in small things, that a headmaster wielded over and through his boys, and Sir Henry was quick to recognize that to offend this centre of influence could only harm A&M.

On the whole Sir Henry was more severe in replying to requests than his colleagues were, but that was not a serious fault in a chairman whose job was not to interpret but to execute the rulings of the Committee. He was not inflexible, as the Uppingham case showed, and not only to be moved by pragmatic reasons. When Sir Henry refused E.H. Bickersteth several hymns for a revised edition of his Hymnal Companion for fear of "diminishing the specialities" of A&M, Harrison and Pulling urged a reversal of the decision. They had been impressed by Bickersteth's "thoroughly Xtian letter,"[190] and indeed, his letters are modest, and yet moving, in their descriptions of the labour and the joys of hymnology. It is a tone generally lacking in the A&M papers, where any reference to the ultimate purpose of their labours is more that of an ecclesiastical politician or a dogmatist, than of a worshipping Christian. Let us find room in this chapter of business to quote Bickersteth:

> Have you felt what I am now so painfully feeling 'sore aweary' of the toil of compilation -- so aweary that it almost seems for a while to take all joy out of singing those hymns over which one has pored so anxiously? I long to be free from the memory of the compiler's travail for the calm of the worshipper's adoration. Still it is a great privilege to have aided in any way the Church's service of song -- but one's heart asks what will the hymns of heaven be, and the song before the Throne.[191]

The exercise of copyright continued to be a problem throughout the nineteenth century. It was not merely a matter of the Proprietors exercising their rights in a field hitherto untouched by copyright, but also one of establishing what those rights were. The Revised edition was published in 1875; in 1876 a Copyright Commission was set up to investigate and rationalize British copyright. In the middle of these enquiries, the Compilers were faced with the even more complicated question of international copyright, and how they might best deal with it in the case of an application for a New Zealand book which might or might not be authorized by Synod.

> I do not think we have had a similar question come before us. The nearest was the application of the 'Irish' Church . . . . It is another

> question 1. whether we should take the same ground in the colonies as we do at home -- Supposing their application comes before us as synodical, representing a desire to have an authorized Hymnal for an integral Colonial Church -- like N.Z. -- Supposing also that they will accept our rule of adopting our words & tunes as they stand in H.A.&M. --
>
> Should we, ex hypothesi, be justified in refusing such an application? ie. in forcing our own private book to the exclusion of a Hymnal of the Church?
>
> Again, the answer to this could depend much on whether it is to be the use of the whole N.Z. Church. If its use is only . . . optional, there would be much less reason for our acceding.[192]

Nor was the question of domestic copyright easily settled: as late as 1904 voices were raised claiming that hymns belonged not to the "original writer, or his heirs, or his commentators" but to "those who have sung the hymn,"[193] and therefore, that the Proprietors were irresponsible and unfaithful in making the radical changes they did in their New edition of 1904. It has been said that the popular outburst against the 1904 edition, which caused its early retirement to the realm of scholarly interest only, was the culmination of forty years' resentment of the Proprietors' exercise of copyright, and their alleged forcing of their book.

That may well be true, but it was extremely unlikely that hymns would have stayed outside copyright if only the Proprietors had not so firmly brought them in, for with the growing numbers of books, and their increasing authority, it was only a matter of time before copyright was invoked to control and protect them. And there is no doubt that the Proprietors of A&M, by initiating this development, ensured the success of their book, and the furtherance of the principles it embodied.

iii. The Competitors

In the preceding section, the use of the law of copyright in the protection and promotion of A&M was discussed. In this section, the competitors of the book, and the principles of uniformity in hymnody are examined more closely.

When the Compilers first began work on A&M, they did not think of producing a book to supersede all other hymnbooks in congregational use in the Church of England. They were simply concerned, as individual editors, to improve their earlier collections, and to reduce unnecessary competition, and the giving-up of old books in order to co-operate in a new one seemed the best way of achieving these two aims. The new volume was compiled on moderately high-church lines, and it was immediately obvious that it was more widely successful than the Compilers had dared hope. At this point, they began to realize that they could be more ambitious for their collection than they had originally been: an Appendix with a broader selection of general and modern hymns would extend its appeal outside the High Church party, and a continuation of the marketing techniques originally adopted to ensure that the Proprietors would not lose their investment could make the book more widely available than any other private venture. The Proprietors began to refer more and more often to their avowed purpose of promoting uniformity in hymnological use, as in the various copyright correspondences.

It is not surprising that resentment was aroused, resentment most forcefully yet politely put by Beadon. The same objection was made by the Rev. Godfrey Thring, who while contributing to the Appendix, fell into the habit of writing long rambling letters to Sir Henry on hymnological and other subjects, as they took his fancy. He had never been entirely happy with A&M:

> ... the great circulation of Hymns A&M I have always thought to be from three causes 1st It was the first respectable book of the kind. 2nd the goodness of the Tunes. 3rd the neverfailing support of the 'Guardian' -- but having obtained this great Circulation they did not move with the times, & the greatly increased knowledge in Hymnody.[194]

Seven months later Thring was conceding in his idiosyncratic way the relative superiority of A&M:

> I am inclined to believe that we shall have to come to HA&M at last! but it is a painful reflection! a very analogous case to what my wife tells me she thought before I married her, 'that all men were beasts but that I was the best of the beasts'. Now I fear as regards 'words' at present H.A.&M. cannot be said to be that. . . . A friend of mine writing to me the other day said . . . every one takes to H.A. & M. in the end, some under protest, some because they can't help themselves some because every one else does, but all take it . . . You must not be put out with my impertinence for I am writing laughing. . . and am not at all the 'cursing' man you might suppose me to be from my anathemas.[195]

The Revised edition he found disappointing, and set himself to overthrow the monopoly he saw A&M to be achieving prematurely:

> ...as to believing with you that the best has been done that can be, and that all the world is to rest content and be bound hand & foot to H A&M, why it is a perfect chimera.[196]

When Harrison reiterated the Proprietors' commitment to promoting uniformity, Thring found it "perfectly astounding":

> Your argument . . . is simply this -- that you think HA&M are so very superior to every other book. that it ought to be forced on the Church at large, and that there should be no other except one, representing an entirely opposite school of thought.[197]

Perfectly astounding or not, it was indeed the Proprietors' argument, and also the argument of W.W. How on behalf of the S.P.C.K.'s Church Hymns.

The possibility of an authorized hymnal for the Church of England was very much in the air in the early seventies when revisions of both A&M and Church Hymns were being prepared. In February 1871 the Bishop of Ely, Edward Browne, presented a petition for an authorized hymnal to the Upper House of the Convocation of Canterbury. The President of the Upper House presented the following resolution to the Lower House:

> That the Lower House be desired to appoint a Committee of their own House who shall prepare a hymn-book, which, if approved by Convocation, may be submitted to the Queen, with a prayer that her Majesty would authorise its use in such congregations of the Church of England as may be disposed to adopt it.[198]

In June of the same year a Committee was duly appointed "with power to confer with any Committee appointed by the Convocation of York and to invite the co-operation of outside experts."[199] The Committee report on the desirability of a uniform hymnbook was presented to Convocation the following year. The points investigated by the Committee were the following:

> 1. The value generally attached to the use of hymns in public worship.
> 2. The law and present practice as to the use of hymns in the public worship of the Church of England.
> 3. The extent to which uniformity prevails in other Communions.
> 4. The character of the hymns most generally prized by worshippers.
> 5. In whom copyright is generally invested and how the proceeds are applied.[200]

After setting out the legal and historical background, and noting that hymns seemed to be of "great value, especially in attaching the young," the Report made the following recommendation, that

> ... a hymn book for the public service of the Church of England is highly desirable and might be compiled on these conditions:
> 1. its use when sanctioned to be optional
> 2. it should be comprehensive and not colourless.

> 3. suggestions to be sought from experts. 'The music to combine purity and elevation of style with simplicity and heartiness of melody'.
> 4. the Committee to be a Standing Committee with power to revise the book and put out special hymns for occasional needs.
> 5. counsel to be taken with sister and daughter churches of the Anglican communion.[201]

Convocation, however, took no action upon the Committee's Report.

It is in the context of this discussion and subsequent inaction that the Proprietors' decision to continue their own work, by revising their own book, must be seen. If Convocation had accepted the challenge of an authorized hymnal, the Proprietors might have felt their own achievement to have been obliterated at one stroke. That they were determined to carry on their work, knowing that their labours might at any moment be nullified by the announcement from Convocation of an official book, is an indication of their belief in the importance of their hymnological work. They may, of course, simply have known better than to delay any project of their own in expectation of prompt action, or any action at all, by Convocation on the recommendation of its Committee. It is, however, very likely that if an authorized book had been undertaken at any time, the Proprietors would not have given up A&M anyway. They may have felt, as Godfrey Thring did, that the Church was not yet ripe for an authorized hymnal, that, although hymnology had developed a great deal in the previous forty years, it could still be much improved, and that the official approval of Convocation would only keep Anglican hymnody in a "groove."[202] Twenty years later, when an unofficial approach was made to the Proprietors about the possibility of a revision of A&M becoming the Convocation hymnal, they would not make an "absolute surrender" of their book because "they desire[d] to present it to the Church in a complete form more nearly approaching the ideal which they [had] set before themselves and propose[d] during the next seven or eight years to make a complete revision."[203] There had been some misunderstanding over procedure between the Proprietors and Canon Henry Twells, then chairman of the Convocation Committee on Hymnbooks, which accounts to some extent but not entirely for the Proprietors' unwillingness to give up their title and their book, although they were willing to allow their words and music to be used in the compilation of an authorized book. The opportunity was lost, for the revision spoken of was the unpopular New edition of 1904, and not long after its publication the _English Hymnal_ appeared (1906), and soon established itself as a serious threat to A&M's predominance. The matter is, however, outside the scope of this study, but it is a case where a knowledge of later events casts doubt upon what might otherwise seem straightforward, the sincerity of the Proprietors' dedication to the principle of "uniformity in Hymnological use."

The period was rightly described at the beginning of this chapter as "this hymn-book-making age," and it is also true that most of the hymnbooks were the work of individuals, reflecting particular tastes and parochial prejudices. These books were more or less easily swept aside by A&M, though not before the Compilers had taken from them what they thought of value.

In displacing very small local collections, the great appeal of A&M was the range and richness of its selection. In displacing rather better collections, it was often the music which first recommended A&M.[204] Music was a prime recommendation to the Rev. Mr. Woodward of Folkestone: he described himself as "an evangelical with moderate high church tendencies," and was a little apprehensive about introducing A&M:

> I do not now fear any trouble beyond a little worry & anxiety & perhaps the absence of a few people from church for a Sunday or two. We have hitherto had Hall's Hymns with a very bad music book the product of our blind organist, so that I anticipate a complete revolution in our church music shortly.[205]

In the event, Woodward seems to have been over-optimistic:

> I was obliged to withdraw the hymn book. . . . I did not anticipate the opposition & it wd have ended in nothing had it not been for a few violent & very wicked persons who stirred up through the little local

> paper (the Editor of which had a large stock of the old hymns on hand) a great deal of ill feeling.[206]

Of the books he ordered from Novello, however, he managed to sell "a great many" of the music editions, and it is clear that he hoped the whole book would in time win acceptance in Folkestone.

A&M had three serious competitors which deserve mention. One of these was E.H. Bickersteth's Hymnal Companion to the Book of Common Prayer, first published in 1870, revised and enlarged in 1878. He had already published Psalms and Hymns in 1858, based upon his father's Christian Psalmody, but the Hymnal Companion was a new project, the intended fruit of a new generation's hymnological knowledge. When planning the Hymnal Companion, Bickersteth appointed a musical committee to help him, recognizing that "a hymnal in these days is of very little use without an edition with tunes."[207] The Hymnal Companion appealed mainly to the low church party: Bickersteth's policy was the conservative one of not admitting "anything wh is not in unison with the Prayer book."[208] These low-church principles in practice offended Sir Henry:

> I cannot help expressing my concern at seeing that you have altered even one of holy John Keble's Hymns just in order to avoid mentioning the name of our dear Lord's dear & blessed Mother -- I wonder how his executors could have given . . . you leave to do so.[209]

In 1876, when Harrison and Pulling urged Sir Henry to give Bickersteth the five copyright hymns he requested,[210] they argued from Mackeson's "Guide to the Churches of London," which gave the Hymnal Companion 73 to A&M's 344 churches, that they had "greatly over rated the risk of any rivalry."[211] Sir Henry did not agree, and gave Bickersteth only one hymn.[212] The Hymnal Companion continued to hold its own share, and even to increase it slightly, according to Mackeson.[213]

The other two serious competitors to A&M were both the work of more than one compiler, and each owed its success largely to the range of their talents as well as their influence. Both books ought to have been even more successful than they were.

The Salisbury Hymn Book, first published in 1857, was revised and published in 1868 as the Sarum Hymnal. The acknowledged similarity between A&M and the Sarum books made the competition particularly serious. When a union of hymnals to become A&M was first planned in 1858, Murray thought that "the Salisbury book ought to be united also -- only they have taken such great, and as I cannot but feel unwarrantable and excessive licence in altering well known hymns."[214] The chief compiler, Lord Nelson, noteworthy as one of the few lay people active in hymnological projects, was invited to a meeting of the Committee of Compilers when A&M was in preparation, but was unable to attend. He did correspond with Sir Henry and help to establish the extent of alterations in some texts by John Keble, and even offered to look over the Specimen:

I really might suggest some

> improvements a fresh eye is a help often times. I was prevented coming to your meeting in London last year -- but looking quickly through your book might enable me to be of more good to you.[215]

The Salisbury collection was notable for its inclusion of ancient hymns, emphasized by the use of the old form "Sarum," with its echoes of the pre-Reformation Sarum Use, but its compilers were concerned to make them acceptable to the moderates of the Church of England, and this moderation of Catholic expression was what Murray, and others, considered unwarrantable alteration. Lord Nelson professed that he made it "a principle to give, as far as possible, the genuine unaltered text, of so much of a composition as I take, (for I do not renounce abridgement), or, when I take a known cento or variation, (which I do in a small number of instances only), to print it expressly as such."[216] The context of this passage in the letter makes it clear, however, that he is referring only to his policy toward modern hymns, and not toward translations of ancient.

The *Salisbury Hymn Book*'s greatest recommendation was the degree to which it had received official episcopal sanction. The Bishop of Salisbury, Walter Kerr Hamilton, and his chaplains took an active part in the compilation, "reviewing" the suggestions put before them by Lord Nelson.[217] In this, the bishop followed the example set by the Archbishop of York when he approved an amended edition of Cotterill's book in 1820.[218] The Bishop of Salisbury even seems to have taken the initiative in ordering a revision of the collection. In 1863, when the Bishop stated his "intention to issue an improved edition of the Diocesan Hymn Book," Perceval Ward renounced his proprietorship in A&M, "having been applied to for assistance [and thinking] it his duty to render it."[219] There is in the unquestioned assumption that proprietorship in A&M is utterly incompatible with help to the Salisbury book more than a trace of Sir Henry's gentlemanly severity. The day after the resignation was accepted, however, the remaining Proprietors resolved to make "an application . . . to the Bishop of Salisbury to co-operate with the Proprietors of Hymns A&M in the production of a revised Edition of the Diocesan Hymn Book."[220] It seems that the Proprietors as a body were willing to offer help to the project, but would not countenance an individual's involvement. Two years of co-operation later, when the Salisbury revision was well advanced, the bishop "advise[d] Ld Nelson to call [the committee] together . . . to consider the subject of amalgamation."[221]

Lord Nelson took the possibility of amalgamation very seriously:

> Our two books have had the greatest run of any, and each successive revision will of course bring them nearer to each other. My idea is, that we should leave our existing books to run their course, till they are naturally superseded by the new one which our joint efforts may compile.

> This leaves us both perfectly free to alter and omit any hymns of the existing versions and opens the way to our bringing out a book for the Province of Canterbury with the Imprimatur of the Archbishop & Bp of Salisbury as presentor. I am for insisting on no particular versions. All I ask is, that we should be so careful in our teaching and expressions that we can fairly expect the sanction of those whose imprimatur we seek. There is an opening for our having the best tunes & the best hymns, & the best versions of hymns ever put together if we will but act together instead of bringing out rival books for the sake of two or three rival hymns or rival versions of hymns which our own wilfulness magnifies into undue importance.[222]

Lord Nelson considered it wilfulness on the part of the Proprietors of A&M to insist that "the present A&M Book must be endorsed [by the Salisbury Committee] -- as to Ancient Hs,"[223] and "after 2 hours hard fighting" in committee, agreed to propose an amalgamation only "on the understanding that 'all the more important Lat: Hs now in A&M . . . shd be accepted, subject to revision'."[224] Several matters were left in abeyance over the next six months: preliminary work on the A&M Appendix was suspended while the Proprietors discussed whether or not they would "produce a revised edition retaining the substance of the present book, but subject to such alterations in revision addition & omission of Hymns, as fair criticism should approve, but without lowering it in tone or doctrine."[225] This reply to Lord Nelson's proposal was actually recorded in the Minute Book, but then scored out, and the Proprietors contented themselves with agreeing to "send a deputation to confer with [a Salisbury subcommittee] on the possibility of united action."[226] The problem of ancient hymns threatened to be so difficult to solve that neither side could show much enthusiasm for the attempt. Lord Nelson sent Sir Henry details of the Salisbury revisions, but without much hope:

> I fear we shall not agree much about a hymnal . . . Our great object has been to throw over all hymns that have no particular merits to make the hymns we do keep as chaste in language and doctrine as possible and rather to raise the taste than to succumb to it.[227]

What Salisbury considered "chaste" in language and doctrine, A&M considered "watered-down," and by November 1865, it was clear that agreement was impossible: the Bishop of Salisbury requested Lord Nelson's committee to complete the revision of their book. The Salisbury subcommittee on amalgamation was dissolved, and upon learning this news the Proprietors considered "the expectation of united action . . . thereby frustrated."[228] Their expectation had not been very sanguine: two days earlier the resolution had been formally made to "take the first steps toward the preparation of an Appendix."[229]

Amalgamation was not proposed again. A&M quite simply outdid the Salisbury, and outdid it for all the reasons given in this chapter: greater range, better music, and harder selling. The language and doctrine to which Lord Nelson objected were more widely acceptable than he had thought, and the Salisbury hymnbooks declined.

There were two S.P.C.K. hymnbooks in competition with A&M. The earlier book was an extension of one of the S.P.C.K.'s much earlier ventures, the reprinting of the New (Tate and Brady) Version of the Metrical Psalter. In 1837 a few hymns were added for festivals and sacraments, together with Thomas Ken's Morning and Evening Hymns. Gradually more hymns were added until their number equalled that of the psalms. The psalms and the hymns could be purchased either separately or bound together. The Hymns had been available separately since 1852, and their sale up to 1862 had been 360,000; the Psalms, available separately since 1854, had had the smaller sale up to 1862 of 125,000. Psalms and Hymns, bound together, had sold 395,000 copies.[230] In 1862, a motion to revise entirely the S.P.C.K. book was defeated, and instead, an Appendix was prepared.[231] In that Appendix were inadvertently included some copyright hymns belonging to A&M. The Proprietors were willing to allow the use of the hymns with an acknowledgement, but S.P.C.K. decided not to be beholden to A&M:

> ... after very full and mature consideration it was thought by the Committee that under all the circumstances and looking to the very

> circulation both of 'Hymns Ancient and Modern' and of the Society's 'Hymns for Public Worship', it would be better that the Books should be entirely independent.[232]

The acknowledged rivalry was not to be constrained by any sense of obligation. When the next Appendix was prepared in 1869, however, the Tract Committee felt they could no longer dispense with the help of A&M, and sought and obtained permission to include copyright hymns. Its own compilers were not much pleased with it:

> There is a very colourless tone of doctrine in it, undoubtedly, but you can imagine what a committee is. . . But something will have been done, if it marks a considerable advance in the poetical taste of SPCK, and if it is the means of raising some congregations above the wretched doggerel which defaces the present SPCK book.[233]

The same writer (Compton) announced the thorough revision of the book in 1871:

> At last the SPCK are going to do what it [sic] ought to have done 2 years ago . . . and bring out a new and amalgamated edition, revising the whole book. Of course it is absurd to entertain any idea of

> finality, but it will be a step of progress, and, I hope, do good.[234]

Compton was the exponent of Catholic principles in the Tract Committee, and was not happy with the compromise which the new _Church Hymns_ turned out to be. Again, the use of copyright hymns belonging to A&M was requested.

> I hope you will let us have these [hymns] to counterpoise an enormous deal of trash, of Watts, Montgomery, & Co. still surviving in the new edition, which will be a standing proof if any one needed it, that no small collection of _gems_ will ever be put out by authority -- seeing that even the shadow of authority to which SPCK pretends is attended with the inevitable system of compromise and of balancing a hymn of Faber or Dix or Wordsworth by a corresponding number of Tate & Brady, or Toplady or Watts.[235]

The irony is that the Compilers of A&M had found an element of compromise to be of immense help in extending the appeal of their book. Their Catholicity was not, like Compton's, paradoxically narrow; they allowed themselves to benefit from the virtues of Christian eclecticism.

The newly revised, newly titled, _Church Hymns_ (with its musical edition under the editorship of

Arthur Sullivan), proved itself a real rival, backed as it was with the authority of the S.P.C.K. and pushed by a country-wide organization capable of generous grants.[236]

W.W. How's prediction that *Church Hymns* and A&M would eventually occupy most of the field did not seem unlikely, though *Church Hymns* had a long way to go to catch A&M's lead, established over the previous ten years. The Proprietors kept a close watch upon the figures of the S.P.C.K.'s circulation, and were delighted to record that S.P.C.K. books had been ousted from 44 churches in 1879, from a further 50 in 1880; from 68 in 1881.[237] Mackeson's survey of London churches showed a declining share: in 1879, 187 (78 *Church Hymns* & 109 *Hymns with Appendix*) out of 872, or 21.4%; in 1880, 179 out of 887, or 20.1%; in 1882, 179 (81 *Church Hymns*; 98 *Hymns with Appendix*) out of 916, or 19.5%. By 1889 its 183 out of 1016 churches, or 18%, was small indeed in comparison with A&M's share, and the rivalry could be reckoned over at last.

NOTES

[1] A.P., Newspaper clipping, *English Churchman*, August 14, 1862.

[2] *English Churchman*, August 14, 1862.

[3] W. Cooke and W. Denton, eds., *The Church Hymnal. A Book of Hymns adapted to the use of the Church of England and Ireland, arranged as they are to be sung in*

Churches, Part 1 Advent to Epiphany, with Advertisement (1852).

[4] The Advertisement was circulated independently, as well as included in the promised first part when published.

[5] A.P., Letter, February 7, 1862, F.H. Murray to W. Denton.

[6] A.P., Letter, July 23, [1858], F.H. Murray to H.W.B.

[7] Letter, July 23, [1858], Murray to H.W.B.

[8] A.P., Letter, February 5, 1862, W. Denton to F.H. Murray.

[9] Letter, February 7, 1862, Murray to Denton.

[10] A.P., Letter, September 6, 1858, W. Denton to W.U. Richards.

[11] See below, Chapter Three, 3, i.

[12] A.P., M.B., April 12, 1877.

[13] A.P., M.B., February 8, 1878.

[14] A.P., M.B., February 10, 1863.

[15] A.P., Letter, November 9, 1858, J.M. Wilkins to [H.W.B.].

[16] A.P., M.B., February 11, 1863.

[17] A.P., Letter, September 7, [1858], J.R. Woodford to [H.W.B.].

[18] Advertisement, The Guardian, 673 (October 27, 1858), 847.

[19] A.P., Letter, July 23, [1858], F.H. Murray to H.W.B.

[20] A.P., Letter, November 18, 1858, W.L. Wigan to [H.W.B.].

[21] A.P., Letter, October 30, 1858, J. Hamilton to H.W.B.

[22] A.P., Letter, October 21, 1858, [W. Braithwaite] to H.W.B.

[23] A.P., Letter, November 13, 1858, W. Braithwaite to [H.W.B.].

[24] A.P., Letters, October 24, 1859, A. Shadwell to H.W.B., and November 25, [1859], W. Braithwaite to [H.W.B.].

[25] A.P., M.B., February 21, 1865.

[26] A.P., M.B., May 2, 1865.

[27] A.P., M.B., April 12, 1864.

[28] A.P., M.B., June 2, 1864.

[29] A.P., M.B., January 30, 1867.

[30] M.B., January 30, 1867.

[31] A.P., Letter, December 15, [1858], H.W.B. to W.U. Richards.

[32] Letter, December 15, [1858], H.W.B. to Richards.

[33] Letter, December 15, [1858], H.W.B. to Richards.

[34] See Chapter Five, 5.

[35] A.P., Draft of Preface to First Specimen book, dated May 20, 1859.

[36] Preface, First Specimen book, May 20, 1859.

[37] A.P., Letter, January 10, 1859, O.L. Chambers to [H.W.B.].

[38] A.P., Second Specimen book, Notice inside back cover, dated November 18, 1859.

[39] A.P., Letter, March 27, 1860, W. Priest to H.W.B.

[40] Letter, March 27, 1860, Priest to H.W.B.

[41] A.P., Draft of Circular, October 30, 1860.

[42] A.P., Letter, April 25, 1876, E.H. Bickersteth to H.W.B.

[43] J. Chandler, ed. *Hymns of the Primitive Church* (1837), ix. Emphasis added.

[44] A.P., M.B., June 2, 1864.

[45] See below, Chapter Three, 3, iii.

[46] A.P., M.B., January 16, 1865.

[47] See Chapter Three, 3, ii and Chapter Four,6.

[48] A.P., Letter, May 29, 1868, M. Bridges to H.W.B.

[49] A.P., M.B., July 3, 1867.

[50] A.P., M.B., February 4, 1869.

[51] A.P., M.B., July 3, 1867.

[52] A detailed list of Appendix expenses is given in M.B., February 4, 1869.

[53] See below, Chapter Three, 3, ii.

[54] A.P., M.B., February 10, 1870.

[55] A copy of a hymn for baptism by Katherine Cornish, "Within our Mother Church's fold," survives in the A.P. archive with the pencilled annotations of those to whom it was sent:

> Rather a nice little hymn, but ? wanted CRH [Harrison]
> Reserve GCW [White]
> Reserve FHM [Murray]

It was eventually printed as "Within the Church's sacred fold" (-/326), with several minor alterations.

[56] A.P., M.B., April 10, 1872; April 23, 1873; November 20, 1873.

[57] A.P., M.B., August 26, 1874.

[58] A.P., Letter, October 30, 1872, R.W. Hutton to G. Thring.

[59] A.P., Letter, [November 1], 1873, J.G. Watton to [H.W.B.]. Watton declared his High-church sympathies not only in the text of his letter, but also by identifying himself as secretary of the West Yorkshire Plain Song Union, and by dating his letter "All Saints Day."

[60] A.P., Letter, June 10, 1873, E. Hoskins to H.W.B.

[61] Letter, June 10, 1873, Hoskins to H.W.B.

[62] Letter, June 10, 1873, Hoskins to H.W.B.

[63] A.P., Letter, January 29, 1872, The Bishop of Oxford to W. Pulling.

[64] A.P., Letter, February 22, 1875, E. Husband to H.W.B.

[65] F.W. Faber, *Jesus and Mary; or, Catholic Hymns* (1849), x-xii.

[66] A.P., Letter, August 11, 1874, F.R. Havergal to H.W.B. In Julian's *Dictionary of Hymnology* (1892), James Davidson wrote that Miss Havergal's "religious views and theological bias are distinctly set forth in her poems, and may be described as mildly Calvinistic, without the severe dogmatic tenet of reprobation" (496). That is to say, she ought not to have been surprised that Evangelicals had greater sympathy with her views than had High churchmen.

[67] A.P., Proof of Preface to Revised edition. In the final version the words in square brackets were omitted.

[68] Simple mathematics disproves this statement, as 273 (1860) + 113 (1868) + 93 (additions 1875) + 10 (litanies) - 18 (omissions 1875) = 471. The two extra hymns are parts 2 and 3 of 142 (1860), "For thee O dear, dear country" and "Jerusalem the golden," which are printed and numbered separately (227 and 228) in the Revised edition.

[69] A.P., M.B., May 4, 1871.

[70] Thomas Hardy, *A Laodicean* (New Wessex edition 1975), 42. *A Laodicean* was first published in 1881.

[71] A.P., Letter, September 24, 1875, ? to [H.W.B.].

[72] A.P., M.B., April 23, 1874.

[73] A.P., M.B., October 3, 1874; April 8, 1875; November 11, 1875; May 17, 1876.

[74] A.P., M.B., February 11, 1863.

[75] A.P., M.B., February 5, 1864.

[76] A.P., Letter, January 14, 1869, H.W.B. to J.M. Wilkins.

[77] A.P., Letter, January 15, 1869, J.M. Wilkins to H.W.B.

[78] A.P., M.B., April 12, 1877.

[79] A.P., Letter, February 16, 1869, C.R. Harrison to H.W.B.

[80] That they did buy is undeniable. A letter from the chaplain in a North American garrison testified that the book was so popular among the common soldiers that they bought their own copies. A.P., Letter, October 8, 1868, J.C. Edghill, Chaplain to H.M. Army at Halifax, Nova Scotia, to [H.W.B.].

[81] A.P., Draft of Circular announcing the Original edition, words only, October 30, 1860. The prices quoted were for "quantities of not less than 100 ordered direct from [H.W.B.]." Clergy who ordered the books could either place them in the church for congregational use, or sell them to parishioners.

[82] A.P., List of "Editions" and Costs prepared by William Clowes and Sons, Ltd., for the Proprietors, 1870.

[83] A.P., M.B., April 21, 1869.

[84] A.P., M.B., June 2, 1864.

[85] A.P., M.B., February 8, 1878.

[86] A.P., M.B., April 12, 1877.

[87] A.P., Draft Letter, December 16, 1875, H.W.B. to W.W. How.

[88] A.P., Letter, January 23, 1876, W.W. How to H.W.B.

[89] A.P., M.B., May 17, 1876.

[90] A.P., Letter, Easter Tuesday 1876, W.W. How to H.W.B., accepting, conditionally, H.W.B.'s offer.

[91] A.P., Draft letter, September 1876, signed G.C. White.

[92] A.P., M.B., October 25, 1877.

[93] A.P., M.B., October 25, 1877.

[94] See above, Chapter One.

[95] A.P., M.B., April 12, 1877.

[96] A.P., M.B., February 8, 1878.

[97] A.P., Letter, August 17, 1876, H. Holloway to H.W.B.

[98] A.P., Letter, February 5, 1862, W.R. Wroth to [G.C. White].

[99] A.P., Letter, May 16, 1862, H.W.B. to B.F. Carlyle.

[100] W.C. Lowther Clarke, _One Hundred Years of Hymns Ancient and Modern_ (1960), 32.

[101] A.P., Letter, February 21, 1861, The Bishop of Hereford to H.W.B. The Bishop was R.D. Hampden, whose Bampton Lectures of 1832 and whose anti-Tractarian attitudes in the 1840s had been notorious.

[102] A.P., Letter, August 29, 1861, The Bishop of Llandaff to H.W.B.

[103] A.P., Letter, October 29, 1861 and December 5, 1861, The Bishop of Fredericton to H.W.B.

[104] A.P., Letter, January 20, 1862, The Archbishop of York to [Adam Clark Smith].

[105] Another attempt to secure influential approval is recorded in a letter from Dean Wellesley of Windsor: "If you would be good enough to send the books to me at the Deanery, Windsor, with whatever words you think proper to place in the beginning, I will take care that they are (being religious books) conveyed to the Queen." (A.P., Letter, November 26, 1863, Dean Wellesley to [H.W.B.]). There is, alas, no record of the Queen's opinion, but one can surmise that A&M (being a religious book) was not rejected.

[106] A.P., Letter, February 5, 1862, W.R. Wroth to [G.C. White].

[107] A.P., M.B., February 5, 1864.

108 A.P., Letter, October 22, 1868, J. Charlesworth to G.C. White.

109 A.P., Letter, May 16, 1864, J.R. Bateman to [H.W.B.?].

110 A.P., Letter, February 8, 1876, Robert N. Young to H.W.B.

111 A.P., M.B., November 11, 1875.

112 A.P., Letter, October 27, 1858, W.W. How to [H.W.B.].

113 A.P., Advertising Circular, before March 20, 1861.

114 A.P., M.B., October 1, 1863.

115 A.P., M.B., February 11, 1863.

116 A.P., M.B., June 2, 1864.

117 A.P., Letter, May 5, 1870, W. Lyall to H.W.B.

118 A.P., M.B., May 4, 1871.

119 A.P., Draft Letter, December 16, 1875, H.W.B. to W.W. How.

120 A.P., Unidentified Newspaper advertisement.

121 A.P., M.B., May 13 and October 13, 1880; April 28 and October 26, 1881; April 25, 1882. Also "Comparative Statement showing Hymn Books in use in the London Churches, Compiled from Mackeson's 'Guide to the Churches of London,'" prepared by Clowes for the Proprietors.

122 A.P., M.B., April 12, 1877.

123 A.P., Letter, February 21, 1860, F. Pott to H.W.B.

124 Letter, February 21, 1860, Pott to H.W.B.

125 A.P., Letter, December 1, 1858, [J.M. Wilkins] to [H.W.B.].

126 A.P., Letter, October 27, 1858, W.W. How to H.W.B.

127 A.P., Letter, May 12, 1868, G. Thring to [H.W.B.].

[128] A.P., Letter, July 7, 1868, G. Thring to H.W.B.

[129] A.P., Letter, January 7, 1860, J.M. Neale to "F.G. Maberly." [From internal evidence, it is clear that Neale is writing to Thomas Maberley, one of the Committee of Compilers, though he has got his correspondent's name wrong.]

[130] Letter, January 7, 1860, Neale to [Maberley].

[131] Letter, January 7, 1860, Neale to [Maberley].

[132] A.P., Letter, April 17, 1862, C. Wordsworth to H.W.B.

[133] A.P., Incomplete Draft Letter, April 22, 1862, H.W.B. to Wordsworth.

[134] A.P., Letters, April 23, August 30, and November 6, 1862, Wordsworth to H.W.B.

[135] A.P., Letter, May 25, 1868, Wordsworth to H.W.B.

[136] A.P., Letters, May 22 and 25, 1868, Wordsworth to H.W.B.

[137] Letter, May 25, 1868, Wordsworth to H.W.B.

[138] A&M was used by the Royal Navy, and a selection from A&M (originally pirated but eventually sanctioned by the Proprietors) was printed for the exclusive use of the Army. A.P., M.B., November 15 and 16, 1865; January 16, 1866; and the Correspondence re the Use of A&M in the Army, 1865-1879.

[139] A.P., Draft Letter, May 28, 1868, H.W.B. to Wordsworth.

[140] Draft Letter, May 28, 1868, H.W.B. to Wordsworth.

[141] A.P., Letter, June 4, 1868, Wordsworth to H.W.B.

[142] A.P., Letter, June 6, 1868, H.W.B. to Wordsworth.

[143] A.P., Letter, May 28, 1868, H.W.B. to Wordsworth.

[144] A.P., Letter, July 4, 1871, Wordsworth to H.W.B.

[145] A.P., Draft Letter, July 7, 1871, H.W.B. to Wordsworth.

[146] A.P., Letter, July 10, 1871, Wordsworth to H.W.B.

[147] A.P., Letter, St. Luke's Day [October 18], [1871], J.B. Dykes to H.W.B.

[148] A.P., Letter, October 23, 1871, H.W.B. to Wordsworth.

[149] A.P., Letter, October 24, 1871, Wordsworth to H.W.B.

[150] A.P., Letter, March 9, 1874, W. Whiting to H.W.B.

[151] A.P., Letter, Feast of the Purification of the Blessed Virgin Mary [February 2], 1875, W. Whiting to H.W.B.

[152] A.P., Letter, October 30, 1871, H.W.B. to Wordsworth.

[153] A.P., Letter, October 29, 1874, Wordsworth to H.W.B.

[154] A.P., Letter, November 11, 1862, W.C. Dix to H.W.B.

[155] A.P., Draft Letter, November [2], 1874, H.W.B. to C.F. Alexander.

[156] A.P., Letter, November 10, 1874, C.F. Alexander to H.W.B.

[157] A.P., Letter, March 26, 1872, W.W. How to [W. Bright].

[158] A.P., Incomplete and undated Letter, [Summer 1860], F. Pott to H.W.B.

[159] In several letters to Sir Henry, Pott had objected to various hymns which he considered to go beyond the Prayer Book or to define "what the Church of England has purposely left undefined" (Letter, October 29, [1859], Pott to H.W.B.). Yet when Sir Henry accused him of "Protestant objections," Pott expressed surprise and amusement at the idea: "It is so new to me to find myself ranked as a Protestant champion, that I can not quite realize my new position; and having so incessantly all my life been in the habit of combatting Protestantism as such, I ought to beg for allowances to be made for me, if I wield my unaccustomed weapons clumsily, and lead you to think me a Protestant unmixed

and intolerant" (Letter, April 18, [1859], Pott to H.W.B.). His objection centered on the hymn "Pange lingua" by Thomas Aquinas, for he felt that its acceptance would prove "a fatal stumbling block to hundreds of men . . . who would I believe otherwise accept [A&M]" (Letter, November 2, [1859], Pott to H.W.B.). The debate over this hymn is discussed in full in Chapter Four, 8.

160 A.P., Letter, December 12, [1860], Pott to H.W.B.

161 Letter, December 12, [1860], Pott to H.W.B.

162 A.P., Letter, January 24, [1861], Pott to H.W.B.

163 A.P., Letter, November 29, [1860], Pott to H.W.B.

164 A.P., Copy of a Letter, November 26, [1861], H.W.B. to Pott. The Proprietors continued to be jealous of their book's appearance. In 1877 they threatened to take to court the Rev. E. Husband for "flagrant piracy" of their title "with the intention and object of deceiving the public." Husband's book was called _Supplemental Tunes to Hymns Ancient and Modern with an Appendix_ (A.P., Letter, August 29, 1877, Freshfield and Williams, solicitors, to E. Husband).

165 A.P., Letter, December 2, 1861, H.W.B. to Pott. Sir Henry's emphasis.

166 Letter, December 2, 1861, H.W.B. to Pott.

167 A.P., Letters, November 29, [1861], and December 2, 1861, Pott to H.W.B.

168 A.P., M.B., Draft Minute, December 11, 1861.

169 A.P., Letter, March 19, 1862, Pott to G.C. White.

170 A.P., Letter, November 25, 1862, J.M. Wilkins to H.W.B.

171 A.P., Letter, March 18, 1863, W. Parke (of Parke and Pollock, Lincoln's Inn Fields) to G.C. White.

172 A.P., M.B., Draft Minute, December 11, 1861.

173 A.P., Printed Correspondence from the _English Churchman_, August 14 and 21, 1862.

174 Correspondence, _English Churchman_, September 4, 1862.

[175] Correspondence, English Churchman, September 11, 1862.

[176] A.P., Letter, August 28, [1862], E. Twells to W. Pulling.

[177] A.P., Letter, August 25, 1862, T.A. Maberley to [H.W.B.].

[178] A.P., Letter, October 21, 1862, H.W.B. to J.B. Trend. Draft and fair copy.

[179] A.P., Letter, October 31, 1862, H.B. Walton to Trend.

[180] A.P., Letter, November 16, 1862, Henry Bailey to Pulling.

[181] A.P., Letter, May 17, 1861, H.W.B. to B.F. Carlyle.

[182] A.P., Newspaper clipping, Literary Churchman, March 2, 1863, Letter to the editor from "Clericus."

[183] A.P., Letter, July 15, [1862], H.W. Beadon to [W. Pulling].

[184] A.P., Draft Letter, July 21, 1862, Pulling to Beadon.

[185] A.P., Draft Letter, [between December 12 and 20, 1862], [Pulling] to Woodford.

[186] A.P., Letter, February 8, 1876, Robert N. Young to H.W.B. Young's emphasis.

[187] A.P., Correspondence re Irish Church Hymnal, 1873-1874, especially Letter, July 19, 1873, H.W.B. to Edward Seymour, Canon of Christ Church, Dublin.

[188] A.P., Letter, December 9, 1870, H.W.B. to Novello & Co., copy.

[189] A.P., Letter, July 24, 1874, E. Thring to H.W.B.

[190] A.P., Letter, Ascension Day, 1876, C.R. Harrison to H.W.B.

[191] A.P., Letter, December 15, 1876, E.H. Bickersteth to H.W.B.

[192] A.P., Letter, April 30, 1877, C.R. Harrison to W. Pulling.

[193] A.P., Newspaper clipping, "'Hymns Ancient and Modern' Revised," _The Spectator_, November 5, 1904.

[194] A.P., Letter, December 13, 1871, G. Thring to H.W.B.

[195] A.P., Letter, July 12, 1872, Thring to H.W.B.

[196] A.P., Letter, April 26, 1877, Thring to C.R. Harrison.

[197] A.P., Letter, June 9, 1877, Thring to Harrison.

[198] W.K. Lowther Clarke, _One Hundred Years of Hymns Ancient and Modern_ (1960), 56.

[199] Clarke, _One Hundred Years_, 57.

[200] Clarke, _One Hundred Years_, 58.

[201] Clarke, _One Hundred Years_, 59.

[202] A.P., Letter, December 13, 1871, G. Thring to H.W.B.

[203] Quoted in Clarke, _One Hundred Years_, 63-64.

[204] Wilkins thought so from the first when he undertook to help the new project: "My feeling about having an edition with the tunes is stronger than ever & I am daily more convinced of its utility & expedience. Mercers book had a large sale almost entirely on this ground & Chope's will have also" (A.P., Letter, June 23, 1859, J.M. Wilkins to H.W.B.).

[205] A.P., Letter, February 12, 1862, M. Woodward to [H.W.B.].

[206] A.P., Letter, March 31, 1862, M. Woodward to [H.W.B.].

[207] A.P., Letter, May 23, 1870, E.H. Bickersteth to H.W.B.

[208] A.P., Letter, May 26, 1870, E.H. Bickersteth to H.W.B.

[209] A.P., Letter, July 19, 1870, H.W.B. to E.H. Bickersteth.

210 See above, Chapter Three, 3, ii.

211 A.P., Letters, Ascension Day 1876, C.R. Harrison to H.W.B.; May 24, 1876, W. Pulling to H.W.B., Pulling's emphasis.

212 A.P., Letter, June 5, 1876, E.H. Bickersteth to H.W.B., expressing thanks.

213 Compare the _Hymnal Companion's_ share of London churches with that of A&M, given in section 3,i.

1879	124/872	14.2%
1880	141/887	15.8%
1881	154/916	16.8%
1889	175/1016	17.2%

214 A.P., Letter, August 10, [1858], F.H. Murray to Perceval Ward.

215 A.P., Letter, August 5, 1860, Lord Nelson to H.W.B.

216 A.P., Incomplete Letter, April 8, 1862, [Lord Nelson] to H.W.B.

217 A.P., Letter, August 5, 1860, Lord Nelson to H.W.B.

218 See Chapter Two, 2, i.

219 A.P., M.B., February 10, 1863.

220 A.P., M.B., February 11, 1863.

221 A.P., Letter marked "Private," April 7, 1865, Rev. A. Codd to F.H. Murray.

222 A.P., Copy of a Letter, April 14, 1865, Lord Nelson to Mr. Tower.

223 A.P., Letter, April 18, 1865, A. Codd to [F.H. Murray?].

224 A.P., Letter, April 24, 1865, A. Codd to [F.H. Murray?]. Codd's emphasis.

225 A.P., M.B., May 2, 1865.

226 A.P., M.B., May 16, 1865.

[227] A.P., Letter, June 18, [1865], Lord Nelson to H.W.B.

[228] A.P., M.B., November 17, 1865.

[229] A.P., M.B., November 15, 1865.

[230] A.P., Letter, February 22, 1862, W. Lyall to H.W.B., sending "the correct statistics of the S.P.C.K. book."

[231] A.P., Letters, February 5, 1862, W.R. Wroth to [G.C.W.?]; February 22, 1862, W. Lyall to H.W.B.

[232] A.P., Letter, November 29, 1862, J. Evans, Secretary of the Tract Committee, to H.W.B.

[233] A.P., Letter, July 26, 1869, B. Compton to H.W.B.

[234] A.P., Letter, October 6, 1871, B. Compton to H.W.B.

[235] A.P., Letter, March 3, [1871], B. Compton to H.W.B.

[236] See above, Chapter Three, 3, i.

[237] A.P., M.B., May 13, and October 13, 1880; April 28 and October 26, 1881; April 25, 1882.

Chapter Four
Editorial Policy and Practice

1. The Size of the Book

It is surprising to realize how small were the collections often considered adequate for congregational use in hymn-singing. In this matter as in others, the distinction has to be made between the source books and the hymnals. Source books (those collections of religious verse, either original or translated, which were not intended for public use, though they might be, and certainly were, used for private devotional purposes) might be large volumes indeed, and were often expensive. Hymnals, on the other hand, were more selections than collections, and sometimes very select indeed: being specifically intended for congregational use, they were subject to much theorizing about their size, contents, and ordering.

The restriction in size is partly due to the fact that many early hymnals were the work of a single and often an amateur editor, and necessarily limited in scope. In addition, it was widely felt that hymns should be proper to their occasion, and as familiar to the people as the Collect of the Day in the Book of Common Prayer. A clear statement of the principle of limitation, and of its practice in a high-church congregation, is found in a letter from the Reverend R. Collins of St. Saviour's, Leeds, who wrote to the Proprietors to explain his preference for the old St. Saviour's collection.

> Then, too, I believe 100 hymns would as much as we should ever require [sic]. I have learnt by experience that hymns & tunes the oftener they are sung the better they are liked -- and that a very great number is a positive disadvantage. Perhaps you are aware that in Yorkshire all sing -- in our Church they certainly do at the top of their voices. Now in the Old book there were hymns for each Sunday after Trinity; but was [sic] never found good to use them[.] the same hymns were used on all those Sundays, unless some festival, which of course, as all minor days were commemorated did not infrequently happen -- but even then there was no great variation . . . And in the other half of the year certain hymns were sung on certain days & seasons & always the same -- This is I think the right course -- most advantageous in fixing the season & its character in the minds of the people.[1]

Thomas Hervey of Alton sent Sir Henry a list of

the ninety-five hymns he thought would serve a congregation adequately, as long as they were arranged according to the Prayer Book order and cross-referenced so that there were four hymns suitable for each Sunday or holy day.[2] J.M. Clarke had made a selection for his Forest Hill church of "about 60 to 80 Hymns & Psalms capable of being distributed through the Christian seasons, -- three being used on each Sunday; -- a small Extension would provide for four each Sunday . . . I have been proving my plan by experiment for two or three years."[3]

Not all hymnals were quite as restricted as these. Braithwaite's Yorkshire committee were planning to include approximately 150 hymns, and forty to fifty metrical psalms in their collection.[4] William Whiting of Winchester wrote to Sir Henry at some length after seeing the Second Specimen, setting out what he thought essential to a Church hymnal. He felt there should be fixed hymns for days of the week and Sundays, invariable except for seasonal doxologies, but richly supplemented by other, what he called miscellaneous, hymns. "300 or there-abouts," he estimated, was a "very useful number, and sufficient for all requirements of Public Worship."[5]

A&M 1860 came quite close to this figure, with its 273 hymns. When the Appendix was published the total reached 386. There were some who thought even the first edition "too large a book in bulk . . . [meaning] that there are too many hymns."[6] The 1875 edition was, however, not only a revision, but an expansion: to 463 hymns and ten Litanies. The great hymnological revival meant that the numbers of contemporary or modern hymns from which to choose had never been higher, and the Compilers wished to borrow hymns proven popular, and to make known little-appreciated hymns of merit.[7]

Perhaps the chief reason for A&M's size was that its Compilers took the advice of John Keble: "If you want to make a hymn book for the use of the Church, make it comprehensive."[8] As the Compilers saw it, a generous provision of hymns was the only way to assure popularity: a strict selection will be adopted only by those whose views coincide exactly with those of the compilers. Furthermore, hymns which are frequently repeated, especially if hymns for the days of the week are sung, must be of a very high quality to withstand the deadening effect of such repetition. There is also a good argument for not associating all the hymns with the fixed part of the prayer book services, but with the variable: to refer to the subject of the homily, for instance, or to some secular circumstance. Of course, the choice of hymns was the parson's, but A&M was large enough to provide as much or as little variety as desired, and also to allow some hymns never to be sung at all if, as occasionally happened, a clerical conscience jibbed at them. Although the Compilers liked to think that their book in being widely acceptable was also thoroughly approved, they knew and sometimes admitted[9] that such was not the case.

Keble's advice also explains much of the policy of the Compilers concerning the kinds of hymns and the ordering of them, matters discussed in the following sections.

It was even more common to restrict the number of hymn tunes than the hymns themselves: J.M. Clarke chose "25 to 30 of the best & most wellknown Tunes" which he thought sufficient for a musically uneducated congregation:

> The same tunes are always used with the same Hymn: the Hymns occur [word illegible] about 3 times in the year, the Hymn Tunes about 6 times: but as soon as the words are given out the people seem to have the tune in their ears with the words: the result is that . . . I have very good congregational singing.[10]

The usual method, if tunes were provided at all, was to print a tune book containing a number of tunes in each of the regular metres, and some irregular, from which the organist chose whichever might be appropriate to the words. Several hymns might thus be identified with the same tune, or a hymn might have no recognizable tune at all, being sung to different ones on different occasions. A good organist might use a number of different tune books at each service, despite the inconvenience, but a lazy or incompetent musician might starve the congregation of musical variety. (Nevertheless, a church with even such an organist might consider itself lucky in comparison with those rural congregations which possessed a barrel organ and only as many tunes as they could afford barrels.) Printing tunes with the words was urged upon the Compilers as a convenience to both choir and organist: it was even suggested by one correspondent that the tunes be printed on separate leaves so that they could be shuffled, and held opposite the hymns for which they were needed.[11] A&M did better: one of its strongest points was the provision of a proper tune for every hymn, and in many cases, a new tune which caught the musical fancy of its hearers.[12] To a very large extent, A&M's success was due to its music, but that aspect does not come within the confines of this study.

2. The Arrangement of the Book

The order of a hymnbook reveals how its compilers expect it to be used. Early English collections, predominantly of metrical psalms, usually took the form of the psalter with an appendix, as the standard form of the Old Version Psalter (1562) had its addenda, and the New Version its 1700 supplement, both containing a miscellany of versions of the canticles, the Lord's Prayer and the Commandments, the Veni Creator, and a few occasional hymns.

Other books preserved a division between Scriptural paraphrases and original hymns, as in George Withers' Hymnes and Songs of the Church, 1623. This book, intended to supplement the Old Version, had two parts, the first containing metrical paraphrases from both the Old and the New Testaments, and the second a collection of hymns for the seasons and holy days of the Prayer book, and for special uses and occasions. Among the latter were hymns when washing, for sheep-shearing, house-warming, and for lovers, tutors, gaolers, prisoners, and members of Parliament.[13]

A similar division was kept in the Olney Hymns of John Newton and William Cowper (1779), which were published in three books: the first "On Select Texts of Scripture," the second "On Occasional Subjects," and the third "On the Progress and Changes of the Spiritual Life." The collection was as original as its authors. The second book, though nominally seasonal, is by no means comprehensive: it contains nothing for Advent, Epiphany, Lent, or Easter, though there are three hymns for Christmas and thirty for the New Year. The third book is the fruit of Evangelical experience, and its hymns are given under such headings as: "Conflict: light shining out of darkness" ("God moves in a mysterious way," Cowper, 192/373) and "Looking upwards in a storm" ("God of our life, to Thee we call," Cowper, 234/374). Of course, these hymns were not intended for use in the regular church services, but at weekly meetings and in private.

Nineteenth-century collections, especially Anglican ones, frequently adopt the seasonal pattern. Heber's book (1827) proclaimed its scheme in its title, Hymns written and adapted to the weekly church service of the year. The immense popularity of Keble's Christian Year (1827) confirmed the predominance of the seasonal arrangment, and to this day there is hardly a hymnal intended for Anglican use which is not to some extent seasonal.

To arrange a book solely according to the Church's calendar necessarily limits it: many of the finest hymns have no immediate seasonal relevance, and would have to be assigned more or less arbitrarily to one another of the Sundays after Trinity. The solution is to have a seasonal selection supplemented by general hymns, and a further selection for the sacraments and special services of the Church. Such a scheme was recommended by John Horner when he wrote to Sir Henry,[14] and Braithwaite discussed this point with Sir Henry on behalf of his Yorkshire committee:

> Our notion was to arrange the Hymns in the order of the Christian Seasons -- but not to classify them, except in a Calendar, which would indicate the Hymns to be used on each Sunday etc. It was not _my_ notion -- I should prefer . . . giving under the Several Seasons those Hymns which are to be used in those Seasons exclusively--& arranging those which are suitable to more than one Season under the head 'Miscellaneous'. In this _I_ agree in what you have written, but I do not agree in the expediency of providing Hymns for days for which our Church has provided no special services. It seems an unnecessary obstacle to the introduction of the Book to many congregations.[15]

Braithwaite's "days for which our Church has provided no special services" are the black-letter saints' days, and his was not the only objection to their proposed commemoration. The Reverend Oswald Chambers of St. John's Church, Leeds, argued that the inclusion of hymns for such days as St. Mary Magdalene and the

Transfiguration would "only create a prejudice against the book needlessly."[16]

Red-letter saints' days are those in the Anglican calendar which are intended for liturgical observance. Black-letter saints' days are simply listed: their observance is not commanded, but they are used as references for law and university terms, or in traditional parlance, as for example, Lammastide and Martinmas. The revived custom of daily celebration of the Eucharist by Anglo-Catholics attracted attention to the lesser saints' days, and the habit of dating by saints' days was regarded by many as a sign of Papist sympathies. Chambers' concern was not idle: the city of Leeds where he ministered had seen the influence of Popery. The church of St. Saviour's, dedicated in 1845, which Pusey had given as a centre for Tractarians working among the lower classes, incurred the suspicion of the Vicar of Leeds, Dr. W.F. Hook, and of the Bishop of Ripon, Dr. Longley, a suspicion which seemed to have been justified when the first vicar of St. Saviour's seceded to Rome with all his curates, and when, in his turn, the third vicar followed.

Braithwaite's committee was not easily reassured on the point: half a year after he first raised it, he wrote again:

> I am desired therefore to enquire . . . what you intend to do in the matter of black-letter days. We have no objection to the insertion of Hymns suitable for the commemoration of martyrs, confessors, etc.

> but not so inserted or particularised as if our own Church had sanctioned the observance of those days in the same way as she has the days of Apostles, etc. With us this could only cause prejudice, & secure the rejection of the Book.[17]

A&M's solution to the problem was to follow as closely as possible the order of the Book of Common Prayer. It begins with the hymns for daily use, as the Prayer Book sets out the order for morning and evening prayer. The hymns for the seasons are set out in the same order as the Collects, Epistles, and Gospels, that is, from Advent through Trinity. After the Collect for the Twenty-fifth Sunday after Trinity, there is another series of Collects, Epistles, and Gospels, beginning with St. Andrew's Day, November 30th, and moving through the year a second time to reach All Saints' Day, November 1st. This second set of Collects, Epistles, and Gospels corresponds to the last division of A&M, which provides proper hymns for some of the days, that is, the Conversion of St. Paul, the Presentation of Christ in the Temple, the Annunciation, Nativity of St. John the Baptist, St. Michael and All Angels, and All Saints' Day.[18] In addition, A&M contains hymns under the separate heading of Apostles, Evangelists, and Martyrs, Etc. (which includes Confessors, Virgins, and Matrons). These hymns are clearly intended for use on those days to which the Prayer Books assigns a Collect, but for which A&M assigned no proper hymn. The advantage of the category of general saints' days is that the possibilities of their use are many: moderates might use them for those feasts in the Prayer

Book, and perhaps at the Festival of the dedication of the church, while those with Anglo- Catholic tendencies could choose among them for any saint they wished to commemorate.

Following the section of the Collects, Epistles, and Gospels in the prayer book are the orders of service for the sacraments of Communion and Baptism, and for confirmation, matrimony, burial of the dead, and the churching of women. The Compilers printed a selection of hymns for use at such services (except the churching of women), and placed them after the general or post-Trinity hymns, and before those for festivals. It is in this section that they allowed themselves a greater flexibility, including a number of occasions of which the Prayer book makes no mention, such as mission, harvest, school festivals, thanksgivings, and "times of trouble." Here the function of hymn-singing beyond the liturgy of the Prayer book and even outside the formal services of the church is recognized. As Tractarian influence may be discerned in the provision for saints' days, so Evangelical traces show in such headings as "times of trouble," where some of Cowper's verses have their place. Similarly, the provision for secular occasions such as harvest is reminiscent of that earlier and much bolder tradition which provided hymns for sheep-shearers, and declared:

> Yea, would God that our minstrels had none other thing to play upon, neither our carters and ploughmen other things to whistle upon, save psalms, hymns, and such godly songs as David is occupied withal! And if

women . . . spinning at the wheels, had none other songs to pass their time withal, than such as Moses' sister, Glehana's wife, Debora, and Mary the mother of Christ have sung before them, they should be better occupied than with _hey_ _nony_ _nony_, _hey_ _troly_ _loly_ and such like phantasies.[19]

3. The Contents of the Book

The examination in Chapter Three of how A&M was compiled has necessarily included some discussion of its contents. It was pointed out there that the Compilers were drawn together by shared principles of what a hymnal should do and what it should contain. There was from the beginning little doubt but that A&M should be, as Keble urged, comprehensive, drawing on the resources of the past made readily available through recent scholarship, enriched by contemporary writing, and left flexible enough to be free of partisan constraint and widely used.

Obviously A&M was not entirely free from party associations: it bore the Tractarian stamp from its inception. Its Compilers, however, succeeded in avoiding the extremes of party prejudice. One correspondent, for example wrote to Sir Henry:

> Will you allow one suggestion to be made to those concerned in [the proposed hymnbook] on the strict adoption of which they will surely find

> their success with all deserving the name of Churchman to depend; the confining of themselves without exception to the productions of Churchmen. The Church has no right to. & has no need of Sectarian hymns.[20]

The Compilers never seriously considered such a policy: their methods were avowedly catholic and eclectic, and their intention was to borrow and adapt whatever excellent material might be made to serve the purposes of the Church of England. Although this correspondent's policy might have allowed the use of mediaeval hymns used in England before the Reformation, it would have severely limited the modern sources and passed over the hymns of Dissent which formed until the nineteenth century the only strong English line of original hymnody.

Several clergy warned against the dangers of arousing anti-Papist feelings by too close an association with the ritualists. J.M. Clarke, whose church was in Forest Hill, south of Peckham, was aware of the strong antipathies which the ritualists had provoked, particularly in London. It was only eight years since the riots at St. Barnabas, Pimlico, and opposition to high-church ceremonial was still strong enough to repeat the scene at St. George's-in-the-East in 1859. Clarke told Sir Henry:

> I do not know the 'All Saints Margt Stt' hymnal; but I do feel strongly that anything bearing the stamp of the Margaret Street services is not

> likely to meet with the approbation of the clergy of this Diocese of London.[21]

To the Compilers, who numbered the Vicar of All Saints, Margaret Street among them, Clarke must have seemed too timid, but they were by no means unaware of the danger which partisan prejudice posed to their book. Their efforts to avoid that danger, without betraying their own standards, are discussed in some detail below.[22]

The Compilers' correspondents focused on three issues which would, they saw, characterize A&M. Two of these were the exclusion of metrical psalms, and the relative proportion of ancient and modern hymns. The third issue, the provision of hymns for saints' days, was discussed above in section 2 of this chapter, on the arrangement of the book.

Both the other principal issues arise in the correspondence between Sir Henry and the Yorkshire clergymen. When Braithwaite first wrote to the A&M Committee, he told them that the Yorkshire book would contain "perhaps 150 Hymns, & 40 to 50 Psalms."[23] The A&M Committee were unwilling to admit any but the few most obvious psalms, for it was their intention to overcome the Church of England's reliance upon the Old and New Versions by an emphasis upon hymns drawn from its Catholic heritage, and from its modern experience. Braithwaite thought Sir Henry's proposed compromise acceptable.

> I see no difficulty in having an edition of selected Psalms which

> might be bound up with the Hymns or omitted as may be desired. For myself I feel very much with you on that subject -- but many of our number are very anxious to have a few Metrical Psalms.[24]

The issue was not raised again. The suggested compromise was not an unusual one, in fact, for A&M was often found with an appendix of hymns in local use which a congregation or a parson was unwilling to see forgotten because the new hymnbook excluded them.

That is not to say that A&M did not contain metrical psalms or psalm paraphrases.[25] There were, in fact, fourteen in A&M 1860, and three in the Appendix, though none was added to the Revised edition (See Table 1). They included the most familiar of the Old and New Versions, such as Kethe's Psalm 100, "All people that on earth do dwell" (136/166), and Tate and Brady's Psalm 34 "Through all the changing scenes of life" (153/290). In addition to these, A&M printed two of Watts's freer renderings, and three of the free paraphrases from H.F. Lyte's _The Spirit of the Psalms_, published in 1834. Two are nineteenth-century recastings of earlier metrical versions: Grant's "O worship the King" (156/167), based on Kethe's Psalm 104, and Sir Henry's "Praise, O praise our God and King" (224/381), after Milton's Psalm 136. The table shows the predominance of later paraphrases over the earlier versions,[26] illustrating A&M's preference for a paraphrase which has the quality of an original hymn, and something more than a Scriptural model to commend it.

Note that of the seventeen paraphrases in 1860 and 1868, twelve are intended for general use, two for Epiphany, and one each for Lent, Missions, and Harvest. In the Revised edition, all are general save those for Missions and Harvest, a change which makes the few psalms A&M does contain as widely useful as possible.

The crucial issue of the proportion of ancient and modern hymns appeared early in the Braithwaite correspondence:

> With regard to the Hymns -- we agree in the main with the principles laid down in your letter. It seems likely however that you would select more ancient and fewer modern Hymns than we have done -- at all events from Advent to Trinity -- our choice in this matter has not been influenced by any preference of the new to the old -- but from the almost impossibility of finding translations of the ancient Hymns -- which are not essentially Latin in their whole structure and expression.[27]

The A&M Compilers, however, were confident of finding, writing, or adapting suitable English translations and were dedicated to the principle of restoring to common use the ancient hymns of the Catholic Church. The predominance of ancient hymns over modern for the seasons of the church year, which was the specific problem Braithwaite raised, was due to the historical peculiarities of English hymnody.[28] Until the nineteenth

1860	1868	1875	First Line of Hymn Paraphrase	Author	Psalm	First Pubn
136		166	All people that on earth do dwell	Kethe	100	1561
81		249	Have mercy, Lord, on me	Tate & Brady	51	1696
153		290	Through all the changing scenes	Tate & Brady	34	1696
161		237	O God of hosts, the mighty Lord	Tate & Brady	84	1696
	310	238	As pants the hart for cooling streams	Tate & Brady	42	1696
196		220	Jesus shall reign where'er the sun	Watts	72	1719
197		165	O God, our help in ages past	Watts	90	1719
174		292	Praise the Lord, ye heavens adore	Anonymous	148	1796
66		219	Hail to the Lord's Anointed	Montgomery	72	1822
	295	294	O praise our great and gracious Lord	Auber	78	1829
156		167	O worship the king	Grant/Kethe	104	1833
63		218	God of mercy, God of grace	Lyte	67	1834
176		284	Far from my heavenly home	Lyte	137	1834
198		298	Praise, my soul, the king of heaven	Lyte	103	1834
219		364	God of grace, O let Thy light	Churton	67	1854
224		381	Praise, o praise our God and King	Baker/Milton	136	1860
	330	197	The King of love my shepherd is	Baker	23	1868

TABLE 1: Psalm Paraphrases on A&M 1860, 1868, 1875

century, most English hymn-writing was either metrical psalmody, or part of the tradition of Dissent, rather than of the established church. Psalms have little to do with the church year: the Prayer Book had appointed that the entire Psalter be read through in the course of a calendar month, but the use of metrical psalms could be entirely arbitrary, for they, like hymns, were governed by no rubric.

The dissenting churches in England after 1662 reformed the Calendar even more drastically than the Book of Common Prayer had done: there is very little attention paid to any but the major festivals, and a subsequent lack of hymns for many of the occasions of the church year. Christmas and Easter have from mediaeval times been supplied with carols in the vernacular, but if the Compilers were not to be put to the task of writing their own hymns for the other occasions, they had to go further back into Catholic hymnody, and translate Latin hymns. Here the Compilers fell into confusion, for not only did they go to the various Uses of England for such hymns, but also to Continental sources. Of course, both English and Continental Uses contained many of the same hymns, but the Compilers found that the Parisian Breviary, chiefly, but other breviaries as well, contained proper hymns which they were glad to borrow and translate. What they overlooked was the fact that many of these hymns were the work of seventeenth- and eighteenth-century Roman Catholics, which found their way into the breviaries soon after their publication. The result was that the number of true ancient hymns for the seasons proposed for A&M was much smaller than Braithwaite realized, but he and his brethren would no doubt not have been comforted by the fact that a number of them were modern but Roman Catholic. In fact, 46% of the Latin hymns in A&M 1860 were written after the Reformation, and a further 2% were late revisions of earlier hymns. The true proportion of ancient to modern is confused by the question of language, but can be seen clearly in Table 2.

The best way to examine the contents of A&M is to compare the editions, and note the changes that were made. The Appendix was intended to broaden the scope of the collection, in tapping new sources, such as Greek hymns, and by increasing the number of modern hymns, especially from the tradition of Dissent, thereby silencing some of the critics of the Original edition.

Nineteenth-century English hymns comprised 36% of the Original edition, and 66% of the Appendix. Pre-nineteenth-century English hymns, including one by Watts and three by Charles Wesley, form 13% of the 1860 book, and 9% of the Appendix, with the result that although not quite half (49%) of the 1860 hymns were originally written in English, fully three quarters (75%) of the 1868 hymns were. The proportion of Latin hymns was accordingly reduced: of the 1860 hymns 25% were pre-Reformation Latin hymns, 21% were post-Reformation; of the 1868 hymns, 10% were pre-Reformation, 1.5% post-Reformation. Hymns from the Eastern Church comprised 10% of the Appendix, either direct translations, or Neale's imitations. The percentage of German hymns remained approximately the same: 4% of 1860, 3.5% of the Appendix.

Contents	Original Edn		Appendix		Revised Edn[1]			
	Nos.	%age[2]	Nos.	%age[2]	Nos.	%age[2]	Additns[3]	Omissns[3]
English Hymns								
16th - 17thC	36	13	10	9	47	10	2	1
19thC	97	36	75	66	244	53	78	6
Sub-total	133	49	85	75	291	63	80	7
Latin Hymns								
mediaeval	61	22	10	9	76	16	9	4
Renaissance	5	2	1	1	7	2	1	0
post-Reformation	58	21	2	1.5	56	12	0	5
med.revd 17thC	3	1	0	0	3	1	0	0
Sub-total	127	46	13	11.5	142	31	10	9
Greek & Syriac Hymns								
translations	0	0	8		8		1	1
Neale versions	0	0	3		3		0	0
Sub-total	0	0	11	10	11	2	1	1
German Hymns								
16th - 17thC	8	3	2		9		0	1
19thC	2	1	2		5		1	0
Sub-total	10	4	4	3.5	14	3	1	1
Other Hymns								
Sub-total	3	1	0	0	4	1	1	0
Total	273	100	113	100	462	100	93	18

[1] Excluding Litanies [2] All percentages approximate [3] Actual figures, not percentages

TABLE 2: Comparative Contents of A&M 1860, 1868, 1875

Where the additions were made is of equal interest. The largest number of Appendix hymns, 51 out of 113, were intended for general use, nearly as many again as were provided in the Original edition (67 out of 273). The number of hymns provided for the sacrament of Holy Communion was more than doubled, six hymns being added to the five in 1860. Other occasional hymns are given: two more for Baptism (1860 had three), two for Confirmation (1860, one), one for the Burial of a child (1860 had three general Burial hymns), one for Ember Days (1860, three), three for Almsgiving (1860, one), two more for Harvest (1860, five), two more for Missions (1860, four), and three for new occasions -- Cattle Plague, Hospitals, and New Year's Eve. A new section of nine hymns for the young was added among the occasional hymns, marking a new comprehensiveness.

Additions to hymns for the Church calendar are fewer: seven evening hymns (1860, ten), and two for Sunday (1860, five), but none for the hours of the day or the days of the week. To the feasts are added only four Lenten hymns (1860, eleven), three for Easter (1860, thirteen), and one each for St. Stephen's Day (1860, one), Epiphany (1860, nine), Passiontide (1860, eighteen), Ascensiontide (1860, five), and the Annunciation (1860, two). Seven new hymns are added to the general section of Martyrs, Confessors, Saints, Matrons, and Virgins (1860, twelve). A new section containing three processional hymns was also included in the Appendix.

What conclusions are to be drawn from these statistics? First, it is clear that with the great expansion of the section of General hymns any notion of proper hymns for each Sunday is given up. Congregations and their priests are given a much wider range of hymns from which to choose, with no guidance but the priest's sense of what is fitting for the day. Second, no more provision is made for very specific occasions within the Church calendar: the great seasons are added to rather than the smaller festivals, general rather than specific provision is made for "Martyrs, etc." The Tractarian emphasis upon the Sacraments is maintained, but no complaint can be made about an excessively Anglo-Catholic fondness for black-letter days.

As important as the increase in General hymns is the additional provision for use outside the formal services of the Church. The new selection of hymns for the young provides Sunday school and catechism classes. Increased reference to external circumstance, harvest and plague, as well as hymns for missions and hospitals, means that hymn-singing is to go beyond the confines of the prayer book and the churchyard, to begin to meet the challenge of modern parishes.

The account of the preparation of the Revised edition in Chapter Three has shown how high-church clergymen urged that the book not be "watered down," fearing that the supplementary material of the Appendix marked a change of direction in the book they had adopted, by and large, as their own. An examination of the comparative statistics of the books indicates this suspected change. Undeniably the English share of the book was gaining over the Latin: their relative proportions in the Revised edition are closer to two thirds and one third (63% vs. 31%) than to the nearly half and half (49% vs. 46%) of the 1860 volume. Most of the new hymns (the eleven Litanies, ten of which were new in 1875, are not included in this account) were contemporary English hymns: 78, or 83% of the additions. Two English hymns from the eighteenth century were also printed. Latin hymns formed only 12% of the additions, and nine of these ten hymns were pre-Reformation. One translation each from Danish, Greek, and German were added.

Against these additions must be set the omissions. One third, that is, six, of these omissions were nineteenth-century English hymns; one eighteenth-century English hymn also was dropped. Translations from Latin were half the omissions, and of these nine casualties, five were post-Reformation. One translation from the German, and a version of a Syrian hymn were also omitted.

These statistics, taken together, indicate quite clearly that the proportions of ancient and modern had not yet been adjusted to the Compilers' final satisfaction. They were turning more to English hymnwriters, though not to the great eighteenth-century writers, but to what was seen and encouraged as the triumphant convergence of two great traditions: those of English (Protestant) hymn-writing, and Catholic belief. Their appreciation of Roman Catholic hymnody was increasingly discriminating: the late Roman element is reduced, and the pre-Reformation, strengthened.

The eleven litanies of the Revised edition were all the work of nineteenth-century writers. One of them, by Sir Henry, had been printed for Rogation Days in the Original edition, but the other litanies were new to A&M, though all but one had been published earlier (five in T.B. Pollock's Metrical Litanies for Special Services and General Use, 1870, and four in the People's Hymnal, 1867). The People's Hymnal, incidentally, was the model Catholic collection which E. Hoskins recommended to the Compilers,[29] and it should have been a reassurance to Hoskins and the Catholic party that A&M had taken over so Catholic a feature as a section of litanies. The subject had been discussed several times during the compilation of the Appendix, but had never been resolved, and the Appendix appeared without them.[30] In addition to the litanies, ceremonialists could approve the addition of another processional hymn to the three printed in the Appendix.

If the increase in English hymns and corresponding decrease in Latin hymns alarmed the high churchmen for fear that A&M was becoming too broad, they could have taken comfort in the uses to which the hymns were put. Most of the new hymns (thirty-one, to be precise) were for general use, it is true, but the specific provision for morning and evening services, and the weekday use, was increased overall by five hymns.[31] There were overall fewer hymns for the seasons of the church year in 1875, as the Compilers removed thirteen hymns from sections which were found to be over-supplied, Advent, Epiphany, Circumcision, Septuagesima, Lent, and Trinity. Ten hymns were added, for Passiontide, Easter, Ascensiontide, and Whitsun, the more dramatic festivals.

The Appendix increase in hymns which looked

beyond the sanctuary was continued in the Revised edition: another hymn for Missions, for Hospitals, in times of trouble, two more each for seamen, for Harvest, and for "lay helpers." Half as many hymns again were printed in 1875 for the young, bringing the total to eighteen. The only losses in these sections were of one almsgiving hymn and Neale's hymn for use in time of cattle plague. The heightened sense of social responsibility implied by the increase in this class of hymns could not be claimed for any one party of the Church of England. Though the Evangelicals had been most active earlier in the century, the high churchmen, having set their own house in order in the Tractarian revivals of Catholic theology, ceremonial and music, were more and more trying their influence in the nation as a whole. Thus the high-church party could not claim "watering down" here, though diffusion there most certainly was. The Tractarian inclination of the Compilers was perhaps nowhere as clearly shown as in the increased provision for the Sacraments, chiefly for the Eucharist. A&M 1860 had contained five Communion hymns; the Appendix added six more, and the Revised edition brought the total to sixteen.

Furthermore, although the Compilers had settled their arrangement of the book in such a way as to provide for saints' days without prescribing for any but the red-letter days, they amplified the final division of the book by printing a series of proper hymns for the Apostles. The idea of proper hymns was pleasingly sympathetic to high churchmen, while low churchmen could not object as the Apostles are singled out for special attention in the Prayer Book itself. In addition, the new hymns were not translations from ancient sources, but the work of living authors, and no fewer than seven of the twelve hitherto unpublished. The whole section may be seen as a compromise between the high and the low, and the ancient and the modern.

That hymns were specially written for a specific purpose in A&M illustrates once more how seriously the Compilers took Keble's advice to make a hymnbook comprehensive. In fact, they intended their book to be complete, and its revision and enlargement in 1875 reflected this intention. No longer were they only selecting from a vast supply of hymns mediocre or masterly to compile a book of practical excellence; they were now commissioning hymns to supply what they thought was lacking. Their compilation of the 1875 edition resembles the solving of a huge puzzle, but with pieces specially cut to order when a stubborn blank could not be fitted. In addition to the series of proper hymns for the Apostles, the Revised edition contains a series on the words of Jesus spoken from the cross, of which six were written for A&M 1875.

There can be no denying that A&M was a high- rather than a low-church collection, though it eschewed the extremes of Anglo-Catholicism. The Revised edition continues the tendencies exhibited in the original edition, taking its form from the Book of Common Prayer, and borrowing freely from its ancient heritage, but more carefully. No longer does a Latin original imply excellence: that quality must be proven in translation and in use, and may after all be found to reside in the work of living authors. A&M reflects that development in the Church of England by which the influence of the Tractarian revival spread throughout the entire church, so that by the end of the century what had once been controversial novelty became the norm. Not that A&M made no concession to other parties of the church, for it could not hope to be generally acceptable without pleasing them in some ways. We have seen the great expansion in hymns for general use, and hymns which refer not to the events of the Christian calendar but to causes and concerns in the larger, sometimes hostile and partly heathen world of England after the Industrial Revolution. The hymns in A&M may not have been much of a practical response to the problems of that world, but it was an acknowledgement of them, and of the whole Church's responsibility.

The tables of authorship which follow reveal some interesting points to supplement the information about sources and uses discussed above. For instance, the increase in English and decrease in Latin hymns is clearly reflected in Table 3, the comparative contribution of select authors. Coffin and de Santeuil are the known Latin[32] authors with the most hymns in A&M, but by 1875 their share overall has dropped by five. The authorship table shows a slight increase in the contribution of the great English hymn-writers. Cowper's share has gone from two to four, Montgomery's from four to seven. Watts has four in 1860, one in the Appendix, and nothing new in 1875; Charles Wesley has the best showing of all the acknowledged masters -- nine in 1860, a further three in 1868, one more in 1875. On the other hand, Heber, Keble, Ken, Newton and Toplady have the same number of hymns in 1875 as in 1860; Doddridge has even lost one. There is certainly no general bias in favour of the classics of English hymn-writing in the first fifteen years of A&M.

It was noted above that the great increase in A&M was in contemporary hymns; nearly 36% of the 244 nineteenth-century hymns (including those of earlier authors such as Heber and Keble) are from the pens of the twelve then-living authors listed in Table 3. Not surprisingly, given his personality and his influence, Sir Henry's own original[33] contribution to A&M is second to that of none but Coffin: twelve in 1860, twenty-one in 1875.

Name of Author	**Number of Hymns**		
	1860	**1868**	**1875**
Alexander, C.F.	1	4	11
Alford, H.	1	1	6
Baker, H.W.	12	5	21
Bright, W.	0	4	7
Cowper, W.	2	1	4
Dix, W.C.	1	1	5
Doddridge, P.	4	0	3
Faber, F.W.	4	3	8
Heber, R.	5	0	5
How, W.W.	1	2	6
Keble, J.	9	0	9
Ken, T.	2	0	2
Lyte, H.F.	4	2	6
Milman, H.H.	3	0	3
Montgomery, J.	4	0	7
Newman, J.H.	0	2	2
Newton, J.	1	0	1
Thring, G.	0	3	4
Toplady, A.M.	1	0	1
Watts, I.	4	1	5
Wesley, C.	9	3	12
Wesley, J.	0	0	1
Wordsworth, C.	0	8	9
Coffin, C.	24	0	22
de Santeuil, J.B.	11	0	8

TABLE 3: Select Authors, A&M 1860, 1868, 1875.

Some of the more frequent names in the Revised edition were unknown in the 1860 book: William Bright,

Godfrey Thring, Newman, and Wordsworth. Others had a small beginning, and expanded quickly: C.F. Alexander from one to eleven; Henry Alford from one to six, William Chatterton Dix from one to five, and William Walsham How from one to six. Still others held or improved their original showing: Faber had four hymns in 1860, and twice that in 1875; Lyte had four in 1860, and two in 1868, but no new ones in 1875; Henry Hart Milman had the same three in the Revised edition as in the original.

The authors in Table 3 may be considered major contributors to A&M: the eighteen English-language authors listed therein for 1860 were responsible for sixty-four hymns, 48% of the English hymns in the book, and nearly 24% of the whole book. The total number of English authors (counting co-authors once only) is sixty-five. The twenty-three English contributors to the Revised edition listed in Table 3 had 138 hymns in 1875, 48% of the English hymns and nearly 30% of the entire book. Of these major contributors, four were Roman Catholic,[34] and four were Dissenters,[35] including, against their will, the two Wesleys under that heading. The rest were Church of England, all but three,[36] clergy, and one of those three a woman. In short, Table 3 sets out the heavily contemporary, clerical and Anglican weight of A&M in its first three volumes.

Analysis of the other tables can be briefer. Table 4 shows the contributions of the relatively few most important translators, and especially the major debt A&M owed to Neale. Note that Sir Henry's pen made a not inconsiderable mark here too.

Name of Translator	Number of Translations 1860	1868	1875
Baker, H.W.	8	0	10
Campbell, R.	6	0	6
Caswall, E.	20	1	21
Chandler, J.	28	1	25
Compilers of A&M	5	2	8
Copeland, W.	4	0	4
Ellerton, J.	0	1	3
Neale, J.M.	36	14	48
Williams, I.	10	0	10

TABLE 4: Select Translators, A & M 1860, 1868, 1875.

Tables 5 and 6 cannot disprove the popular notion that hymn-writing was a favourite pastime of Victorian women, but do show just how few women's hymns were published for congregational use.

Name of Author	Number of Hymns 1860	1868	1875
Adams, S.F.	1	0	1
Alderson, E.S.	0	1	2
Alexander, C.F.	1	4	11
Auber, H.	1	1	2
Cornish, K.	0	0	1
Elliott, C.	1	1	3
Flowerdew, A.	1	0	1
Havergal, F.R.	0	0	5
Leeson, J.E.	0	*1	2
Leslie, E.(Mrs. Toke)	2	0	2
Maitland, F.S.F.	*1	0	*1
Maude, M.F.	0	1	1
Miller, E.	0	0	1
Noel, C.M.	0	0	1

* denotes joint authorship

TABLE 5: Women Authors, A & M 1860, 1868, 1875

Name of Translator	Number of Translations		
	1860	1868	1875
Borthwick, J.L.	0	0	1
Campbell, J.M.	0	1	1
Cox, F.E.	3	1	4
Leeson, J.E.	1	0	1
Winkworth, C.	6	1	6

TABLE 6: Women Translators, A & M 1860, 1868, 1875.

Ten women were responsible for eighteen of the 273 hymns in 1860, of which only eight were original verses. By 1875, A&M's female contributors numbered nineteen, and were responsible for forty-seven hymns, thirty-four of them original. Only C.F. Alexander qualifies as a major contributor, with eleven hymns in 1875. The distinctive contribution of the women to A&M was translations from German; only one hymn in all Table 6, that of Jane Leeson, is from the Latin. Frances Cox and Catherine Winkworth were acknowledged translators, and their books, important sources.[37]

4. On Translation

The revival of interest in Catholic hymnody which was part of the Oxford Movement's influence stimulated great interest in the problems of translation. Newman himself had called attention to Latin hymns neglected by the English church, in the seventy-fifth of the *Tracts for the Times*, "On the Roman Breviary" (1836), which contained fourteen of his own translations. Another of the Tract authors, Isaac Williams, whose "On Reserve in the Communication of Religious Knowledge" has been referred to in Chapter 2, published his *Hymns translated from the Parisian Breviary* in 1839. His translations had already appeared occasionally in the *British Magazine*, where they had attracted the attention of John Chandler, who was stimulated by them to "collect, translate, and arrange" his *Hymns of the Primitive Church* (first published in 1837, and in a revised edition "for Public Use" in 1841). These men, with Edward Caswall, whose *Lyra Catholica* was first published in 1849, the year before he joined the Roman Catholic Church, were among the most important translators, though none was so influential as Neale. He was chief among those clergymen who were concerned to distinguish what was the Church of England's rightful inheritance, from the early and mediaeval church, from what was Roman. In hymnody as in ceremony, the Tractarians and their followers were concerned to restore to the English church its own tradition and to make that tradition accessible to the churchgoer as well as to the clergyman with his classical education. Neale's work in the Hymnal Noted, published in two parts in 1851 and 1854, is to some extent written as a corrective to Caswall's more Romanizing book, and strictly according to ecclesiological principles.

One of Neale's prime concerns was that translated hymns should be in the authentic English tradition, texts that were, in Neale's words, "in general use through the Western Church, before the so-called reform of Urban [the revision of the Breviary ordered by Pope Urban VIII in 1629]."[38] This distinction is of considerable importance, and merits some attention.

The reform to which Neale refers was the recasting of the hymns in the Roman Breviary done by a committee of four Jesuits at the order of the Pope in 1629. Their revised Breviary was published in 1632. Most of the revisions were "corrections" of mediaeval into classical Latin, and the results were drastic. Compare, for instance, two versions of a stanza from the sixth or seventh century hymn "Urbs beata Jerusalem":

11th C. Ms

Angularis fundamentum lapis Christus missus est
Qui conpage parietis in utroque nectitur,

Quem Sion sancta suscepit, in quo
credens permanet.

Christ is made the sure foundation
Christ the head and corner-stone,
Who, the two walls underlying,
Bound in each, binds both in one:
Holy Sion's help forever
And her confidence alone.

1632

Alto ex Olympi vertice Summi
Parentis Filius
Ceu monte desectus lapis terras in
imas decidens
Domus supernae, et infimae utrumque
iunxit angulum.

From the high peak of Olympus the Son of the Almighty Father, like a stone cut from the mountain descending to the lowest lands, joined together both corners of the upper and the lower abode.[39]

Perhaps the most incongruous alteration, and the one immediately noticeable, is the introduction of the terminology of pagan classicism into Christian poetry: it were better to leave Olympus to Jupiter. Neale frankly condemned the revised prosody:

> The literati of the court of Urban VIII . . . bound themselves down to

> those classical chains, which the Church had deliberately flung away, and sacrificed beauty, piety, fervour, poetry, to cramp the grand old hymns into the rules of prosody.... In fact, the hymns of the modern Roman Breviary are, emphatically, <u>spoilt</u>.[40]

The scarcity of translations of the unrevised Breviary hymns, "our own hymns," according to Neale, was the first reason he gave for publishing the <u>Hymnal Noted</u>. The compilers of A&M, however, did not always prefer the Sarum to the Roman versions of a hymn. Indeed, in every edition of A&M there appear translations of both versions of one of the hymns. The first (111/128) is "The Lamb's high banquet called to share," Neale's translation, altered by the Compilers, of the older "Ad cenam Agni providi." The second (113/127) is "At the Lamb's high feast we sing," a translation by Robert Campbell of the regularized Roman Breviary form "Ad regias Agni dapes," which came to A&M slightly altered from Cooke and Denton's <u>Church Hymnal</u> (1852).

If authenticity of sources was Neale's first concern in translation, his second was what may be called excellence. The criteria of excellence in translation are as difficult to establish objectively as in any art. Three considerations are paramount, however, and recur frequently with reference to A&M: first, the choice of metre, second, technical accuracy, and third, "Englishness," or fluency of style.

The first question is relatively straightforward.

The translator's first decision, after choosing a text, is whether or not to keep to the original metre of the verse. One of Neale's chief objections to Caswall's work was how infrequently he retained the metre of the original, "a point to us, clearly of absolute necessity."[41] Neale's reason was that he wished to make available for general use, not only the old hymns, but also their proper ancient melodies, fitting them to the new English words with as little alteration as possible. It was originally Sir Henry's intention to follow Neale's lead in this matter, but he found that "practically it wd not do," for the predominance of ancient hymns for the seasons would mean little but long measures, and that lack of variety would displease "those who do not use the old tunes."[42] Even without objecting to the use of ancient melodies, doubts were expressed about the number of hymns in long measure, perhaps most memorably by the Rev. George Ironside, who wrote to G.C. White to record his generally favourable opinion of the second Specimen:

> We are quite aware that in Translations long measure has generally advantages over any other -- It allows the rendering to be more literal -- & admits of the adoption of the ancient music -- which in some cases, is most desirable; but notwithstanding this, the measure is so heavy, that, where the Hymn is long -- as is often the case, the singing of it by an untrained country congregation is very difficult. Perhaps this is not felt so much in England, where

> the people naturally sing faster than in Scotland, just as they speak faster; but in a congregation such as mine -- or others consisting chiefly of the working classes, the singing of eight or nine verses in long measure (& frequently the Hymn cannot be divided) would be really more an act of penitence than of praise --[43]

The compromise which Sir Henry suggested was to preserve the Sarum hymns in their original metres, to be sung to Hymnal Noted tunes, but that translations of hymns from other sources need not be so strictly bound. Thus, for example, the translation indicated in the first Specimen of the hymn "Instantis adventum Dei," by Charles Coffin, is the L.M. one by Gerard Moultrie "The Advent of our God and King," but it is replaced in 1860 by the S.M. "The Advent of our King," based on John Chandler's translation. Its S.M. form enabled it to be set to the eighteenth-century German tune "Franconia." In the case of the two translations of the Easter hymn noticed above, the Sarum version ("The Lamb's high banquet called to share") is in L.M., and is set to the ancient melody arranged by Monk; the Roman version ("At the Lamb's high feast we sing") is in double sevens (eight seven-syllable lines) and is set to a modern tune, a seventeenth-century German melody harmonized by Bach.

The second criterion by which a translation is to be judged is that of technical accuracy, particularly in conveying exactly the meaning of the original, but also in producing English verses in correct rhythm and rhyme. Again, it is Neale who set the standard, and who did not hesitate to criticize the compilers when they fell short of it. The successive translations of "Ad cenam Agni providi" reveal the scrupulous accuracy Neale urged. In his first published translation (in the prospectus of the Hymnal Noted, February 1851) he wrote "The Lamb's high banquet stands displayed," but altered it two months later to "The Lamb's high banquet we await," when he came to understand that "providi" did not modify "Agni" ("of the Lamb Who provides the feast"), but was nominative plural ("We who look forward to"), because, as he explained, the hymn was not "originally an Easter one: it was a baptismal hymn, sung between the regeneration of the Catechumens & their first reception of the Holy Communion: first, that is, when they were Providi."[44] He was, not surprisingly, distressed to see the mistake he had first made and then corrected recur in the second A&M Specimen, and warned the Committee to be careful of correcting anything without diligent study beforehand. In the 1860 edition, the stanza was altered ("The Lamb's high banquet called to share"), though not restored to Neale's own Hymnal Noted version.

Another criticism of an A&M alteration of the same hymn was a matter not of syntax but of shades of meaning, and literally of shades of colour. In the second stanza, A&M printed "His crimson blood" to translate "cruore eius roseo." Neale had given "roseate blood," arguing that:

> Blood is crimson when it first begins to flow: but the longer it

> flows, the paler it becomes, till at last it is quite a light rose colour. The poet then would tell us that, our Lord shed not merely a portion of, but all, His Blood for our sakes; & the very word you have cut out, is the most appropriate of the whole Hymn.[45]

The Committee, however, refused to restore "roseate," feeling no doubt that its significance would be lost or that the word would only baffle that majority of hymn-singers who did not follow his arguments. Neale felt so strongly about the matter that he returned to it in the preface to the second edition of his Mediaeval Hymns and Sequences, published in 1862. In the Revised edition of 1875, the Compilers evaded the question by printing, with even less accuracy, "His precious Blood."[46] It is a justifiable generalization that many of the banalities of hymns are the results of such unresolved disagreements, and though that does not make the unsatisfactory compromise any more acceptable, it makes it harmless at least, and comprehensible.

Neale's work, however, was by no means faultless, and the Committee made a number of undeniable improvements in the simple matter of sense. Take, for instance, another stanza from "Urbs beata Jerusalem."

> nova veniens e caelo
>   nuptiali thalamo
> praeparata, ut sponsata
>   copuletur Domino;
> plateae et muri eius
>   ex auro purissimo

> New[ly] coming from heaven, prepared for the nuptial chamber, that she may be joined as a bride to the Lord; her streets and walls [are] of purest gold.[47]

Neale translates this stanza as follows:

> Coming new from highest heaven,
> Ready for the nuptial bed,
> Decked with jewels, to His Presence
> By her Lord shall she be led:
> All her streets and all her bulwarks
> Of pure gold are fashioned.

The image of the city with its architectural attributes so closely bound up with the image of the bride of Christ is confusing enough in the original Latin, though the image is an old one, and has the strength of familiarity. Neale's further confusion of the bridal image is incomprehensible: without having recourse to the doctrine of the Holy Trinity it is nigh impossible to explain how the bride can be led into the presence of the bridegroom by that bridegroom himself, though this is certainly what Neale has written. The fault lies in the need to fill out the lines of eight and seven syllables, when nearly all the English words are much shorter than their Latin equivalents, even with their attendant prepositions. Hence the number of words in Neale's version for which there is no Latin original. The Compilers of A & M, recognizing the problem, took bolder advantage of the solution Neale had indicated, and discarded literalness in favour of sense, even if expanded:

From celestial realms descending,
Bridal glory round thee shed,
Meet for Him whose love espoused thee,
To thy Lord shalt thou be led;
All thy streets and all thy bulwarks,
Of pure gold are fashioned.
(243/396i)

Though there may be conflicts and objections, the task of translating can be rewarding, for translation can often be a useful tool in literary appreciation. Neale found this to be true, and wrote warmly of "some of the happiest and most instructive hours of [his] life," spent on translation in committee:

> It was my business to lay before it the translations I had prepared, and theirs to correct. The study which this required drew out the beauties of the original in a way which nothing else could have done, and the friendly collision of various minds elicited ideas which a single translator would in all probability have missed.[48]

The Committee of A&M compilers worked in much the same way as Neale described, considering a given translation, often one of Neale's or Caswall's, but sometimes one submitted to them by one of their correspondents. The deliberations of the Committee can only be guessed from a comparison of translations in their original, specimen, and final versions. Among the A&M papers, however, are some of Harrison's notes on suggested versions and alterations. One of them in particular contains a tactful interchange between Harrison and Sir Henry. The hymn in question is one for Circumcision, Abbé Besnault's "Felix dies quam proprio," the translation of which in 1860 is based upon John Chandler's. Indeed, the choice of that translation was never much doubted: it appears in the first Specimen in almost the final A&M version (56/71). Sir Henry, however, proposed his own translation, the chief virtue of which, he claimed, was its accuracy. The second stanza, for instance, runs as follows in Sir Henry's translation:

> He was but born a week ago
> And now the precious blood drops flow
> Those first soft notes of mercy's strain
> That pledge of Calvary's bitter pain.
>
> (Vix natus ecce lacteum
> profundit infans sanguinem;
> Libamen est hoc funeris,
> Amoris hoc praeludium.)[49]

Sir Henry remarked in the margin against the last two lines of his stanza "I think I have caught the Latin." Harrison commented: "?Is this correct idea of praeludium." Harrison is being very cautious: another more dedicated to Neale's scrupulous standards might have questioned Sir Henry's right to substitute "mercy" for "love," "pledge" for "foretaste" or "preamble," and to import a musical metaphor -- all in two lines. The previous lines are equally free from literalness: "but born a week ago" is not the same as "vix natus," and the phrase "precious blood drops" is both awkward and commonplace.[50] Harrison's comment on the whole translation is "This trans^{n} more literal but not so good a hymn," and Sir Henry seems to have yielded. The stanza continued to give trouble: although the meaning was clear enough in the first Specimen (despite the need for seven words to express "vix natus")

> Scarce entered on this life of woe,
> His infant blood begins to flow;
> The earnest of His love for men,
> The foretaste of Death's bitter pain,

the rhyme was unsatisfactory until the last two lines were transposed and touched up as follows:

> A foretaste of His death He feels,
> An earnest of His love reveals.

Translations from other languages than Latin do not seem to have caused quite the same problems. The first edition contained no hymns from the Greek; the Appendix contained one from the Syriac, seven from Greek, and three on Greek models by Neale. On the whole these translations were not much altered by the A&M committee. Quite simply, there were far fewer versions from which to choose, and interest in Greek translations was relatively slight. When Neale published his *Hymns of the Eastern Church* in 1862, he wrote in the preface that "it is a remarkable fact, and one which shows how very little interest has hitherto been felt in the Eastern Church, that these are literally, I believe, the only English versions of any part of the treasures of Oriental Hymnology."[51] The next year, 1863, Richard Littledale published his *Offices of* the Holy Eastern Church, but the growing interest did not much infect the Committee, who were amateurs of Latin verse rather than Greek.

Nor did the Committee quibble much with translations from German, though they did ask Catherine Winkworth to recast lines they thought obscure or awkward. Only rarely did she use literalness as a defence, as for example, in the case of her hymn for the burial of a child, (358/402), from the German of J.W. Meinhold (published 1835). The first two lines originally read "Tender Shepherd, Thou hast stilled/Now Thy little Lamb's long weeping," and though she remarked to Sir Henry that it had clearly been written about some "special case [indeed, the author's own fifteen-month-old son] where the child must have been a great sufferer,"[52] she allowed the Committee to change "long" to "brief" -- a change which turns painfulness into poignancy. Other alterations of adjectives are merely matters of choosing more melodious combinations of adjectives ("To the sunny heavenly plain" in the second stanza of the same hymn becomes "To Thy meadows bright and fair"). Much of the last stanza of this hymn was recast, in particular the last couplet which was, Sir Henry suggested, awkward.

> Then the gain of death we prove,
> Though Thou take what most we love.

Winkworth replied:

> I suppose [the lines] mean that in heaven we shall see how death itself even when it takes our best-loved

> treasure may prove a gain, if it makes us desire to reach the same place of reunion & happiness.
> I can't put all that neatly into two lines, but I give a slightly modified version . . . if you like it.[53]

The 1875 edition duly contained the revision:

> Lost awhile our treasured love,
> Gained for ever, safe above,

which, though it loses the virtue of literalness, has at least a better rhyme than the earlier version.

It is not easy to discuss accuracy without impinging on the third criterion of a good translation -- its fluency. Certainly it was a frequent criticism of available translations, especially of Latin hymns, that they were un-English: Woodford complained of "laboured renderings, without flow,"[54] and recounted with some chagrin how a clerical acquaintance had laughed out loud at one of the specimen translations. Even earlier Braithwaite of Yorkshire had lamented "the almost impossibility of finding translations of the ancient Hymns -- which are not essentially Latin in their whole structure and expression -- & hardly adapted to the use & understanding of the poor. Could we have translations in flowing English & simple language we should only to be [sic] too glad to admit them."[55] J.M. Clarke expressed a similar concern that the poor understand: his objection to Mozley's hymnbook was that its translations were "so un-English in their words and idiom & rhythm, that I am sure with poor people they would fail to awaken the emotions they ought."[56]

A good example of the kind of Latinate structure objected to is to found in the Christmas hymn "Of the Father's love begotten" (46/56 "Corde natus ex parentis," a fourth/fifth century hymn of Prudentius). The eighth stanza was translated in the first Specimen as

> Thee let old men, Thee let young men,
>   Thee let boys in chorus sing;
> Thee the matrons and the virgins,
>   Little maidens answering;
> Let their guileless songs re-echo,
>   And the heart its praises bring,
>   Evermore and evermore!

That this is an accurate translation of the Latin words is undeniable, but that it conveys equally accurately the Latin structure is not so justifiable.

> Te senes et te iuventus
>   Parvulorum te chorus
> Turba matrum virginumque
>   Simplices puellulae
> Voce concordes pudicis
>   Perstrepant concentibus.

The pronoun "te," by its position first in the line and in the stanza, and by its reiteration, is given the central emphasis: the worshippers assemble behind the pronoun in phrase upon phrase, and the stanza comes to a resonating climax with the long-delayed verb (with its emphatic prefix "per"). It is effective in the Latin poem, but cannot work in English. The inversion is unnatural, but might have been acceptable if used only once; the English need for a verb means that the climax is dissipated in the weak anticipation "sing," and the women's chorus is left without any verbal support save the participle "answering," and of that one is not even sure to which noun it refers, and is left with the suspicion that it was introduced solely for its rhyme. This confusion is abated in the version published in 1860, but it is not a great improvement:

> Matrons, virgins, little maidens
> With glad voices answering.

Neale had a fondness for Latinate words, which manifests itself in the frequent doxology "Consubstantial, co-eternal,/ While unending ages run," which is nearly as frequently altered in A&M 1860 to "One in might and One in glory/While eternal ages run" (though restored in 1875, in keeping with the professed policy in that edition not to make, or keep, alterations without strong reason. See for example, "Blessed City, heavenly Salem" 243/396i). There is a weight and dignity in Neale's two words which conveys something of the majesty of the Trinity. Similarly, in stanza 3 of his version of "Jerusalem the golden" (142iii/ 228) Neale wrote "They stand, those halls of Sion,/ Conjubilant with song," and the word expresses far more strongly the heavenly unity and community of praise than the weaker A&M "All jubilant." Neale's multisyllabic words convey some impression of the original Latin texts, which usually have no more than three or four words per line, and which make the English translations look overcrowded by comparison. Again, a good example can be drawn from "Urbs beata Jerusalem," part ii, stanza 2:

All that dedicated City
   Dearly loved by God on high,
In exultant jubilation
   Pours perpetual melody;
God the One, and God the Trinal
   Lauding everlastingly.[57]

Neale's translation contains only five words more than the Latin, many of them derived from Latin themselves. The A&M Committee objected to the use of the word Trinal, perhaps on the grounds that it sounded too technical: certainly their alteration expressed the essential mystery of the Trinity in the plainest English: "God the One in Three."

Their alteration of another Neale Latinism in the immediately previous stanza is certainly acceptable. Neale concisely translated "quem Sion sancta suscepit/ in quo credens permanet" as "Holy Sion's acceptation,/ And her confidence alone." The A&M Committee no doubt realized that "acceptation"[58] was unhappily obscure, though it is a good rendering of the equally imprecise Latin "suscepit."[59] In this case as elsewhere, literalness was eschewed in favour of clear sense: "Holy Sion's help for ever."

Latin structure was one undeniable problem; Latin conceits another. The hymn for St. Stephen's Day (50/65) "First of martyrs," is a translation of de Santeuil's "O qui tuo dux martyrorum" in the Cluniac Breviary of 1686. It has been ingeniously constructed around the fact that the Greek name "Stephen" means a "crown." The first stanza is fairly straightforward, making the point about the name Stephen, and drawing a contrast between the martyr's crown and a garland of flowers:

> First of Martyrs, thou whose name
> Doth thy golden crown proclaim,
> Not of flowers that fade away
> Weave we this thy crown today.

> O qui tuo dux martyrorum
> Praefers coronam nomine
> Non de caducis floribus
> Tibi coronam nectimus.

The conceit is not entirely clear but may be explained thus: those singing the hymn are making a crown of praise for the martyr, not of flowers but of the details of the martyrdom -- stones and wounds and blood. Both the crown and the hymn are devised, woven, contrived in conceit. The translator's insertion of the word "golden" into the second line detracts from the effectiveness of the contrivance: a golden crown is a conventional contrast with a garland of flowers, but the hymn-writer is concerned to present an unconventional contrast. On the other hand, it is still closer to the Latin than the translation upon which the A&M version is based, which neglects entirely the Stephen word-play:

> Rightful prince of martyrs thou,
> Bind thy crown about thy brow.

It goes on to make explicit the point that this is a crown won in death, a very crown of death: a striking image anticipating the details of the following stanzas, but sadly weakened by the false note of its rhyme:

> Fairer far than fading wreath,
> Weave we this thy crown of death.

The hymn is intended to be a thing of contrasts: the second stanza compares the bloodied stones, the instruments of martyrdom, with a diadem made of stars:

> Bright the stones, which bruise thee, gleam,
> Sprinkled with thy life-blood's stream;
> Stars around thy sainted head
> Never could such radiance shed.
>
> Tuo cruenta sanguine
> Quam saxa fulgent pulchrius
> Aptata sacro vertici
> Non sic micarent sidera.

The third stanza is the extreme of the conceit:

> Every wound upon thy brow
> Sparkles with unearthly glow

is the translator's version. The crown is now nor name, nor flowers, nor stones, nor stars, but the wounds themselves. If the singers paused upon the thought, they might well be revolted by the image, but they are moved on immediately to a comparison which is paradoxically a contrast:

> Like an angel's is thy face
> Beaming with celestial grace.

The image shares a graphic quality with some of the more lurid products of popular iconography which cheaper methods of colour reproduction were making more widely available, and which "Protestants" abhorred on principle. The curious point about the image is that it is largely the work of the translator. The Latin reads:

> Quot facta fronti vulnera
> Tot tela lucis emicant.
> (As many wounds as are made on the brow, so many beams of light shine forth.)

The crown is one of light. The translator, in avoiding the awkwardness of that Latin structure "quot...tot," simplified the thought also, making it more literal or, as we have seen, more graphic. Even more than usual, the translator must be criticized for an unnatural rendering. The translation is, in fact, anonymous, "supplied by a friend" to Isaac Williams for his <u>Hymns translated from the Parisian Breviary</u>, 1839, and much revised by the Committee of A&M.

The lack of fluency in translation is exemplified best perhaps in doxologies, though it is not limited to them. The compression of a Latin doxology is hard to emulate in English, where reference has to be made to each of the Three Persons of the Trinity (and also, if possible, to one of the major points or to the occasion of the hymn, in order to maintain a connection between the body of the hymn and its doxology), all in four lines. The basic Latin doxology is simple enough:

Deo Patri sit gloria
Eiusque soli Filio
Sancto simul cum Spiritu
Nunc et per omne saeculum,

and can be adapted to C.M.:

All glory to the Father be,
All glory to the Son,
All glory, Holy Ghost, to Thee,
While endless ages run, (12/13)

or to L.M.:

All praise to God the Father be;
All praise, Eternal Son, to Thee;
Whom with the Spirit we adore
For ever and for evermore. (3/2)

Strict accuracy in translation is not necessary in a stock doxology, but a degree of fluency is. In the shorter metre, awkwardness is hard to avoid:

All glory to the Son,
Who comes to set us free,
With Father, Spirit, ever One,
Through all eternity. (34/48)

This short stanza (6.6.8.6.) manages to squeeze in a seasonal reference to Advent, but at the cost of a conjunction which makes the third line uneven, though not unintelligible.

An uninflected language means less flexibility

because position rather than accord determines which words are modified. The following doxology is strictly correct:

> Jesu, in mercy bring us
>   To that dear land of rest;
> Who art, with God the Father,
>   And Spirit, ever blest. (142/227)

The form "art" makes it clear that "who" can only refer to "Jesu," and not to "us," though it might be possible for an uneducated person to make the mistake. The Committee seems to have feared as much, in placing a semicolon at the end of the second line (in the Specimens they tried a colon) to break the connection between the relative pronoun and the preceding thought. It is not the simplest English, but it is not too serious a weakness, though the disrupted pattern can be found elsewhere:

> O Lord, the Virgin-born, to Thee
> Eternal praise and glory be;
> Whom with the Father we adore
> And Holy Ghost for evermore. (45/57)

Worse examples of unusually placed phrases can be found. In the same hymn as the above doxology are the lines:

> And heaven, and earth, and sea, and shore
> His love Who sent Thee here adore.
> (stanza 5, ll.3-4)

Normal English syntax would suggest "Heaven etc. . . . adore the love of Him Who sent Thee here," or even better, "adore Him Whose love sent Thee here." The effect of this non-idiomatic structure, together with the obtrusively compounded subject and the delayed principal verb is undeniably foreign. It was Sir Henry himself who was responsible for this translation.

Braithwaite and others had held up the importance of a hymn's being adapted to the use and understanding of the poor. Inversion within sentences, however, is not necessarily an obstacle to their understanding. The writers of street literature had no compunction about altering simple sentence structure in order to assure a rhyme at the end of a line or a sufficiency of syllables. Take, almost at random, a stanza from a sensational ballad printed in the 1860's by Disley of St. Giles:

> To the police he did a letter send,
> That he was about this life to end,
> And that he had poisoned, he did declare,
> His wife, and his six children dear.[60]

Nearly every phrase or word has been shifted which could have been without destroying the sense or the impetus of the lines. A&M rarely descends to that level, but it does contain, unlike that ballad stanza, syntax less clear and comprehensible. Those lines quoted above, from "O Christ, Redeemer of our Race," (45/57) could distract the singer from the act of praise to puzzle and doubt, and that is a potentially grave fault.

It could be argued that any regular churchgoer would not be confused by complexity of phrasing, having been long accustomed to the resonant but undeniably archaic language of the services of the Book of Common Prayer, with its doubled phrases and clause built upon clause. It would be hard to find, for example, more inverted a structure than those lines in the second collect at Evensong:

> ... and also that by Thee we being defended from the fear of our enemies may pass our time in rest and quietness.

The advantage that the services have over hymns is the frequency of their use, whereby what was obscure at first hearing may make sense after repetition. Furthermore, though it is not always the case, the congregation's understanding is aided by the parson's intonation (if the service is spoken) or phrasing (if sung). A hymn, on the other hand, may be sung only at very infrequent intervals, and there is very little opportunity in congregational singing to give the spacing and emphasis which might clarify the meaning. On the whole, the hymn editor's best policy is to preserve the hymns in as lucid, though not necessarily as simple, a form as possible.

Criticism of the A&M translations is frequent but often unsupported and difficult to illustrate. The Rev. J.A. Skinner wrote to Pulling a year after publication to record his complaints:

> I think every -- let me say <u>almost</u> every -- translation of Neales [sic] wch has been altered in H.A.M. has

> been altered for the worse. -- The Hymn has lost in spirit & vigour, & in the original effect, -- even where it may seem to have gained in exactness of rendering.[61]

In the preceding pages this generalization has been refuted by a number of counter-examples, but against Skinner's largely subjective judgment may be set Neale's own specific and honest approbation:

> I will freely & thankfully allow that, in some of your translations I think you have improved on our versions. . . . in 'Jesu, the very thought is sweet', you have got rid of the honey very well.[62]

The stanza as altered by the Committee reads:

> Jesu! the very thought is sweet!
> In that dear name all heart-joys meet:
> But oh! than honey sweeter far
> The glimpses of His presence are.

Neale's third line originally read "But sweeter than the honey far," where the insertion of the definite article is dictated by the metre, but is not English idiom. Skinner might, of course, have objected that the insertion of the interjection and exclamation was a greater weakness, being destructive of vigour, than Neale's article, except that stanza 3 contains a similar structure, "To them that seek Thee, oh how kind!" for which Neale is solely responsible.

5. Which Version?

In the section "On Translation," reference has been made to the two versions of "The Lamb's High Banquet" which were printed in A&M. Another hymn appeared twice in the collection, "Jesu dulcis memoria," long thought to be by St. Bernard, but now claimed by the Hymn Society of Great Britain and Ireland as the work of a twelfth-century English writer. It is a long poem of over thirty stanzas, and both Neale and Caswall made and translated centos of it. Caswall's is fifteen stanzas divided into three parts, and was published in _Lyra Catholica_, 1849. Neale's six-stanza cento was included in the _Hymnal Noted_, 1852. The Committee seemed unable to decide between the two versions, though neither of them entirely escaped alteration. The whole of Neale's hymn (65/177) and the corresponding stanzas of Caswall's (157/178) are given below together with the Latin text.

Jesu dulcis memoria,
Dans vera cordi gaudia:
Sed super mel et omnia
Dulcis eius praesentia.

Nil canitur suavius,
Nil auditur iucundius,
Nil cogitatur dulcius,
Quam Jesus Dei Filius.

Jesu, spes paenitentibus,
Quem pius es petentibus,
Quam bonus te quaerentibus,
Sed quid invenientibus?

Nec lingua valet dicere,
Nec littera exprimere;
Expertus novit credere,
Quid sit Jesum diligere.

Jesu, rex admirabilis,
Et triumphator nobilis,
Dulcedo ineffabilis,
Totus desiderabilis.

Neale's version amended in A&M:

Jesu! the very thought is sweet!
In that dear Name all heart-joys meet:
But oh! than honey sweeter far
The glimpses of His presence are.

No word is sung more sweet than this,
No sound is heard more full of bliss,
No thought brings sweeter comfort nigh,
Than Jesus, Son of God most High.

Jesu, the hope of souls forlorn,
How good to them for sin that mourn!

To them that seek Thee, oh how kind!
But what art Thou to them that find?

No tongue of mortal can express,
No pen can write the blessedness,
He only who hath proved it knows
What bliss from love of Jesus flows.

O Jesu, King of wondrous might!
O Victor, glorious from the fight!
Sweetness that may not be expressed,
And altogether loveliest!

Abide with us, O Lord, to-day,
Fulfil us with thy grace, we pray;
And with Thine own true sweetness feed
Our souls from sin and darkness freed.

Caswall's version, as amended in A&M:

Jesu, the very thought of Thee
   With sweetness fills the breast;
But sweeter far Thy face to see,
   And in Thy presence rest.

No voice can sing, no heart can frame,
   Nor can the memory find
A sweeter sound than Jesu's Name
   The Saviour of mankind.

O Hope of every contrite heart,
   O Joy of all the meek,
To those who fall how kind Thou art,
   How good to those who seek!

But what to those who find? Ah! this
Nor tongue nor pen can show;
The love of Jesus, what it is
None but His loved ones know.

Part II

O Jesus, King most wonderful,
Thou Conqueror renowned,
Thou sweetness most ineffable,
In Whom all joys are found!

Part III

Abide with us, and let Thy Light
Shine, Lord, on every heart;
Dispel the darkness of our night,
And joy to all impart.

Neale's version is in L.M., Caswall's, C.M. On the whole, Caswall's translation is more free. Neale, for example, gives the full force of the Latin participles in the third stanza "paenitentibus. . . quaerentibus . . . invenientibus," "that mourn . . . that seek . . . that find," but at the cost of smoothness, though the ejaculation might be claimed as a justifiable overflowing of emotion. Caswall's stanza, on the other hand, is altogether more flowing, so much so indeed that it spills over into the following stanza. This in turn forces Caswall to compress his translation where Neale has had to import words to fill out the lines (stanza 4). Neither translation expresses exactly the sense of the last line of the fourth stanza "Quid sit Jesum diligere" -- "What it is to love Jesus"; instead they both refer to the "love of Jesus," and it is not clear whether the genitive is objective or subjective.

These lines in Neale's version are not actually his at all, but the A&M Committee's. The Hymnal Noted stanza is one of Neale's more inept handlings. Literalness has sabotaged English in the second line, by keeping "letters" for "littera," and the verb in the active voice, when it would be more natural to speak either of letters being written, or of some instrument writing (which is what both Caswall and A&M choose):

> No tongue of mortal can express,
> No letters write its blessedness.

The last two lines of the stanza are in a structure not unusual in Neale: the subject is a clause, and the verb is delayed to the following line, together with an interjected apostrophe:

> Alone who hath thee in his heart
> Knows, love of Jesus! what thou art.

It is by turning the verses into prose that one really notices the distortion: "[He] alone who hath it in his heart knows what the love of Jesus is." Obviously one does not apply the standards of prose syntax to verse, but there is a danger of succumbing too readily to the pressure to distort the form which is determined by sense, in order to fit the form determined by the conventions of versification.

These are small points, but of interest to critics of translations. To critics of hymns, other points will be more important. They will criticize both versions in that fourth stanza for the inversions of syntax which mean that the third line must run on.

The untrained lungs of a congregation will demand a break, at the risk of a break in sense. This is not too serious a fault, for with a choir trained perhaps by Thomas Helmore or his brother, or by one of the graduates of St. Mark's College, Chelsea,[63] the hymn could be carried without serious loss.

Neale's version, largely because it is shorter, is more unified than Caswall's, where the development is more complex and the connections occasionally more vague. Neale's hymn has four stanzas dealing with humanity's experience and expression of the love of Jesus: the last two stanzas come from elsewhere in the poem, but they are tied in by the word "sweetness," which is contrasted with the might and majesty of the king who conquers death. The place of the singers is kept humble: there is no first person in the hymn until the supplication of the final stanza "Abide with us, O Lord, to-day." The very first stanza of Caswall's version originally contained a pronoun in the first person singular, which the A&M Committee quickly removed: "With sweetness fills my breast." The first person plural is frequent in the second and third parts of the hymn, where the poem concentrates on the duty and response of Christians to their Lord. On the whole, then, Neale's hymn is a tauter composition and a more literal translation than Caswall's: its singleness of purpose made the Compilers place it with the hymns for Epiphany in the Original edition, where it was intended to celebrate the manifestation of God in human form. In the Revised edition they printed it among the general hymns, where Caswall's version -- more diffuse in structure, more personal in tone, more free in translation -- had already found its place.

6. Alterations

The question of alterations has already been touched upon in the section above on translation, and also in the discussion of copyright in Chapter Three. In the first case, the alterations of translations may be considered a form of joint work or unasked-for collaboration; in the second case the chief question, particularly in the matter of Wordsworth's hymns, is not whether hymns ought to be altered, but whether they were altered against the author's will. In this section the more fundamental issues will be examined: the integrity of the original texts and the defensibility of adaptations of those texts for specific purposes.

The first and chief point to be made is that the editorial responsibility of a hymnal compiler is unlike that of a scholar whose first responsibility is to the text. The scholarly editor must establish an authoritative reading of the author's original or, where drafts and corrections survive, reveal this evidence of the processes of creation and refinement, of the author's struggle after finality. The integrity of the text is paramount. The hymnal compiler's first responsibility lies outside the text: it is to the purpose that the text will serve. That purpose is primarily the worship of God in its various aspects: adoration, praise, and thanksgiving. Inasmuch as a hymnal is designed for congregational worship it must conform to certain standards of suitability either in objectivity and sincerity, or in the more practical matter of suitability for singing. The diversity of sources from which hymns are drawn gives hymnody its richness, but also means that all hymns are not equally suitable for public worship in any one form in any given age. Thus the religious verses intended for private devotional purposes will not be immediately suitable for public use, or the hymns sung by a religious community will not serve the needs of an ordinary congregation, or a hymn which expresses some universal truth of Christian experience may do so in doctrinal terms which a particular denomination will be unable to accept. For all these reasons, alteration or adaptation is an essential tool in hymnal editing. The point was summarized by one editor, E.H. Bickersteth, who had evidently confronted the problem himself, and wrote of his father and predecessor in the same task:

> He saw with his strong practical sense that a hymnbook, drawn up for general use, stands on a footing entirely distinct from a literary edition of an author's work, where the first excellence is historical fidelity; and that there was no good reason why a beautiful hymn should be sacrificed because of some doctrinal or critical flaw in a single

> verse; or why real faults should be perpetuated and imposed upon thousands of congregations, in order to secure the integrity of a brief, and perhaps hasty, composition, as it first came from the author's pen.[64]

As Bickersteth goes on to say, the principle may well be sound, but is nonetheless subject to abuse. Alterations on doctrinal grounds are easier to justify than those on grounds of taste: sometimes it is not easy to distinguish to a nicety whether an objection to a particular form of words, or to a whole vocabulary, is a matter of doctrine or taste. Excessive alteration is equally difficult to establish: it would be foolish to set up either an optimum or a maximum number of permissible changes, though it would only be wise to question whether a hymn which had to be entirely recast was worth the attention. Nor should it be forgotten that hymns are verse, and sometimes poetry, not articles of belief, and that a hymn rendered unobjectionable by a zealous editor may at the same time lose all its real merits.

A contemporary parallel can be drawn between hymnal editors and ecclesiologists. Neither finds much of interest in the variants, irregularities, and exceptions which fascinate more scholarly minds. The Compilers of A&M were more concerned to establish correct versions, using doctrine and suitability for public worship as the standard of correctness which would, they hoped, eventually inform an official hymnal. In this respect, they were like those followers of the precepts of the Cambridge Camden Society who felt that

Decorated was the best Gothic, and who wished to restore all old churches in keeping with the fragments of Decorated which most of them possessed, all for the sake of correctness in ecclesiastical architecture.[65]

Neale's influence on hymnal editors is very strong. He allowed a hymn compiler "the most perfect right to make any alteration which he thinks advantageous to its general effect, if he only acknowledges his alterations or additions, or mutilations."[66] Neale was himself willing to countenance alterations in his translations that he considered improvements, but would have argued strenuously against anything he thought a mutilation. Yet he seemed unwilling to set a limit on alteration:

> ... there are some hymns which, unless they were almost entirely altered, would be out of the question for our future Church [authorized] Hymnal; but which, if they received the necessary corrections, might be none the worse when admitted.[67]

The examples he cites are "Rock of Ages" (150/184) as altered by himself, and "Guide me, O Thou great Jehovah" (338/196) as "transfigured by Mr. Keble for the Sarum Hymnal."[68] The second hymn is not quite a straightforward case, for it is a translation from the Welsh, though Keble's is a variation on the translation by Peter and William Williams:

> Guide me, O Thou great Jehovah,
> Pilgrim through this barren land;

I am weak, but Thou art mighty,
   Hold me with Thy pow'rful hand:
Bread of heaven, bread of heaven,
Feed me till I want no more.

Open now the chrystal fountain,
   Whence the healing stream doth flow;
Let the fire and cloudy pillar
   Lead me all my journey thro':
Strong Deliv'rer, strong Deliv'rer,
Be Thou still my strength and shield.

When I tread the verge of Jordan,
   Bid my anxious fears subside;
Death of death, and hell's
                    destruction,
   Land me safe on Canaan's side:
Songs of praises, songs of praises,
I will ever give to Thee.[69]

The references to the Old Testament God and the sustained imagery of the Exodus which give the hymn its shape sound well from the pen of the Welsh preacher, but Keble found them insufficiently Christian, and in his version, Jehovah makes way for Christ:

Guide us, Thou whose name is Saviour,
   Pilgrims in the barren land,
We are weak, and Thou Almighty,
   Hold us with Thy strong right-hand,
      As in Egypt,
   As upon the Red Sea strand.

Let the cloud and fire supernal
   Day and night before us go:

Lead us to the rock and fountain
Where the living waters flow:
Bread of Heaven,
Feed us, till no want we know.

When we touch the cold, dark river,
Cleave for us the swelling tide;
Through the flood and through the whirlpool
Let Thine Ark our footsteps guide:
Jesu, lead us,
Land us safe on Canaan's side.

Praise the Father, God of Heaven,
Him who reigns supreme on high;
Praise the Son, for sinners given,
E'en to suffer and to die;
Praise the Spirit,
Guiding us so lovingly.[70]

The use of the first person singular Keble considered uncongregational, and the robustness of the appeal seems to have displeased him. The straightforward "Feed me, till I want no more" is displaced from its original position, and replaced by a further reference to the Exodus, which is meant to underline the parallel with the Christian pilgrimage through life, ("Hold us... As in Egypt, As upon the Red Sea strand"), but serves only to reinforce the narrative or historical level of the hymn, rather than its immediacy. Furthermore, the overtones of human satisfaction are removed when Keble alters the original sentence to read "Feed us, till no want we know." It is weaker: one cannot quite imagine the pilgrims of Keble's version hungering and thirsting after righteousness with quite the same fervour as Williams'. Presumably Keble also objected to the suggestion of a bargain in the third stanza, instead of the undeserved grace of salvation. His alteration deprives the stanza of its greatest poetry, the contrast between human weakness ("my anxious fears") and the magnificently phrased version of the all-conquering God Who triumphs over death ("Death of death, and hell's destruction"), and yet may be called upon to care for one timid soul. Keble's literalness ("the cold, dark river," "the swelling tide," "the flood," "the whirlpool") is tedious in comparison, and for all his direct invocation ("Jesu, lead us") this stanza is further from the triumph of the New Testament than Williams', where the ransomed Christian's rapture of praise is the correct final note -- "and all the trumpets sounded for him on the other side." Keble's pilgrims, plodding behind their symbol of the Old Testament convenant, ("Let Thine Ark our footsteps guide"), cross the Jordan but it is no climax. One feels that their arrival, like that of the people of Israel after forty years in the wilderness, is only another beginning, not a consummation, and this impression is confirmed when the hymn does not end even there, but continues into a doxology.

The version which appeared in the A&M Appendix is largely the early translation, though it too deposes "Jehovah" in favour of "Redeemer," which is an improvement on Keble's roundabout phrase; furthermore, it avoids the suggestion of appetite and satiety in the last line of the first stanza by substituting "Feed me now and evermore."

The case of "Rock of Ages" reveals Neale in two minds about alterations and highlights the difficulties an editor faces. Neale had publicly praised the hymn as "absolutely in the first class of hymns" with "Vexilla regis" and both "Pange lingua," declaring that it would "live as long as the world lasts . . . spite of vile rhyme, vulgar expressions, and doctrine, not necessarily false, but from such an author more than questionable."[71] Before its publication, he had written to object to A&M's proposed version:

> 'Rock of Ages' is completely spoilt: that humble, however coarse, second verse you have filed all the sharpness off. . . . Now by a very slight alteration you might easily get rid of one or two jarring words, & save a verse which I confess I can never repeat without the tears coming into my eyes.[72]

The A&M version is in three stanzas of which the second is a pastiche of the second and third stanzas of the original. The texts are set out below, of Toplady's original, A&M's 1860 version, and Neale's improvements. The alterations in the later versions are indicated.

Toplady, Psalms and Hymns, 1776.

Rock of ages, cleft for me,
Let me hide myself in Thee!
Let the Water and the Blood
From Thy riven Side which flow'd,
Be of sin the double cure;
Cleanse me from it's [sic] guilt and pow'r.

Not the labours of my hands
Can fulfill thy law's demands:
Could my zeal no respite know,
Could my tears for ever flow,
All for sin could not atone:
Thou must save, and Thou alone.

Nothing in my hand I bring;
Simply to thy Cross I cling;
Naked, come to Thee for dress;
Helpless, look to Thee for grace;
Foul, I to the Fountain fly:
Wash me, Savior, or I die!

While I draw this fleeting breath --
When my eye-strings break in death --
When I soar through tracts unknown --
See Thee on thy judgment throne --
Rock of ages, cleft for me,
Let me hide myself in Thee!

A&M 1860

Rock of ages, cleft for me,
Let me hide myself in Thee;
Let the Water and the Blood,
From Thy wounded Side which flowed,
Be of sin the double cure,
Save from wrath and make me pure.

Nothing in my hand I bring,
Simply to Thy Cross I cling:
Could my tears for ever flow,
Could my zeal no languor know,

All for sin would not atone,
Thou must save and Thou alone.

While I draw this fleeting breath,
When *mine eyelids close* in death,
When I *rise to worlds* unknown,
See Thee on Thy judgment throne,
Rock of ages, cleft for me,
Let me hide myself in Thee.

Neale's amended version (*Christian Remembrancer*)

Rock of Ages cleft for me,
Let me hide myself in Thee!
Let the Water and the Blood,
From Thy riven Side's *dear flood*,
Be of sin the double cure,
Cleanse from guilt and keep me pure.

Not the labours of my hands
Can *fulfil Thine own commands*;
Could my zeal no respite know,
Could my tears for ever flow,
All for sin could not atone;
Thou must save and Thou alone.

Nothing in my hand I bring;
Only to Thy Cross I cling;
Naked, come to Thee for dress;
Helpless, come in *helplessness*;
Vile, *to David's* Fountain fly:
Cleanse me, Saviour, or I die.

Fourth stanza as original.

Neale seems to have been in two minds about the roughness of the hymn's expression: he altered the first stanza to improve the rhymes "blood/flowed" and "cure/power." Similarly he reworked the penultimate line of the stanza he found most moving, the third, to avoid the awkwardness of "Foul, I to the Fountain fly," with the assonance and alliteration which make it difficult to sing. Nevertheless he had scornful words for those who "prettified" the hymn:

> In the third verse [of the A&M version] you have substituted the pretty lady-like expression 'eyelids closed', [sic] instead of the strong phrase of the original, 'eye strings break'.[73]

One is allowed to improve the sound of the lines, it seems, but not to tamper with the images. One wonders, therefore, how Neale justified his substitution of the word "cleanse" for the more literal verb "wash" in the third stanza: it is dangerously close to prettifying, in contrast with the uncompromisingly blunt words which precede it: "naked . . . helpless . . . foul."

"Rock of Ages" remained an editorial problem: there were others who praised its "grand roughness, boldness & force," and saw it as a "kind of protest against what is the danger of modern hymns, an over softness of phrase."[74] Not all agreed that the phrase "eyestrings break" should be restored, though Dean Church was sure that once "people got used to it, as they soon would, they would no longer be startled, & then, the force, & not the strangeness, would remain."[75] The Proprietors considered printing both the original and an amended version in the Revised edition as a kind of uneasy compromise, but "it was finally settled that the original version be printed alone."[76] The controversial "eyestrings" was the only expression not restored, but on the whole "Rock of Ages" exemplifies the policy announced by the Proprietors in their 1875 Preface: "The general desire is rather to have a Hymn as its author wrote it; and the Compilers are expected not to make changes in it without strong reason."

A lesser instance of the Proprietors' implementing this policy is in "Thou Whose almighty Word" (220/360) by John Marriott, whose son had complained of the alteration of a phrase:

> 'Spreading the beams of grace' is printed instead of 'Bearing the lamp of grace' -- which is the original & better for singing -- & I don't see anything gained in sense or imagery by the alteration. As a rule, I dislike altering a man's own way of putting things on principle -- & certainly, where the improvement is not manifest, it is a pity.[77]

The Proprietors apparently appreciated the complaint when it reached them, for the original is restored in 1875.

Alterations are justifiable on four chief grounds: briefly, those of doctrine, circumstance or occasion, intelligibility, and musicality. No one is unequivocally in favour of printing what authors wrote: the question is the extent to which alterations are permissible. In the two cases discussed above, the Compilers of A&M faced the problem and worked out their own solution. Let us look now at some more detailed cases for alteration.

Doctrinal grounds are immediately understandable. The Church of England, being both Catholic and Reformed, has an immense heritage from its past, and close ties with its fellow churches. Obviously, as Bickersteth had seen, it was wasteful to deprive the church of its inheritance, if doctrinal alterations could be silent, and no more objectionable than the kind of scientific updating, for instance, in Neale's translation of the eighth-century Greek hymn "The Day of Resurrection" (290/132). No one who paused to think would attribute to St. John Damascene the Copernican revelation implicit in the third stanza "Now let . . . . The <u>round world</u> keep high triumph" [emphasis added]. The principle is the same as the one which Isaac Watts practised more boldly and on a wider scale, when he wrote his paraphrases of the Psalms, in which the Old Testament is presented in the light of the subsequent Christian revelation. Watts had deplored the possibly pernicious effect of the unmodified psalms upon his congregation:

> Here I may with Courage address myself to the Heart and Conscience of many pious and observing Christians, and ask them, Whether they have not found a most divine Pleasure in

> Singing, when the Words of the Psalm have happily express'd their Frame of Soul? . . . Have not your Spirits taken Wing, and mounted up near to God and Glory with the Song of David on your Tongue? But on a sudden the Clerk has proposed the next Line to your Lips with dark Sayings and Prophecies, with Burnt-Offerings and Hyssop, with New-Moons, and Trumpets and Timbrels in it, with Confession of Sins which you never committed, with Complaints of Sorrows such as you never felt, cursing such Enemies as you never had, giving thanks for such Victories as you never obtained, or leading you to speak in your own Person of Things, Places and Actions, that you never knew. And how have all your Souls been discomposed at once, and the Strings of Harmony all untuned! You could not proceed in the Song with your Hearts, and your Lips have sunk their Joy and faultered [sic] in the Tune; you have been baulked and ashamed, and knew not whether it were best to be silent or to follow on with the Clerk and the Multitude, and sing with cold Devotion, and perhaps in Darkness too, without Thought or Meaning.[78]

In the next century the correct use of the Psalms

in public worship was still a subject of discussion for the same reasons. Their place in the Book of Common Prayer was unquestioned, even though the Shortened Services Act of 1872 had allowed the use of only one psalm for weekday services. The clerical attitude is expressed by H.P. Liddon:

> The Psalms surely are an ideal expression of religious life -- proper to the Collective Church or to Our Lord but only aimed at and accepted with necessary reservations and limits by the sinful individual member.[79]

The objection is of course that one cannot be sure that one's less well-educated congregation will make the necessary mental reservations. The Psalms by tradition occupy such an important place in the Anglican liturgy that the objection may be waived in their case, but there seemed no reason why hymns should not be utterly unexceptionable. The efforts of the Compilers to make them doctrinally so are discussed at some length in the following section of this chapter.

Alterations on circumstantial grounds are those which are made to fit for congregational singing hymns originally sung in different circumstances, or verses written for other uses. The simplest alteration of this kind has already been seen in Keble's change of the first person singular to the plural in Williams' "Guide me, O Thou great Jehovah," though it was not an alteration the Compilers adopted. They did, however, alter the pronouns in Part 3 of Edward Caswall's translation of "Jesu dulcis memoria," (157/178) where one stanza is particularly egocentric:

Caswall:

O my sweet Jesu! hear the sighs
Which unto Thee I send;
To Thee my inmost spirit cries,
My being's hope and end!

A&M 1860:

O most sweet Jesu, hear the sighs
Which unto Thee we send;
To Thee our inmost spirit cries,
To Thee our prayers ascend.

Elsewhere, Caswall used the first person plural, which the Compilers retained. Similarly, a Lenten hymn by Isaac Williams "Lord, in this Thy mercy's day" (82/94) originally contained both singular and plural pronouns, but in A&M they are all plural.

The principle was not an invariable one: many hymns written in the first person singular are untouched in that respect, when the pronoun brings home the intensity of the experience related ("When I survey the wondrous Cross" 101/108) or the individual commitment and resolve of the Christian ("Awake, my soul, and with the sun" 1/3). Thus did John Ellerton defend his usage to Sir Henry when challenged about his "Throned upon the awful Tree" (--/118):

> I have not thought it objectionable, in a meditative hymn of this sort, to speak in the first person *singular*. It seems to me more pointed.[80]

Conversely, an original plural may be made singular, as in "Be Thou my Guardian and my Guide" (334/282), a version of one of Isaac Williams' Hymns on the Catechism (1842), which he based on the petition "Lead us not into temptation" in the Lord's Prayer. The Compilers clearly felt that the pleas of this hymn might be sung with more fervour if the temptations appeared particular rather than general, and throughout the hymn "we" becomes "I":

> Be Thou my Guardian and my Guide,
>   And hear me when I call;
> Let not my slippery footsteps slide;
>   And hold me lest I fall.

In most cases the Revised edition repeats these alterations from 1860. In one hymn, however, ("All ye who seek for sure relief" 158/112) by Edward Caswall, a first person singular which had stood in both the original and A&M 1860 was altered in 1875, not because the singular was in itself objectionable, but because in the previous stanza Christ's words were paraphrased "All ye that labour, come to Me,/And I will give you rest." The Compilers wished to remove any potential source of confusion by changing every other "I" in the hymn to "we."

A particular example of changing a hymn to suit the changed circumstances of its use is one of C.F. Alexander's hymns which was published in the Appendix (363/331), "We are but little children weak." As she explained in a letter to Sir Henry:

> It was written exclusively for very

> poor children at a crowded city Sunday school. I have endeavoured to alter the first verse so as to make it more fit for a mixed congregation, but I am afraid I have done it badly.[81]

The original opening read "We are but little children poor/ And born in very low estate"; the Appendix prints: "We are but little children weak,/ Nor born in any high estate." Similarly the seventh stanza is recast in order to avoid a reference to "our dwellings dim." The alterations make the hymn more generally useful, though it is still primarily intended for the young. Alexander considered it suitable "for a mixed congregation," and the Compilers did not preclude the possibility of its being so used. Christian humility will accept on a metaphorical level the frequent use of "child" by adults. A stanza which is harder to read mataphorically is omitted by A&M:

> When adverse seems our parents' will,
> 　And hard the effort to obey,
> Then we may cross our own desire;
> 　'Tis thus he bids us die to-day.[82]

That best-known of Victorian hymns "Abide with me" (14/27) was written in terms and circumstances which would seem to disqualify it from congregational use. The Rev. H.F. Lyte wrote it before leaving his parish to die abroad: it is suitable for an evening service only if one resolutely reads its metaphors literally, though it might be justified on the grounds that Christians need fear death no more than nightfall, and that it is a daily rehearsal of their deathbed. The last stanza must be sung as a statement of faith, for none can speak truthfully of any experience of "heaven's morning," though they can sing with sincerity what is a poetic affirmation of the creed's "And I look for the Resurrection of the dead, and the life of the world to come." Not all the stanzas are suitable for such use, however, and the Compilers found the fifth stanza of the original[83] too autobiographical:

> Thou on my head in early youth didst smile;
> And, though rebellious and perverse
> meanwhile,
> Thou hast not left me, oft as I left Thee,
> On to the close, O Lord, abide with me.

The stanza is reminiscent of the second stanza of Newman's "Lead, kindly Light," printed in the A&M Appendix, in which he confesses "Pride ruled my will: remember not past years." Indeed, Lyte may well have known Newman's poem, which was first published in 1834, thirteen years before Lyte's death.

Two hymns caused the Compilers problems because of certain expressions which might have been considered unsuitable for congregational use. One of these hymns is Faber's "O come and mourn with me awhile" (100/114) which is discussed at length below. The other hymn is John Newton's "How sweet the Name of Jesus sounds" (185/176), where the fourth stanza is an effusion of grateful praise:

> Jesus! my Shepherd, Husband, Friend,
> My Prophet, Priest, and King,

> My Lord, my Life, my Way, mine End,
> Accept the praise I bring.

The stanza is a striking expression of the complete and loving surrender to the Lord in which Christians find their freedom. The doubtful expression is that "Husband": the Compilers allowed it in 1860, but during the preparation of the Revised edition, they consulted a number of clergymen whose opinions might have some authority. Their responses are worth quoting for their range. Dr. Pusey felt that "in a <u>mixed congregation</u>" the title were better avoided, though he confessed his "knowledge of hymns . . . very limited."[84] Christopher Wordsworth held an opposite view, though his reasons were more subjective than rational:

> Though I do not go so far as you do in saying that to change the word 'husband' would deny scriptural truth: yet I confess that I should mourn if the alteration were made. The best side of the early evangelical movement was a passionate love of our Lord. Would that we had it in these days.
>
> It is an assumed precept that in a hymn you may use warmer language than the mass of the Congregation feel, with a view to the words drawing them upwards.[85]

Dr. Bright's contrary opinion is clearly stated:

> I own that I am on the side of those

> who think that it is not for any individual christian, as a general rule, to apply for himself that sort of language as regards Our Lord: it is, I am disposed to think, the whole church only that can with propriety . . . call Him Spouse or Husband: unless exception be made, as, no doubt, from ancient times has been made, for women dedicated to His special service. In this Hymn we have the language put into the mouth of a devout individual Christian, and I think it had better not be so used even in private, -- for the sake of reverence. When it comes to be used congregationally, I think the objection is rather increased than lessened: no one reading or hearing the Hymn will suppose that the Church is meant to be the speaker; and when the congregation is largely composed of men, I think that a peculiar sense of incongruity results.[86]

These arguments do not seem to have touched the Compilers, for the word remains in the Revised edition. Sir Henry himself seems to have had no doubt about the propriety of the expression, and seems deliberately to have sought support for his view. Of the three authorities to be consulted mentioned in the Minute Book (Dr. Pusey, Dr. Bright, and the Bishop of Brechin)[87] two opposed the usage, and no letter from the third has been preserved, though it may be inferred that the Bishop would not have objected. In an earlier letter he had described an unspecified hymn:

> ... The one you send me is in exquisite bad taste but still there is a swing about it which . . . account [sic] for its popularity. With the Song of Solomon in the Canon we cannot except at the verses you have marked theologically.[88]

The Minute Book does not record Christopher Wordsworth's name as an authority to be consulted; nevertheless, the draft of Sir Henry's letter to him begins "I am desired by my colleagues . . . to ask you a question which I shd not myself have thought capable of doubt."[89] Although one cannot now be certain, it seems as if Sir Henry was deliberately seeking an opinion to counteract the strong statement he expected and received from Dr. Bright. The case reveals both the strength and a weakness in the editorial method of A&M: the willingness of the Proprietors to listen to more authoritative voices than their own, and the manipulation, however well-intended, to which the Proprietors, functioning as a committee, were subject.

There was considerable correspondence between Sir Henry and Henry Twells on the subject of the latter's "At even ere the sun was set" (276/20). The grounds for its alteration may be called circumstantial, in that both gentlemen were concerned to print a hymn to be sung at an evening service by an ordinary congregation without their falling into either hypocrisy or ridicule. It is to Sir Henry's great credit that he disregarded many of the minor points raised by Twells, who may have been too scrupulous and literal. With reference to his third stanza ("O Saviour Christ, our woes dispel;/For some are sick, and some are sad") Twells ventured:

> What do you say to substituting 'weak' for 'sick' . . .? Perhaps weakly people are more likely to be at Church than 'sick' people.[90]

A&M printed 'sick.' Sir Henry, however, was equally concerned about some of the implications of the hymn. Twells' fourth stanza ran:

> And some are pressed with worldly care,
> And some are tried with sinful doubt;
> And some such grievous passions tear
> That only Thou canst cast them out.

Sir Henry considered the construction of the last two lines unclear; Twells promptly offered two variations:

> And some whom grievous passions tear
> (Have fail'd themselves) to cast them out.
> (Entreat Thy aid)[91]

Sir Henry, however, accused him of preaching demoniacal possession, and threatened to relegate the hymn to "special missions." Twells made another attempt to salvage the stanza, but conceded that it might be better omitted:

(weigh'd down)
And some (oppress'd) by earthly care
Have anxious nights & weary days:
And some have wandering thoughts in prayer,
And (only lukewarm) hearts in praise.
(far too sluggish)[92]

The stanza was omitted.

Such joint revisions are not the same as an editor's unilateral alterations, but they do illustrate some of the same concerns. The frequent requests of contemporary writers, such as Godfrey Thring, to be allowed to approve alterations proposed by the Compilers were heeded, though it may be inferred that Sir Henry was happier with those hymn-writers who were more willing to defer to his judgment.

It is interesting to note to what extreme the principle of congregational suitability might have been carried. There is in an early letter to Sir Henry a passing reference to a proposed "Expurgate Edition for popular use."[93] No further mention is made of it: one must assume that the Committee felt that such an edition would only prove that their editorial powers were inadequate to the task of preparing a book for use at all levels of society, as one book served for common prayer, and would betray their own first principle of promoting uniformity in hymnody.

Alterations on grounds of intelligibility are usually quite straightforward: the subject is touched upon in the section on translation, and was one that troubled conscientious editors. Woodford, writing when A&M had just been conceived, spoke of his own policy, the "exclusion of every technical or scholastic word such as abound in Neale's translations, and the omission of any verse in which the allusions seemed too remote for popular appreciation."[94] In section 4 of this chapter are given three examples of "technical or scholastic" words, "acceptation," "conjubilant," and "Trinal," which the Compilers excised in accordance with a policy like Woodford's. Only in the first case is the Compilers' substitution unquestionably preferable to Neale's original choice.

It has been seen that complex structures were not necessarily a problem to even an uneducated congregation, and certainly not to one familiar with the complexities of the language of the Book of Common Prayer. Nevertheless, the Compilers were careful to identify potential causes of misunderstanding. A good example is W.C. Dix's hymn, "Come unto Me, ye weary," which was the subject of some correspondence before it was printed in the Revised edition (--/256). In the second stanza, Dix describes how Christ refreshes benighted wanderers:

> But morning brings us gladness,
> And songs the break of day.

In reply to Sir Henry's query, Dix wrote:

> I think poor people <u>ought</u> to understand that it is the 'break of day' which brings the 'songs' & not v.v.

In case they might not, he kindly offered a number of variations:

But morn shall bring the gladness
   Of full Salvation's day
               or
But, o the joy & gladness
   When Christ reveals the Day!
               or
But Jesu's Voice brings gladness
   We hear it as we pray.
               or
your own[95]

Eventually the lines read

But He has brought us gladness
   And songs at break of day,

which has the virtue of being clear and at the same time close to what Dix originally wrote.

Other problems were not so easily solved. One of the stickiest was "My God, I love Thee" (88/106), a translation, chiefly by Caswall, of the Latin hymn "O Deus ego amo te," said to be a seventeenth-century religious sonnet from the Portuguese. The first two lines read:

My God, I love Thee; not because
   I hope for heaven thereby.

The fear was that, especially when sung, the punctuation might be disregarded, and the shocking and heretical nonsense be heard. When asked for an opinion on the subject, H.P. Liddon ventured:

> If the reading 'I love Thee; not because', were properly punctuated (;--) the objection you feel vanishes.
> To begin with 'My God' instead of "I love Thee Lord' is less egoistic?[96]

The hymn being popular in Tractarian circles, it was left as written, although when the 1875 revision was undertaken the question was raised again. By that time the hymn was far more widely known, and it was too late to change it. As Sabine Baring Gould noted:

> Do not see advantage of change which will only perplex. 'My God I love thee' is so familiarised with us now that an alteration will irritate if made in the first line.[97]

The unexpected construction probably had only a good effect, as even unenthusiastic churchgoers could not fail to reject the reading "My God, I love Thee not," and begin to consider more closely than usual the sense of the words they were singing.

A similar case is that of the German hymn for Easter by C.F. Gellert, the first line of which in Frances Cox's translation is "Jesus lives! no longer now" (117/140). In print, the lines offer little problem: the exclamation mark is unmistakable and the line is not end-stopped:

> Jesus lives! no longer now
> Can thy terrors, Death, appal us.

In singing, however, the immediate sense is a direct contradiction of the spirit of Easter, and there seems no real justification for perpetuating the confusion. It would not have been difficult to amend the line to remove the stumbling-block, but the hymn remained unchanged in the Revised edition, although _Church Hymns_ had printed "Jesus lives! Thy terrors now/ Can no longer, Death, appal us" in 1871. _Church Hymns_ was, however, one of A&M's chief competitors, and the Proprietors were not accustomed to borrowing from it. In 1880 Thring published in his _A Church of England Hymnbook Adapted to the Daily Services of the Church throughout the Year_, a variation which received Cox's approval, and has since become the usual form: "Jesus lives! thy terrors now/ Can, O Death, no more appal us."

A hymn which caused Sir Henry great uneasiness was "All hail the power of Jesu's Name" (301/300). In this case he could not correspond with an obliging author, for Edward Perronet died in 1792. The chief problem was not so much one of intelligibility, as of interpretation. The third line of the fourth stanza in the original (the third stanza in A&M) reads "Extol the stem of Jesse's rod." Not long before the publication of the Appendix, Sir Henry was seized by a doubt.

> Are you _quite_ sure that we are right in altering the original line
> 'Extol the stem of Jesse's rod'
> into
> 'Of Jesse's stem extol the rod'?
> It is a serious matter to make such a change unless we are _quite_

> sure. . . . Are [the commentators] wrong in saying that the rod is the B.V.M., and Christ the Branch or Flower growing from her? In verse 11th of Isaiah xi is not Christ meant by the 'root' or stem? . . . I don't think the subject was ever properly discussed at our meetings: I admit that I for one spoke too hastily about it.
> . . . Far better just give the original untouched, unless we are **quite** clear that it must be altered. . . . I am inclined on the whole to **omit** that verse altogether.[98]

Dr. Pusey, when appealed to, opined that "the most literal reading would be 'of Jesse's stump extol the Rod' but stump is undignified in English."[99] The alteration was allowed in the Appendix, though in the Revised edition, the words were restored to their original order, while the Appendix sense was retained by the use of hyphens: "Extol the stem-of-Jesse's Rod." The Compilers' reliance upon punctuation to convey such an important change, and silent punctuation, too, (that is, which could not be expressed by the voice to those who could not see the text) seems an unhappy and dishonest compromise. Sir Henry does not seem to have recovered the confidence which he had so badly lost over this hymn. In the same letter to Pulling in 1868, he had suggested printing Perronet's original final stanza, the second line of which is unclear:

> Let every tribe and every tongue
> That bound creation's call,
> Now shout in universal song
> The crownèd Lord of all.

The alteration proposed was

> Let every tribe and every tongue
> Before Him prostrate fall,
> And shout etc.

Sir Henry wrote:

> And in that last verse the prostrate 'tongue' is not very good. Shall we restore the original . . .? Far better let the original be blamed than us for altering: but we may omit.[100]

The stanza was not omitted, but it was altered, and no better alteration has yet found its way into common use.

Alterations on grounds of musicality are usually simple. By musicality is meant those characteristics which are conducive to good singing. Thus changes which improve rhymes, as long as they do not interfere with some other beauty of the hymn or with its sense, are good in that the ring of a true rhyme is satisfying, and is perhaps the poetic quality most easily recognizable to an unsophisticated ear. Neale had a strong view on this matter too: all common metre hymns ought to rhyme a b a b, not just a b c b. C.M., he wrote, citing Chapman's Homer, is the metre of English historic narrative, but when it is used in lyric, "as all hymns are but short odes -- then all graces of sound, as well as all the fascination of sense, ought to coalesce."[101] These desiderata are better instructions for translators than for editors, for the recasting of someone else's lines in order to secure better rhymes is fraught with danger. Wisely, the Compilers did not attempt to improve rhymes unless a hymn or a translation was to be recast anyway. An amusing letter on the subject of rhyme was written by the Rev. John Monsell to Sir Henry, who had apparently sent him some comments upon his latest book, probably _The Parish Hymnal after the Order of the Book of Common Prayer_, 1873. Monsell wrote:

> I see we do not judge in these matters by the same laws, wh may acct for your occasional censure of what I wd deem correct. You for example judge of rhymes by the eye, I by the ear. You condemn 'risen' & 'prison' . . . 'true' & 'do' -- while you sanction 'hour' & 'pour', 'live' & 'strive', 'door' & 'poor'. Now I consider my rhymes in these words to be better than yours for _sound_, & sound in the reading & singing of Poetry is I deem all important. Then again you don't on other occasions seem to be guided by either sight or sound. [He cites Charles Wesley's "Lo He comes" (39/51) where] 'bears' & 'worshippers' &

> 'scars' [are] supposed to rhyme, but without evidence of it to _eye_ or _ear_.[102]

Such criticism serves little purpose: one can easily find numerous examples of imperfect rhymes at random in any collection, and A&M is no exception. Charles Wesley is particularly prone to such "faults": his first hymn in A&M 1860, "Forth in Thy Name" (6/8) rhymes "pursue/or do," "yoke/look," and "given/Heaven," but one must be grateful that they have not been improved.

For hymns to be suitable for singing they must be limited rhythmically; that is to say, the shifts of rhythmic stress and speed which give poetry much of its force, are overridden by the regular stresses of modern barred music. (The freer Gregorian chants which were revived in the nineteenth century were not so restrictive, but that subject lies outside this study.) Hence it is important that the rhythm of the words not conflict with that of the music, and hymns are often rhythmically tedious when merely read aloud. This necessity makes it difficult to use as a hymn poems which were not intended for such use, especially if the poems are very good, for they are more likely than mere versification to contain subtle rhythmic effects. This is not a real problem in the early editions of A&M, which do not contain hymns drawn from the unusual sources later collections sometimes tapped. Verses written for private devotional purposes often have more irregularities which only become obvious when they are put to congregational use. One of the stanzas omitted from the A&M version of "Abide with me" runs thus:

Not a brief glance, I beg, a passing
word;
But as Thou dwellest with Thy
disciples, Lord;
Familiar, condescending, patient, free,
Come not to sojourn, but abide with me.

The short words and light stresses of the first line give it a speed which reflects its meaning, but the rhythm of those first words is not the same as that of the other stanzas, where the stress falls on the second syllable, making an iambic foot. (Set to music, the natural stress at the beginning of a bar also emphasizes the first syllable, so that the total effect is spondaic: Abíde, I féar, Hóld Thóu.) This irregularity would not be enough to warrant the omission of the stanza, for the second stanza printed has a similar initial trochaic foot, "Swíft to its clóse," but the third line is another musical problem. Monk's tune "Eventide" was composed especially for the hymn in A&M 1861, a good example of Monk's popular facility. The shape of the third musical line, however, with its slow second bar and pathetic series of descending notes does not fit the words of the stanza in question: "Familiar, condescending, patient, free" -- for the second word is stretched to the breaking point over the slow interval, and the rest of the word "-descending" literally descends the scale. It is an unfortunate effect. These two problems of "musicality," together with the slightly extraneous nature of the stanza, are enough to justify its omission.

There is evidence of the Compilers' attention to "musicality" or rhythm in the correspondence with the authors of new hymns. C.F. Alexander sent a hymn on St. Mark the Evangelist for the Revised edition (--/410) beginning "Out of the cloud of amber light,' which she altered to "From out the cloud," realizing that the initial trochee in an iambic line was not as good for singing as the more regular rhythm of the more unusual phrase "from out."[103]

The conventions of hymn-singing make some "musical" alterations unnecessary, as, for instance, in Charlotte Elliott's hymn "Just as I am" (--/255), which was first included in the Revised edition. The second line of the second stanza there printed "With many a conflict, many a doubt" strictly contains two syllables more than it ought, but the syllables disappear in singing: "With man-ya conflict, man-ya doubt," by a kind of elision in which the "y" acts more as a consonant than as a vowel. This effect is so usual in singing that there was no need to indicate it when printing the hymn. Similarly, the Compilers did not indicate the most common elisions: the word "heaven," for example, is fully spelled out, even though it is almost always pronounced "heav'n"; only rarely is it given its two full syllables as in "God, Who madest earth and heaven" (18/26), but there is no easy way to indicate this in the text. Conversely, there are some elisions most carefully noted: "O the wisdom of th' Eternal!" ("He Who once in righteous vengeance," 90/102), and in the case of past participles, the syllable is marked when it is to be pronounced, as in "Blessèd city, heavenly Salem" (243/396i), which contains the unusual usage "fashionèd" to rhyme with "led." Even when the participles can be differentiated by their spellings, the marking is not omitted: "Again the Lord's own day is here" (22/35) contains "blest" in the third stanza (to rhyme with "possest" -- which seems to be a case, to use Monsell's words, of rhyming by eye, as there is only the purest phonetic reason for not printing "possessed"), while "blessèd" appears in the fourth.

Having noted various reasons for editorial alterations, and examples thereof, let us look at one hymn and analyze the changes it has undergone to be fitted for A&M. The hymn is Faber's for Passiontide, "O come and mourn with me awhile" (100/114). The original hymn was published in _Jesus and Mary_ (1849) in the following form:

1 O come and mourn with me awhile;
See, Mary calls us to her side;
O come and let us mourn with her, --
Jesus, our Love, is crucified!

2 Have we no tears to shed for Him,
While soldiers scoff and Jews deride?
Ah! look how patiently He hangs,--
Jesus, our Love, is crucified!

3 How fast His Hands and Feet are nailed;
His blessed Tongue with thirst is tied,
His failing Eyes are blind with blood,--
Jesus, our Love, is crucified!

4 His Mother cannot reach His Face;
She stands in helplessness beside,
Her heart is martyred with her Son's,--
Jesus, our Love, is crucified!

5 Seven times He spoke, seven words of love,
And all three hours His silence cried
For mercy on the souls of men;--
Jesus, our Love, is crucified!

6 What was Thy crime, my dearest Lord?
By earth, by heaven, Thou hast been tried,
And guilty found of too much love;--
Jesus, our Love, is crucified!

7 Found guilty of excess of love,
It was Thine own sweet will that tied
Thee tighter far than helpless nails;--
Jesus, our Love, is crucified!

8 Death came, and Jesus meekly bowed;
His falling Eyes He strove to guide
With mindful love to Mary's face;--
Jesus, our Love, is crucified!

9 O break, o break, hard heart of mine!
Thy weak self-love and guilty pride
His Pilate and His Judas were;--
Jesus, our Love, is crucified!

10 Come, take thy stand beneath the Cross,
And let the Blood from out that Side
Fall gently on thee drop by drop;--
Jesus, our Love, is crucified!

11 A broken heart, a fount of tears,--
Ask, and they will not be denied;
A broken heart love's cradle is;--
Jesus, our Love, is crucified!

12 O Love of God! O Sin of Man!
In this dread act your strength is tried;
And victory remains with love,
For He, our Love, is crucified!

The A&M version is only half as long:

1 O come and mourn with me awhile;
O come ye to the Saviour's side;
O come, together let us mourn;
Jesus, our Lord, is crucified.

2 Have we no tears to shed for Him,
While soldiers scoff and Jews deride?
Ah! look how patiently He hangs;
Jesus, our Lord, is crucified.

3 How fast His Hands and Feet are nailed;
His Throat with parching Thirst is dried;
His failing Eyes are dimmed with blood;
Jesus, our Lord, is crucified.

5 Seven times He spake, seven words of love;
And all three hours His silence cried
For mercy on the souls of men;
Jesus, our Lord, is crucified.

10 Come, let us stand beneath the Cross;
So may the Blood from out His Side
Fall gently on us drop by drop;
Jesus, our Lord, is crucified.

11 A broken heart, a fount of tears
Ask, and they will not be denied;
Lord Jesus, may we love and weep,
Since Thou for us art crucified.

It will not be necessary to note all the alterations. Intended for Passiontide, and set to an emotional tune by Dykes, the hymn is to be sung rather slowly and with feeling: it is therefore important that it not be overlong. The reasons for which some stanzas were omitted are not always obvious. The ninth stanza, however, could easily be criticized for excessive emotionalism and too great a personal emphasis: the metaphor is a striking one, and brings home the nature of the sacrifice, that the salvation assured thereby is both universal and particular, but it could be charged that the thought, when voiced by an entire congregation in song, is a breast-beating pose rather than an awful revelation. On the other hand, it would have been better to include the twelfth stanza, in which the essence of the struggle and of the victory is rather subtly understated ("And victory remains with love") and the understated abstraction is juxtaposed with the human reality ("He, our Love, is crucified"), and omit the tenth, which seems to revel in gory detail from a safely non-literal distance. Such detail is not of course to be omitted simply out of any squeamish sense of propriety, but to allow it without excellent reason is to risk a charge of morbidity. When Toplady writes of "the Water and the Blood/ From Thy riven Side which flowed," he gives equal emphasis to the "double cure," for he is exploring the paradoxical truth of the healing sacrifice, the life-giving death. Similarly, Isaac Watts, in "When I survey the wondrous cross," is not afraid to face the reality of the Crucifixion, though he speaks not of blood and water but of "sorrow and love [flowing] from His head, His hands, His feet." His recognition of the enormity of the sacrifice and his own unworthiness is weakened when the fourth stanza of that hymn is omitted, as it is in A&M:

His dying crimson like a robe
Spreads o'er His body on the Tree
Then am I dead to all the globe
And all the globe is dead to me.

One does not feel that the integrity of Faber's poem, or the effectiveness of the hymn, would be violated or diminished by the omission of his tenth stanza.

The A&M alterations are for the most part understandable. When the Compilers removed the references to Mary from the first stanza, they avoided giving offence to the many Anglicans who were suspicious of Mariolatry. Since the references to Mary are not essential to Faber's hymn, the Compilers preferred to leave them out, knowing that there were other more defensible hymns where they would face heavy criticism. Any loss of pathetic effect in the first stanza might be considered compensated by the new parallel structure of reiterated pleas. The changes in the A&M third stanza are all changes of sense: the tongue-tied Christ is an exaggeration which makes incongruous the following stanza's reference to the Seven Words from the Cross. Similarly the blindness is an exaggeration, for St. John's Gospel records how Jesus saw His mother at the foot of the cross and commended her to the care of His disciple. Such details are small, but the Compilers may have been right to correct unwarrantable exaggerations in a hymn already emotionally highly-charged. The final stanza in the A&M version is badly mutilated: Faber's version only barely makes sense when one remembers that he has already asked for a broken heart, and that this broken heart is the acceptable temple of the Lord: "A broken heart love's cradle is," or as the Psalmist says, "The sacrifices of God are a broken spirit: a broken and a contrite heart, O God, thou wilt not despise."[104] In the A&M version the stanza's fragile sense is destroyed by the common plea the Compilers thought proper to conclude a congregational hymn: "Lord Jesus, may we love and w-eep,/ Since Thou for us art crucified."

The most notorious alteration is that of "our Love" to "our Lord" in the final line of each stanza, by which Faber obviously had intended a cumulative emotional effect. The Compilers were very wary of what seemed to them excessive emotionalism: a depth of feeling that might be permissible in a poem for private devotion may appear to be paraded when sung by a congregation. Of course, the members of the congregation may sing in all sincerity, finding the words the appropriate expression of their religious feelings, but propriety suggests rather more restraint. Hence the substitution of "Lord" for "Love" in both 1860 and 1875, a choice of word which not only avoids the emotionalism, but also succeeds in establishing the complex relation between Christians and their suffering sacrificed Master. That, at least, was the Compilers' justification, though there are dissenting voices. William Brooke, for instance, cites the antiquity of the expression, used in the first century by St. Ignatius, and throughout the middle ages, and in Charles Wesley's "O Love divine, what hast Thou done?" which has the refrain "My Lord, my Love, is crucified." "It is a beautiful thought, and full of spiritual meaning. Its tenderness is not intensified by the change of '<u>our Love</u>' to '<u>Our Lord</u>.'"[105] William Whiting, in his comments to Sir Henry on the second Specimen, was not quite so dogmatic:

> P.S. I think the sweet hymn in your Book No 74 should be more fully given, and regret the alteration in the last line of each verse: . . . though I suppose this is done to render the hymn more generally acceptable; but I venture to doubt if it will do so; & those who know the original will regret the change; and those who don't must have admired the more correct version, if it had been presented to them before the one printed.[106]

This hymn has been examined in some detail in order to show the overall effect of the Compilers' alterations. It is not intended as a typical example, save that it does contain both justifiable and unnecessary alterations, both improvements and weakenings.

It is difficult to judge the rightness of A&M's alterations, and to draw final conclusions: the book's very popularity made its versions so well-known that they have acquired an unwarranted authority. On the whole one can say that the Compilers were perhaps too attentive to details, too concerned with accuracy and afraid of admitting excess or exaggeration, or any exercise of poetic licence. In their concern for congregational suitability they were reflecting their generation's interest in the nature and needs of worship, and if they were tied a little too closely by their self-imposed rules, they were so no more than were the Ecclesiologists in architecture, and without such drastic and lasting effects as in their corrections and restorations of old parish churches. As the century wore on, and the revivals became familiarities, there was a chance to re-examine and relax regulations, to admit the exceptional and the original. With more widespread education and the traditional relationship between clergy and people changed in and by new circumstances, editors came to place more confidence in the discernment of their congregations, and could allow their authors to speak for themselves.[107]

7. Originality in Paraphrase: The Achievement of Sir Henry Baker

At several points in this chapter the question of paraphrase has been touched on. In Section 3, on the contents of A&M, the small number of metrical paraphrases of Scripture printed in A&M was discussed. The distinction was drawn between the relatively straightforward versifications of the Old and New Versions of the Psalter, and the freer renderings of Watts and those who followed his example, in expressing Old Testament truths in forms of Christian experience.

The translations discussed in Section 4 were for the most part metaphrase, the almost word-for-word rendering of the texts into English. Accuracy is the chief criterion of excellence in metaphrase, though when the translations are intended for use in public worship in a tradition alien to that of the original, an editor may alter them in accordance with some practical or doctrinal standard. The resultant renderings may seem quite far removed from the original. Not all hymns from foreign languages are even basically metaphrastic: some of Neale's translations from the Greek in the A&M Appendix are very free indeed ("Let our choir new anthems raise" 380/441) and for some, undeniably Greek in inspiration and feeling, no actual sources exist ("Art thou weary, art thou languid" 299/254 and "O happy band of pilgrims" 297/224).

In the section on alteration, Watts's justification for recasting the psalms in the language of the New Testament is quoted. It is here that the real problem of paraphrase begins. When does alteration become paraphrase? At what point does an editor assume the responsibility of authorship?

There is no doubt about most examples of A&M alteration: the changes are so slight, being a matter only of emphasis, taste, or a reference foreign to Anglicanism. Other examples raise interesting questions about originality, poetic integrity, and editorial responsibility.

Take, for example, John Keble's version of "Guide me, O Thou great Jehovah," discussed above in Section 6. Neale considered it a "transfiguration" of the original, but it is argued that it is rather less than that, in fact, and that Keble weakened the impact of the hymn and dissipated its vigour by confusing the images of its pilgrim theme. The fault is paradoxically both too great a timidity and too little respect: the original hymn has its own integrity of form and concept, based on the strong tradition of Welsh Dissent out of which it was written, and with its characteristic theme of pilgrimage, and the language and stern tone of the Old Testament. Keble should either have left the hymn intact, or taken it apart and woven its elements together with his own into a new whole. As it is, Keble's hymn can neither supersede nor stand beside the original.

The point can be illustrated from Watts's paraphrases. "Jesus shall reign where'er the sun" (196/220) is a bold interpretation of the later verses of Psalm 72. Watts writes what he is certain the Psalmist would have written if he had known Christ: the king of Israel becomes Jesus, and the attributes of his kingdom are transformed. Might makes way for love, and the Old Testament images are broadened into more universal ones:

> They that dwell in the wilderness shall bow before him; and his enemies shall lick the dust. The kings of Tarshish and of the isles shall bring presents: the kings of Sheba and Seba shall offer gifts. Yea, all kings shall fall down before him: all nations shall serve him. (Psalm 72:9-11, Authorized Version)

These verses are rendered thus by Watts:

> People and realms of every tongue
> Dwell on His love with sweetest song,
> And infant voices shall proclaim
> Their early blessings on His Name.
> (stanza 2)

Not all Watts's paraphrases are as bold as this one. A&M also prints "O God, our help in ages past" (197/165), which is a versification of Psalm 90, not without Christian overtones (for example, in its emphasis on "our eternal home") but largely on the Old Testament images.

> Before the mountains were brought
> forth, or ever thou hadst formed the
> earth and the world, even from ever-
> lasting to everlasting, thou art
> God. (Psalm 90: 2, A.V.)

> Before the hills in order stood
> Or earth received her frame,
> From everlasting Thou art God,
> To endless years the same.
> (stanza 3)

These paraphrases have the integrity of original compositions. They neither detract from nor conflict with their Old Testament sources, but rather cast upon them the light of Christian revelation.

It is obviously unfair to compare Keble's touching-up with Watts's creation, but the examples show a standard of originality and integrity against which to measure the hymns under discussion in the rest of this section. They are three: "We love the place, O God" (164/242), "Praise, o praise our God and King" (224/381), and "The King of love my Shepherd is" (330/197). They come from various sources and through different forms before being printed in A&M, but the common factor is that they are all, as printed in A&M, substantially the work of Sir Henry Baker.

Sir Henry has appeared in this study as a

practical and persistent innovator, and as a pains-taking and perhaps fussy editor; in this section there is an opportunity to examine a remarkable achievement which is peculiarly his own.

The first hymn stands halfway between an altered original and a paraphrase. The original was written by William Bullock, Dean of Nova Scotia, and published in 1854. The first four stanzas in A&M are largely as Bullock wrote them, with the following amendments by Sir Henry. In the first stanza, "other" is replaced by "earthly," in "the joy of Thine abode/ All earthly joy excels," in keeping with the contrast which Sir Henry wishes to emphasize between earth and heaven. The third stanza is slightly improved when Bullock's

> We love the sacred Font
> Wherein the Holy Dove
> Pours out, as He is wont,
> The effluence from above.[108]

is changed to

> We love the sacred Font;
> For there the Holy Dove
> To pour is ever wont
> His blessing from above.

The awkwardness of Bullock's "wherein . . . pours out," and "effluence" is not missed, though Sir Henry has managed to cut off both subject and object from their respective verbs in his inverted construction: "the Dove to pour is wont his blessing," and left only one breathing place in the whole stanza. Again, in his version of the fourth stanza, Sir Henry implies a contrast between earth and heaven, and is not afraid to call the Communion table an outright altar, in true Tractarian style.

> We love our Father's board;
> Its Altar-steps are dear; (Bullock)
>
> We love Thine Altar, Lord;
> Oh what on earth so dear? (Baker)

He is even bolder when he comes to finish the hymn. Bullock concluded the original as follows:

> We love Thy Saints who come
> Thy mercy to proclaim,
> To call the wanderers home,
> And magnify Thy Name.
>
> Our first and latest love
> To Zion shall be given,
> The house of God above,
> On earth the gate of heaven.

These lines pose several questions, perhaps the gravest of which is, where is Christ? Why are "Saints" performing the functions of the Son of God, in proclaiming the mercy of God, and calling the sinful to repentance? And why is Zion, even Zion in its most abstract sense, the "first and latest" love of Christians? Even in the enthusiasm of verse, such a sentiment may justly be called an exaggeration. The effect of these doubts, together with the general cloudiness of the concept of "Zion" in the last stanza, is to prevent any real climax and conclusion of the hymn. Sir Henry's conclusion not only remedies that weakness, but also builds new strength into the hymn as a whole. His new stanzas are as follows:

> We love the Word of Life,
> The Word that tells of peace,
> Of comfort in the strife,
> And joys that never cease.
>
> We love to sing below
> For mercies freely given;
> But oh! we long to know
> The triumph-song of heaven.
>
> Lord Jesus, give us grace
> On earth to love Thee more,
> In heaven to see Thy Face,
> And with Thy saints adore.

Sir Henry's stanzas expand the idea presented in Bullock's final line, of the church on earth being the gate of heaven. The first of the stanzas above marks a transition from the church building itself, with its architectural features, and with Christ more or less "contained" in the church, His presence being found there, to the Word of life itself, heard, it is implied, in the church, but permeating the struggles of life and informing eternity. The second stanza makes explicit the contrast between heaven and earth, between what is known ("for mercies freely given") and what is promised ("the triumph-song of heaven"). In the final stanza the emphasis on the worshipper is less: it is a straightforward plea for grace so that both on earth and in heaven all love and all worship may be returned to their source. Having underlined the differences, Sir Henry allows them to begin to dissolve in the essential unity of the Christian universe.

Sir Henry's free hand with Bullock's hymn has changed it from a journeyman's occasional piece, serviceable enough and not seriously flawed, to a small work of mastery, with a shape and a force of its own. When A&M published the names of its hymnwriters (in the index to the Revised edition), Sir Henry's name took its rightful place with Bullock's.

If Sir Henry was bold to rewrite Bullock's hymn, he was even bolder to rewrite a paraphrase by John Milton, even if the poet was only fifteen years old when he wrote it. "Let us with a gladsome mind" is Milton's paraphrase of Psalm 136, which is characterized by its refrain in every verse "for his mercy endureth forever", and its summary of God's goodness toward Israel, from the creation, through the delivery from Egypt, to the catalogue of enemy kings slain. Milton kept the refrain, but condensed the psalm, making its brief lines rich with compound epithets and striking images: compare his summary of the escape from Egypt with part of the psalmist's:

> He with his thunder-clasping hand
> Smote the first-born of Egypt land,...
> And in despite of Pharoah fell,
> He brought from thence his Israel.
>
> (Milton)[109]

> To him that smote Egypt in their first-born . . . and brought out Israel from among them . . . with a strong hand, and with a stretched out arm. (Psalm 136:10-12 A.V.)

It is not, however, the historic account which attracts Sir Henry: he picks out the penultimate verse of the psalm ("Who giveth food to all flesh," v. 25), and on that bases a harvest hymn of thanksgiving (224/381). To that end his first stanza is a general call to worship, using Milton's refrain, but substituting "still" for "aye," avoiding thereby a potential archaism and an uncertainty of pronunciation:

> Praise, O praise our God and King!
> Hymns of adoration sing;
> For his mercies still endure
> Ever faithful, ever sure.

Sir Henry's one stanza will hardly stand comparison with either the psalm or the Miltonic paraphrase: both build from a relatively quiet beginning through phrase after phrase, until the only response is not Sir Henry's adoration, but awe:

> O give thanks unto the Lord; for he is good . . . O give thanks unto the God of gods . . . O give thanks to the Lord of lords . . . To him who alone doeth great wonders. (Psalm 136: 1-4, A. V.)

> Let us with a gladsome mind
> Praise the Lord, for He is kind. . .

Let us blaze His name abroad,
For of gods He is the God. . .
O let us His praises tell
Who doth the wrathful tyrants quell. . .
Who with his miracles doth make
Amazèd heav'n and earth to shake.
(Milton)

Sir Henry's theme is the cycle of seasons that brings the harvest: two stanzas paraphrase Milton, but without the idiosyncratic descriptions with which the poet delights:

Praise Him that He made the Sun
Day by day his course to run. . .
And the silver Moon by night,
Shining with her gentle light.
(Baker)

And caused the golden-tressèd sun
All day long his course to run. . .
The hornèd moon to shine by night,
Amongst her spangled sisters bright.
(Milton)

At this point Sir Henry takes leave of both the psalm and Milton to write three stanzas explicitly about weather and the harvest, loosely based on passages in Deuteronomy (11:14), the Psalms (65:11, 147:8), and Jeremiah (5:24). The penultimate stanza is an infusion of Christianity into the Old Testament psalm: a Tractarian reminder that man cannot live by bread alone, however grateful for it he is:

And for richer Food than this,
Pledge of everlasting bliss.

The hymn concludes with another call for praise, and a much compressed doxology.

It is not easy to judge fairly the merits of this paraphrase by Sir Henry. As a harvest hymn, it could not be meant to replace Milton's more general paraphrase, which is probably unfit for congregational singing precisely because of its peculiar felicities of expression. On the other hand, there seems to be no compelling reason to turn this psalm into a harvest-hymn, except that it does contain a germ, and that the short lines and frequent refrain provide an attractive framework. It is almost as if Sir Henry could not let the opportunity pass, and he has made a creditable hymn of it, sufficiently logical and unified to withstand the constant tug of the refrain, convincingly directed to its Christian end, but finally, a little too uninspired, its rejoicing not exuberant enough. Its dutiful praise must suffer in comparison with the spirit which made Milton write

Let us therefore warble forth
His mighty majesty and worth,

in which the very incongruity of the expression makes a valid point of the contrast between mighty Creator and humble creation. It is, after all, a pity that Sir Henry should have ousted Milton.

Sir Henry's best paraphrase was first printed in the Appendix; "The King of love my Shepherd is"

(330/197) is his version of the twenty-third psalm. It is hard to fault. At first glance it seems that Sir Henry has once again been unable to work directly from the Scriptural text, for the first line inevitably recalls George Herbert's own paraphrase of the psalm, "The God of love my shepherd is." Apart from the unavoidable similarities between the two paraphrases (both have the same number of verses as the psalm, and follow its pattern exactly), the likeness ends with the first line. Sir Henry's hymn is a Christianized version. If his first stanza is fairly literal, his second contains two adjectives which point beyond the experience of the psalm:

> Where streams of living water flow
> My _ransomed_ soul He leadeth,
> And, where the verdant pastures grow,
> With food _celestial_ feedeth.

Even more explicit is the addition of the cross to the supports mentioned in the fourth stanza, and the explicit identification of the table of the psalm with the sacrament of the Eucharist, even to the Tractarian "chalice," in the fifth:

> In death's dark vale I fear no ill
> With Thee, dear Lord, beside me;
> Thy rod and staff my comfort still,
> Thy Cross before to guide me.
>
> Thou spread'st a Table in my sight,
> Thy Unction grace bestoweth,
> And oh! what transport of delight
> From Thy pure Chalice floweth.

> Yea, though I walk through the valley of the shadow of death, I will fear no evil: for thou art with me; thy rod and thy staff they comfort me. Thou preparest a table before me in the presence of mine enemies: thou anointest my head with oil; my cup runneth over. (Psalm 23:4-5, A. V.)

The changes in the final stanza are very slight, but give a distinctly Christian emphasis. The psalm ends with a declaration:

> Surely goodness and mercy shall follow me all the days of my life: and I will dwell in the house of the Lord forever. (verse 6)

Herbert's conclusion is also a declaration, but he is not content simply to dwell, he must praise his Maker while he lives:

> Surely Thy sweet and wondrous love
> Shall measure all my days;
> And, as it never shall remove,
> So neither shall my praise.[110]

In his final stanza, Sir Henry goes beyond the limits of the psalm to the Christian prospect of life everlasting by simply avoiding the personal pronoun ("_the_ length of days" instead of "_my_ days"), and humbled by that prospect, he ends his hymn with a petition rather than a declaration:

> And so through all the length of days
> Thy goodness faileth never;
> Good Shepherd, may I sing Thy praise[111]
> Within Thy house for ever.

The result of Sir Henry's small changes is to bring closer to Christian understanding the experiences of the Old Testament, so that, paradoxically, the echoes of Christian eternity that he imports make the hymn more personal and immediate. It is, however, the stanza not yet discussed which is the most "human." When David wrote "He restoreth my soul: he leadeth me in the paths of righteousness for his name's sake," he made no claim for his own worth or virtue; Herbert expresses the implied unworthiness:

> Or *if I stray*, He doth convert,
> And bring my mind in frame:
> And all this not for my desert,
> But for His holy name.
> [emphasis added]

Sir Henry expands Herbert's phrase into a little drama of sin and redemption. The stanza builds from the initial confession of sin and weakness, through an attractive but by no means original image of the good shepherd, to joy, which, by the ambiguous placing of a participle, embraces both Saviour and saved, and is not even quite quenched by the grimmer immediate prospect of the stanza following ("death's dark vale"), which itself soon dissolves in the hope of the cross.

> Perverse and foolish oft I strayed,
> And yet in love He sought me,

And on His shoulder gently laid,
And home, rejoicing, brought me.

The impact of this stanza is no doubt due to the personal conviction which fired it.[112] It was Sir Henry's own drama, as he admitted when he whispered these words on his deathbed, and as his assessment ("perverse and foolish") is so far demonstrably accurate, let us accept also the assurance of his pardon.

8. Theology and Doctrine

The use of hymns as theological propaganda was discussed in Chapter Two; therefore this section will be restricted to specific examples of editorial concern with theological or doctrinal matters. Much of this concern is over evidence of either excessive Popery or Protestantism, as the Compilers tried to assemble a book true to the principles of the Church of England, as they saw them, while offending as few of the varieties of churchgoers as possible. The Anglican _via media_ has always been generously defined or, rather, left undefined. The English Reformation, without the strong immediate influence of either a Luther or a Calvin, concentrated not on redefining and re-establishing a systematic structure of theology, but on reforming the abuses of the mother church. Thus the Articles of Religion were not intended to be a complete statement, but, as the title of the Forty-Two Articles of 1553 explained, "Articles agreed on . . . for the auoiding of controuersie in opinions and the establishment of a godlie concorde in certeine matiers of Religion."[113] The Nicene Creed is the core of the Church's theology, and churchgoers who recite it declare their belief in "one Catholic and Apostolic Church," but reformed in "certeine matiers" to suit English consciences. In the Book of Common Prayer the form of the Church's public worship is laid down in accordance with the Creed and the Articles of Religion, and established by a legal Act of Uniformity. No attempt, however, is made to establish the forms and patterns of private worship; they may be as idiosyncratic or as derivative as the individual wishes. Thus evangelical or low-church Anglicans will use little but a well-read and pondered Bible in their private devotions, while Anglo-Catholics may use a Roman Catholic breviary or missal.

The discretion of the Reformers who drew up the Book of Common Prayer was formidable, and the Compilers found it very difficult to imitate. Again and again warning voices were raised against a proposed hymn on the grounds that it exceeded authority, either that of the Bible itself, or of the Book of Common Prayer. Let us consider Scriptural authority first.

It was no longer thought that hymns, not being directly drawn from Holy Writ, should be excluded from public worship, though it was properly assumed that hymns so used should not contain statements not found in the Bible. The association of unsupported statements with the formal worship of the Church might lend them an entirely spurious authority. Non-scriptural details are frequent in popular Christian literature, especially detail about the life of Christ, for the gospel narratives are for the most part sketchy biography. Carols, for instance, often humanize Jesus, by describing recognizable (sometimes anachronistic) features of his life, as for instance in the carol of "The Holy Well."[114] This carol tells the story of

Jesus as a boy, who goes out to play on a May morning, and is scorned by "the lords' and ladies' sons" whom he meets. Old Testament stories are also embellished, as in the Chester miracle play of the Flood, in which Noah's wife is portrayed for comic effect as a shrew and a scold.

Hymns, however, are taken much more seriously, and the smallest details do not escape scrutiny. W.C. Dix's Epiphany hymn "As with gladness men of old" (64/79) was criticized for its statement that the wise men found Jesus in the manger, though St. Matthew's gospel makes it clear that by the time the wise men came to Bethlehem, the boy was a "young child" (Matthew 2:8), though not more than two years old, and that the family had long since left the stable and were living in a house (Matthew 2:11). Dix wrote rather testily to Murray:

> I must say I think the objection rather hyper-critical. In all art representations of the adoration our Lord is on a manger-bed I think--

Nevertheless, he dashed off several possible alterations.

> As with joyful steps they sped --
> 1.? <u>Where</u> was laid the lowly Head;
> 2.? <u>Where</u> the Light Divine was shed
> 3. To that lowly Monarch's bed;
> 4. To that lowly Infant's bed;
> 5. To that royal Infant's bed;[115]

The Compilers appear to have accepted Dix's reproach, for the "manger-bed" remains in the 1860 edition.

The wise men were the occasion of other doubts: in his translation of "O sola magnarum urbium" of Prudentius, Caswall rendered "magi" as "Eastern kings" in the third stanza: "By its rays divinely guided,/See the Eastern kings appear!"[116] Wilkins was troubled: "Their kingship is not even a primitive or very ancient tradition - sh[d] we not hesitate before we dogmatically assume & teach it as a fact?"[117] In fact, the whole translation was so radically altered by the Compilers, that it was not difficult to change these lines too.

> Eastern sages at His cradle
> Make oblations rich and rare.

Nor were these isolated examples. Christopher Wordsworth criticized an unspecified hymn in A&M because it contained a reference to the pierced feet of Jesus, for which, he pointed out, there is no gospel authority; but only the reference in Psalm 22 "They pierced my hands and my feet":[118]

> ... it seems to me that Hymn Writers should be extremely jealous & cautious, in admitting anything which may expose them to the charge of being 'wise above what is written'.[119]

The Compilers' willingness to exceed written authority in some of these small points in order to follow popular tradition is very much to their credit. To strip popular images of their accepted details is unnecessarily harsh, and Wordsworth's attitude is one that became increasingly uncommon as the century progressed. As Biblical scholarship became bolder, and the various storms over _Essays and Reviews_ (1860) and Colenso's _The Pentateuch and the Book of Joshua critically examined_ (1862-63) shook churchgoers and unsettled church authorities, excessive literalness of interpretation waned, even among the clergy. Of course, Sir Henry's willingness to embroider the gospel outlines with a few innocuous details has little in common with the scholarly scepticism being turned upon the Biblical accounts of the Creation or the nature of miracles.

In at least one case the Compilers deferred to unsupported popular tradition. W.D. Maclagan's hymn for Passion-tide, "It is finish'd! Blessed Jesu" (--/122) was among those proposed for the Revised edition. At their general meeting the Proprietors passed the following motion, that "the Hymn be so modified as not to appear to contradict the received tradition that our Ld led the Spirits out of the prison into Paradise."[120] The reference is to the sixth and eighth stanzas:

> For Himself proclaims the story
>   Of His own Incarnate life,
> And the death He died to save us,
>   Victor in that awful strife.
>
> Oh, the bliss to which He calls them,
>   Ransom'd by His precious Blood,
> From the gloomy realm of darkness
>   To the Paradise of God!

(Both stanzas were subsequently omitted from the New edition of 1904.)

The problems of exceeding Scriptural authority are simple in comparison with the problems of exceeding that of the Book of Common Prayer. Again and again a warning note is sounded. Before the first edition was published, Braithwaite wrote on behalf of the Yorkshire Committee:

> It is difficult to know how to express our feelings upon this. We do not wish for any concealment or abandonment of truth -- but we do not desire statements of truth in words more exclusive than those adopted in our formularies, or in such a form as is undoubtedly liable to misinterpretation, & misjudgment.[121]

More fears were expressed in anticipation of the Appendix. Archdeacon John Allen conveyed to Sir Henry the doubts of his neighbour and friend, a 'moderate High Churchman':

> I am greatly concerned to find from excellent authority that the proposed Supplement to Hymns A&M exceeds in many particulars the teaching of our Church, and is even startling to very high Churchmen. Thus we shall have a weight on the neck of our H. Book that will sink it.[122]

It will be best to take the case of a particular hymn, one that was notorious for the controversy surrounding it, in order to see how the fears were provoked, and how the Compilers handled the problem. The hymn is Thomas Aquinas' "Pange lingua gloriosi corporis mysterium" (203/309), written for the office of Corpus Christi in 1263, and modelled on a much earlier hymn by Venantius Fortunatus (c530/609). The Compilers proposed its use for Holy Communion, and had a number of English versions to choose from, as it had been translated by Isaac Williams, Edward Caswall, Robert Campbell, and J.M. Neale, to name only the four chief talents it attracted.

It was this hymn that Braithwaite had in mind when he wrote the passage quoted above. It was this hymn that Francis Pott found impossible to accept, precipitating his resignation from the Compilers. Pott wrote to Sir Henry about his doubts:

> I have thought over the question of the 'Pange lingua' a great deal and have talked it over with several of my friends, . . . and they all say that . . . they could not accept it as it stands, because it defines what the Church of England has purposely left undefined.[123]

A few days later he wrote again, setting out more fully the points upon which he was uneasy. Inasmuch as the hymn is a narrative of the Last Supper, it cannot be faulted; the problems concern the extent to which the hymn describes what actually happens in the Mass or Eucharist.

Pott's doubts first arose in the third stanza:

> in supremae nocte cenae
> recumbens cum fratribus
> observata lege plene
> cibis in legalibus,
> cibum turbae duodenae
> se dat suis manibus.

A&M 1860, based on Caswall:

> That last night at Supper lying
> 'Mid the Twelve, His chosen band,
> Jesus, with the law complying,
> Keeps the feast its rites demand;
> Then, more precious Food supplying,
> Gives Himself with His own Hand.

A literal translation of the Latin makes it clear in the last two lines that Christ gives Himself, with His own Hands, as food for the Twelve. Pott points out that

> ... if it be true, then '_se_ dat' applies to the case of Judas Iscariot, as a matter of history, and to the case of all who receive unworthily, as a matter of doctrine and present belief and practice and this many hold to be questionable.[124]

Article XXIX of the Book of Common Prayer says clearly enough that

> The Wicked, and such as be void of a lively faith, although they do carnally and visibly press with their teeth (as Saint Augustine saith) the Sacrament of the Body and Blood of Christ, yet in no wise are they partakers of Christ: but rather, to their condemnation, do eat and drink the sign or Sacrament of so great a thing.

That is to say, that the Latin says that the Twelve, hence Iscariot, hence the wicked, received and receive Christ Himself in the rite, whereas the Church of England declares that Judas and the wicked received and receive only the outward sign of the Body of Christ, the species or appearance, as the theologians call it. Pott put it this way:

> ... it is very generally believed that the Church of England holds (and certainly allows her members to hold) that the giving of the Body and Blood is simultaneous but not identical, with the giving of the Bread & Wine. -- and that though it be universally true that Christ is 'Really' and, in a sense, 'Corporally' present in the Holy Eucharist, it is not universally true that He is received by every communicant. But as I said before I will not enter into the argument as to the truth of the doctrine conveyed by

> the Hymn (only let it suffice that many acknowledged divines have held and do hold with either side). . . All I shall content myself with, is urging, that the Hymn in this part does define what the Church of England has left (I believe purposely) undefined.[125]

The A&M translation of this stanza is Caswall's rewritten, and the Compilers have avoided the issue as much as possible without ignoring the Latin, by moving the reference to the Twelve to the beginning of the stanza (where the Latin has "fratribus"), and thus not drawing attention to the recipients of the giving. The avoidance, the refusal to say too exactly what they mean, exemplifies a skill long perfected in Anglican theology.

The fourth stanza also caused Pott trouble.

> Verbum caro panem verum
> verbo carnem efficit,
> fitque sanguis Christi merum,
> etsi sensus deficit
> ad firmandum cor sincerum
> sola fides sufficit.

The stanza is beautifully and tightly written: it takes no knowledge of Latin, for example, to notice the alliteration throughout of v,c,f, and s. A strictly literal translation would be:

> The Word/Flesh (Word-made-Flesh)

> makes very (real, actual) bread into flesh by word, and wine becomes the blood of Christ; even if senses fail, faith alone is sufficient to strengthen (assure, confirm) the pure heart.

The problem is not that the narrative, such as it is, is inaccurate, for the Gospel records that Christ declared "This is my Body, this is my Blood," and the breaking of the bread foretold the sacrifice to come, and the shared cup of wine symbolized the new covenant between God and man, which was to be sealed in that sacrifice, and by that blood. Christ commanded His followers to commemorate Him in the Sacrament of the Last Supper, but the issue of what actually happens to the elements when consecrated in the Sacrament is one that has divided Christendom since the Reformation. The issue is transubstantiation.

The doctrine was expressed by St. Thomas Aquinas in his _Summa Theologia_, in the terms of Aristotelian philosophy: that the substance of the bread and wine are transmuted, while their "accidents" or "appearances" (_species_) remain. Whether or not the people understood the distinction is a question that can be debated, but Christians believe many things they cannot understand except by faith, such as the doctrine of the Trinity, and must say with Tertullian "Certum est quia impossible est." The danger with a doctrine such as transubstantiation is that a failure to understand the philosophical-theological rationale leads to nonsense, or as Article XXVIII puts it, to "many superstitions."

The Church of England's position is set out in the Catechism and the Articles, and can be summarized for the laity as follows: a Sacrament is "an outward and visible sign of an inward and spiritual grace,. . . ordained by Christ Himself, as a means whereby we receive the same, and a pledge to assure us thereof." A Sacrament has two parts, the "outward visible sign" (which in the Eucharist is the "Bread and Wine, which the Lord hath commanded to be received"), and the "inward spiritual grace," (which is the "Body and Blood of Christ which are verily and indeed taken and received by the faithful"). Thus the Catechism. Article XXVIII denies that the elements are identical with Christ: "The Body of Christ is given, taken, and eaten, in the Supper, only after an heavenly and spiritual manner," for "Transubstantiation (or the change of the substance of Bread and Wine) in the Supper of the Lord, cannot be proved by holy Writ; but it is repugnant to the plain words of Scripture, overthroweth the nature of a Sacrament, and hath given occasion to many superstitions."

The Anglican acceptability of the hymn itself depends on the meaning of the words of the translation. When Aquinas says "efficit," we may be sure that he means "makes" in the sense of "transforms." The A&M translation says simply "maketh," and Pott points out that

> If 'efficit' is 'making' in the sense of unalterably changing the nature, (whether positively in themselves or relatively to the recipient) of the elements, it . . . comes

> under the objection urged against 'se dat suis manibus', of defining beyond (if not contrary to) our Church's statements.[126]

It could be argued that, again, the Compilers are using great discretion: they are using words which can be interpreted according to the user's predilections, and are not defining what the Prayer Book leaves undefined. Unfortunately the words are susceptible to unacceptable interpretations as well, as in the case of Pott's third objection. The fifth stanza begins:

> tantum ergo sacramentum
> veneremur cernui,

and the question is, what does the verb mean? It is a clear case of Humpty Dumptyism: "When I use a word," Humpty Dumpty said in a rather scornful tone, "it means just what I choose it to mean, -- neither more nor less." If by "sacramentum" is meant the mystery whereby spiritual grace is shown by an outward sign, ordained by Christ, and commemorative of His sacrifice, then the correct attitude is one of awe and wonder and reverence:

> Therefore we, before Him bending,
> This great Sacrament revere.

If, however,

> 'veneremur cernui' means 'adoration' and 'Sacramentum' means the 'elements' -- as scholastically it would

> -- as distinguished from the 'Res Sacramenti' -- and still further distinguished from the 'Real Presence', then it certainly militates against the last words of the XXVIII Article.[127]

This possibility of manifold meanings greatly disturbed Pott:

> You see that in the above remarks I have assumed that the words mean just what would be objected to; whereas you no doubt would say, we do not take them in that sense. But to this, it is I must confess fairly replied; -- by those I have consulted; -- 'If we accept a Hymn, the original of which will bear, and doubtless by the author was intended to bear a sense, which you yourselves would own to be an unsound (i.e. a Roman) sense, and if we take simply a literal unmodified translation of it, which of course can be made to bear the same sense, it will be fairly cast in our teeth that we accept the Roman doctrine, whatever we may say about taking it in another, ie an Anglican sense'. . . . And moreover we must not forget that the public, in the church, both clergy and laity will not stop to ask us what we understand by this or

> that hymn -- but will put <u>their own</u> interpretation upon it and reject the book accordingly.[128]

The final A&M versions of the two suspect stanzas are as follows:

> Word-made-Flesh true bread He maketh
> By His word His Flesh to be;
> Wine, His Blood; which whoso taketh
> Must from carnal thoughts be free;
> Faith alone, though sight forsaketh,
> Shows true hearts the mystery.
>
> Therefore we, before Him bending,
> This great Sacrament revere;
> Types and shadows have their ending,
> For the newer rite is here;
> Faith, our outward sense befriending,
> Makes our inward vision clear.
>
> (stanzas 3,4)

Neale called the fourth stanza the bow of Ulysses to translators, and found fault with most of the current attempts. The A&M version he criticized for its third and fourth lines, for most of which there is no Latin original: "Wine His Blood: <u>which whoso taketh/ Must from carnal thoughts be free</u>." These lines were not added simply to fill out the lines, however, for they can be read as a deliberate attempt by the Compilers to make clear where they stood on the issue of unworthy communion.[129]

Pott's fear that the public will not stop to ask

what meaning the Compilers intended is voiced again over other hymns and other expressions. Sir Henry drafted the following response to a criticism of Dix's "Alleluia sing to Jesus" (350/316) which contains the lines:

> Thou on earth both Priest and Victim
> In the Eucharistic feast.
> (stanza 4)

Sir Henry wrote:

> I admit that it is capable of an interpretation that would contradict the 31st Article[130] & be indeed a fearful heresy. For any second or repeated offering of our dear Lord as Victim in the same way in which He was once offered on Calvary we know there cannot be. But just because we do know this: because every English priest says so whenever he celebrates: because in another Hymn in H.A. & M. we, the compilers only of H.A. & M., do distinctly assert it: 'Once, only once, & once for all' etc. . . .-- for these clear reasons surely. . . every fair reader ought to feel sure that we could not mean anything except a spiritual & mystical offering by the words used in ['Alleluia sing to Jesus'].[131]

The objector was sufficiently content with Sir Henry's sincerity and logic to order A&M for his church, though he pointed out that hymns are sung singly, and that congregations do not compare and contrast what they sing.[132] Sir Henry acknowledged the point, though he argued that congregations do judge the whole, and that they receive a cumulative impression from familiarity with the contents of the book. He also recommended that if his correspondent's scruples were too strong, the hymn be omitted and never sung; others, Sir Henry admitted, had taken that course, and omitted what they could not approve.[133] The Proprietors were sufficiently convinced of the superior merits of their book to be confident that, despite objections, most clergy would be reluctant to accept another book. This case only confirmed them in their confidence.

A good example of a Compilers' alteration on dogmatic grounds is in the hymn "Days and moments quickly flying" (375/ 289). This hymn was written by Edward Caswall and published under the heading "The Swiftness of Time" in his _Masque of Mary and other Poems_, 1858, together with the following "Warning," to be sung after the final stanza:

> As the tree falls, so must it lie;
> As the man lives, so will he die;
> As the man dies, such must he be,
> All through the days of eternity.

The Compilers printed it in the Appendix for use on "New Year's Eve," noting also its suitability for Lent and for the burial service. To discuss thoroughly what is at issue in this stanza would demand an understanding of all that is meant by the Communion of Saints, Purgatory, and prayer for the dead, in short, of the nature of the Life everlasting. The subject is immensely complex and controversial, and the differences between denominations are marked. The Anglican position is not anywhere defined, neither in Creed, Articles, nor the burial service (save for the repudiation of the "Romish doctrine concerning Purgatory" in Article XXII).[134]

Many found it difficult to accept Caswall's stanza, because its implications seem contrary to Christian hope, even on the death bed, and because it states what the Prayer Book does not. The strongest expression of such objections comes from the Reverend H. Percy Smith of Great Barton, Suffolk:

> I, for one, am deprived of the use of the Appendix in service, because I dare not put into the hands of my people a tremendous statement, which as _a matter of fact_, is not in the Prayer Book.
>
> The Three Creeds, the 39 Articles, the Formularies, are absolutely devoid of every least hint of this assumed impossibility of any the least moral improvement in the impenitent dead. Its appearance therefore in a Hymn Book, not hinted, but dogmatically stated, I most respectfully contend, cannot by any possibility be defended.
>
> Even if this impossibility and

> hopelessness be a fact, our Church plainly regards it as a secret locked up in the bosom of the Almighty.
>
> Many clergymen, myself amongst them, would at once throw up their livings, if they believed our Church made this most awful statement.[135]

The Compilers saw the force of the objection, and in their Revised edition they replaced Caswall's "Warning" with their own prayer:

> O by Thy power grant, Lord, that we
> At our last hour fall not from Thee;
> Saved by Thy grace, Thine may we be
> All through the days of eternity.

Concern for implication, even in small details and mere phrases is exemplified in the hymn "Saviour when in dust to Thee" (104/251) by Sir Robert Grant. This hymn was given for use at Passiontide in A&M 1860, in a much revised version taken from Murray's book. Some of the changes are indeed improvements, as when the internal rhyme and the awkward repetition in "By the boding tears that flowed/ Over Salem's loved abode" is avoided by the substitution of "gracious" for "boding." In 1875, however, the Compilers restored the hymn to its original form, according to their declared principle of altering as little as possible. The one phrase they did not restore was a reference to Christ's "dire despair," because despair is one of the greatest sins, and the Compilers did not wish anyone to attribute it to Christ, even in His human agony on the cross. The Compilers preferred "whelming fear," and brought the author's nephew to bow to their judgment, though unenthusiastically:

> I never took it in such a sense that it would be inapplicable to our Lord, though I admit it may have such an interpretation I think it may express the state described in the Gospels when the words "My God, my God, why hast Thou forsaken me' were used. No doubt, in the sense of utter desperation, it would be wrong.[136]

One of the hymns which occasioned much criticism is one by Sir Henry himself, "Shall we not love thee, Mother dear" (376/ 450). Dean Howson of Chester feared that the hymn might lead congregations "further than the Prayer Book sanctions."[137] Another clergyman asked that it be replaced by "others more in harmony with the spirit of our Reformed & Protestant church!"[138] This appeal was unlikely to be favourably heard, for to Sir Henry, "Protestant" was a term of opprobrium.[139] L.C. Biggs assured Sir Henry that he found no heresy in the hymn, but feared that his "choir and parish would rebel against addressing a hymn to the Blessed Virgin," and wondered "'how shall he that occupieth the room of the <u>unlearned</u>' make the distinction (clear enough to you and to me) between the address to GOD which we make as knowing that He hears us, and the address to the Blessed V. of which at least we must own that we make it with no such <u>certainty</u>, I should add with no such idea."[140] The place of Mary in Anglican theology is discussed below in section 9, "No Popery": suffice it to say here that Sir Henry was entirely unwilling to discard his hymn. In the Revised edition it was, however, removed from under the heading "Annunciation," for which it was too general to be entirely suitable, to the more appropriate and less conspicuous section "Festivals of Martyrs and other Holy Days: For the B.V.M." Sir Henry also altered the last lines of his first and seventh stanzas from

> And in His Temple, year by year,
> Thy joy and glory tell,

to

> And, to His glory, year by year,
> Thy joy and honour tell.

These changes make Christ rather more prominent -- it is His glory which is paramount -- and bring Mary closer to the saints, as one to whom dulia (due honour) is owed, rather than hyperdulia (the supreme degree of honour which is implied in Sir Henry's term "glory").

An excellent example of editorial alteration from one edition to another is the hymn "Come, Thou Holy Spirit, come" (128/156) for Whitsun, in a translation based on Caswall's in *Lyra Catholica*, 1849. The third stanza of the Latin contains the lines:

> Sine tuo numine
> Nihil est in homine
> Nihil est innoxium

> (without thy presence there is nothing in man, nothing is innocent/harmless.)

In 1860, A&M printed the following translation:

> If Thou take Thy grace away,
> Nothing pure in man will stay,
> All our good is turned to ill.

In 1875, the A&M compilers borrowed a line and a rhyme from Neale's translation in the Hymnal Noted, Part 2 (1854) of the same hymn ("Where Thou art not, man hath nought;/ Every holy deed and thought/ Comes from Thy Divinity"), and gave as their revised version:

> Where Thou art not, man hath nought,
> Nothing good in deed or thought,
> Nothing free from taint of ill.

The translation is still an expansion of the original, but not so much as the 1860 edition or Neale's version. The significance of the revision lies in the implications of the reference to grace. As it stands, the suggestion that individuals can lose the grace of God is a disturbing one, for it means either that they can utterly forfeit grace, despite Christ's promise of redemption for all, or that it could be more or less arbitrarily withdrawn. The second alternative is unthinkable in an unchanging God of love; the first implies that the individual must be worthy of grace, and that grace and merit belong together. The repudiation of that doctrine and the assertion of the exclusive connection of grace with faith is a chief point of Protestant doctrine. In altering the implication, that is to say, the Compilers were asserting their Reformed faith.

It is sometimes difficult to say exactly where a particular alteration is made on grounds of doctrine or of congregational suitability. Frequent evidence has already been seen of a kind of double standard: words that the priest would not repudiate are kept from a congregation for fear they might be misunderstood, or taken too literally. On the other hand, the clergy were perhaps too protective of their singing congregations, hardly admitting that common sense is just that -- common.

When Dean Alford criticized the Compilers for altering his harvest hymn "Come ye thankful people, come" (223/382) without his permission, Sir Henry set out the reasons why he had found part of the original objectionable:

> Tho' good and bad are mingled in the Church, it is nevertheless utterly opposed to the whole structure of our services to teach each little Choir or congregation to say 'we are wheat and tares' -- I never could do it. nor would any members of our committee do it I am sure -- 'The world', 'earth', is the field: 'therein' wheat and tares are sown -- both 'ripening with wondrous power till etc': (but it is incorrect to say 'then the full corn etc' of the tares) -- [141]

The stanza referred to is the second in Alford's original:

> We ourselves are God's own field,
> Fruit unto His praise to yield;
> Wheat and tares together sown,
> Unto joy or sorrow grown;
> First the blade and then the ear,
> Then the full corn shall appear;
> Grant, O harvest Lord, that we
> Wholesome grain and pure may be.[142]

A&M 1860 printed the following version:

> *What* *is* *earth* *but* God's own field,
> Fruit unto His praise to yield?
> Wheat and tares *therein* are sown,
> Unto joy or sorrow grown;
> *Ripening* *with* *a* *wondrous* *power*,
> *Till* *the* *final* *Harvest-hour*:
> Grant, *O* *Lord* *of* *life*, that we
> *Holy* grain and pure may be.

Alford was strongly indignant about A&M's treatment of this hymn:

> You first take my hymn, . . . without taking even the commonest pains to ascertain whose it is. Then you proceed to alter it, obliterating the symbolism, and introducing into it what I believe to be false doctrine.[143]

Alford's judgment seems unnecessarily harsh, for Sir Henry's alterations are little more than a matter of sense, though perhaps too literally taken.

The other unauthorized alterations were chiefly in the final stanza, where Alford had written "Then, Thou Church triumphant come,/Raise the song of Harvest-home."[144] Sir Henry felt that these lines were no more than a "poetical appeal to the Church," and "preferred a prayer to our Lord that He would cause us to sing the great Harvest Home . . . [otherwise] there is no prayer at all in the whole Hymn -- "[145] A&M therefore printed:

> Come then, Lord of mercy, come,
> Bid us sing Thy Harvest-Home!

Alford admitted the strength of this objection, and himself altered the stanza in his later publications (Poetical Works, 1865 and Year of Praise, 1867) to

> Even so, Lord, quickly come
> To Thy final Harvest-home.[146]

These alterations reflect not so much a doctrinal concern as an understanding of the nature and function of a hymn in worship, that all things be centered on and directed to God.

It is not only in statements that the Compilers had to be careful of doctrine, but in omissions also. Earlier examples have shown how frequently a statement can be found objectionable through too much precision, but there are also cases where a refusal to define, or an oversight, is equally reprehensible. In Chapter 3, mention has already been made of Christopher Wordsworth's public criticism of the A&M alterations of his almsgiving hymn "O Lord of heaven and earth and sea"

(370/365). His chief complaint was not about the more regular refrain "Who givest all" which the Compilers printed, but about the omission of his fourth and fifth stanzas. The first three stanzas are an effusion of praise and thankfulness for the blessings of life; the omitted stanzas refer to God's gifts, first of the Son, and second of the Holy Spirit. The last stanzas concern the Christian's responsibility to use well and gratefully God's gifts. Wordsworth charged that the omission made him as author of the hymn "culpable and guilty in a certain sense of the sin of heresy,"[147] the heresy, as he told Sir Henry, "of silence."[148] That Christians must acknowledge their redemption as the greatest gift of all is Wordsworth's point. The Proprietors protested that their fourth stanza[149] contained enough about grace and redemption to forestall a charge of heresy of silence. Wordsworth's refusal to be mollified caused the Proprietors to restore the omitted stanzas in the Revised edition. The controversial lines are:

> Thou didst not spare Thine Only Son,
> But gav'st Him for a world undone,
> And freely with that Blessèd One
> Thou givest all.
>
> Thou giv'st the Holy Spirit's dower,
> Spirit of life, and love, and power,
> And dost His sevenfold graces shower
> Upon us all. (stanzas 4,5, 1875)

It was not only Anglican clergy who were much exercised over matters of doctrine in hymnody. One very bitter controversy among Congregationalists took place over the publication in 1855 of The Rivulet A Contribution to Sacred Song, by Thomas Toke Lynch. The collection was published for his congregation, as a supplement to Watts, though not all the hymns therein were intended for public use. The chief criticism levelled at the collection was that it was insufficiently dogmatic: the editor of the Morning Advertiser thought the hymns might have been written by Deists and sung by Freethinkers. Eventually Lynch responded satirically in his Songs Controversial, by Silent Long. There was much in what he had to say to his detractors with which the A&M Compilers, or indeed, any hymnbook editor, could sympathize. One of Lynch's poems can put this whole section into perspective.

When sugar in the lump I see,
I know that it is there,
Melt it, and then I soon suspect
A negative affair:
Where is the sugar, Sir? I say,
Let me both touch and see;
Sweetness instead of sugar, Sir,
You'll not palm off on me.

Don't tell me that the sugar-lumps,
When dropt in water clear,
That they to make the water sweet,
Themselves must disappear;
For commonsense, Sir, such as mine,
The lumps themselves must see;
Sweetness instead of sugar, Sir,
You'll not palm off on me.

For instance, Sir, in every hymn
   Sound doctrine you should state
As clearly as a dead man's name
   Is on his coffin plate:
Religion, Sir, is only fudge,
   Let's have theology;
Sweetness instead of sugar, Sir,
   You'll not palm off on me.[150]

9. No Popery

The accusation of Roman Catholic sympathies among the Proprietors and Compilers of A&M was not one to be lightly shaken off. Anglicizing, and Anglicanizing, Roman hymns was an important part of the Compilers' editorial responsibility, and it was not slighted: their conscientious discussion of the choice, the ordering, and the theological implications of the hymns has been seen throughout this chapter. The Compilers were, we have seen, second-generation Tractarians, applying their Catholic principles in a new area. The public reception was mixed, but on the whole extraordinarily favourable and successful beyond precedent or prediction. Many had minor criticisms or reservations, but the number of avowed enemies of the book was small, and these detractors were perhaps the more vociferous for being few.

One of the most vociferous was the Reverend James Ormiston, who seems rarely to have missed an opportunity to address a public meeting or stir up feeling against A&M. The Proprietors were evidently wary of him, for newspaper clippings and reports of his speeches have been kept in the archive, some of the very few such items there.

Ormiston was unashamedly anti-Tractarian. One report of a speech contains the following declarations:

> He would call their Church of England a Protestant church (applause). Its Protestation was now practically ignored by a section of the clergy. He openly avowed himself a thorough Protestant and evangelist [sic]. He held by the thirty-nine Articles, and the Book of Common Prayer, as thoroughly scriptural. He was satisfied with things as they were originally, because he believed them to be thoroughly Protestant (applause).[151]

The whole concept of the Church of England as Catholic and Apostolic seems to have escaped him.

Ormiston did more than address public meetings: he published in 1875 a tract entitled _Hymns Ancient and Modern, and their Romanizing Teaching_, prompted by the publication of the Revised edition, which he saw as the third step in a "_progressive scheme_ for Romanizing the congregations of our land."[152] In it he argued the same points he had put in his lectures: that the Church of England contained an "organized body whose declared aim was to undo the grand work of the Reformation,"[153] and one of whose means was A&M, "a Jesuitical stratagem [of] the Ritualists, . . . for Romanizing the Church and for promoting her re-union with the Church of Rome."[154] Hymns, he said, had been used for propaganda purposes throughout Christian history, but "unsanctified by God's grace" they present only "sensuous religion," playing on the emotions at the expense of judgment (3). Reinforced by attractive music, the hymns in A&M were "pernicious and perilous,"[155] because they taught 1.Mariolatry, 2.Idolatry, 3.Transubstantiation, 4.Baptismal Regeneration, _ex opere operato_, 5.Prayer for the Dead, and 6.Salvation by human works (5). Ormiston's pamphlet discusses and illustrates each of these accusations in turn.

He was distressed to discover in A&M evidence of Mariolatry, "one of the most prominent features of the fallen Church of Rome" (5). This is not the place for an extended treatise on Mariology, but the following points may be noted. Not even Ormiston took exception to the doctrine affirmed in the Creeds that Jesus was "conceived by the Holy Ghost, born of the Virgin Mary": there is adequate Scriptural authority for this miraculous parthenogenesis. Protestants object rather to excessive devotion paid to Mary, excess they especially saw in Counter-Reformation Catholicism. Ormiston singles out "At the Cross her station keeping" (98/-117), a hymn for the Passion from the thirteenth-century Latin "Stabat Mater." Ormiston claimed that "the sufferings and sorrows of Mary are magnified in order to attract sympathy, and to deepen reverential feelings toward her" (8). The "Stabat Mater" he attributed to "the darkest and most corrupt ages of Christendom . . . 1350," and his association is not entirely wrong, for though the hymn was written earlier, it is connected with the flagellant movement of the mid-fourteenth century. The public spectacle of penitents singing this hymn while walking from town to town in a procession, beating one another, would have been abhorrent to Victorian church people, or, indeed, to any who preferred rather more reticence in religion.

The Proprietors who printed this hymn would have argued against Ormiston that the "Stabat Mater" is not a celebration of Mary's sufferings, but a genuine penitential cry -- penitential in a way which the flagellants seem to have recognized. That is, the hymn brings Christians to a realization in human terms of the enormity of Christ's suffering, and a sense of their own ingratitude and unworthiness. Of the five stanzas of the A&M hymn, only the first two are solely about the *mater dolorosa* herself. The third calls Christians to imitate her grief and sense of loss:

> Who, on Christ's dear Mother gazing
> Pierced by anguish so amazing,
> Born of woman, would not weep?
> Who, on Christ's dear Mother thinking
> Such a cup of sorrow drinking,
> Would not share her sorrows deep?

The fourth stanza is essentially an exposition of Atonement: "For His people's sins chastisèd,/ She beheld her Son despisèd," and the final stanza calls for greater devotion (not a turmoil of repentance and breastbeating) and is addressed to the Redeemer -- the human Mother is kept undeniably subordinate.

> Jesu, may her deep devotion[156]
> Stir in me the same emotion,

Fount of love, Redeemer kind,
That my heart fresh ardour gaining,
And a purer love attaining,
May with Thee acceptance find.

Ormiston was concerned lest the worship properly owed to God be usurped: Sir Henry's hymn "Shall we not love thee, Mother dear" (376/450) is criticized for "direct address of worship to the Virgin Mary" (9), whereas modern readers are more likely to consider it a discreditable example of misplaced Victorian sentimentality.

He admits that he cannot accuse A&M of referring to Mary as the mother of God, a usage "monstrously absurd . . . that the creature is superior to the Creator" (6), but the very mention of the expression is a tract-writer's device, for it will be associated with A&M in the mind of a hasty and prejudiced reader. The reason for which the Third Ecumenical Council (at Ephesus A.D. 431) declared Mary "Theotokos" (Bearer of God) was not in order to exalt Mary, but to counter the claims of Nestorian heretics that Jesus was not divine, but only human. Thus far Mariology is impeccable; it is with the development of beliefs in Mary's perpetual virginity, her assumption, and her freedom from original sin that fears grew that excessive attention and honour was being paid to her, and that the cult becomes Mariolatry.

Although Ormiston could not find the usage "mother of God" in A&M, he did find what he considered an inordinate number of references to Jesus as the "son of Mary": "Obviously the purpose of this reiteration is to familiarize the mind with the relation in which the

Son of God is by Romanists placed to the Virgin, and to exalt the Virgin at the expense of the Son" (7). The hymn which most occasioned his anger was H.H. Milman's "When our heads are bowed with woe" (163/399) for general use in 1860, and for the burial of the dead in 1875, where every stanza ends with the appeal "Jesu, Son of Mary, hear." The justification is that the hymn is an appeal to Christ for strength to bear suffering and especially, grief, and that Christians are confident their appeal is heard because Christ Himself knew human griefs. The reference to His mother underlines the humanity in which His divinity was clothed:

> Thou our throbbing flesh hast worn,
> Thou our mortal griefs hast borne,
> Thou hast shed the human tear;
> Jesu, Son of Mary, hear. (stanza 2)

Ormiston seems to have felt that the fact that Christ had a mother at all were better entirely forgotten: "Did Jesus, the Son of God, once call Mary -- Mother?" (7). Such an example of narrow literalism and utter lack of sympathetic imagination reflects more upon Ormiston's shortcomings than on the supposed errors of A&M's writers.

Allied to the charge of Mariolatry is that of "idolatry, or the worship of material things," specifically of the material cross.

> We live in a day when the material cross has actually become a fashionable ornament. Crosses surmount our church roofs; crosses meet us within

> on every side; the congregations display crosses; the clergy wear crosses, make crosses, carry crosses. Crosses decorate the service books, and hymnals celebrate them(9).

The purely symbolic or even emblematic function of a cross hardly seems to occur to Ormiston. A cross on a church roof is nothing like a graven image for pagans to worship, but a reminder to those engaged in secular activities of the religious purposes which should underlie and sustain those activities. As church spires point upwards to heaven, the cross points inward.

Ormiston's particular objections are to two of the noblest Latin hymns by Venantius Fortunatus, his "Vexilla regis" (84/96) and "Pange lingua" (289/97). The stanza in the first to which he objected is the fourth, in the A&M translation (based on Neale):

> O Tree of glory, Tree most fair,
> Ordained those Holy Limbs to bear,
> How bright in purple robe it stood,
> The purple of a Saviour's Blood!

The stanza is a statement of the paradox that the means of a shameful death should become the emblem of triumph: the real emphasis is on the burden borne by the cross.

The stanzas in the "Panga Lingua" are perhaps a little more doubtful:

> Faithful Cross, above all other
> One and only noble Tree,

None in foliage, none in blossom,
None in fruit thy peer may be;
Sweetest wood, and sweetest iron;
Sweetest weight is hung on thee.

Bend, O lofty Tree, thy branches,
Thy too rigid sinews bend;
And awhile the stubborn hardness,
Which thy birth bestow'd, suspend;
And the Limbs of Heav'n's high Monarch
Gently on thine arms extend.
(II, st. 3,4)

Taken alone, the first of these stanzas might seem idolatrous, unless one made allowance, as Ormiston evidently does not, for poetry. The conceit is well-contrived, and shares a quality of vision which is characteristically mediaeval, and produced in Anglo-Saxon _The Dream of the Rood_. The patent impossibility of the appeal in the second of the above stanzas only enhances the immediacy of what is described: the poet and the singer are helpless in view of the suffering of their God, itself an almost impossible concept. Again, Ormiston's literal approach and his evident lack of poetic imagination utterly prevent intelligent criticism.

Ormiston's third charge is that A&M preaches the doctrine of transubstantiation: he is one who reads Aquinas' "Pange lingua" in exactly the sense that Pott feared. His criticisms of other hymns are not specific, their "priestly pretensions," he says, "are too palpable to need comment" (12). He does attack a second hymn by Aquinas in Woodford's translation, "Thee we adore, O hidden Saviour, Thee" (206/312), which, he claims, preaches adoration of the consecrated elements. The first lines are the ones referred to:

> Thee we adore, O hidden Saviour, Thee,
> Who in Thy sacrament dost deign to be.

Ormiston's interpretation is not the only one -- the hymn does not declare the Real Presence of Christ in the bread and wine, and the words do not in themselves contradict the Articles. The first line could hardly be more emphatic, with the pronoun placed first and repeated last in the line, and the reference to a hidden Saviour does not imply that Christ is present though disguised as bread and wine, but connects with the final stanza "O Christ, whom now beneath a veil we see," and with the well-known words in the thirteenth chapter of I Corinthians: "For now we see through a glass, darkly; but then face to face."[157]

The question of Baptismal regeneration, Ormiston's fourth criticism, was the cause of great controversy in the nineteenth century. Baptism has from apostolic times been the rite of initiation of new members into the Church, and is seen as a dying to self and a rebirth in Christ, that is, regeneration. The rite of initiation has been divided into two stages, however, infant baptism, and confirmation and first communion. In infant baptism, the child's sponsors or parents renounce the devil and all his works and affirm the creed and the intention to keep God's will and commandments, on the child's behalf. Confirmation means, in the words of the Book of Common Prayer, that

> children, being now come to the years of discretion, and having learned what their Godfathers and Godmothers promised for them in Baptism, they may themselves, with their own mouth and consent, openly before the Church, ratify and confirm the same; and also promise, that by the grace of God they will evermore endeavour themselves faithfully to observe such things, as they, by their own confession, have assented unto.[158]

Many Evangelical Anglicans or low-church adherents who preached or accepted the necessity of personal conversion as the occasion of rebirth, objected to the words of the call to prayer in the Baptismal service which follows the signing of the child with the sign of the cross, when the priest says "Seeing now . . . that <u>this Child is regenerate</u>, and grafted into the body of Christ's Church, let us give thanks."[159] They felt that regeneration was conditional upon the worthy reception of the sacrament of Baptism, and that no infant had the discretion to chose worthily or to experience conversion. It is said that it was not uncommon for evangelicals to have their infants baptized by nonconformists, in order to avoid that declaration of regeneration.[160]

The notorious Gorham case concerned George Cornelius Gorham, who, after lengthy examination, was refused institution in 1847 by his bishop (Phillpots of Exeter) on the grounds that his denial of Baptismal regeneration contradicted the teaching of the Church. When Gorham took the case to the Court of Arches, the chief church court in the Province of Canterbury, his bishop's refusal was upheld, but on appeal to the Privy Council, which since 1832 had been the ecclesiastical court of final appeal, the decision was reversed. The court did not pronounce Gorham's teaching either right or wrong, but only "not inconsistent" with the declared doctrine of the Church: legally, therefore, clergy were freed to believe or disbelieve the doctrine of Baptismal regeneration according to their own consciences.[161]

Ormiston argued from Article XXVII that Baptism, as a sign of regeneration, was not to be confused with the thing signified: "Baptism . . . is also a sign of Regeneration or new Birth, whereby, as by an instrument, they that receive Baptism _rightly_ are grafted into the Church" [emphasis added]. Again, he says that forgiveness, grace and faith are not conveyed by the rite itself (_ex opere operato_), but that God's promise of them is sealed, and that prayer to God, rather than details of the act, is "the secret of spiritual blessing" (13). "The promises of the forgiveness of sin, and of our adoption to be the sons of God by the Holy Ghost, are visibly signed and sealed; Faith is confirmed, and Grace increased by virtue of prayer unto God" (Article XXVII). Ormiston does not accept the suggestion that the prayers of the priest and the child's parents and godparents may be just as efficacious on the child's behalf: he allows no subtlety of interpretation, but again, only literalness. Curiously, the hymns he criticizes, and in which he finds evidence of "priestly ambition," are not the hymns especially for Baptism. There, such lines as "An heir before of son and shame,/Now in the Holy Triune Name/ His guilt is washed away" (from "Within the Church's sacred fold" (--/326) are presumably sufficiently qualified in other stanzas that they may be allowed to stand. In the same hymn, for example, the prayer is voiced that "divinely trained this babe may be/ In faith and hope and love;/ So may he gain, earth's waves o'erpast,/ His bright inheritance at last/ With all Thy Saints above." Similarly, though the declaration of the first stanza of another hymn for Baptism (209/327) is unmistakable:

> 'Tis done! that new and heavenly birth,
> Which recreates the sons of earth,
> Has cleansed from guilt of Adam's sin
> A soul which Jesus died to win,

it is followed by four stanzas emphasizing the dangers and the struggles which must be gone through before the kingdom is won.

The hymns Ormiston criticizes are those which contain only a passing reference to Baptism, and the theology of which is therefore neither qualified nor expanded. Thus "O Word of God above" (242/395), for the festival of the dedication of a Church, mentions among other architectural features the font, whence is "poured/ Grace on each sinful child," instead of saying that the font is where the promise of Grace through prayer is sealed. Similarly, the fifth stanza of "O Christ the heavens' Eternal King" (115/129) for Easter, is considered dangerously unqualified:

Eternal Shepherd, Thou art wont
To cleanse Thy sheep within the font,
That mystic bath, that grave of sin,
Where ransomed souls new life begin.

Ormiston has not been able to find very good examples for his Protestant purposes, but he is concerned only to make his points, and is not overscrupulous about how he does so: here as elsewhere he does not discuss the hymns he cites as objectionable, but only lists them by number.

Ormiston's fifth point is that A&M preaches the efficacy of prayer for the dead, his evidence being the translation of the "Dies irae" by W.J. Irons, "Day of wrath! O day of mourning!" (221/398), and the last lines thereof in particular:

Ah! that day of tears and mourning!
From the dust of earth returning
Man for judgment must prepare him
Spare, O God, in mercy spare him!
Lord, all pitying, Jesu Blest,
Grant them Thine eternal rest.

Ormiston's text was the 1875 edition, but it is worthwhile to note that in 1860 the last line reads "Grant <u>him</u> Thine eternal rest." The pronoun might have mistakenly been thought to refer to the dead person at whose funeral the hymn was being sung, instead of to the noun "Man" three lines above. The authority Ormiston quotes is the Homily of The Church "Concerning Prayer," in which it is declared that:

> ... the sentence of God is unchangeable, and cannot be revoked again. Therefore let us not deceive ourselves, thinking, that either we may help other, or other [sic] may help us by their good and charitable prayers in time to come (14).

That is clear enough, and no human would be foolish enough or could be bold enough to question or challenge the judgment of God,[162] certainly no one in the state imaginatively anticipated in the "Dies irae":

> Low I kneel, with heart submission,
> See, like ashes, my contrition;
> Help me in my last condition.

The answer to Ormiston's objection lies here, in the fact that the hymn is an imaginative anticipation of the day of judgment, intended to strike fear and inspire repentance in the hearts of the living. The reference in the final line (it is clearer in 1860 than in 1875) is not to "the dead," but to "humankind," including, presumably, both those now living and the dead. The appeal for mercy and peace is not an appeal against judgment, but in anticipation of it: just as the Anglican comes to Communion with these words of humility:

> We do not presume to come to this thy Table, O merciful Lord, trusting in our own righteousness, but in thy manifold and great mercies. We are not worthy so much as to gather up

> the crumbs under thy Table. But Thou art the same Lord, whose property is always to have mercy.[163]

No one is righteous enough to be saved by individual merit, but only through the grace and mercy of God. The "Dies irae," even when sung at the burial of the dead, is sung for the living, as the final prayer of the service is for the living, that they may themselves repent, and that they may find comfort in the thought that even the dead have not gone beyond the reach of God's mercy.

The word merit has been used in the discussion of prayer for the dead, and it is the essential term for an understanding of Ormiston's final accusation, that A&M teaches "salvation by human works." On this point the Church of England is thoroughly Protestant: its Articles XI-XIV make clear its views "Of the Justification of Man" (XI), "Of Good Works" (XII), "Of Works before Justification" (XIII), and "Of Works of Supererogation" (XIV). Article XI states:

> We are accounted righteous before God, only for the merit of our Lord and Saviour Jesus Christ by Faith, and not for our own works or deservings: Wherefore, that we are justified by Faith only is a most wholesome Doctrine, and very full of comfort.

Unqualified, "by Faith only" can be misconstrued: either that keeping the faith is easier than keeping the law, which it manifestly is not, or that one's qualification for salvation is a correct inward disposition, which leads one into either self-satisfaction or despair. To avoid potential misinterpretation of the doctrine "by Faith alone," Article XII was written to qualify it:

> Albeit that Good Works, which are the fruits of Faith, and follow after Justification, cannot put away our sins, and endure the severity of God's Judgement; yet are they pleasing and acceptable to God in Christ, and do spring out necessarily of a true and lively Faith; insomuch that by them a lively Faith may be as evidently known as a tree discerned by the fruit.

Roman Catholics hold that individuals can do something to prepare themselves for the reception of grace, and thereafter can by good works merit more grace and eventually salvation.[164] This teaching is expressly denied in the Articles, and it is this teaching that Ormiston claims to find in A&M hymns.

The first hymn he cites is a translation from the Latin of the Roman Catholic Charles Coffin, for use on Thursday, "The fish in wave, the bird on wing" (28/42). The most frequent word in the hymn is "Faith," but this emphasis for Ormiston is contradicted by the fourth stanza:

> Its light the joy of Heav'n reveals
> To hearts made pure within;

> And bids them [1860: us] seek by
> worthy deeds
> Eternal crowns to win.

The lines can be understood in two senses, both of them contrary to Anglican teaching, either that worthy deeds are the means to procure salvation, or that they are supererogatory, and gain crowns to embellish salvation already won. Ormiston's objection will have to be allowed unless one agrees that anyone reading or singing these lines will find their meaning greatly modified by the insistence on Faith and the pure heart.

Ormiston's objection to another hymn "Lo! now is our accepted day" (76/88) for Lent is presumably based on the third stanza:

> Then let us all with earnest care,
> And contrite fast, and tear, and prayer,
> And works of mercy and of love,
> Entreat for pardon from above.

but it would only stand if "earn" or "merit" were substituted for "entreat" in the fourth line. After all the entreaties, one must still wait for the "gifts of grace" of the fourth stanza, for which faith alone is needed, however supported and exercised and strengthened in fasting, prayer, and deeds.

On this point as on all others, Ormiston is excessively literal, and errs on the Protestant side of the _via media_. Four Articles were needed to summarize adequately the complex relation between faith and works; any reference in a hymn will necessarily be a simplification, and prone to error, as we have seen. To refuse to admit the complexities is, however, another form of error, and one to which Ormiston and his like are subject. Common sense and careful reading are capable of dealing with the cries of "No Popery," but those who cry it allow their hearers no opportunity to see for themselves. Ormiston does not discuss the texts of the hymns mentioned in his tract: his tactic is to oppose Protestant and Roman points of dogma, and then to quote the numbers of the hymns where the Roman doctrine is supposedly to be found. The Proprietors were right not to argue the points, but to let their book speak for itself. Only where people were ignorant of its contents could they dismiss it on Ormiston's authority alone, but the places where the book was utterly unknown were few, thanks to its rapid sale and unprecedented popularity. A&M was a phenomenon that could not be dismissed out of hand, as Ormiston eventually discovered.

NOTES

[1] A.P., Undated Letter ca. 1875, R. Collins to [H.W.B.].

[2] A.P., Letter, October 21, 1858, Thomas Hervey to H.W.B.

[3] A.P., Letter, October 29, 1858, J.M. Clarke to H.W.B.

[4] A.P., Letter, October 21, 1858, [W. Braithwaite] to H.W.B.

[5] A.P., Undated Letter ca. 1859, W. Whiting to H.W.B.

[6] A.P., Letter, November 18, 1862, J.A. Skinner to W. Pulling.

[7] The book continued to grow: there have been more A&M supplements than revisions, largely because supplements are easier to prepare, but also because people do not readily accept changes in what is familiar to them.

[8] A.P., Notes of a speech given by William Pulling at a Church Conference, Swansea, 1879.

[9] See Chapter Four, 8.

[10] A.P., Letter, October 29, 1858, J.M. Clarke to H.W.B.

[11] A.P., Letter, November 6, 1858, W.L. Wigan to [H.W.B.].

[12] If not a new tune, then an old one revised, preserving its old musical associations even in its new harmonies. Thomas Hardy in several poems ("Afternoon Service at Mellstock," "On the Tune called the Old-Hundred-and-Fourth," "The Chapel Organist") gave eloquent if nostalgic testimony to the effect the church tunes had on him. The following stanzas come from "Apostrophe to an Old Psalm Tune," written in 1916.

> I met you first--ah, when did I first meet you?
> When I was full of wonder, and innocent,
> Standing meek-eyed with those of choral bent,
> While dimming day grew dimmer
> In the pulpit-glimmer.
>
> Much riper in years I met you--in a temple
> Where summer sunset streamed upon our shapes,
> And you spread over me like a gauze that drapes,
> And flapped from floor to rafters,
> Sweet as angels' laughters.
>
> But you had been stripped of some of your old vesture
> By Monk, or another. Now you wore no frill
> And at first you startled me. But I knew you still,
> Though I missed the minim's waver,
> And the dotted quaver.

The Collected Poems of Thomas Hardy, 4th ed. (1930, reprinted 1968), 404-405.

[13] Winfred Douglas, Church Music in History and Practice: Studies in the Praise of God (1937), 222-223. The provision for such secular occasions is a clear precedent for the provision in A&M of hymns which reach beyond the church services and calendar. See Chapter Four, 3.

[14] A.P., Letter, September 25, 1958, John Horner to H.W.B.

[15] A.P., Letter, November 24, 1858, W. Braithwaite to [H.W.B.].

[16] A.P., Letter, January 10, 1859, Oswald L. Chambers to [H.W.B.].

[17] A.P., Letter, June 25, 1859, W. Braithwaite to [H.W.B.].

[18] In 1860. In 1875, the Apostles and Evangelists are all provided for under their own headings.

[19] Miles Coverdale, Goostly Psalmes and Spiritual Songes (date uncertain but not before 1543), Preface, in Remains of Myles Coverdale, Bishop of Exeter, ed. George Pearson (Cambridge: Parker Society, 1846), 537.

[20] A.P., Letter, October 22, 1858, H.W. [identity unknown] to [H.W.B.].

[21] A.P., Letter, November 30, 1858, J.M. Clarke to H.W.B. Bishop Blomfield of London had resigned in 1856, and had been succeeded by A.C. Tait, whose opposition to ritualism was thoroughgoing and notorious.

[22] See Chapter Four, 8.

[23] A.P., Letter, October 21, 1858, [W. Braithwaite] to H.W.B.

[24] A.P., Letter, Festival of Saints Simon and Jude [October 28], 1858, W. Braithwaite to H.W.B.

[25] See also Chapter Four, 7.

[26] The real debt A&M owed to metrical psalmody was for the tunes: even a cursory glance through the index of tunes reveals more psalm tunes than psalm paraphrases. A total of twenty-one tunes were borrowed from various psalters for the Music edition of 1861, seven of which bear the proud designation "Old," as in "Old 100th."

[27] A.P., Letter, November 13, 1858, W. Braithwaite to [H.W.B.].

[28] Although Braithwaite and his colleagues disliked the predominance of ancient hymns for the seasons, there were others for whom it was a principle. An unidentified correspondent wrote to the Proprietors from St. Leonard's on Sea, stating that

> H.A.M. are, to my mind, more defective in respect to the ancient hymns than in any other way. . . . It is a principle with me to give every office, as far as possible, its old hymn, just as it is the general rule of our English Church to give it its old collect, or at least one framed upon a like plan. (A.P., Incomplete letter, January 21, 1872, ? to [H.W.B.].)

[29] See Chapter Three, 1, iii.

[30] A.P., M.B., January 30, 1868; March 18, 1868; May 14, 1868.

[31] One of Sir Henry's projects for the Revised edition had been a new series of hymns for the days of the week, either to supplement or to supplant the hymns printed for that use in A&M 1860, all of which were translations from the eighteenth-century Latin of Charles Coffin. The proposed series was actually printed in the 1873 specimen of the Revised edition, but they caused so much comment, and evoked so much criticism, that they were finally omitted. Their author, Godfrey Thring, had described them as hymns on the creation, and had explained to Sir Henry: "I took great pains to reconcile . . . modern thought & the discoveries of geology with the account given in Genesis, the one I imagine when it is true always agreeing with the other" (A.P., Letter, July 27, 1872, Godfrey Thring to H.W.B.). The difficulties of such a task of reconciliation explain why the hymns could not generally please.

[32] Most of the Latin hymns are anonymous, or ascribed more or less inaccurately to known authors. They can be dated by manuscript information and by internal evidence of style, but the authorship of very few of the genuine ancient hymns can be authenticated.

[33] Or nearly original -- his paraphrases are included in this figure rather than among the translations.

[34] Faber, Newman, Coffin and de Santeuil.

[35] Doddridge, Watts, and Charles and John Wesley.

[36] C.F. Alexander, Cowper, and Montgomery, the last of whom was at one time a Dissenter, but later an Anglican communicant.

[37] Sacred Hymns from the German (1841) and a second edition, Hymns from the German (1864), by Frances Cox; Lyra Germanica, First and second series (1855 and 1858), Chorale Book for England (1863), and Christian Singers of Germany (1869), by Catherine Winkworth.

[38] J.M. Neale, The Ecclesiologist, n.s. vol. viii (October 1850), 175

[39] Latin texts from John Julian, ed., A Dictionary of Hymnology (1892), 1198-1199. First English translation by J.M. Neale, as altered in Salisbury Hymn Book, 1857; second translation by the present writer.

[40] J.M. Neale, The Ecclesiologist, n.s. vol. ix (February 1851), 11-12. Neale's emphasis.

[41] Neale, Ecclesiologist (February 1851), 12.

[42] A.P., Letter, December 15, [1858], H.W.B. to W.U. Richards. H.W.B.'s emphasis.

[43] A.P., Letter, October 13, 1860, G. Ironside to G.C. White.

[44] A.P., Letter, January 7, 1860, J.M. Neale to [Maberley].

[45] Letter, January 7, 1860, Neale to [Maberley].

[46] Sabine Baring Gould objected to this alteration when he read the specimen of the Revised edition, saying that "crimson gives an idea & character, precious is commonplace." A.P., Letter, March 11, 1873, S. Baring Gould to [H.W.B.].

[47] Unless otherwise specified, all Latin texts in this chapter are those given in Maurice Frost, ed., A Historical Companion to Hymns Ancient and Modern (1962), and English "trots" are by the present writer.

[48] J.M. Neale, Mediaeval Hymns and Sequences, 2nd edition (1863), vii-viii.

[49] Latin text from L.C. Biggs, ed., Hymns Ancient and Modern . . . with Annotations, etc. (1867).

[50] In addition, it overlooks the much-compressed sense of "lacteum . . . sanguinem," a sense which is not brought out until the 1904 translation, where the lines read "While from His Mother's bosom fed,/ His precious blood He wills to shed."

[51] Quoted in Julian, ed., Dictionary of Hymnology (1892), 788.

[52] A.P., Letter, May 29, 1868, C. Winkworth to [H.W.B.].

[53] A.P., Letter, July 15, 1874, C. Winkworth to H.W.B.

[54] A.P., Letter, April 24, [1859], J. Woodford to H.W.B. Woodford's emphasis.

[55] A.P., Letter, November 13, 1858, W. Braithwaite to [H.W.B.].

[56] A.P., Letter, November 30, 1858, J.M. Clarke to H.W.B.

[57] J.M. Neale, Mediaeval Hymns (1851), 19.

[58] It almost seems as if Neale wished to suggest by the choice of the word "acceptation" the term from Roman law "acceptilation," the remission of a debt by acquittance without payment, or figuratively, free remission, which has its theological parallel in mankind's release through God's grace from its inheritance of sin.

[59] Suscipio: to catch; to support; to pick up, resume; to bear (children); to accept, receive (under one's protection); to take up, undertake; to acknowledge, recognize (a child) as one's own.

[60] Victor E. Neuburg, "The Literature of the Streets," Plate 47 in The Victorian City: Images and Realities, eds. H.J. Dyos and Michael Wolff, Vol. I (1977), facing 199.

[61] A.P., Letter, November 18, 1862, J.A. Skinner to W. Pulling.

[62] A.P., Letter, January 7, 1860, J.M. Neale to [Maberley]. Neale's emphasis.

[63] See Chapter One, 2.

[64] E.H. Bickersteth, Life of Edward Bickersteth, vol. 2, 38. Quoted by J.M. Neale, "Hymns and Hymnals," The Christian Remembrancer, vol. xlvi, no. cxxi (July 1863), 115-116.

[65] See Kenneth Clark, The Gothic Revival (1928), especially Chapter 8, "Ecclesiology."

[66] J.M. Neale, Christian Remembrancer (July 1863), 115.

[67] J.M. Neale, Christian Remembrancer (July 1863), 116.

[68] J.M. Neale, Christian Remembrancer (July 1863), 116. Neale's emphasis.

[69] "A Favourite Hymn, sung by Lady Huntingdon's Young Collegians," undated leaflet, c. 1772. The first stanza comes from Peter Williams' Hymns on Various Subjects (1771); the second and third stanzas are by William Williams.

[70] John Keble, Miscellaneous Poems (1869), viii.

[71] J.M. Neale, Christian Remembrancer (July 1863), 108.

[72] A.P., Letter, January 7, 1860, J.M. Neale to [Maberley].

[73] Letter, January 7, 1860, Neale to [Maberley].

[74] A.P., Letter, Ascension Day 1874, Dean R.W. Church to H.W.B.

[75] Letter, Ascension Day 1874, Church to H.W.B.

[76] A.P., M.B., November 20, 1873.

[77] A.P., Letter, December 9, 1872. J. Marriott to "his cousin Fitzherbert."

[78] Isaac Watts, Preface, The Psalms of David, imitated in the language of the New Testament, and apply'd to the Christian State and Worship (1719), xiv-xv. Watts's emphasis.

[79] A.P., Fragment of a Letter, probably before October 5, 1860, H.P. Liddon to [R.M. Benson?].

[80] A.P., Letter, August 22, 1874, John Ellerton to H.W.B. Ellerton's emphasis.

[81] A.P., Letter, May 20, 1868, C.F. Alexander to [H.W.B.].

[82] Stanza 5 of the hymn as printed in Dr. Hook's Leeds Church Sunday School Hymn Book, 1850.

[83] Original English texts, unless otherwise specified, are those given in Frost, ed., Historical Companion to A&M (1962).

[84] A.P., Letter, [January 15, 1874], Pusey to H.W.B.

[85] A.P., Letter, January 15, 1874, C. Wordsworth to H.W.B.

[86] A.P., Letter, January 17, 1874, W. Bright to H.W.B.

[87] A.P., M.B., November 20, 1873.

[88] A.P., Letter, July 13, 1872, Bishop of Brechin to W. Pulling.

[89] A.P., Draft Letter, [January 1874], H.W.B. to C. Wordsworth.

[90] A.P., Letter, May 12, 1868, H. Twells to H.W.B.

[91] A.P., Letter, July 11, 1868, H. Twells to H.W.B.

[92] A.P., Letter, July 18, 1868, H. Twells to H.W.B.

[93] A.P., Letter, September 25, 1858, John Horner to H.W.B. "I will only add that Mr. [W.H. Perceval] Ward spoke of an Expurgate Edition for popular use, to this I confess I strongly objected."

[94] A.P., Letter, September 7, [1858], J.R. Woodford to H.W.B.

[95] A.P., Letter, January 21, 1874, W.C. Dix to H.W.B.

[96] A.P., Letter, October 5, 1860, H.P. Liddon to R.M. Benson.

[97] A.P., Letter, March 11, 1873, S. Baring Gould to [H.W.B.].

[98] A.P., Letter, August 21, 1868, H.W.B. to W. Pulling.

[99] A.P., Letter, August 31, [1868], Pusey to H.W.B.

[100] Letter, August 21, 1868, H.W.B. to Pulling.

[101] Neale, _Christian Remembrancer_ (July 1863), 121.

[102] A.P., Letter, [ca. April 1874], J. Monsell to H.W.B. Monsell's emphasis.

[103] A.P., Letters, June 14 and November 12, 1874, C.F. Alexander to H.W.B.

[104] Psalm 51:17, Authorized Version.

[105] William T. Brooke, "My Lord, my Love was crucified," _Dictionary of Hymnology_, ed. Julian (1892), 781. Brooke's emphasis.

[106] A.P., Letter, [1859], W. Whiting to H.W.B., Comments on the Second Specimen.

[107] It was a development which A&M greatly advanced, and hardly enjoyed. Although it falls outside the scope of this study, it is worth noting that the Proprietors of A&M persevered in their constant revision of their book in committee, culminating in the New edition of 1904, which was in part an attempt to restore to common use originals which A&M versions had long ousted. The changes were met with outraged protests, exemplified by the popular rejection of Charles Wesley's own "Hark! how all the welkin rings" in favour of the familiar "Hark! the herald-angels sing." When the novelty had worn off, many accepted the more authentic versions, but from the pages of the _English Hymnal_ (1906), not from the A&M New edition.

[108] Bullock's original from Biggs, ed., _A&M with Annotations_ (1867).

[109] Milton's text here and below from Douglas Bush, ed., _The Complete Poetical Works of John Milton_ (1965), 6-8.

[110] F.E. Hutchinson, ed., _The Works of George Herbert_ (1941), 172-173.

[111] The use of "praise," especially in its prominent rhyming position, may seem a borrowing from Herbert,

but it has been seen (cf. the final stanza of "We love the place, O God") that an image of the faithful rapt in wonder and worship of God is for Sir Henry a frequent vision of heaven.

112 The post-script of a letter from Henry Twells to Sir Henry testifies to the hymn's appeal:

> I cannot forbear telling you that a dear old lady, a parishioner of mine, aetat 87, who is now upon her deathbed, sent for one of our choristers the other day that she might hear once more "The King of Love my Shepherd is," which the child duly sung to her. I told her, when I heard of it, that the author of that hymn might perhaps come to the Dedication Festival. Her face lighted up for an instant, and then she said -- 'I shall not be here then, or I should so like to thank him for that hymn!' (A.P., Letter, July 9, 1873, Henry Twells to H.W.B.)

113 S.L. Ollard and Gordon Crosse, eds., _A Dictionary of English Church History_ (1912), 31.

114 Percy Dearmer, Martin Shaw, and Ralph Vaughan Williams, eds., _The Oxford Bood of Carols_ (1928), no. 56.

115 A.P., Letter, July 2, [1860?], W.C. Dix to F.H. Murray. Dix's emphasis.

116 A.P., First specimen (1859), no. 21, "Earth has many a noble city" (59/76).

117 A.P., Letter, June 23, 1859, J.M. Wilkins to H.W.B.

118 Psalm 22 begins "My God, my God, why hast thou forsaken me?" -- Jesus' words from the cross (Matthew 27:46). Later in the psalm are the words "They pierced my hands and my feet . . . they part my garments among them, and cast lots upon my vesture" (vv. 16,18 Authorized Version), which are read as prophecy.

119 A.P., Letter, April 23, 1862, C. Wordsworth to H.W.B.

120 A.P., M.B., August 26, 1874.

121 A.P., Letter, June 25, 1859, W. Braithwaite to [H.W.B.].

[122] A.P., Letter, February 13, 1868, J. Allen to H.W.B.

[123] A.P., Letter, October 28, [1859], F. Pott to H.W.B.

[124] A.P., Letter, November 2, [1859], F. Pott to H.W.B. Pott's emphasis.

[125] Letter, November 2, [1859], Pott to H.W.B. Pott's emphasis.

[126] Letter, November 2, [1859], Pott to H.W.B.

[127] Letter, November 2, [1859], Pott to H.W.B. The last words of the Article are "The Sacrament of the Lord's Supper was not by Christ's ordinance reserved, carried about, lifted up, or worshipped."

[128] Letter, November 2, [1859], Pott to H.W.B. Pott's emphasis.

[129] The reference is to the Passover: it has been said that the Last Supper of Christ and His disciples was the passover meal which, in its commemoration of the deliverance of the people of Israel from Egypt, also foretold the true deliverance from the bondage of sin and death, when the true paschal lamb was sacrificed: "Christ our passover is sacrificed for us: therefore let us keep the feast" (I Corinthians 5:7). The third stanza of the hymn had already mentioned the feast and the rites demanded by the law.

[130] Article XXXI. "Of the one Oblation of Christ finished upon the Cross. The offering of Christ once made is that perfect redemption, propitiation, and satisfaction, for all the sins of the whole world, both original and actual; and there is none other satisfaction for sin, but that alone. Wherefore the sacrifices of Masses, in the which it was commonly said, that the Priest did offer Christ for the quick and the dead, to have remission of pain or guilt, were blasphemous fables, and dangerous deceits."

[131] A.P., Copy of a Letter, [early September 1875], H.W.B. to R.A. Maunsele. H.W.B.'s emphasis.

[132] A.P., Letter, September 10, 1875, R.A. Maunsele to H.W.B.

[133] A.P., Copy of a Letter, September 13, 1875, H.W.B. to R.A. Maunsele.

[134] Article XXII: "Of Purgatory. The Romish Doctrine concerning Purgatory, Pardons, Worshipping and Adoration, as well of Images as of Reliques, and also invocation of Saints, is a fond thing vainly invented, and grounded upon no warranty of Scripture, but rather repugnant to the Word of God."

[135] A.P., Letter, April 28, 1874, H. Percy Smith to [H.W.B.]. Smith's emphasis.

[136] A.P., Letter, December 4, 1871, Sir R. Grant to H.W.B.

[137] A.P., Letter, October 22, 1868, Dean Howson to H.W.B.

[138] A.P., Letter, December 7, 1874, H. Downton to H.W.B.

[139] See Chapter Three, 3, ii re: correspondence between H.W.B. and Francis Pott.

[140] A.P., Letter, March 15, 1873, L.C. Biggs to H.W.B. Biggs's emphasis.

[141] A.P., Letter, October 1, 1864, H.W.B. to G.C. White. H.W.B's emphasis.

[142] Original text of 1844 as given in Biggs, ed., _A&M with Annotations_ (1867).

[143] A.P., Letter, October 26, 1864, H. Alford to H.W.B.

[144] In Biggs, ed., _A&M with Annotations_ (1867).

[145] Letter, October 1, 1864, H.W.B. to G.C. White. H.W.B.'s emphasis.

[146] In Frost, ed., _Historical Companion to A&M_ (1962).

[147] A.P., Cutting from _Guardian_, October 18, 1871, Report of a speech by C. Wordsworth to Nottingham Church Congress.

[148] A.P., Letter, July 4, 1871, C. Wordsworth to H.W.B.

[149] (Sixth stanza in Wordsworth's original)
For souls redeemed, for sins forgiven,
For means of grace and hopes of heaven,

What can to Thee, O Lord, be given,
Who givest all?

150 T.T. Lynch, Songs Controversial, by Silent Long (1856), no. 8, "A Negative Affair."

151 A.P., Cutting from an unidentified newspaper, [May 1879], "Report of a lecture on 'Hymns Ancient and Modern' given in the Vestry Hall, Turnham Green, on Monday evening last, by the Rev. J. Ormiston, vicar of Old Hill, Dudley."

152 J. Ormiston, Hymns Ancient and Modern, and their Romanizing Teaching (Church Association Tracts, no. 21, 1875), 4. Subsequent page references to this tract will be given in parentheses in the text.

153 Newspaper cutting, Turnham Green lecture.

154 A.P., Cutting from an unidentified newspaper, "Report of a lecture by J. Ormiston at Blackburn" [where the congregation and Sunday-school teachers of St. Peter's Church had refused to use A&M as their vicar wished].

155 Newspaper cutting, Turnham Green lecture.

156 In 1860, the line reads "Jesu, may such deep devotion."

157 I Corinthians 13:12.

158 Preface to The Order of Confirmation, Book of Common Prayer.

159 The Ministration of Publick Baptism of Infants, Book of Common Prayer. Emphasis added.

160 G.M. Young, Victorian England: Portrait of an Age (1960), 119n.

161 The hostility toward the Privy Council aroused by the Gorham judgment and by those in later cases of ceremonial greatly undermined the whole structure of Church law and authority, for many refused to acknowledge the moral authority of a court created solely by Parliament. Though some high churchmen, chief among them Manning, took the occasion to secede to Rome, other influential figures such as Keble, Samuel Wilberforce, and Gladstone held that a ruling by the Privy Council was a mere State decision, and did not compromise the Church.

[162] The question centers on when that judgment will be given, and Christians including Anglicans declare their belief that Christ "shall come again with glory to judge both the quick and the dead" (Nicene Creed) and that at this coming "all men shall rise again with their bodies: and shall give account for their own works. And they that have done good shall go into life everlasting: and they that have done evil into everlasting fire" (Athanasian Creed). Judgment is suspended until that last day, and Roman Catholics have allowed for a process of purification by fire (Purgatory) between death and judgment, and that "souls there detained are helped by the intercessions of the faithful, but most of all by the acceptable sacrifice of the altar" (Council of Trent, quoted in A.T. Hanson, "The Christian Hope," A Dictionary of Christian Theology, ed. Alan Richardson (1969), 160). The Church of England, in repudiating Purgatory, also repudiated or, more accurately, made irrelevant, the intercession through prayer of the living for the dead.

[163] The Order of the Administration of the Lord's Supper, or Holy Communion, Book of Common Prayer.

[164] P.S. Watson, "Good Works," A Dictionary of Christian Theology, ed. Alan Richardson (1969), 146.

Chapter Five
The Inculcation and Reflection of Anglican Attitudes

1. The Middle-Class Bias

That hymns convey the attitudes of those who write them is undeniable, and the social attitudes expressed in a wide range of Victorian hymns have been examined in Susan Tamke's _Make a Joyful Noise Unto the Lord_ (1978). A&M contains a more restricted sample of hymns, but they, too, repay scrutiny. Some attitudes are conscious and were discussed above: deliberate propaganda and dogmatic declaration in Chapter Two, and the importance attached to the didactic function of the hymns in A&M in the doctrinal section of Chapter Four. This section concentrates upon the more subtle evidence of Anglican attitude and bias.

The whole question is a complicated one. Obviously, a great deal can be inferred from the church's hymns. If no other evidence of the existence of this particular form of Christianity survived, one could nevertheless draw a fairly accurate picture of the Church of England from one of its hymnbooks. Thus, even a quick glance through A&M will reveal the pattern of the church year with its feasts and fasts, the sacraments and saints, and the episcopal and parochial organization. Reading the book closely will reveal the doctrines and articles of faith, and also suggest the degree of latitude in interpretation that is allowed. Finally, the book sets out a pattern of Christian life, which exists in tension with the implicit pattern of society.

A&M is not, however, the only surviving relic of Victorian Anglicanism. It is, nevertheless, a source quite unlike ecclesiastical or historical documents, in that it cuts across all levels of Christian life: the corporate, and the individual, the ideal and the practical. Such a book is essentially conservative: it almost always reflects rather than projects, and is sometimes extraordinarily slow to reflect changes. This time lapse, over centuries in extreme cases, sets up tensions between the language and imagery of the hymns and the experience of those who sing them.[1] The hymn may then be only a dim shadow, its significance distorted or blurred by changed circumstance. An example of this shift is discussed below in the section on urban imagery, where a vision of perfection has been eroded because the terms in which it was expressed have been devalued. In other cases, the hymn may survive intact, like a fly preserved in amber, complete and curious, a reminder of what has gone before, and sometimes, a salutary reminder. The hymns which survive thus are those which have a deeper integrity than others, a poetic integrity, and the force which preserves them is imagination.

When a hymn collection reflects more immediately, it is not a complete picture, but a vivid and often an unusual one. The section on mission hymns below gives an example. The historian records that foreign missions evoked considerable popular interest after 1871. The hymns themselves, with their new emphasis on personal responsibility, and a lively awareness of the drama of missions, show how the writers' imaginations were fired and a general popular interest given direction. It would, however, be foolish to pretend that the hymns give any real idea of the full extent of Victorian missionary endeavour.

Other attitudes are harder to pin down and to appreciate, largely because the contents of the book have been filtered through so many minds, often through a translator and several editors and critics, before assuming their A&M form. The difficulty is increased because the kinds of bias being sought are rarely blatant, or at the centre of a hymn, but are to be detected in the odd phrase or illustration. Children's hymns are often an exception, for many of them are very prescriptive and thus reveal their authors' assumptions. Moreover, one must be cautious about misinterpreting the often compressed language of verse, and basing condemnation on misunderstanding. The notorious stanza in C.F. Alexander's hymn (not published in A&M 1860, 1868 or 1875) "All things bright and beautiful" is an excellent cautionary example:

> The rich man in his castle,
> The poor man at his gate,
> He made them, high or lowly,
> And ordered their estate.

At first sight, the sentiment seems a reactionary one, perhaps deliberately so in response to the turmoil of the times in which the hymn was published (1848). But one must not overlook the commas and the range of meaning of the word "ordered" -- what the lines really say is that for all their obvious disparity, whether they are rich or poor, people are part of God's orderly creation.

One must be careful to distinguish between attitudes inculcated and attitudes reflected. For "inculcated" might be substituted the words "recommended" or "reinforced." Obviously a hymn reflects most immediately the attitudes of its writer, which may or may not be those of its singers. Sometimes the recommendations may be so forceful as to be didacticism. For example, there is throughout A&M an attitude of respect for clergy, but when J.M. Neale writes a hymn for Ember Days about the Apostolic Succession, "Christ is gone up; yet ere He passed" (214/352), he is actually preaching a doctrine, and at the same time encouraging a deeper respect, even reverence, among the people for the priesthood. The lines quoted above from "All things bright and beautiful" may be considered a reflection of Alexander's views, and a recommendation of those views among those who sing her words. When dealing with the complexities and the nuances of this matter of attitudes, it is imperative to pay close attention to the voice, to know whether it is that of an individual, or of a group (whether class or profession), or of an individual speaking for or interpreting a group (whether from within or from without).

Sometimes attitudes are more straightforward. A prevailing view may be reflected in hymns only to be criticized. C. F. Alexander fretted about the materialism of her age, measuring it by an Apostolic standard, and finding it wanting. Her hymn for St. Andrew, "Jesus calls us; o'er the tumult" (--/403), was written for the S.P.C.K. book of 1852, and its third stanza reads:

> Jesus calls us from the worship
>   Of the vain world's golden store,
> From each idol that would keep us,
>   Saying, 'Christian, love Me more'.

More than twenty years later she was still concerned about this form of idolatry, and wrote for A&M 1875 a hymn for St. Matthew (--/420). The evangelist is only the occasion of the discourse: he is memorable to Alexander mostly for his renunciation of commerce. The hymn is fired by her concern, and plunges without pause through three stanzas, containing some vivid images:

> Dear Lord, on this Thy servant's day,
> Who left for Thee the gold and mart,
> Who heard Thee whisper, 'Come away,'
> And followed with a single heart,
>
> Give us, amid earth's weary moil,
> And wealth for which men cark and care,
> 'Mid fortune's pride, and need's wild toil,
> And broken hearts in purple rare,[2]
>
> Give us Thy grace to rise above
> The glare of this world's smelting fires;
> Let God's great love put out the love
> Of gold, and gain, and low desires.

The fourth stanza is a deliberate contrast: the evangelist's presence in the hymn is made startlingly clear in a simile utterly unlike any other image:

> Still, like a breath from scented lime
> Borne into rooms where sick men faint,
> His voice comes floating through all
> time,
> Thine own Evangelist and Saint.

The final stanza is a recapitulation, but it is weakened by Alexander's inability to escape the metaphors she is attempting to devalue. Partly it is the fault of the gospel itself to which the hymn refers: the epigraph is "Lay up for yourselves treasures in heaven." However much she despises it, gold is the pre-eminent standard of value; earthly treasure rusts, but the gold of heaven is incorruptible. The gospel itself has the ring of true metal, and even when she tries to downplay gold as mere yellow dust, the contrast she sets up conceals an inadvertent monetary pun:

> Still sweetly rings the gospel strain
> Of golden store that knows not rust:
> The love of Christ is more than gain,
> And heavenly crowns than yellow dust.

The most fascinating attitudes are not those easily identifiable, but those which can be traced through slighter references, which accumulate, and are convincing in their very number. Individually they do not attract much attention: they are neither doubted nor questioned. What editors, as sensitive to implication as the A&M Compilers assuredly were, pass without comment must be unexceptionable indeed.

Take, for instance, the references to labour in the hymns, which reflect both the professional and the social assumptions of the writers. The word labour itself is used in a very general sense, to mean all human activity through which Christian love can be manifested. There is rarely any sense of labour as heart- and body-wearing toil undertaken to earn a living. The most concrete reference to manual labour is in a children's hymn, "Come, sing with holy gladness" (366/341):

> O boys, be strong in Jesus,
> To toil for Him is gain,
> And Jesus wrought with Joseph
> With chisel, saw, and plane.

One can imagine what a caricature Dickens would have made of anyone who had come canting that sentiment to David Copperfield's companions in the warehouse.

The common use of metaphors of pilgrimage and battle both dramatize and distance the reality of daily living. Those who were trapped in repetitive labour may find such metaphors enheartening, but they cannot always have been sure that they were travelling anywhere or gaining any ground. Those whose lives were more comfortable were kept so by those metaphors.

It may well be argued that a hymnbook is not the place for startling reappraisals, that a hymn should not introduce controversy into divine worship. On the other hand, it ought not to ignore, or belittle, or make it easy to condone the suffering or the wrong that humans have made of God's creation. It is not the hymn-writers' intention to ignore or belittle or condone. Rather, it is their intention to dignify all work, making it all equally acceptable in the sight of God. Unfortunately those who wrote the hymns and taught that <u>laborare est orare</u>, were rarely those who could not hear themselves think in the noise of a great mill.

Faber's evening hymn, "Sweet Saviour, bless us ere we go" (17/28), contains an excellent example of the glibness of inexperience. It was infinitely easier for Faber to pen the following lines than for a worker to enact the sentiment: "Labour is sweet, for Thou hast toiled;/ And care is light, for Thou has cared." The stanza which contains these lines (the fifth) was omitted when the hymn was revised for A&M 1875.

What the hymn-writers are guilty of is a failure of nerve, a failure to confront their understanding of work with the reality of working-class life. It is not their task, finally, to solve the problem, but the task of theologians and Christian apologists. In shirking that confrontation, however, the hymn-writers betray the poetic qualities of their verse, for poetry ought to have the necessary nerve and imagination. Instead, the problem is, generally, evaded: the number of hymns about Paradise is proof both of the failure of nerve, and of the uneasy conscience that resulted.

That is not to say that the related problems of labour, injustice, and pain are not dealt with at all in the A&M hymns, but that there is a significant failure to admit their part in Christianity. Nowhere is the middle-class bias of Anglicanism more evident than in a hymn such as Eliza Alderson's almsgiving verses "Lord of glory, who hast bought us" (372/367). She perceives poverty as something with which Christians must cope, but not something which they must share. The fourth stanza of her hymn requires careful reading:

> Yes: the sorrow and the suffering,
>   Which on every hand we see,
> Channels are for tithes and offerings
>   Due by solemn right to Thee;
> Right of which we may not rob Thee,
>   Debt we may not choose but pay,
> Lest that Face of love and pity
>   Turn from us another day.

Clearly she does not mean that God must not be deprived of Creation's sorrow and suffering, though it almost appears so from the uncertainty about the antecedent of the relative pronoun, in "Right of which we may not rob Thee." That charity and almsgiving are enjoined upon Christ's people has ample gospel authority, and Alderson's hymn is a reminder of that. It also, however, suggests that sorrow and suffering are ultimately irremediable, and that they exist in order that Christians may practice charity for the good of their souls.

The suggestion is faint, however, and the sentiment is not general. To set against that hymn is one by Sir Henry Baker, for "Friendly Societies," "O praise our God today" (232/380), which is a hearty blend of muscular Christianity and mild Christian socialism:

> O praise our God today,
>   His constant mercy bless,

Whose love hath helped us on our way,
And granted us success.

His Arm the strength imparts
Our daily toil to bear;
His grace alone inspires our hearts
Each other's load to share.
(stanzas 1-2)

The friendly society, in Sir Henry's view, attributes the success of its work equally to self-help, and to God. The very use of the word "success" strikes an unusual note on first hearing: Christians rarely speak of success, but more often of repeated attempt and failure, and ultimately a triumph undeserved by their own efforts. The note of congratulation in Sir Henry's hymn is meant to encourage the members to renewed efforts. "If God be with us, who can be against us?" and "The Lord helps those who help themselves" are the popular sentiments which underlie the hymn.

Their success, however, is limited, and their help does not penetrate the depths of human misery. It never occurred to Sir Henry, or at least, he did not think it fit for a popular hymn, that some ills might be eradicated at source, and that the cure must touch the cause of the disease, and not alleviate its symptoms merely. One does not expect a hymn-writer to suggest large-scale economic reforms, but when one considers some aspects of Victorian society, it seems feebly inadequate to sing of sweetening "many a cup of woe/By deeds of holy love!"(stanza 3) or rejoicing "with them that do rejoice,/And [weeping] with them that weep" (stanza 4).

Christianity is a religion both radical and non-revolutionary. It is radical in that, if believers lived out the teachings of Jesus, their society would be unrecognizable, its social, economic, and political structure axed at the roots, and utterly remade. It is non-revolutionary in that the many are not to be overthrown by the few, and what is Caesar's must be rendered unto Caesar. His own followers were disappointed when the Messiah did not wish to appropriate a throne, and impose a new order.

One problem with the Church of Christ, and particularly of the established Church, is that its members are too ready to render unto Caesar, and may neglect the things that are God's. The people's physical and mental well-being is Caesar's; their souls are God's: let them live in slums so long as they praise their Maker. (These are extreme sentiments but they point at truth.) Acts of charity are to be performed, but it takes a special kind of seer to perceive, when Christ says, "I was in prison, and you visited me," that it is not enough merely to visit the prisons when they are in crying need of reform. On the other hand, it is unjust to condemn a Victorian hymn-writer for a common failure: who would cast the first stone?

Sir Henry's hymn may not be the work of a radical imagination, but it is important for its sense of a community of people ministering to one another as equals, without the condescension of Alderson's hymn. He thought of it only in terms of a friendly society, however, and not of the entire congregation or society at large; it is nevertheless an unusual hymn, and worthy of notice.

This introductory section has indicated some of the difficulties inherent in an attempt to search beneath the surface meaning of a hymn, and has also suggested how subtle an appreciation one can develop of the minds of the hymn-writers. In the sections which follow, different groups of hymns are studied for their treatment of theme, their use of imagery, their judgments and evaluations, and their response to a variety of challenges to imagination and expression.

2. Hymns of Paradise

It was suggested above that the number of hymns about Paradise is evidence of the inability of the hymn-writer to come to terms with the reality of industrial Britain, especially at the working-class level. This section discusses, first, what is meant by Paradise hymns, and second, the extent to which they are an escapist device, both for writer and singer.

By Paradise hymns is meant those hymns which describe a local heaven in some vivid detail or which express a strong yearning for heaven. They may or may not set up an explicit contrast between the vision of heaven and the experience of earth.

Paradise is a theme which has never palled, though the majority of the Paradise hymns in A&M are either mediaeval or Victorian. An increase in their popularity is reflected in the successive editions of A&M: 1860 has half a dozen; the Appendix adds nine more; the Revised edition omits none of these and prints two new ones.[3] In that edition they form a sub-section of fifteen general hymns (222 to 236). A few of these were grouped together in the Appendix (322 to

325), otherwise the hymns were more widely scattered. The new grouping emphasizes the Compilers' recognition of the type of "Paradise hymn."

The mediaeval Paradise hymns are characterized by their vivid imagery and lack of self-consciousness. The imagery is largely that of the book of Revelations, with a wealth of precise and colourful detail. The unselfconsciousness shows in the simplicity with which the details are given, even the most exotic being accepted. The authority of the Scriptures suffices to lend credibility, and it is important that the heaven for which one longs is a heaven in which one believes. That is not to say that the writers took literally every image that St. John dreamed, although they delight in them. Even the most concrete of images will slide into obvious metaphor. An example of this is one of the hymns from "De contemptu mundi," "For thee, O dear, dear Country" (142ii/227). Two stanzas in the middle of the hymn celebrate the holy city as a material place, though the materials are unimaginably precious:

> With jasper glow thy bulwarks,
> Thy streets with emerald blaze;
> The sardius and the topaz
> Unite in thee their rays.
> (stanza 5)

The architectural description culminates, however, in what is undeniably metaphor, which casts back over the preceding passage its non-literal light. The poet lets us know that the images do not have to be taken literally to be taken seriously, and that seriousness does not preclude delight.

Thine ageless walls are bonded
With amethyst unpriced;
The saints build up its fabric,
And the corner-stone is Christ.
(stanza 6)

Perhaps unselfconscious is the wrong adjective, for these ancient artists know exactly what they are doing. The more appropriate word may be confident: the writer does not necessarily believe the images, but does believe in their force.

The modern hymns of Paradise reduce the richness to a minimum, as if the writers were afraid to be caught out in the midst of such credulous exuberance. C.F. Alexander's hymn "The roseate hues of early dawn" (167/229) contrasts earth and heaven, but the colour and detail are reserved for earth, while heaven is given a pair of perfunctory clichés and a metaphor:

The roseate hues of early dawn,
The brightness of the day,
The crimson of the sunset sky,
How fast they fade away!
Oh, for the pearly gates of heaven,
Oh, for the golden floor,
Oh, for the Sun of Righteousness,
That setteth nevermore!

From that stanza alone it is hard to see why anyone would trade the beauty of the earth for such a stilted heaven. Alexander lacks confidence in her vision.

The mediaeval vision is often surprisingly real,

and sometimes even earthy. In "Jerusalem the golden" (142iii/228), the sounds of heaven come from real throats:

> There is the throne of David;
> And there, from care released,
> The shout of them that triumph,
> The song of them that feast.
> (stanza 5)

There is honest gusto in that heavenly song. Compare a hymn by Sir Henry, "There is a blessed Home" (182/230), which is characterized by abstractions (faith, hope, light and peace -- no amethyst or topaz here) and in which the music is disembodied: "Glad songs that never cease/Within its portals swell" (stanza 2).

It would be unfair to suggest that the ancient hymns without exception are more vividly attractive than the modern ones. A counter-example must be Peter Abelard's hymn "O quanta qualia," which appears in A&M (343/235) in an altered form of Neale's translation, as "O what the joy and the glory must be." Part of the unattractiveness of the hymn is its dactylic trisyllables, which canter with heavy and monotonous regularity throughout. Furthermore, there is hardly a sentence which is not inverted ("Now in the meanwhile with hearts raised on high,/We for that country must yearn and must sigh," stanza 6). Its doxology is a marvel of grammatical and theological precision, but out of keeping with the supposed yearning of the hymn:

> Low before Him with our praises we fall,
> Of Whom, and in Whom, and through Whom are all:

> Of Whom, the Father; and in Whom, the Son;
> Through Whom, the Spirit, with Them ever
> One.

It is rather pedantry than praise.

These faults are largely attributable to the translator, but the central comparison of the hymn is Abelard's, and it is this comparison which is least attractive:

> O what the joy and the glory must be
> Those endless Sabbaths the blessèd ones
> see.

and

> There dawns no Sabbath, no Sabbath is
> o'er,
> Those Sabbath-keepers have one evermore.
> (stanzas 1,5)

Such a prospect is enough to daunt any middle-class child who found Sundays intolerably dreary. Nor is Sabbath a name to appeal to the worker, whose day of rest was declared a day of idleness and boredom by those who would keep the Sabbath by restricting amusement and proscribing pleasure. This is a good example of an ancient hymn sorely weakened by a new association of meaning. In itself it is not a great or serious difference, but it becomes necessary for the modern reader to make a deliberate allowance for the change. Immediacy is gone; there is no ready recognition of or identification with the mood of the hymn, and therein lies its weakness, for the major level of the hymn is the emotional one of anticipation and jubilation.

In fact, the Paradise hymns are what may be called subjective rather than objective. By definition they deal in things unseen save in a dream, and they embody a longing for salvation, peace, life, light and the fulfilment of all the promises of God, which is at once general and intensely personal. When the hymn-writers lost confidence in their images of Paradise, they began to write more fervently about the hope rather than the vision of heaven.

Of course, any hymn about heaven implies, at least, a contrast with earth, and it is the attitudes about life on earth to be detected in these hymns which are of chief interest here. Sometimes the contrast between earth and heaven is explicit. In the "De contemptu mundi" hymns the point is brusquely made in the opening lines:

> Brief life is here our portion;
> Brief sorrow, short-lived care;
> The life that knows no ending,
> The tearless life, is <u>there</u>.
> (142i/225. Emphasis in 1860 only)

> The world is very evil,
> The times are waxing late.
> (298/222)

For the mediaeval writer the world is a struggle: the metaphors are the traditional ones of warfare.

And now we fight the battle,
   But then shall wear the crown
Of full and everlasting
   And passionless renown;

And now we watch and struggle,
   And now we live in hope,
And Sion in her anguish
   With Babylon must cope.(142i/225,
                     stanzas 3-4)

The chief point, however, is that the struggle of this world is the essential preliminary to the attainment of heaven, and not to be entered half-heartedly.

Be sober and keep vigil,
   The Judge is at the gate.

Arise, arise, good Christian,
   Let right to wrong succeed.

Strive, man, to win that glory;
   Toil, man, to gain that light;
Send hope before to grasp it,
   Till hope be lost in sight.
         (298/226, stanzas 1,2,4)

In this world-view, mortal life is a preliminary, and not to be valued in itself, but only as a way-stage to eternity. It is at this point that a danger arises -- the danger of emphasizing heaven at the expense of and to the detriment of earth. It is a common and mistaken criticism of Christianity that it condones oppression by promising rewards for passive suffering, and that it is an obstacle to reform of all kinds, because misery is established in its system, not to be displaced. This is not the place to debate or defend the theology of the subject, but to examine the hymns for evidence of an undue concentration on heaven.

It has already been noted that the number of Paradise hymns in A&M grew from edition to edition, and were increasingly recognized as a particular type. The reason is that they were understood to fill a popular need. The nature of that need has been hinted at above; it is none other than the need for the life of the working classes to be dignified and to make sense in itself, not just as a dehumanized part of an economic machine. Some hymn-writers gave a metaphorical dignity to labour through the use of their images of warfare and battle. The socialist reformers wanted to restore human dignity to workers, making them proud of their labour as a commodity, and making sense of their lives by centering the economic structure on their labour. The church wanted to invest all humanity with a spiritual and sacred dignity, by ordering human life not by its internal relations between individuals or classes, but by reference to a greater being and another world. None of these three approaches is entirely false, nor is any of them entirely adequate to supply that human need.

Hymn-writers have not been able, until quite recently, to embrace the reality of labour and modern life and include it in the song of the church. Section 3 of this chapter shows how the language and imagery of Biblical and ecclesiastical tradition shaped the vision and straitened the expression of its writers, and were inadequate to serve a changed reality. There are many examples of hymns which either avoid the problem of making sense of contemporary life, or subordinate it to their larger vision.

Several characteristics of the modern Paradise hymns in A&M have already been made clear by comparison with the ancient hymns. They lack the sureness of tone and certainty of vision, and are almost anxious in their eagerness for heaven, rather than joyous in their expectation.

C.F. Alexander's hymn "The roseate hues of early dawn" has already received some attention for its earthly vividness and heavenly abstraction. She expresses her longing for heaven in short gasps:

> Oh, for a heart that never sins,
> Oh, for a soul washed white,
> Oh, for a voice to praise our King,
> Nor weary day nor night.
> (stanza 2)

She concludes with a prayer which is hardly confident, or even very trusting, as it seems to remind Christ of a contracted responsibility:

> Oh, by Thy love and anguish, Lord,
> And by Thy life laid down,
> Grant that we fall not from Thy grace,
> Nor cast away our crown. (stanza 3)

The imagery of Sir Henry's hymn "There is a blessed Home" is on the whole restrained, but its tone, like its short lines, is rather abrupt and not to be questioned; the second person pronoun and the imperative in the final stanza make it difficult to consider this the song of a Christian community. Its exhortation is hardly mutual, and the final impression is that the author has distanced himself from the people he is admonishing and encouraging.

> Look up ye saints of God,
> Nor fear to tread below
> The path your Savior trod
> Of daily toil and woe;
> Wait but a little while
> In uncomplaining love,
> His own most gracious smile
> Shall welcome you above. (stanza 4)

The emotionalism of Faber's hymns presents a sharp contrast to the tone of Sir Henry's hymn. Faber's two Paradise hymns in A&M are "Hark! hark, my soul; Angelic songs are swelling" (325/223) and "O Paradise, O Paradise" (324/234), the second of which came to represent everything that was emotional and suspect in hymnody. The first-named is an imaginative composition, woven round the idea that the music of heaven can be heard and ought to encourage Christians. Faber does not attempt to describe a real Paradise: his hymn is a general promise of rest for the weary, and otherwise depends on the suggestiveness of his "Sweet fragments of the songs above." Indeed, the hymn as printed in A&M is a small masterpiece of vagueness and suggestion, held together by emotional hunger and a pretty refrain.

Angels, sing on! your faithful
watches keeping;
Sing us sweet fragments of the
songs above;
Till morning's joy shall end the
night of weeping,
And life's long shadows break in
cloudless love.
Angels of Jesus, Angels of light,
Singing to welcome the pilgrims
of the night.[4]

"O Paradise, O Paradise" has been represented as the epitome of escapist hymnody: an irresponsible, self-pitying, dressed-up but not disguised version of the "grass-is-greener" cry. It proved extraordinarily popular, partly because of the tune by Dykes with which the A&M Compilers printed it. In an emotional context, the hymn works; it intensifies vague feelings into a strongly directed, because self-directed, force. Read dispassionately, it is merely petulant.

O Paradise, O Paradise,
Who doth not crave for rest?
Who would not seek the happy land
Where they that love are blest?
Where loyal hearts and true
Stand ever in the light,
All rapture through and through,
In God's most holy sight.

O Paradise, O Paradise,
'Tis weary waiting here;
I long to be where Jesus is,

To feel, to see Him near;
Where loyal hearts and true, etc.
(st. 1,3)

Faber's original hymn expressed a distinct longing for sudden death, as a means of hastening the coming to Paradise. The Compilers excised those sentiments.

Much later, when the hymn was omitted from the New edition of A&M (1904), some popular protest was made, and a writer in the Church Times[5] attempted to defend the hymn. His justification was that "sentiment" in popular singing had a practical effect on souls and that it made for holiness, but to illustrate his point he had to quote the only stanza of "O Paradise" (with the exception of the last, written by the Compilers of A&M) which says anything at all about holiness or Christian life:

O Paradise, O Paradise,
I want to sin no more,
I want to be as pure on earth
As on thy spotless shore;
Where loyal hearts and true, etc.
(stanza 4)

The hymn, in short, is an example of Faber's emotional self-indulgence. If it is uplifting, it is so in the same way that hot air is: it provides no support for the soul that would attain, and not just imitate, exaltation. It tackles no serious question, neither the nature of everlasting life nor the rationalization of the earthly one. Its theory is that we shall all feel better for a good cry, and go away comforted. It exemplifies the worst of Christian hymnody. It also prompts fascinating speculation about the man who wrote it, and the people in whose hearts it struck such a resounding chord.

Most of the Paradise hymns that have been discussed avoid problems of human suffering and concentrate on the heavenly reward. J.M. Neale, however, put into words much of what is only implied by other hymn-writers: that the trials of this life are a necessary prelude to eternal bliss, and are to be meekly borne without complaint. Liberal reformers would accuse his hymn, "O happy band of pilgrims" (297/224), of preaching acquiescence and compliance, and of condoning suffering and injustice.

> O happy if ye labour
> As Jesus did for men:
> O happy if ye hunger
> As Jesus hungered then.
>
> The trials that beset you,
> The sorrows ye endure,
> The manifold temptations
> That death alone can cure,
>
> What are they but His jewels
> Of right celestial worth?
> What are they but the ladder
> Set up to heaven from earth?
> (stanzas 2,5,6)

In contrast with the discontentedness of Faber's "O Paradise," however, Neale's hymn is pleasantly strong-hearted and determined. None of the Paradise hymns attempts to distinguish between trials and persecution (trial meaning the suffering which is part of the human condition, and persecution meaning the suffering which is caused or exacerbated by human inhumanity), to which resignation and rebellion are, respectively, the appropriate responses. Paradise hymns avoid the problem of pain, being concerned only to present a coherent picture culminating in a vision of heaven. One may regret the failure of hymnody to do more, and one may explain or excuse that failure, but one cannot deny the attractive persistence of the hope of heaven, and the sometimes obvious, sometimes subtle, heart-stirring reaction of sympathy it provokes.

3. Urban and Pastoral Imagery: The City of God and Harvest Hymns

Most of the predominant imagery in hymnody is drawn from Scripture, for obvious reasons. Moreover, the old Calvinist proscription of any language in a hymn which does not have Scriptural authority means that hymn-writers were not encouraged to explore other patterns of imagery to express or illuminate the spiritual life to which hymn-singing contributes. Imagery serves its purpose of expression or illumination by making abstractions vivid and indicating ideas not susceptible to easy formulation: this latter use of imagery is metaphor, the presentation of something unknown in terms of something known. Metaphor in extended use is, of course, allegory, a favourite device of religious writers confronted with a subject beyond the powers of simple telling. The success of an allegory depends to a large extent upon its consistency, both on the allegorical plane, and in relation to its indicated meaning. That is to say, the development of the allegory must have its own logic, and at the same time, the vehicle at any point of the allegory must be appropriate to its particular tenor. The same consistency is required of any extended metaphors or image-cluster.

Metaphor or allegory is vulnerable when the imagery of the vehicle undergoes a change of meaning or value. Declaring "The Lord is my Shepherd," the Psalmist employs a series of metaphors which have their origin in the culture of the Israelites as a sheep-herding people. The traditional images were still valid when Jesus used them in his parables, and the usage culminates in the image of Jesus the Good Shepherd. By the time hymn-writers employ the same imagery in the nineteenth century, however, there is little vitality left in it. "Shepherd" becomes a mere synonym for Jesus, rather than a comparison which illuminates. The reality of sheep-herding is far from the experience of the majority of those who sing the hymns, and certainly far from the experience of those who write them. In addition, the weight of the long tradition of pastoral idyll hangs on the imagery, blurring its sturdy outline and washing away the shadows and dangers with sunshine and prettiness. Thus the meaning of the vehicle is confused, because it is remote from its original reality and associated with a literary tradition and convention. The vitality of the imagery is lost, not so much in Scripture itself, where the imagery remains in an appropriate historical and cultural context, but in the hymns and verses which borrow the image without the substance, either leaving the singers suspended between two unrealities, or distorting or diminishing their perception of the image's significance.

Pastoral imagery is one example; a slightly different one is another image-cluster of Scriptural origin, that of the city. When the Israelites were a nomadic tribe, the idea of a city was all that was wonderful and utterly different from their life of tents and travelling arks. When they took possession of Canaan and settled, each tribe had its cities of refuge, strongholds in the midst of their lands.[6] When they took their first king, Jerusalem became the chief of cities,[7] the centre of pilgrimage and the city of God's Temple. No doubt Jerusalem was a shabby town to those who knew it, but far more people never saw it, and knew only that it contained wonders of architecture and richness beyond their experience. Furthermore, a city was exclusive: its people were citizens, and had special rights and privileges. In the Greco-Roman world, civilization centered in the city-states, and was finally identified with the city-empire of Rome. In mediaeval times, cities were few, and the great majority of people lived rural lives. The unknown city contained palaces, and even the common streets might be paved with gold. The reality of the city was sufficiently distant and unknown not to jeopardize the image.

It is from this background that the concept of the new Jerusalem, heavenly Sion, the city of God, took shape. It is a natural extension of the Hebrew idea: as Jerusalem to Judea, so heaven to earth, but magnified and glorified. There is Scriptural authority for the image, in the Epistle to the Hebrews (Chapter 12:22) and, with consistent imaginative power, in Revelations (especially Chapter 21).

The imagery of Revelations informs mediaeval and later writings about the world to come, as was seen in the preceding section. Eventually the image of the city glorified became so well-established that it was hard to speak of heaven without employing it. John Bunyan's Celestial City is the end and goal of his pilgrim's progress, the city that was pure gold. When

Bunyan was writing, the city was not yet the normal dwelling-place of his countrymen, so that his Scriptural imagery was reinforced by a common feeling that the city was a place to travel to out of the daily realm.

With the industrialization of England, however, came urbanization and a move from the country into the crowded cities. For larger numbers than ever before, cities meant slums and filth and disease, sweated labour, and death. The opening statement of Prudentius Aurelius Clemens' fourth-century "Earth has many a noble city" (59/76) might well be questioned by nineteenth-century hymn-singers, although it does not really detract from the overall point of the hymn for Epiphany -- the humble village of Bethlehem excels all the noble cities. The image of the heavenly city, however, is weaker because of its remoteness from nineteenth-century experience. Is it inconceivable and meaningless to minds assailed by the wretchedness and squalor and hardship of a slum life? Or does the image draw force from its very unreality and distance, strengthened by the unfamiliar language -- the walls and bulwarks, and the catalogue of gems and precious things beyond imagination? We cannot be sure of the effect of the image on those who sang the hymns, but the suspicion remains that it had less to do with an imaginative apprehension of life after death than with an inarticulate, confused longing for something better than present existence.

The image does seem to have had a hold on the nineteenth-century hymn-writers, partly because of the authority of their mediaeval predecessors, and partly because it served as a kind of shorthand reference.

James Montgomery's "'For ever with the Lord'" (--/231) equates Jerusalem with the "bright inheritance of Saints" (stanza 2), and Edward Hayes Plumptre's "Rejoice ye pure in heart" (386/393) urges pilgrims onward to "their Father's House,/ Jerusalem the blest" (stanza 9). The significance of the metaphor depends on a welter of Scriptural, literary, and geographical associations, rather than the experience in which the most telling metaphors are grounded.

When a Victorian hymn-writer like Henry Alford attempted to expand the shorthand in his processional hymn "Forward! be our watchword" (--/392), he had recourse to the traditional imagery:

> Far o'er yon horizon
> Rise the city towers,
> Where our God abideth;
> That fair home is ours:
>
> Flash the streets with jasper,
> Shine the gates with gold;
> Flows the gladdening river
> Shedding joys untold. (stanza 5)

His city of God is as unreal as a painted backdrop, despite the illusion of life given in the prominent verbs. This failure of imagination, this inability or refusal to go beyond the traditional limitations underlines the real imaginative boldness of Blake's juxtaposition, and his grasp of the mental as well as geographical gap between the images: "And was Jerusalem builded here/ Among these dark satanic mills?"

The same imaginative limitation that perpetuates

the imagery of the city of God perpetuates a vision of the earth as essentially rural and pastoral. Blake admitted the existence of satanic mills, but nineteenth-century hymns in general are devoid of any suggestion that God's world is anything but the world of Nature (and not a nature red in tooth and claw). Again, the reliance upon Biblical imagery explains this incompleteness, in part, and the ancient hymns give no other precedent, but the absence of imagery more appropriate to an increasingly urban and industrial world is nonetheless odd. Sir Henry, it is true, lived in a rural parish, as did several of the A&M Proprietors, but there were several London parsons among them as well, whose daily horizons were brick walls and chimney pots, rather than glebeland. They preferred, apparently, the resolutely sunny vision of Christopher Wordsworth's almsgiving hymn, "O Lord of heaven, and earth, and sea" (370/365):

> The golden sunshine, vernal air,
> Sweet flowers and fruit Thy love declare:
> When harvests ripen, Thou art there,
> Who givest all. (stanza 2)

The beauties of nature include the more beautiful aspects of human nature:

> For peaceful homes, and healthful days,
> For all the blessings earth displays,
> We owe Thee thankfulness and praise,
> Who givest all. (stanza 3)

One suspects that all this emphasis on nature is, in fact, evidence of the shadow of industrialization, just as the harvest festival only became a general custom in the middle of the nineteenth century,[8] though there had been earlier local English feasts, the dedication of the first-fruits of harvest at Loafmass, or Lammastide (August 1st). Prayers for abundant harvests were issued from time to time after 1796, and a complete form of prayer in 1847. A form of service was prepared in 1862 by the Convocation of Canterbury, but was not legally authorized. It was to supply this newly popular custom that five harvest hymns were printed in A&M 1860, two more in the Appendix, and nine altogether in the Revised edition.

In rural parishes a service of harvest thanksgiving has an obvious significance for lives in close contact with agriculture. In the city, too, it is a good thing to acknowledge the round of the seasons and humanity's dependence upon the success or failure of the harvest. The tie is otherwise rarely apparent: the rain which is cursed for turning the city's courts and alleys to mud and for drenching the unsheltered may be the very rain that was longed for to save the corn. Thus the service may fitly be used to remind the people of their place not only in the natural, but also in the economic order. The dangers of incongruity arise in the hymns written for the service. The hymn ought not to be so literal that its use is manifestly absurd in any other than a strictly rural context. For instance, "We plough the fields and scatter/The good seed on the land" (360/383) would be inappropriate on the lips of urban churchgoers, were it not that the main emphasis of the hymn is on the contrast between what little "we" humans can do, and the benevolent omnipotence of God. On the whole it may be said that the A&M harvest hymns have been judiciously chosen. The imagery of open air, sunshine, vigour and growth is undeniably attractive, but is never exploited for its own sake, or out of romantic fancy or pastoral nostalgia. Even where the hymns enumerate the beauties of nature, as in the hymn mentioned above (Jane Campbell's translation of the German of Matthias Claudius), those beauties are always explicit evidence of God's goodness and power:

> He only is the Maker
> Of all things near and far,
> He paints the wayside flower,
> He lights the evening star;
> The winds and waves obey Him,
> By Him the birds are fed;
> Much more to us, His children,
> He gives our daily bread.
> (stanza 2)

The hymn-writers also expand the harvest imagery to teach further theological lessons. Sir Henry, for instance, in his second-hand paraphrase of Psalm 136, "Praise, O praise our God and King" (224/381),[9] leads from agriculture and harvest to the Eucharist and the promise of eternal life:

> Praise Him that He gave the rain
> To mature the swelling grain;
>
> And hath bid the fruitful field
> Crops of precious increase yield;
>
> And for richer food than this,
> Pledge of everlasting bliss.
> (stanzas 4,5,7)

Similarly, Henry Alford links harvest with the parable of the wheat and the tares, and his imagination inflates the metaphors into an apocalyptic vision of death and the last judgment as God's own harvest-home.

> What is earth but God's own field,
> Fruit unto His praise to yield?
> Wheat and tares therein are sown,
> Unto joy or sorrow grown;
> Ripening with a wondrous power,
> Till the final Harvest-Hour:
> Grant, O Lord of Life, that we
> Holy grain and pure may be.[10]

Similar parallels are drawn by W.C. Dix in his hymn "To Thee, O Lord, our hearts we raise" (--/384), both between daily bread and the bread of life:

> Thou, Who dost give us earthly bread,
> Give us the Bread Eternal,
> (stanza 2)

and between harvest and death and resurrection:

> May we, the Angel-reaping o'er,
> Stand at the last accepted,
> Christ's golden sheaves for evermore
> To garners bright elected.
> (stanza 3)

If Dix's attention to the details of the metaphor seems excessively picturesque, it is at least in keeping with the hyperbole of Psalm 65 on which it is partly based.

> Bright robes of gold the fields adorn,
> The hills with joy are ringing,

> The valleys stand so thick with corn
>   That even they are singing.
>   (stanza 1)

> The pastures are clothed with flocks; the valleys also are covered over with corn; they shout for joy, they also sing. (Psalm 65:13)

Dix's literalness is cheerfully hyperbolic, but William St. H. Bourne is more sombre. His hymn "The sower went forth sowing" (--/386) explores the agricultural metaphor through more than one level. His first stanza is straightforward harvest thanksgiving; his second recalls the parable of the sower:

> Behold! the heavenly Sower
>   Goes forth with better seed,
> The Word of sure Salvation.

His third and fourth stanza are yet another parallel between harvest and death, but far more grimly literal than in any other hymn:

> Within a hallowed acre
>   He sows yet other grain,
> When peaceful earth receiveth
>   The dead He died to gain;
> For though the growth be hidden,
>   We know that they shall rise;
> Yea even now they ripen
>   In sunny Paradise.

> One day the heavenly Sower
>   Shall reap where He hath sown,

And come again rejoicing,
   And with Him bring His own;
And then the fan of judgment
   Shall winnow from His floor
The chaff into the furnace
   That flameth evermore.
O holy, awful Reaper,
   Have mercy in the day
Thou puttest in Thy sickle,
   And cast us not away.

The hymn was written in 1874, but the fear and trembling it evokes in its final stanza seem to belong to an earlier time, or to another occasion than a thanksgiving. Nevertheless, in its move from a local and particular event to the universal, it cannot be said to be suitable for only limited parochial use.

It would be unfair, however, to say that the descriptions of earthy reality in A&M's hymns, even the thanksgiving ones, are entirely bucolic. In contrast to Wordsworth's vision of "peaceful homes and healthful days," W.W. How allows the darker side of human nature to appear in "We give Thee but Thine own" (371/366): "Oh! hearts are bruised and dead,/And homes are bare and cold." The glimpse of unpleasantness is brief, however, and How takes refuge in pastoral metaphor again: "And lambs, for whom the Saviour bled,/Are straying from the fold" (stanza 3).

There are two more unusual hymns in the early editions of A&M, unusual in that they deal directly with the dark side of nature. An eighteenth-century hymn by Benjamin Schmolck appears among the harvest hymns in a version by Sir Henry Baker, "What our Father does is well" (227/389). In parentheses it is explained that the hymn is "to be used when there is a deficiency in the crops."

> What our Father does is well;
> Blessed truth His children tell!
> Though He send, for plenty, want,
> Though the harvest-store be scant,
> Yet we rest upon His love,
> Seeking better things above.
>
> (stanza 1)

The syntax is a little odd, and the whole translation somewhat stilted, but the hymn is an honest attempt to embrace a situation usually overlooked: to embrace, not to rationalize or to justify or to explain the mysterious ways of God. The faithful Christian's response is to recall the promises of God (of "better things above"), and to remember that, despite chastisement, God is all-sufficient to human needs:

> What our Father does is well;
> May the thought within us dwell;
> Though nor milk nor honey flow
> In our barren Canaan now,
> God can save us in our need,
> God can bless us, God can feed.
>
> (stanza 4)

The Compilers added a doxology to reaffirm the duty of God's people despite the lack of apparent cause for rejoicing:

Therefore, unto Him we raise
Hymns of glory, songs of praise.

No doubt this hymn never lessened the complaints during a time of scarcity, but its very existence in the pages of A&M is proof that the Compilers of that book intended it to be of use in a significant service, connecting the worship of God with external circumstance. To them, then, harvest festival was not solely the occasion for flights of pleasant metaphor and picturesque imagery. It was to be an occasion of uniting all parishes in recognition of their dependence upon God in both life and death.

The same sense of realism is manifest in another hymn, which confronts an ugly problem in terms of Christian trust and hope. The problem is a rural one: the hymn is for use in times of cattle plague, Neale's "All creation groans and travails" (374/---). The hymn was not reprinted after its initial appearance in the Appendix, presumably because its usefulness was extremely limited, and the Compilers decided not to supply hymns for the more unusual occasions. The hymn is a straightforward call for mercy; again, it offers no explanations, but only a confession:

Pity then Thy guiltless creatures,
Who, not less, man's sufferings share;
For our sins it is they perish;
Let them profit from our prayer.
(stanza 2)

Human helplessness is also recognized, and prayed for; the attitude, however, is like that of Alderson's

Almsgiving hymn (see section 1) in that the poor do not appear to be part of the church, though the church graciously offers prayers on their behalf.

> For the widow, for the orphan,
> For the helpless, hopeless poor:
> Helpless, hopeless, if Thou spare not
> Of their basket and their store.
> So -- while these her earnest accents
> Day by day Thy Church repeats, --
> (stanzas 7,8)

The harvest hymns in A&M show that, when the challenge is a new one -- a newly popular service requiring new hymns -- the limitations of their imagery did not prevent Victorian writers from supplying meaningful hymns. The rural imagery is not inappropriate, after all, for singing about crops, even if the singers are not farmers or farm-labourers. Nevertheless, for the most part, the inherited imagery is blurred by its distance from nineteenth-century reality. Though the provision of special hymns for scanty harvest and for cattle plague argues that realism might have had a place in Victorian hymnody, their rapid disappearance from A&M suggests a lack of clerical nerve as well as imagination. There is a certain irony that the lines most appropriate to the British landscape and population in that century were applied in a mission hymn to the other side of the world:

> What though the spicy breezes
> Blow soft o'er Ceylon's isle,
> Though every prospect pleases,
> And only man is vile.[11]

4. Children's Hymns

Children's hymns furnish especially good illustrations of matters of attitude. The concept of hymns for children is itself an interesting one, and a relatively recent one. Isaac Watts' Divine and Moral Songs for the Use of Children (1715) is an early precedent and may be related to other eighteenth-century innovative books such as those by Mrs. Barbauld and Thomas Day, for the use and instruction of children. Children's religious verses were used rarely in services of worship, but more often for lessons. The adoption of children's hymns for less pedagogical purposes was gradual, but the hymns did not lose their instructive qualities. Much that is implicit elsewhere is here explicit; as a result, the A&M selection of children's hymns generously repays study.

In the first edition there was not, in fact, a special section of hymns "for the young"; only in the Appendix was there thought to be such a need. The original edition had three hymns for School Festivals among its occasional hymns, all of them written within a few years of one another. They are all rather clumsy, each in a different way. The first is Sir Henry Baker's "Lord Jesus, God and Man" (228/344), which resembles in part Faber's "O Jesu, God and Man,/ For love of children once a Child," from his Jesus and Mary, 1849. The hymn invokes the child Jesus on an unspecified "festal day" to grant "gifts of grace" such as "childlike hearts," "gentle holy love" and "simple faith." A single reference to "friends around us here" recalls that this is a hymn for schools, but there is no real child in the whole hymn. It is a hymn for adults, whose view of children in general is pleasantly Romantic, full of innocence and trailing clouds of glory. It is not quite sentimental, as it would be if the adults were totally absorbed in their idealized children, for there is a strong tension between that potential absorption and a commitment to God and a Christian life. The childlike hearts and gentle love of the third stanza, for instance, are balanced with "strength to do Thy will below/As angels do above."

Even more an adult's hymn is W.W. How's "O holy Lord, content to dwell" (230/---), never reprinted in A&M. Despite How's heading "A Child's Hymn," it is actually an adult's prayer and pattern for a Christian child. It is not quite as bad as C.F. Alexander's lessons in deportment,[12] but it expresses an adult's condescension and romanticism:

> Lead every child that bears Thy name
> To walk in Thy pure upright way,
> To shun the paths of sin and shame,
> And humbly, like Thyself, obey.

Let not this world's unhallowed glow
The fresh baptismal dew efface,
Nor blast of sin too roughly blow,
And quench the trembling flame of
grace. (stanzas 3-4)

It is hard to imagine how this hymn could be used for school festivals, unless at a gathering of Pecksniffian trustees and teachers. Any schoolchild within hearing ought to feel thoroughly uncomfortable and embarrassed.

The other hymn for schools in A&M 1860 is by the Rev. James Elwin Millard, "God eternal, mighty King" (229/343) and is by far the best of the three. It is essentially a hymn of robust praise (Millard called it a "Te Deum"), which children aspire to join. Instead of being set apart as objects of adult musing, the children claim their own place:

God eternal, mighty King,
Unto Thee our praise we bring;
All the earth doth worship Thee,
We amid the throng would be.

Glorified Apostles raise
Night and day continual praise;
Hast not Thou a mission too
For Thy children here to do?
(stanzas 1,3)

This confident enthusiasm verges on smugness in the fourth stanza, when the singers declare:

With the Prophets' goodly line
We in mystic bond combine;
For Thou hast to us revealed
Things that to the wise were sealed.

In 1875, "us" is altered to "babes," which avoids the hint of smugness and makes explicit the reference to the babes and sucklings of Psalm 8 and Matthew 11 and 21.

There are two conclusions to be drawn from these hymns: first, that the editors had not yet properly grasped the idea of hymns for children themselves (rather than about them), and the related, but seemingly contradictory conclusion that the best children's hymns are those which are as little self-conscious as possible. Further evidence from the later A&M editions will confirm these conclusions.

The 1868 Appendix contained nine hymns "For the Young." Of these, only one, Wordsworth's "Heavenly Father, send Thy blessing" (364/338), is actually an adult's hymn about children:

Heavenly Father, send Thy blessing
   On Thy children gathered here,
May they all, Thy Name confessing,
   Be to Thee for ever dear:
May they be like Joseph, loving,
   Dutiful, and chaste, and pure;
And their faith, like David, proving,
   Steadfast unto death endure.
(stanza 1)

If children are "they" in Wordsworth's hymn, they are "you" in John Jeremiah Daniell's "Come, sing with holy gladness" (366/341), a long exhortation to praise and prompting to gratitude, for

> 'Tis good for boys and maidens
> Sweet hymns to Christ to sing,
> 'Tis meet that children's voices
> Should praise the children's King;
> For Jesus is salvation,
> And glory, grace, and rest;
> To babe and boy and maiden
> The one Redeemer Blest. (stanza 2)

The Compilers omitted the more exuberant stanzas of the original, feeling perhaps that children could not be expected to sing the multisyllabic exclamations with the requisite enthusiasm, or that the sudden intrusion of the first person is incongruous, as the prompter turns chorus.

> For us, O exultation!
> O exstacy of joy!
> Jesus was born an infant,
> And Jesus grew a boy;
> For us, O speechless mercy!
> Upon the wood He bled
> And on the children richly
> Th'atoning sprinklings shed.[13]

The omission of the final image is also not to be regretted, given the literal turn of children's minds. Similarly, the Compilers omitted the author's sixth stanza with its warnings of the perils awaiting those who leave the sole security of the church:

> Ye are the Church's glory
> The Church's strength and pride--
> Love ye the Church that bare you,
> Cleave to the Church's side.
> Through dread pollution stainless,
> Unharmed through perils wild,
> Safe to the arms of Jesus
> She leads each blessed child.[14]

What is left of the original hymn is, again, a pattern, not only of Christian behaviour but of social roles. Boys are to sing a chorus, girls (who are never girls, but "gentle maidens"), a "sweet responsive lay." The original calls for boys to "be strong in Jesus -- /Work bravely -- toil is gain --" following the example of Jesus the carpenter's son. A&M corrects the Samuel Smiles-like worldly maxim to "To toil <u>for Him</u> is gain," but in neither version are the girls given any active or precise responsibilities.

> O maidens, live for Jesus,
> Who was a maiden's Son;
> Be patient, pure, and gentle,
> And perfect grace begun. (stanza 3)

The clumsiness of the misplaced emphasis in that last line is entirely in keeping with the heavy hand that wrote this guide for childhood.

Other Appendix hymns typify other modes of writing for children. "Gracious Saviour, gentle Shepherd" (365/342) is a cento of three hymns from Jane

Leeson's Hymns and Scenes of Childhood (1842) with alterations and additions by John Keble. It is a prayer for guidance and protection, using the metaphor of shepherd and sheep, hard to fault save for some excessive prettiness ("Taught to lisp the holy praises"), but otherwise keeping a good balance between the ideal and the real.

The sheep-keeping metaphor runs close to pastoral convention, but there is also something more robust: "Thy Cross, O Lord, the holy sign" (367/--) by Hugh Stowell (1840), written for his Salford Sunday schools. The militarism noted elsewhere shows defiant here, though not unrealistically so:

> . . . before the vain,
> The proud, the scoffing, the profane,
> We will, through grace, our Lord confess,
> His faint but faithful witnesses.
>
> (stanza 2)

Apart from the self-consciousness of "we, His little soldiers" in stanza 3, it is hard to find a reason for the omission of this hymn from the 1875 edition, unless the criticism is that few could sing it with complete sincerity. In children's hymns, however, if nowhere else, aspiration and enthusiasm ought to have their place. The Revised edition would be the better for it.

Three of the Appendix hymns have become classics and not only for children: two of C.F. Alexander's, "Once in royal David's City" (361/329), and "There is a green hill far away" (362/332), and Baring Gould's "Now the day is over" (368/346). The explicit references to childhood in these hymns are relatively few: there are none at all in "There is a green hill far away." Baring Gould's hymn contains a sixth stanza reminiscent of a nursery prayer:

> Through the long night watches
> May Thine Angels spread
> Their white wings above me,
> Watching round my bed.

There is no lingering over the other references, "Grant to little children/Visions bright of Thee" in the fourth stanza, for the imagination must leap from children to sailors to sufferers and wrong-doers within eight lines. "Once in royal David's City" contains two stanzas (3 and 4) in Alexander's most governess-like manner, containing such lines as "Christian children all must be/ Mild, obedient, good as He," and "For He is our childhood's Pattern." Otherwise, what makes these hymns suitable for children is their simplicity of language. There is no obscuring of the essential concepts of redemption ("There is a green hill far away"), and of incarnation ("Once in royal David's City"), nor is there any watering down. "There is a green hill far away" is undoubtedly the best of these three hymns. It is entirely free from the infelicities of expression (the repeated "ands") of "Once in royal David's City," and from the touch of prettiness in Baring Gould's "peeping stars" and "birds and beasts and flowers." The awesomeness of the beliefs in "There is a green hill far away" is fully revealed in the utter simplicity of word and phrase, and at the same time the wholly inadequate but necessary response of the Christian ("O, dearly, dearly has He loved,/And we must love Him too") has its own dignity of simplicity.

Alexander at her best illustrates the precepts of John Keble about writing for children, that "puerility, in contradistinction to simplicity is a sort of insult"[15] and that children's hymns ought to be of "real use and comfort to them, when recalled to their memories, in whole or in part, by the events of their after life, such as they may dwell on continually, and find deeper and deeper meanings in them as they grow older, and consult their consciences more."[16]

The Revised edition of A&M contains eighteen hymns for the young, eight of which are new. The special needs of children have been fully recognized, though not necessarily met. In the 1860 hymns, the viewpoint was decidedly adult; by 1875 it has changed considerably. All the new hymns are written in the first person, two of them in the first person singular. The level, however, has generally fallen. Where Alexander set out the great truth of the incarnation, Emily Miller puzzles "though I cannot see Him/I know He hears my praise" ("I love to hear the story" --/330). In sharp contrast with the earlier pattern hymns, the new ones in 1875 are much less precise in their instructions: Emily Miller allows "I am both weak and sinful," but speaks only vaguely of "try[ing] to follow/ His footsteps here below." The children of William Bourne's "Christ Who once amongst us" (---/333) are even more passive: "If [they] keep [their] promise/ Made Him at the Font," they will be "carried/Safe from all alarms" and will "rest/ In His Arms for ever,/ Leaning on His Breast." There is no hint here of muscular Christians in training. There are lambs in both Bourne's hymn and Jane Leeson's "Loving Shepherd of Thy sheep" (--/334), but they rather languish than gambol. If this selection lacks the robust note, it is at least more cheerful, its praise less dutiful. There is the repeated declaration "I love to hear the story," and "Hosanna we sing, like the children dear" (--/340) by G.S. Hodges, with its basically anapestic bounce. Praise is associated with heaven, and there are more angels in the children's section of A&M than anywhere else, as the writers seek to capture the children's imagination. Emily Miller hears her story not in Sunday School but directly from Angel voices, a fanciful touch which can claim only imaginative authority. Neale's only hymn for children in A&M, "Around the throne of God a band" (--/335), is full of the imagery of angels in all its mediaeval detail, of harps and crowns, of hymn and errand. He invokes the presence of guiding and guardian angels, and the hymn is full of serene and confident strength, utterly unlike the insecurity or passivity noted in some of the other hymns. In John Chandler's hymn "Above the clear blue sky" (--/336), the angels' praise inspires the "cheerful songs" of the children. Chandler is perhaps a little optimistic when he speaks of infant tongues managing "sweet accord," but no doubt even the uncertain singing of children is part of a larger harmony. Certainly, his refrain with its repeated Alleluias and jingling "sing/King" rhyme is a good device, and one surprisingly unexploited in these children's hymns.

As frequent a theme as the angels is Paradise, echoing the popularity of the idea among the hymn-writers for adults. Almost every one of the new hymns in the 1875 edition ends with a vision of Paradise, whether it is singing with the angels ("I love to hear the story," "Around the Throne of God," "Hosanna we sing") or the heavenly pastures of "Christ, Who once amongst us." What is remarkable is the wealth of detail in such a hymn as Albert Midlane's "There's a Friend for little children" (--/337) with its emphasis on a physical heaven "above the bright blue sky," and all its attributes both concrete and abstract, robe, crown and psalm, rest and home. It sets forth heaven as a compensation for the realities of earth, more explicitly than many of the Paradise hymns discussed in section two of this chapter:

> A rest from every turmoil,
> From sin and sorrow free,
> Where every little pilgrim
> Shall rest eternally.
>
> No home on earth is like it
> Nor can with it compare;
> For everyone is happy,
> Nor could be happier, there.
> (stanzas 2,3)

Just when the compensatory fantasies of the hymn, and its reiterated "for little children/Above the bright blue sky" begin to annoy, Midlane disarms his critic. His fifth stanza anticipates the complaint, and puts it to use as a standard of comparison:

> There's a song for little children
> Above the bright blue sky,
> A song that will not weary
> Though sung continually.

Then follows a contrast which is breathtakingly simple and meaningful:

A song which even Angels
  Can never, never sing;
They know not Christ as Saviour,
  But worship Him as King.

It is a passage that Keble must have approved, for it yields its full significance slowly. Furthermore, that sense of awesome privilege is a happy change from the persistent dutifulness of other hymns.

This detailed look at the children's hymns in A&M has revealed some of the hymn-writers' attitudes toward those for whom they wrote. Those attitudes range from the extremes of Romantic idealization or strict instruction, to uncondescending respect, though rarely are they found unmixed. The hymns reflect not so much what Victorian childhood was like, as what adults thought childhood was and ought to be, both on a spiritual and on a social plane. Nevertheless, the hymn-writers and editors had accepted that children are not merely adults not fully grown, but beings with special attributes and particular needs, deserving serious attention. They were helped to this realization by a general interest in and concern for children and their well-being, which was the result of Romanticism and modern philanthropy, and partly by the example of Christ Himself, who had stern words for those who ignored or excluded the children. The true measure of the importance attached to these small Christians is the simple fact that a whole section of a hymnbook for general use was designated for their especial edification and pleasure in the praise of their Creator.

5. Mission Hymns

There are two kinds of missions commonly referred to in nineteenth-century church affairs, the foreign, and home missions.

Foreign missions have the authority of Christ's own command to His disciples, after His resurrection: "Go ye therefore, and teach all nations, baptizing them in the name of the Father, and of the Son, and of the Holy Ghost: Teaching them to observe all things whatsoever I have commanded you."[17] The Church of Christ is to be Catholic, that is, universal, not limited to a small sect in Judea and Galilee. After the Reformation, the Church of England assumed the responsibility of sending Christianity after the explorers and colonizers. English missionary efforts were coextensive with the British Empire, and as the empire grew, so foreign missions were increasingly well-organized. The first English missionary society, the Society for the Propagation of the Gospel in New England, was founded in 1649. The Society for the Promotion of Christian Knowledge was formed in 1698, the Society for the Propagation of the Gospel in 1701, and the Church Missionary Society in 1799.

The work of these societies was considered so important that support was requested from the English church as a whole. On Whitsunday in 1819, for example, collections were authorized by royal letter in every church and chapel of England for the work of the S.P.G. It was for this occasion that Reginald Heber wrote "From Greenland's icy mountains" (217/358).

A great revival of interest in foreign missions began in 1871, when John Coleridge Patteson, Bishop of Melanesia, was killed on one of the little Pacific islands which made up his diocese and mission field. Charlotte Yonge wrote his life, and made the "martyr bishop" widely known. In 1872 the Day of Intercession was inaugurated by the S.P.G., and from this time Anglican missions expanded quite wonderfully.

The pattern of general interest in missions is reflected in the Mission Hymns in A&M. The Original edition contains four hymns, only two of which, Heber's "From Greenland's icy mountains," and John Marriott's "Thou Whose Almighty Word" (220/260), were specifically about missions. Heber's hymn was written and first sung in 1819; Marriott's was probably written about 1813, was quoted by a speaker at a meeting of the London Missionary Society in 1825, and thence found its way into print and common use.

"The earth, O Lord, is one wide field" (218/354) is from Neale's <u>Hymns for the Young</u>, 1843, where it is intended for Ember Week in Lent, according to the ancient and originally pagan tradition of fasting for a good crop. In its original form the hymn began with a request for "timely sun and rain"; from this literal level, the hymn develops on a metaphorical level (where the A&M version begins), with prayers for help in the nurture of Christian souls. This concern is as much domestic as foreign:

> Not for our land alone we pray,
> Though that above the rest,
> The realms and islands far away,
> O let them all be blest.
> (stanza 3, A&M version)

In fact, in its prayers for the bishops, priests, deacons, and people in turn, the hymn refers rather to an organized church than to an exploring mission. In the Revised edition, the hymn was returned to the section for Ember Days for which Neale had intended it, and the Mission Hymns section was kept for hymns dealing more specifically with conversion than with consolidation.

The other mission hymn in A&M 1860 is in fact a paraphrase of Psalm 67 by Edward Churton for his Cleveland Psalter of 1854. "God of grace, O let Thy light" (219/364) is appropriate to a mission theme on the strength of its expansion of the Psalm verse "That Thy way may be known upon earth, thy saving health among all nations."[18]

> To the nations led astray
> Thine eternal love display;
> Let Thy Truth direct their way
> Till the world be Thine.
> (stanza 2)

Where the psalm is exhortation and exultation ("O let

the nations be glad and sing for joy: for thou shalt judge the people righteously, and govern the nations upon earth," v.4), the hymn is heavier, its reiterated "let them" more imperative than hortatory. The nations' joy is the dutiful response of an enlightened people, rather than the celebration of a saved nation. It is hard not to hear in Churton's stanzas the tone of a weighty responsibility not unlike the British imperial burden:

> Let them moved to gladness sing,
> Owning Thee their Judge and King;
> Righteous Truth shall bloom and spring
> Where Thy rule shall be.
>
> While His grace our life shall cheer
> Furthest lands shall own His fear,
> Brought to Him in worship near,
> Taught His mercy's ways.
> (stanzas 4,7)

It is, however, a difficult task to write a hymn for foreign missions which is neither pedestrian and precise nor uninspiringly vague. Marriott's hymn runs the second risk, but escapes. Its primary metaphor is light, but it is not allowed to be an empty metaphor which leaves its concepts as hopelessly abstract as ever. The hymn possesses grandeur by virtue of its creation imagery, and it has human immediacy from the person of Christ the Redeemer: the whole is shaped and ordered by the Trinitarian structure of the hymn. The first stanza is the most dramatic:

Thou, Whose almighty Word
Chaos and darkness heard,
And took their flight.

The very light of creation is here identified with the good news which must be spread:

Hear us, we humbly pray,
And where the Gospel-day
Sheds not its glorious ray
Let there be light!

The second stanza manifests that light to human beings:

Thou Who didst come to bring
On Thy redeeming wing
Healing and sight,[19]
Health to the sick in mind
Sight to the inly blind,
Oh, now to all mankind
Let there be light!

The "Spirit of truth and love" of the third stanza is caught up in the creation imagery again, and identified with the Spirit that moved upon the face of the deep, so that the conquest of darkness by light is extremely vivid. The final stanza of the hymn is not so much a close as the releasing of the forces evoked in the first three stanzas. The grandeur of the creation imagery combines with the deliberate rhythm of the final invocation:

Blessèd and Holy Three,
Glorious Trinity,
Grace, Love, and Might,[20]

and with the final simile to make an inexorable climax:

> Boundless as ocean's tide,
> Rolling in fullest pride,
> Through the world, far and wide,
> Let there be light!
> (stanza 4, 1860)

There is no mention in this hymn of the part that societies and boards and special collections will play in the achievement of this grand climax. The hymn's business is to provide sufficient exaltation of purpose and impetus to carry the gospel through the necessary practicalities.

Heber's technique is similar in method but very different in effect. His task is the same as Marriott's -- to write a convincing hymn about missions in general, without ineffective or vague gesturing. Both hymns borrow their strength from their imagery: Marriott's from the grandeur of the act of creation, Heber's from the sensual vividness of creation itself. Heber's scale is much smaller than Marriott's; though his vision encompasses the globe, he scatters it with recognizable landmarks and placenames.

> From Greenland's icy mountains,
> From India's coral strand,
> Where Afric's sunny fountains
> Roll down their golden sand.
> (stanza 1)

There is no chaos and darkness in this universe, save where error and idolatry linger in strange and deliberate contrast to the lavish kindness of God. Divine gifts are present to touch and sight and scent and their vividness carries over to the more difficult-to-realize images of wisdom, life, salvation, and glory. Nevertheless the hymn begins to falter. The very heart of the hymn is the contrast between the "heathen in his blindness" and "we whose souls are lighted/With wisdom from on high," but what ought to be the crux, Heber's rhetorical question "Can we to men benighted/The lamp of life deny?" is not allowed to reverberate in individual consciences. He rushes quickly past, and the question is lost in the reiterated shout "Salvation! oh, Salvation!" The individual arena disappears in the expansion to "each remotest nation." In the fourth stanza there is an unfortunate suggestion of a second great flood:

> Waft, waft, ye winds, His story,
> And you, ye waters, roll,
> Till like a sea of glory
> It spreads from pole to pole,

and any recognizable human element is utterly effaced. Humanity is reduced to a "ransomed nature" and submerged in inverted sentence structure and an unfortunate final bad-weather pun:

> Till o'er our ransomed nature
> The Lamb for sinners slain,
> Redeemer, King, Creator,
> In bliss returns to reign.

Where Marriott's hymn builds to a climax which is not yet a conclusion -- "Let there be light" -- Heber's comes to a conclusion which is an anticlimax. The impression persists that there was greater vitality before idolatry was expunged. In sum, Heber's hymn is dominated neither by a sense of individual Christian responsibility, nor by the certainty of God's purposes unfolding. Fallen between these two, it owes its limited strength to the unusual sensual vividness of its first images.

Of the two new mission hymns in the Appendix, one is specifically for foreign missions, and was, indeed, published in _Verses for 1851 in Commemoration of the third Jubilee of the Society for the Propagation of the Gospel_ (edited by E. Hawkins, 1851). It is A.C. Coxe's "Saviour, sprinkle many nations" (356/359) and in contrast with the 1860 hymns it is rather personal than grand, though it concludes with the almost obligatory picture of the isles awaiting "Love's pure flame and wisdom's light." Christ the Saviour is the dominant figure, but He is a very human Christ. It is His sorrows, pains, and consolations which shall win the Gentiles, who in their turn are longing for Him in human and individual weakness:

> Far and wide, though all unknowing
> Pants for Thee each mortal breast;
> Human tears for Thee are flowing,
> Human hearts in Thee would rest.
> (stanza 2)

The hymn recognizes also the humanity of the means by which these needs will be supplied; in the final stanza, between the vision of the waiting isles and the prospect of worldwide Christendom, there is a real and urgent prayer: "Give the word, and of the preacher/ Speed the foot, and touch the tongue" (stanza 3). The lines are almost bathetic, but they do express the real and chief concern of those who are singing. Theirs is not pure flame and light, nor the universal hymn, but what they can pray for and do is, nevertheless, at the very core of the vision.

The two new hymns in the Revised edition are products of the increasing interest in foreign missions. One of them, "Through midnight gloom from Macedon" (--/361), was written by S.J. Stone specifically for the first Day of Intercession for Foreign Missions in 1872. Both hymns have the personal note which was lacking in the first A&M mission hymns, but which began to appear in the Appendix. There is nothing inevitable about the process of converting the world in these hymns: it is rather a serious responsibility, to be faced by every Christian.

Henry Downton wrote "Lord, her watch Thy Church is keeping" (--/362) for the annual meeting of the Church Missionary Society in 1866. Its insistent questions were supposed to prod the consciences of those whose declared business was missions; by 1875, its appearance in A&M suggests that the whole Church ought to share that concern.

> Lord, her watch Thy Church is keeping;
> When shall earth Thy rule obey?
> When shall end the night of weeping?
> When shall break the promised day?
> See the whitening harvest languish,
> Waiting still the labourer's toil;

Was it vain, Thy Son's deep anguish?
Shall the strong retain the spoil?

The concern in Stone's hymn is even more dramatic,[21] and literally so, for there are three voices in the hymn -- those of the heathen and the Christians, and that of Christ. The hymn sets out the need in eloquent and expressive language:

Through midnight gloom from Macedon[22]
The cry of myriads as of one,
The voiceful silence of despair,
Is eloquent in awful prayer,
The soul's exceeding bitter cry,
'Come o'er and help us, or we die.'

The cry falls on ears deafened by the sounds of the world (stanza three), until Christ wakes them:

'My voice is crying in their cry;
Help ye the dying, lest ye die.'

Christians cannot overlook their responsibility to their unconverted brethren without putting their own souls in grave peril, because both Christians and heathens are united in the humanity Christ died to save:

O by the kingdom and the power
And glory of Thine Advent hour,
Wake heart and will to hear their cry;
Help us to help them, lest we die![23]

Home missions were quite distinct from foreign

missions, not only because of the proximity of the field, but because they were differently organized. The initiative had originally been local, and in emulation of the early Methodist practice of open-air revival meetings. When it became apparent by mid-century that urban churches were not drawing the working population to their services, some Evangelical clergymen began to leave their church premises to preach on street corners or in halls and meeting rooms. Those parochial missions were largely urban, and by 1885 it was estimated that nearly every urban parish held regular mission services. A Clergy Mission College was founded to supply clerical assistants trained for such work.[24] Eventually it was recognized that the parish was too small a unit for effective work, and the diocese came to be the missionary unit. Tait, while Bishop of London, set up the innovative London diocesan home mission, and later canon-missioners were appointed, whose sole responsibility was evangelistic preaching. Not all parochial missions were for converting the ungodly: many parishes held sessions of preaching and prayer intended to encourage and revitalize the faith of those who were already churchgoers.[25]

Music played an important role in both proselytizing and sustaining missions, though perhaps more dramatically in the former. When Moody came to England in 1874-1875, Sankey sang heart-stirring solos at his services. When Booth's Salvation Army began to march, they had martial hymns to attract followers and brass bands to drown the jeers. Hymn collections such as A&M, compiled for the regular services of the church, contained relatively few hymns which were considered suitable for such services. Those that were used tended to be the more subjective and emotional ones, for they would contribute to the heightened emotion considered essential to any mass conversion or resolution. The S.P.C.K. had printed a small mission collection, but by 1875 its enlargement was considered necessary, and this task was undertaken by W.W. How. He was prompted to write to Sir Henry to request the use of several A&M hymns and tunes,[26] and this request led eventually to the co-operation between How and the Proprietors which resulted in the A&M mission collection.[27]

The correspondence reveals just what was expected of the book. The hymns How had originally requested were the more personal and more imaginative, as well as more modern ones: Emily Miller's "I love to hear the story," and C.F. Alexander's hymns on the words from the Cross, "Forgive them, O my Father" (--/115) and "His are the thousand sparkling rills" (--/119). Among the book's hundred hymns were to be several "preparatory" hymns, and some jubilant, and some penitential,[28] and rather shorter litanies than the ones in A&M, as "the poor cannot sustain the Spirit of devotion in singing so long as the entire Litany."[29] The book itself was to be cheap (How recommended a penny and the A&M Committee twopence),[30] without Scriptural headings, numbered verses, or an index, and above all, to be in clear black type, "legible to the poor with gaslight."[31]

Mission hymns might be used in several ways, but one clergyman, engaged in compiling a collection, outlined his ideal pattern of use.

> The Book is sent to the parish 6 months or so beforehand & the people have a full opportunity of getting to know the tunes. A large number of books will be purchased privately and used in families and thus the music becomes well-known and all is ready as far as music is concerned by the time the mission begins.[32]

This was the ideal, but the basic pattern of the congregational mission is there: an outside preacher, whether the canon-missioner, or a friend of the incumbent, and an occasion long planned and awaited, expectation building to an emotional, and, ideally, a spiritual, climax.

Thus home missions, being outside the regular services of the church, were supplied by separate hymn collections. Their existence, however, and the need for evangelizing and encouraging the nation and the church itself, are acknowledged in the mission section of A&M itself.

"Almighty God, Whose only Son" (357/363) was written by Sir Henry Baker for the 1868 Appendix, and intercedes for "all who err and go astray."

> There are who never yet have heard
> The tidings of Thy blessèd Word,
> But still in heathen darkness dwell,
> Without one thought of heaven or hell.
> (stanza 3)

Sir Henry refuses to distance the heathen darkness with exotic or picturesque attributes: he allows that it might be just beyond the church door. The sense of immediacy is heightened when he looks within the church itself and spies godlessness even there:

> And some within Thy sacred Fold
> To holy things are dead and cold,
> And waste the precious hours of life
> In selfish ease, or toil, or strife:
>
> And many a quickened soul within
> There lurks the secret love of sin;
> A wayward will, or anxious fears,
> Or lingering taint of bygone years.
> (stanzas 4-5)

He is not shocked; he merely sets out clearly and with a little touch of distaste what he sees, and reserves his warmth of expression not for castigation but for aspiration:

> O give repentance true and deep
> To all Thy lost and wandering sheep;
> And kindle in their hearts the fire
> Of holy love and pure desire.
> (stanza 6)

Sir Henry's hymn is a reminder that not all the mission fields are remote, and that the task is not to be left entirely to the professionals, to the societies and the boards, or even to the preachers. In this, it is an unusual hymn.

Christian missions, like the commercial and political empires of the western world, can be criticized. The study of comparative religion leads to an appreciation of so-called heathen practices in their own cultural contexts, and finds them no worse and sometimes even better than transplanted Christianity, and condemns the religious imperialism which went hand in hand with the expansion of the British Empire, as Anglican missionaries followed David Livingstone's route into Central Africa. This is not the place to pursue this argument: let it here be stated only that the Victorian missionaries saw it as their Lord's own commission, which they strove to carry out not only for the good of those whom they perceived to be languishing in error, but also because their disobedience in this matter would be grave indeed -- "Help us to help them, lest we die!" Divine mission or unsympathetic imposition, it is pleasant to hear in Sir Henry's hymn a note of humility, a rare acknowledgment of the beam in the cleric's eye at the same time as he strives to remove the mote from his neighbour's eye.

More evidence of the Church of England's domestic missions can be found in the Revised edition of A&M, between the hymns for Ember Days and those for missions. These are two hymns for "lay helpers": Frances Havergal's "Lord, speak to me that I may speak" (--/356), and Jane Borthwick's translation of a German hymn by C.J.P. Spitta, "How blessèd from the bonds of sin" (--/357). The Church had long made use of district visitors and Scripture readers, but in 1836 the Church Pastoral Aid Society was founded to provide for the maintenance of curates and lay-agents in poor and crowded parishes. By mid-century the usefulness of such help was widely recognized: a lay-helpers' association was established in the diocese of London in 1865, and received formal episcopal approval at a Lambeth meeting the following year. Lay readers were active in mission halls in both city and country, and in Sunday schools, but permission for them to preach in consecrated buildings was granted very slowly and diocese by diocese. The A&M hymns describe an ideal of committed service to God's people. Havergal's hymn defines rather more precisely than Borthwick's what that service may entail. The plea is that one may be an effective instrument:

> O teach me, Lord, that I may teach
> The precious things Thou dost impart;
> And wing my words, that they may reach
> The hidden depths of many a heart.
> (stanza 4)

Miss Borthwick's hymn is more metaphorical:

> How blessèd, from the bonds of sin
> And earthly fetters free,. . .
> With willing heart and longing eyes
> To watch before Thy gate,
> Ready to run the weary race
> To bear the heavy weight,
> (stanzas 1,2)

and rather more vague, though enthusiastic, in speaking of undertaking the "hardest toil . . . with joy at Thy command" (stanza 1), and of how "happily the working days/ In this dear service fly" (stanza 4). Both hymns are properly humble: Borthwick offers "The meanest office to receive/With meekness at Thy hand" (stanza 1), while Havergal pleads "O use me, Lord, use even me" (stanza 7). The attitude becomes the office of lay-helper, the lowliest of parochial assistants.

The inclusion of these hymns in A&M is evidence that, as suggested earlier, the title "Hymns . . . for use in the services of the church" is to be more generously interpreted than before. The church is moving beyond the limits of its statutory services and its traditional role, to embrace and bless different practices and new instruments in its changing world.

NOTES

[1] For a thorough examination of the changing imagery and emphases of their hymns, see Lionel Adey, Hymns and the Christian 'Myth' (1986).

[2] The use of the unusual verb "cark" tempts one to speculate that, as she wrote this hymn, Mrs. Alexander was remembering Dombey and Son, Dickens' earlier (1846-1848, in parts) tale of fortune's pride and broken hearts.

[3] These figures are representative but not absolute; the total comprises only those hymns the major theme of which is Paradise. Others may wish to include other hymns with more peripheral references to Paradise.

[4] In Faber's original (in his Hymns, 1861, no. 137 "The pilgrims of the night") the third and fourth lines read "While we toil on, and soothe ourselves with weeping,/ Till life's long night shall break in endless love." The emotional self-indulgence of these lines was evidently more than the Compilers could accept. Nor were they willing to print two other stanzas (Faber's second and sixth):

Darker than night life's shadows fall around us,
And, like benighted men, we miss our mark;
God hides Himself, and grace hath scarcely found us,
Ere death finds out his victims in the dark.
Angels of Jesus, etc.

Cheer up, my soul! faith's moonbeams softly glisten
Upon the breast of life's most troubled sea;
And it will cheer thy drooping heart to listen
To those brave songs which angels mean for Thee.
Angels of Jesus, etc.

If the former stanza presents salvation as depressing, doubtful, and ungenerous, the latter is an incongruous blend of homely admonition and would-be poeticism. Neither stanza is much missed.

[5] G.C. Ommaney, "Correspondence," *The Church Times*, LII 2182 (November 18, 1904), 652-653.

[6] Numbers 35:1-15; Joshua 21.

[7] Psalm 87. See also the Lamentations of Jeremiah.

[8] W. Lowther Clarke, *Liturgy and Worship* (1932), 239.

[9] See Chapter Four, 7.

[10] "Come, ye thankful people, come" (223/382), stanza 2, altered from the original by the Compilers. See Chapter Four, 8. The hymn was further altered in A&M 1875, and revised by Alford himself in 1865.

[11] Reginald Heber, "From Greenland's icy mountains" (217/358), stanza 2, written in 1819. Heber's MS and the A&M version give "Ceylon," though Heber's text in *Hymns* (1827) reads "Java," for no known reason.

[12] See Chapter Two, 1, vi.

[13] A.P., Manuscript text, signed John J. Daniell, dated February 8, 1868, stanza 3.

[14] A.P., Manuscript text by J.J. Daniell, stanza 6.

[15] C.M. Yonge, *Musings over the Christian Year and Lyra Innocentium*, (1871), xvii.

[16] J. Keble, Preface to *The Child's Christian Year*, by Mrs. Yonge (1841), iii-iv.

[17] Matthew 28: 19-20.

[18] Psalm 76:2, Authorized Version.

[19] "Sight" was misprinted as "light," in some copies of A&M 1860, but was corrected in later printings and in A&M 1875. A.P., Letter, December 9, 1872, John Marriott [son of author] to "his cousin Fitzherbert."

[20] John Marriott's original manuscript read:

Blessèd and holy and
Glorious Trinity,
Wisdom, Love, Might.

The A&M version improves the enjambement, and relates the three abstractions, as attributes of the persons of the Trinity, more directly to the preceding stanzas. In response to a protest from the author's son, they restored the original third line (and also "earth" for "world" in the penultimate line of the stanza), but reordered their first line to read "Holy and blessèd Three," in the Revised edition.

[21] Indeed, Stone wondered whether it was not "more a poem than a Hymn [although] I do not think it is too little of the latter to make that an objection." A.P., Letter, May 29, 1874, S.J. Stone to H.W.B.

[22] Reference to the vision which appeared to Paul in Acts 16: 9-16.

[23] The A&M version ends on this ominous note, although Stone's original hymn ended much more cheerfully:

Yet fair the hope that speeds us on,
With psalms of praise for Macedon!
Thy blessing given, Thy promise bright,
An earnest sweet of morning light,
Till 'Alleluia' be the cry
Of souls that live and shall not die!

The A&M Compilers wanted to emphasize the need rather than the promise, to awaken conscience rather than hopefulness.

[24] Inglis, _Churches and the Working Classes_ (1963), 28.

[25] In his great study of London, Charles Booth wrote that, despite the best efforts of those involved, church missions were generally ineffective:

> In almost every case the bulk of those who attend are regular churchgoers, and it may be questioned whether they really profit by

> these high-pressure experiences. As to outsiders, for whose sake more particularly the missions are held, the attempt is always practically a failure, some will be attracted, and of them a few may be deeply moved to adopt a new life; but, as with ordinary missions, such success is a question of a few individuals, difficult to win, and still more difficult to hold. The mass remain untouched. (Life and Labour of the People in London, third series, Religious Influences (1902), VII, 275.)

The cleric would counter that in the matter of souls, the salvation of even one would justify the effort.

[26] A.P., Letter, December 15, 1875, W.W. How to H.W.B.

[27] See above, Chapter Three, 2, ii.

[28] A.P., Letter, May 29, 1876, W.W. How to H.W.B.

[29] A.P., Letter, August 15, 1876, W.W. How to H.W.B.

[30] A.P., Circular signed G.C. White requesting help with the Mission Book, [September] 1876.

[31] A.P., Letter, Easter Tuesday 1876, W.W. How to H.W.B.

[32] A.P., Letter, January 13, 1874, W.H.M.H. Aitken to [H.W.B.?]

Chapter Six
Conclusions and Directions

Until recently, hymnody as a literary endeavour has been neglected save by a few specialist scholars. The writing and editing of hymns is not an activity undertaken for its own sake, and is therefore not subject to the same aesthetic criteria as other literary forms. Indeed, literary criticism has hardly touched hymns, a failure which is not to be deplored insofar as such criticism is only literary, and does not take into account the many factors, historical, theological, ecclesiastical, and social, which influence hymnody. The reluctance of critics to approach the subject is, however, unnecessarily extreme, and is probably best exemplified by Helen Gardner's refusal to judge hymns, claiming that her appreciation of them has been prejudiced beyond correction by childhood acquaintance and association.[1] It may be possible in this more secular age than the Victorian to read hymns without being susceptible to their influence, but hymns on the printed page are only skeletons. Their real existence is in the voices of singers: the element of song at once severely limits and heightens them. Critics who know their own susceptibility are the critics who will be most sensitive to hymns, conscious of their peculiar character and able to make allowance for undue influence, without needing to pin the words to a silent page before studying them. The drama critic who refused to see a production of King Lear, for fear he might weep at Cordelia's death, and who consequently confined himself solely to the reading of the text, would rightly be condemned for doing scant justice to the play. Similarly, Hymns Ancient and Modern is only really appreciated in the context of Victorian worship, and at the same time as it needs that background to be most meaningful, it also illuminates whole areas of Victorian worship, and of the tastes and prejudices, needs and fancies which informed it.

The success of A&M can be understood in three areas: material, hymnological, and spiritual. Material success is easier to measure than either of the others, and was recorded in Chapter Three. A&M was certainly a publishing success. Its sales were immense, and were widespread, covering most of England and extending abroad to English churches on the Continent and to those colonies where the Church of England flourished. Its variety of available editions brought it conveniently and attractively within the price range of almost any buyer, and ensured that its adoption for church use would be sealed by individual purchases, and the people's liking of the book enhanced by their possession of it, and by their chance to learn its contents more thoroughly than those of a borrowed book. The success of the book in ousting lesser collections from public use culminated in the honour of being unofficially considered for adoption by

Convocation as the authorized hymnal, or at least as the basis for one. A&M's music gave it even wider circulation, because of the Proprietors' policy of protecting the tunes of which they owned the copyright. As has been seen, the Proprietors' use of the copyright laws virtually assured the success of A&M, by not permitting the book to be torn apart for the sake of its best elements. The material success of A&M is proven by the Proprietors' financial records of the dividends they were able to pay themselves, and of the charities they were able to support.

The hymnological success of A&M is equally impressive. A&M was a demonstrable improvement over its predecessors, by being at once comprehensive, eclectic, and Catholic. It provided liberally for the formal services of the Church, and for many of its concerns beyond, by means of its occasional hymns. Represented in its volumes are most of the great traditions of Christian hymnody, though the first edition was more limited in scope, and even the Revised edition gave less emphasis to the hymns of English Dissent than did later supplements and editions. The Compilers of A&M were not innovators in the same way as Neale was, for example, but they were intelligent popularizers, able to take advantage of the discoveries of others, and make them widely acceptable by eschewing extremes and placing the novel hymn among the familiar ones, or combining it with a tune which would be an assured success. Their cautious progress from a limited book of Latin translations and contemporary imitations to a rich compendium of Latin, Greek, German, and English hymns reflecting most of the divisions of Christianity, meant that the ordinary congregation was gradually accustomed to its new richness of fare with relatively little objection. In this matter, too, the Compilers' exercise of copyright laws had a decided effect, for by keeping the book intact, they pressed upon some clergy material to which they might have objected, but were prepared to overlook for the sake of other hymns they wished to use. In this way whole congregations might be taught to tolerate the presence, if not the use, of hymns of which they did not approve. They might even be encouraged to experiment with new hymns and new uses for hymns, from seeing them in A&M. Thus the high-church bias, more pronounced in the first edition of A&M than in successive volumes, became even less noticeable as its hymns became familiar and people became accustomed to the idea of hymns for saints' days, even if they never sang them. The ubiquity of A&M came gradually to influence the general idea of a hymnbook, so that it was often imitated, sometimes unintentionally, as if no other form were conceivable. Furthermore, the popularity of the book, based partly on the excellence of some of its translations, lent authority and acceptance to the rest of its contents. The poorer hymns became as familiar as the good ones, and were warmly defended, by people who were uncritically fond of them, against attempts to change them, omit them, or even to restore them to their original form. The Proprietors of A&M came to rue their own free hand when they later adopted a policy of as few alterations as possible, and had to face the popularity they themselves had established.

The real achievement of A&M was to consolidate Anglican hymnody by replacing many local books with one that was more comprehensive, less partisan, better organized, more thoroughly edited and painstakingly compiled, and supplied with more attractive music. Two streams of hymnological interest met in the Compilers: the popular and the scholarly. On the one hand they asserted the Church's right to its song at the primary and practical level of the parish, thus preventing hymns from becoming the exclusive preserve of scholars, antiquarians, and liturgiologists. On the other hand, they insisted that hymnody to be popular had not to be exempt from all criteria of good taste or good scholarship. Popularity, they asserted, need not be synonymous with sentimentality, vulgarity, or doggerel. They were themselves a new kind of hymnologist, neither too seriously intellectual to be concerned with practicality and popularity, nor so intellectually irresponsible as to be lax over such questions as the reliability and authenticity of sources, or to indulge themselves in their own idiosyncrasies, as did so many of the amateurs.

The spiritual achievement is far harder to assess objectively than any other. Obviously the tone of the book and its contents were congruent with the spiritual needs and expressions of many Victorian Anglicans. That much can be inferred from its popularity in both churches and homes. It may be spiritual achievement enough to provide a voice both to express a sense of Christian community and to echo the Christian experience of the individual.

There were those, however, who attributed to A&M an extraordinary power to capture the imagination of ordinary people, and to further the work of the clergy in ways beyond mere usefulness in teaching. The theoretical aspects of the appeal, whether intellectual or emotional, and the usefulness of hymns were discussed in Chapter Two. The ways in which A&M reflected and perhaps reinforced some Victorian pre-occupations were the subject of Chapter Five. In those chapters are found the reasons for A&M's popularity: what is important here is the first-hand testimony to the appeal and effectiveness of the book.

People take possession of hymns in many ways, and not always within the formal context envisioned by hymnal editors. In the biography of William Walsham How is recounted an anecdote concerning one of his aged parishioners, who had made Bishop Ken's Evening Hymn peculiarly her own, and had incorporated it into a private ritual with strong personal significance. She told the new Rector in 1851:

> The old man and me, sir, never go to bed without singing the Evening Hymn. Not that I've got any voice left, for I haven't, and as for him, he's like a bee in a bottle; and then he don't humour the tune, for he don't rightly know one tune from another, and he can't remember the words neither; so when he leaves out a word, I puts it in, and when I can't sing I dances, and so we gets through it somehow.[2]

Such a practice might be abhorrent to a liturgiologist or hymnologist, but it does exemplify a popular adoption of hymns which made possible A&M's huge success both in formal worship and among individuals.

Archdeacon John Allen of Prees wrote to Sir Henry and testified to the effect the use of A&M had had in his parish.

> I believe that you are greatly helping our Master's cause, if we may say as much with reverence, by your publication.
> I was very unwilling to introduce the book at Prees.
> I am greatly thankful that have [sic] introduced it.
> I find that poor widows, living on alms, receiving parish relief, read the book in their loneliness, learn the hymns by heart and repeat them as they lie awake at night.
> One baptist, a woman, strong in dissent, has by reading these hymns almost been drawn to the Church. She has been an attendant at Church occasionally & I hope will in the end worship here continually.
> . . . [Our congregations] never were so large D.G. as at this time.[3]

A similar tribute was relayed at second-hand to the Compilers:

> Only a few days since a Yorkshire clergyman (quite a moderate man) was saying what effect the Book had had

> in his Parish, & that it had been the means of bringing many Dissenters to church, by teaching them to love the church service. He also said that one young man, who had a lingering illness, found the book of the utmost use to him on his sick-bed. He learned nearly all the Hymns by heart before his death, and was constantly saying or singing them to himself.[4]

The most fascinating testimony came from a Dorset clergyman, who declared that "to Hymns Ancient & Modern I trace as regards earthly causes a great deal of the spiritual life of the village."

> Fourteen years ago when I came into the place . . . there was, in the church, an old 'Grinder' with one barrel, having three available tunes, and two chants: the hymn book being a collection, compounded of Dr. Watts hymns and didactic moral pieces. Dissent flourished. but such dissent as few can have any idea of. The church congregation did not amount to 12; the communicants were three! but there were innumerable private meetings where Denham Smith's[5] hymns were shouted and most horrible rubbish talked. Smuggling, card playing, drinking, and gross immorality prevailed on a

> Sunday evening; whilst I myself and my children were even stoned in the street. I know that God's blessing accompanied the means, but amongst the chief means to better things I rank foremost Hymns Ancient & Modern. I saw nothing before me but a coup de force, and almost every sort of abuse I swept away Grinder, hymn book etc etc and taught . . . the tunes in Hymns A&M. They won my people over. They had singing at church, they could join in it, it was easy musical & varied and the tunes which they took to especially were many of them those of Dr. Dykes. Now I have no Dissent here. I have no public house. I have full and even overflowing congregations and of my 150 parishioners I have generally 25, sometimes more at the Holy Table.[6]

Whether or not everything Burrows says is strictly true is not important. He believed it to be true, and no doubt there was a great change in his parish during his ministry there. He is probably being modest when he gives much of the credit to A&M, for in most cases it is not the trappings of the ministry, but the character of the minister which attracts and holds the people.[7] Nevertheless A&M was one of the means by which Burrows ministered, and if its music made the first impression, the words must have in their turn taken hold of the people's thoughts and imagination.

It is not surprising that the Compilers took themselves and their task seriously, when one realizes what testimony they were given of its effectiveness, and what enormous expectations their success occasioned. Their pride in and ambition for their book never caused them to lose sight of the real arena where it would be tested -- in the parish, where hymns enter a dimension of spirituality and imagination, and can be justified only insofar as they are the expression of a living faith. To contribute in even a small way to the harmony, both literal and figurative, of the Christian church is a worthy achievement. To offer *Hymns Ancient and Modern* for the use and comfort of the Church of England is a great one.

This study of A&M has served to indicate what wealth of material is available for the scholar who seeks a better understanding of the Victorian church in its everyday relations, where the concerns of the clergy meet those of the people. Those concerns are manifold and complex, but the use of such a method of study as A&M provides enables the researcher to seize and comprehend some part of them, without denying or diminishing either multiplicity or complexity. The study of a church's hymns is thus both a focal point of study, and a starting point for further research. The scholar whose discipline is English literature finds the church's hymns a worthy study in themselves, though they cannot be fully appreciated in isolation. Nor is their only relevant context the religious one of liturgy and theology, for hymns also reflect the education, tastes, prejudices and purposes both of individuals and of the classes of society.

An interdisciplinary approach to Victorian studies is not new, and has proved its usefulness many times over, but the choice of hymnody and hymnology as a serious study outside the narrower limits of liturgiology and for purposes not those of religion has not been a common one. A&M is at once the subject of this study, and the means to investigate another and larger subject, Victorian life and thought. The limits of this larger study have not been reached, and indeed, have not even been indicated in these pages. As far as A&M itself is concerned, some conclusions are ventured and some judgments passed, but in the larger sphere this study is exploratory rather than conclusive. Such exploration demands an open-ness which, though not uncritical, sometimes comes close to sympathy, in order to counteract a longstanding reluctance to admit hymns, and the people who write and sing them, as a serious subject for intellectual study. Judgment and conclusions will come in time. If this study has kept and communicated some of the curiosity in which it was conceived and the excitement in which it was pursued, it has achieved its first and most important purpose.

NOTES

[1] See also Lionel Adey, *Hymns and the Christian 'Myth'* (1986), 1.

[2] F.D. How, *Bishop Walsham How: A Memoir* (1898), 46. How's appreciation of that kind of popularity certainly affected his own writing and editing.

[3] A.P., Letter, October 29, 1868, John Allen to H.W.B.

[4] A.P., Letter, August 28, [1862], Edward Twells to William Pulling.

[5] Joseph Denham Smith, a Congregationalist minister whose evangelizing work and hymns flourished in the 1860s.

[6] A.P., Letter, May 8, 1876, E.D. Burrows to H.W.B.

[7] See Chapter One, 2.

A Select Bibliography

(Unless otherwise specified, the place of publication is London.)

Primary Sources

Royal School of Church Music, Addington Palace. Archive Belonging to the Proprietors of *Hymns Ancient and Modern*.

Hymns Ancient and Modern for Use in the Services of the Church. [First] Specimen. 1859.

Hymns Ancient and Modern. [Second] Specimen. 1859.

Hymns Ancient and Modern. Words only edition. 1860.

Hymns Ancient and Modern. Music edition. 1861.

Hymns Ancient and Modern with Appendix. 1868.

Hymns Ancient and Modern. Draft of Revised edition. 1873.

Hymns Ancient and Modern. Revised edition. 1875.

Secondary Sources

Companions to *Hymns Ancient and Modern*

Biggs, Louis Coutier, ed. *Hymns Ancient and Modern for Use in the Services of the Church with Annotations, Originals, References, Authors' and Translators' Names with some Metrical Translations of the Hymns in Latin and Greek*. 1867.

Clarke, W.K. Lowther. _One Hundred Years of Hymns Ancient and Modern_. 1960.

Cottage, R.M. _The Writers of Hymns Ancient and Modern, In their Order of Time and According to their Churches, with Notes and Index giving the Greek, Latin, and German First Lines_. Cambridge, [1884].

Frere, W.H., ed. _Historical Edition of Hymns Ancient and Modern_. 1909.

Frost, Maurice, ed. _Historical Companion to Hymns Ancient and Modern_. 1962.

Jeayes, I.H. _Choirmaster's Companion to Hymns Ancient and Modern_. [1889].

Moorsom, Robert M., ed. _A Historical Companion to Hymns Ancient and Modern; containing the Greek and Latin; the German, Italian, French, Danish and Welsh Hymns; the First Lines of the English Hymns; the Names of all Authors and Translators; Notes and Dates_. _1889_.

Reference Books

Crockford's Clerical Directory. Volumes for 1858 to 1880 inclusive.

Cross, F.L., ed. _The Oxford Dictionary of the Christian Church_. 1957.

Davies, J.G., ed. _A Dictionary of Liturgy and Worship_. 1972.

Hayden, Andrew J. and Robert F. Newton. _British Hymn Writers and Composers: A Check-List_. 1977.

Julian, John, ed. _A Dictionary of Hymnology, setting forth the Origin and History of Christian hymns of all ages and nations, with special reference to those contained in the Hymn Books of English-speaking Countries_. 1892. Second edition revised with Supplement, 1907.

Ollard, S.L., G. Crosse, and M.F. Bond, eds. _A Dictionary of English Church History_. Third edition. 1948.

Richardson, Alan, ed. *A Dictionary of Christian Theology*. 1969.

Sedgwick, Daniel. *Comprehensive Index of Names of Original Authors of Hymns, Versifiers of Psalms, and Translators, of every Denomination and Age, with the Dates of their various Works*. Second edition. 1863.

Syndor, James Rawlings, ed. *A Short Bibliography for the Study of Hymns*. New York, 1964.

Other Hymn Books

Beadon, H.W., G. Phillimore, and J.R. Woodford, eds. *The Parish Hymn Book*. 1863. Enlarged edition, 1875.

Bickersteth, E.H., ed. *The Hymnal Companion to the Book of Common Prayer*. 1875. Second edition, revised and enlarged, 1977. Third edition, 1880.

Caswall, Edward. *Lyra Catholica: containing all the Breviary and Missal Hymns, with Others from various sources*. 1849.

Chandler, John. *The Hymns of the Primitive Church: now first collected, translated, and arranged*. 1837.

Cooke, William and William Denton, eds. *The Church Hymnal. A Book of Hymns adapted to the use of the Church of England and Ireland, arranged as they are to be sung in Churches*. 1853.

Faber, F.W. *Hymns*. 1862.

-----. *Jesus and Mary: or, Catholic Hymns*. 1849.

Helmore, Thomas and John Mason Neale. *The Hymnal Noted*. Two parts, 1851 and 1854.

Helmore, Thomas. *Manual of Plainsong*. 1850.

C.F.H. [Cecil Frances Alexander, nee Humphreys]. *Hymns for Little Children*. 1848.

Neale, John Mason. *Mediaeval Hymns and Sequences*. First edition, 1851; second edition, 1863.

-----. Hymns of the Eastern Church, translated with notes and an introduction. 1862.

Nelson, Horatio, ed. The Salisbury Hymn Book. 1857.

Nelson, Horatio, J.R. Woodford, and E.A. Dayman, eds. The Sarum Hymnal. 1868.

Pott, Francis, ed. Hymns Fitted to the Order of Common Prayer and Administration of the Sacraments. 1861.

S.P.C.K. Hymns. 1852.

-----. Psalms and Hymns. 1855. First Appendix, 1863. Second Appendix, 1869.

-----. Church Hymns. 1871.

Trend, J.B., ed. A Hymnal for Use in the Services of the Church. 1862.

Williams, Isaac. Hymns Translated from the Parisian Breviary. 1839.

Wordsworth, Christopher, ed. The Holy Year; or, Hymns for Sundays and Holydays, and Other Occasions. 1862.

Yonge, Mrs., ed. The Child's Christian Year: Hymns for every Sunday and Holy-Day, Compiled for the Use of Parochial Schools. 1841.

Historical, Literary, Hymnological and Theological Works

Adey, Lionel. Class and Idol in the English Hymn, Vancouver, 1988.

-----. "Great Aunt Tilly's Beautiful 'ymns: A Victorian Sub-culture." Wascana Review, vol. 12 (1977), 21-47.

-----. Hymns and the Christian 'Myth.' Vancouver, 1986.

A Layman. Hymns Ancient and Modern: Their Tendency Not Romanizing. 1876.

Bailey, Edward Albert. The Gospel in Hymns. 1950.

Balleine, G.R. Sing with Understanding. 1954.

Baring Gould, Sabine. The Church Revival. 1914.

Benson, Louis F. The English Hymn: Its Use and Development. New York, 1915.

-----. The Hymnody of the Christian Church. New York, 1927.

-----. Studies in Familiar Hymns. Philadelphia, 1903.

Beresford Hope, A.J. Worship in the Church of England. 1874.

Bett, Henry. The Hymns of Methodism in their Literary Relations. 1945.

Biggs, Louis Coutier. English Hymnology. 1873.

Bowen, Desmond. The Idea of the Victorian Church: A Study of the Church of England 1833-1889. Montreal, 1968.

Box, C. Church Music in the Metropolis. 1884.

Bradley, Ian. The Call to Seriousness: The Evangelical Impact on the Victorians. 1976.

Brook, Stella. The Language of the Book of Common Prayer. 1965.

Brose, O.J. Church and Parliament: The Reshaping of the Church of England 1828-1860. Stanford, 1959.

Brown, C.K. Francis. A History of the English Clergy, 1800-1900. 1953.

Burge, W. On the Choral Service of the Anglo-Catholic Church. 1844.

Burkitt, F.C. Christian Hymns. Oxford, 1908.

Cairns, W.T. "The Constituents of a Good Hymn," The Religion of Dr. Johnson and Other Essays. 1946.

Campbell, F. Hymns and Hymn Makers. Edinburgh, 1895.

Carpenter, S.C. *Church and People, 1789-1889*. 1933.

Chadwick, Owen. *The Victorian Church*. Part 1, third edition, 1971. Part 2, second edition, 1972.

Church, R.W. *The Oxford Movement, 1833-1845*. 1891.

Clark, Kenneth. *The Gothic Revival*. Third edition. 1962.

Clarke, C.P.S. *The Oxford Movement and After*. 1932.

Clarke, W.K. Lowther. *A History of the S.P.C.K.* 1959.

Clarke, W.K. Lowther and Charles Harris, eds. *Liturgy and Worship: A Companion to the Prayer Books of the Anglican Communion*. 1932.

Cockshut, A.O.J. *Anglican Attitudes*. 1959.

-----, ed. *Religious Controversies of the Nineteenth Century: Selected Documents*. 1966.

Copinger, Walter Arthur. *The Law of Copyright, in Works of Literature and Art: including that of the Drama, Music, Engraving, Sculpture, Painting, Photography, and Ornamental and Useful Designs* etc. 1870. Second edition, 1881.

Cornish, F.W. *The English Church in the Nineteenth Century*. Two vols. 1910.

Crowther, M.A. *Church Embattled: Religious Controversy in Mid-Victorian England*. Newton Abbott, 1970.

Cuming, G.J. *A History of Anglican Liturgy*. 1969.

Danielou, J., A.H. Couratin, and John Kent. *Historical Theology* . Vol 2 of *The Pelican Guide to Modern Theology*. Edited by R.P.C. Hanson. 1969.

Davie, Donald. *A Gathered Church: The Literature of the English Dissenting Interest 1700-1930*. 1978.

Davies, W. Horton. Worship and Theology in England. Vol. 3 From Watts and Wesley to Maurice. 1961; Vol. 4 From Newman to Martineau. 1962.

Dearing, Trevor. Wesleyan and Tractarian Worship: An Ecumenical Study. 1966.

Douglas, Winfred. Church Music in History and Practice: Studies in the Praise of God. 1937. Revised with additional material by Leonard Ellinwood, 1963.

Duffield, S.W. English Hymns, their Authors and History. 1886.

Duncan-Jones, C. Anglican Revival in Sussex. Chichester, 1933.

Elliott-Binns, L.E. The Early Evangelicals: A Religious and Social Study. 1953.

-----. English Thought 1860-1900: The Theological Aspect. 1956.

-----. Religion in the Victorian Era. 1935.

England, Martha and J.H.S. Sparrow. Hymns Unbidden. New York, 1966.

Faber, Geoffrey. Oxford Apostles: A Character Study of the Oxford Movement. Second edition, 1936.

Fairchild, Hoxie N. Religious Trends in English Poetry. Vol 4. 1830-1880 Christianity and Romanticism in the Victorian Era. New York, 1957.

Fellowes, Edmund H. English Cathedral Music. 1941. Fifth edition, revised by J.A. Westrup, 1969.

Fowler, J.T., ed. J.B. Dykes: Life and Letters. 1897.

Gardner, Helen. Religion and Literature. 1971.

Gillman, F.J. The Evolution of the English Hymn: An Historical Survey of the Origins and Development of the Hymns of the Christian Church. 1927.

Gregory, A.S. Praises with Understanding. 1936.

Hart, A. Tindal and Edward Carpenter. The Nineteenth Century Country Parson. 1954.

Heeney, Brian. *A Different Kind of Gentleman: Parish Clergy as Professional Men in Early and Mid-Victorian England*. Hamden, Connecticut, 1976.

Helmore, Frederick. *Choristers' Instruction Book*. 1872.

-----. *Church Choirs*. Fourth edition. 1879.

Helmstadter, Richard J. "The Victorian Churches" in *Victorian Prose: A Guide to Research*. Edited by David DeLaura. New York, 1973.

Heywood, John. *Our Church Hymnody: An Essay and Review*. [1881].

Horder, W.G. *The Hymn Lover: An Account of the Rise and Growth of English Hymnody*. 1889.

Housman, H. *John Ellerton: Life and Writings on Hymnology*. 1896.

How, F.D. *Bishop Walsham How: A Memoir*. Second edition. 1899.

Hutchings, Arthur. *Church Music in the Nineteenth Century*. 1967.

Inglis, K.S. *Churches and the Working Classes in Victorian England*. 1963.

Ingram, Tom and Douglas Newton, eds. *Hymns as Poetry: An Anthology*. 1956.

Jackson, M.J. *The Sociology of Religion: Theory and Practice*. 1974.

Jefferson, H.A.L. *Hymns in Christian Worship*. 1950.

Johnson, Samuel. *Works*. Vol. 2. *The Lives of the Most Eminent English Poets*. 1787.

Keble, John. *The Christian Year*. 1827.

-----. *Lectures on Poetry 1832-1841*. Translated by Edward Kershaw Francis. 2 vols. Oxford, 1912.

King, J. *Anglican Hymnology*. 1885.

Kitson Clark, G. *Churchmen and the Condition of England 1832-1885. A Study in the Development of Social Ideas and Practice from the Old Regime to the Modern State*. 1973.

-----. "The Romantic Element -- 1830 to 1850" in *Studies in Social History: A Tribute to J.M. Trevelyan*. Edited by J.H. Plumb. 1955.

La Trobe, J.A. *The Music of the Church, Considered in its Various Branches, Congregational and Choral*. 1831.

Lawson, Mary Sackville, ed. *The Letters of John Mason Neale, D.D*. 1910.

Leask, G.A. *Nineteenth-Century Hymn Writers*. 1902.

Longford, Elizabeth. *Piety in Queen Victoria's Reign*. 1973.

Lough, A.G. *The Influence of John Mason Neale*. 1962.

MacDermott, K.H. *The Old Church Gallery Minstrels. An Account of the Church Bands and Singers in England from about 1660 to 1860*. 1948.

Mackarness, Charles Coleridge. *The Poetry of Keble as a Guide to the Clergy in their Pastoral Work*. 1918.

Mackerness, E.D. *A Social History of English Music*. 1964.

Maclagan, W.D. *The Church and the People*. 1882.

Maison, Margaret. *Search your Soul, Eustace: A Survey of the Religious Mind in the Victorian Age*. 1961.

Manning, B.L. *The Hymns of Wesley and Watts*. 1942.

Marsh, P.T. *The Victorian Church in Decline: Archbishop Tait and the Church of England 1868-1882*. 1969.

Mason, Lowell. *Musical Letters from Abroad*. New York, 1854. Reprinted, 1967.

McLeod, Hugh. Class and Religion in the Late Victorian City. 1974.

Meacham, Standish. "The Church in the Victorian City." Victorian Studies, XI (1968), 359-78.

Miall, Edward. The British Churches in relation to the British People. 1849.

Miller, Josiah. Singers and Songs of the Church. Second edition. 1869.

Mudie-Smith, Richard. The Religious Life of London. 1904.

Neale, John Mason. "Hymns and Hymnals." The Christian Remembrancer, XLVI (July 1863), 105-144.

Newman, John Henry. "On the Roman Breviary as embodying the Substance of the Devotional Services of the Church Catholic." Tracts for the Times, no. 75. 1836.

Norman, E.R. Anti-Catholicism in Victorian England. 1968.

Ollard, S.L. A Short History of the Oxford Movement. Revised edition. 1932.

Ormiston, James. Hymns Ancient and Modern, and their Romanizing Teaching. Church Association Tracts, no. 21. n.d.

Overton, J.H. The English Church in the Nineteenth Century. 1894.

Palmer, Roundell. Hymns: their History and Development. 1892.

Parry, K.L. Christian Hymns. 1956.

Patrick, Millar. The Story of the Church's Song. Second edition. Edinburgh, 1947.

Pearsall, Ronald. Victorian Popular Music. Newton Abbott, 1973.

Phillips, C. Henry. The Singing Church. An Outline History of the Music Sung by Choir and People. 1945.

Phillips, C.S. Hymnody Past and Present. 1937.

Phillips, P.T., ed. The View from the Pulpit: Victorian Ministers and Society. Toronto, 1978.

Pitman, Mrs. E.R. Lady Hymn Writers. 1892.

Pollard, Arthur. English Hymns. 1960.

Prothero, R.E. The Psalms in Human Life. 1902.

Pugin, A.W.N. Contrasts. Second edition. 1841.

Purcell, William. Onward Christian Soldier. A Life of Sabine Baring Gould, Parson, Squire, Novelist, Antiquary 1834-1924. 1957.

Rainbow, Bernarr. The Choral Revival in the Anglican Church 1839-1872. 1970.

-----. The Land Without Music: Musical Education in England 1800-1860 and its Continental Antecedents. 1967.

Reeves, J.B. The Hymn as Literature. 1924.

Robinson, Ian. The Survival of English: Essays in Criticism of Language. Cambridge, 1973.

Routley, Erik. Hymns and the Faith. 1955.

-----. Hymns and Human Life. Second edition. 1959.

-----. The Musical Wesleys. 1968.

-----. A Short History of English Church Music. 1977.

-----. Words, Music, and the Church. 1968.

Smith, Alan. The Established Church and Popular Religion 1750-1850. 1971.

Soloway, R.A. Prelates and People: Ecclesiastical Social Thought in England 1783-1852. 1969.

Symondson, Anthony. The Victorian Crisis of Faith. 1970.

Tamke, Susan S. "Hymns for Children: Cultural Imperialism in Victorian England." _Victorian Newsletter_, 49 (Spring 1976), 18-22.

-----. _Make a Joyful Noise Unto the Lord: Hymns as a Reflection of Victorian Social Attitudes_. Columbus, 1978.

Thompson, D.A. _Bureaucracy and Church Reform: The Organizational Response of the Church of England to Social Change, 1800-1865_. 1970.

Thompson, David M. _Nonconformity in the Nineteenth Century_. 1972.

Thompson, E.P. _The Making of the English Working Class_. 1964.

Towle, Eleanor A. _John Mason Neale D.D.: A Memoir_. 1907.

Trollope, Anthony. _Clergymen of the Church of England_. 1866.

Tulloch, John. _Movements of Religious Thought in Britain During the Nineteenth Century_. 1885.

Vidler, Alec. R. _The Church in an Age of Revolution_. Vol. 5 of _The Pelican History of the Church_. Edited by Owen Chadwick. 1974.

Wagner, D.O. _The Church of England and Social Reform Since 1854_. New York, 1930.

Walsh, Walter. _The Secret History of the Oxford Movement_. Fourth edition. 1898.

Webb, C.C.J. _A Study of Religious Thought in England from 1850_. Oxford, 1933.

Weir, A. and W.D. Maclagan. _The Church and the Age_. 1870.

White, James F. _The Cambridge Movement: The Ecclesiologists and the Gothic Revival_. Cambridge, 1962.

Whitley, W.T. _Congregational Hymn-singing_. 1942.

Wickham, E.R. _Church and People in an Industrial City_. 1957.

Williams, Isaac. "On Reserve in Communicating Religious Knowledge." _Tracts for the Times_, nos. 80 and 87. Vol. 4, 1838. _Vol. 5, 1840_.

Yonge, Charlotte Mary. _Musings over the 'Christian Year' and 'Lyra Innocentium,' together with a few Gleanings of Recollections of the Rev. John Keble, Gathered by Several Friends_. 1871.

Index of First Lines

General Index

TEXTS AND STUDIES IN RELIGION

1. Elizabeth A. Clark, **Clement's Use of Aristotle: The Aristotelian Contribution to Clement of Alexandria's Refutation of Gnosticism**
2. Richard DeMaria, **Communal Love at Oneida: A Perfectionist Vision of Authority, Property and Sexual Order**
3. David F. Kelly, **The Emergence of Roman Catholic Medical Ethics in North America: An Historical-Methodological-Bibliographical Study**
4. David Rausch, **Zionism Within Early American Fundamentalism, 1878-1918: A Convergence of Two Traditions**
5. Janine Marie Idziak, **Divine Command Morality: Historical and Contemporary Readings**
6. Marcus Braybrooke, **Inter-Faith Organizations, 1893-1979: An Historical Directory**
7. L. William Countryman, **The Rich Christian in the Church of the Early Empire: Contradictions and Accommodations**
8. Irving Hexham, **The Irony of Apartheid: The Struggle for National Independence of Afrikaner Calvinism Against British Imperialism**
9. Michael Ryan, editor, **Human Responses to the Holocaust: Perpetrators and Victims, Bystanders and Resisters**
10. G. Stanley Kane, **Anselm's Doctrine of Freedom and the Will**
11. Bruce Bubacz, **St. Augustine's Theory of Knowledge: A Contemporary Analysis**
12. Anne Barstow, **Married Priests and the Reforming Papacy: The Eleventh-Century Debates**
13. Denis Janz, editor, **Three Reformation Catechisms: Catholic, Anabaptist, Lutheran**
14. David Rausch, **Messianic Judaism: Its History, Theology, and Polity**
15. Ernest E. Best, **Religion and Society in Transition: The Church and Social Change in England, 1560-1850**
16. Donald V. Stump *et al.*, editors, ***Hamartia*: The Concept of Error in the Western Tradition**
17. Louis Meyer, **Eminent Hebrew Christians of the Nineteenth Century: Brief Biographical Sketches**, edited by David Rausch
18. J. William Frost, editor, **The Records and Recollections of James Jenkins**
19. Joseph R. Washington, Jr., **Anti-Blackness in English Religion 1500-1800**
20. Joyce E. Salisbury, **Iberian Popular Religion, 600 B.C. to 700 A.D., Celts, Romans and Visigoths**

21. Longinus, **On the Sublime,** translated by James A. Arieti and John M. Crossett
22. James Gollnick, ***Flesh* as Transformation Symbol in the Theology of Anselm of Canterbury,**
23. William Lane Craig, **The Historical Argument for the Resurrection of Jesus During the Deist Controversy**
24. Steven H. Simpler, **Roland H. Bainton: An Examination of His Reformation Historiography**
25. Charles W. Brockwell, **Bishop Reginald Pecock and the Lancastrian Church: Securing the Foundations of Cultural Authority**
26. Sebastian Franck, **280 Paradoxes or Wondrous Sayings,** Translated & Introduced by E. J. Furcha
27. James Heft, **John XXII and Papal Teaching Authority**
28. Shelley Baranowski, **The Confessing Church, Conservative Elites, and the Nazi State**
29. Jan Lindhardt, **Martin Luther: Knowledge and Mediation in the Renaissance**
30. Kenneth L. Campbell, **The Intellectual Struggle of the English Papists in the Seventeenth Century: The Catholic Dilemma**
31. William R. Everdell, **Christian Apologetics in France, 1730-1790: The Roots of Romantic Religion**
32. Paul J. Morman, **Noel Aubert De Verse: A Study in the Concept of Toleration**
33. Nigel M. de S. Cameron, **Biblical Higher Criticism and the Defense of Infallibilism in 19th Century Britian**
34. Samuel J. Rogal, **John Wesley's London: A Guidebook**
35. Andre Seguenny, **The Christology of Caspar Schwenckfeld: Spirit and Flesh in the Process of Life Transformation,** translated by Peter C. Erb and Simone S. Nieuwolt
36. Donald E. Demaray, **The Innovation of John Newton (1725-1807): Synergism of Word and Music in Eighteenth Century Evangelism**
37. Thomas Chase, **The English Religious Lexis**
38. R.G. Moyles, **A Bibliography of Salvation Army Literature in English, 1865-1987**
39. Vincent A.Lapomarda, **The Jesuits and the Third Reich**
40. Susan Drain, **The Anglican Church in the 19th Century Britain**
41. Aegidius of Rome, **On Ecclesiastical Power: De Ecclesiastica Potestate,** Arthur P. Monahan (trans.)
42. John R.Eastman, **Papal Abdication in Later Medieval Thought**
43. Paul Badham, editor, **Religion, State, and Society in Modern Britain**

44. Hans Denck, **Selected Writings of Hans Denck, 1500-1527,** E.J.Furcha (trans.)
45. Dietmar Lage, **Martin Luther on the *Imitatio Christi* and *Conformitas Christi* and Their Relationship To Good Works**
46. Jean Calvin, ***Sermons on the Books of Jeremiah and the Lamentations,*** Blair Reynolds (trans.)
47. David Lee Wheeler, **A Relational View of the Atonement: Prolegomenon to a Reconstruction of the Doctrine**
48. Alexander Sandor Unghvary, **The Hungarian Protestant Reformation in the Sixteenth Century Under the Ottoman Impact: Essays and Profiles**